MW01028587

ALL OR NOTHING

ALSO BY MICHAEL WOLFF

The Fall: The End of Fox News

Too Famous: The Rich, the Powerful,
the Wishful, the Notorious, the Damned

Landslide: The Final Days of the Trump White House

Siege: Trump Under Fire

Fire and Fury: Inside the Trump White House

Television Is the New Television:
The Unexpected Triumph of Old Media in the Digital Age

The Man Who Owns the News:
Inside the Secret World of Rupert Murdoch

Autumn of the Moguls:
My Misadventures with the Titans, Poseurs,
and Money Guys Who Mastered and Messed Up Big Media

Burn Rate: How I Survived the
Gold Rush Years on the Internet

Where We Stand

White Kids

ALL OR NOTHING

How Trump Recaptured America

. . .

MICHAEL WOLFF

CROWN
NEW YORK

CROWN
An imprint of the Crown Publishing Group
A division of Penguin Random House LLC
1745 Broadway,
New York, NY 10019
crownpublishing.com
penguinrandomhouse.com

Copyright © 2025 by Michael Wolff
Penguin Random House values and supports copyright. Copyright fuels
creativity, encourages diverse voices, promotes free speech, and creates a vibrant
culture. Thank you for buying an authorized edition of this book and for
complying with copyright laws by not reproducing, scanning, or distributing any
part of it in any form without permission. You are supporting writers and
allowing Penguin Random House to continue to publish books for every reader.
Please note that no part of this book may be used or reproduced in any manner
for the purpose of training artificial intelligence technologies or systems.

CROWN and the Crown colophon are registered trademarks of
Penguin Random House LLC.

Library of Congress Control Number: 2024952084

Hardcover ISBN 978-0-593-73538-1
Ebook ISBN 978-0-593-73539-8

Editor: Gillian Blake
Editorial assistant: Jess Scott
Production editor: Patricia Shaw
Text designer: Andrea Lau
Production manager: Heather Williamson
Copy editor: Jenna Dolan
Proofreaders: Rob Sternitzky, Tricia Wygal, Navorn Johnson, and Judy Kiviat

Manufactured in the United States of America

9 8 7 6 5 4 3 2 1

First Edition

The authorized representative in the EU for product safety and compliance is
Penguin Random House Ireland, Morrison Chambers, 32 Nassau Street,
Dublin D02 YH68, Ireland, https://eu-contact.penguin.ie.

For Victoria

Contents

Author's Note

This is my fourth book about Donald Trump's political journey. It is a story about character, a singular one. I have used the firsthand observations of people who have been in personal, often daily, contact with him to create as much as possible an intimate portrait of Donald Trump at significant and revealing moments during his third run for the presidency. Here are the moment-by-moment gyrations of his whims, needs, furies, survival instincts, and, arguably, bursts of genius. To tell the story of a man who sees himself as having a special status and destiny—who is, indubitably, not like you or me—requires, ideally, the confidence of his butler; in Trump's case, his many butlers. I have offered anonymity to anyone who can help me see into his private chambers. Such protections become ever more important in what I fear is a new climate of retribution, with more power than ever before in the hands of loyalty enforcers (and more paranoia among them, too). My hope is that the insights so many people have provided me, out of both personal alarm and because the story is too extraordinary not to tell, into the real-time temper of the star and his entourage of enablers offers a different sort of window from the daily news coverage into Donald Trump's character and the upended politics of our time.

ALL OR NOTHING

Prologue

Mar-a-Lago

When Donald Trump returned to Mar-a-Lago on Inauguration Day, January 20, 2021, a dwindling band seeing him off from Andrews Air Force Base, it was at best a loser's fantasy that he could run for president again. In the orbits around him (family, White House aides, Republican leaders, donors), there certainly weren't many cogent voices encouraging him in this fantasy. If you were close to him, you tended to be at best circumspect, if not mortified, on his behalf—defeat; crazy, *Keystone Cops* efforts to deny his loss; January 6; exile.

Most immediately, he faced another impeachment trial in the Senate and could hardly even marshal a competent legal team to put up his defense—a ragtag band of small-time practitioners was assembled only after a wide casting call. He was saved—and his ability to hold office again preserved—only by Republican Senate leader Mitch McConnell's pity and desire to wash his hands of him. Through conventional eyes, this trial was just one more coffin nail. (Still, an advantage perhaps evident only to him, it did keep him in the news.)

His finances were in disarray. His sons, with their own livelihoods at issue, were counting on a level of calm and distance, with him necessarily out of the news, to help re-establish the brand, with hope that in a year or two or three, "Trump," would be *old* news. There were several open outbursts at Mar-a-Lago between them and him, with the sons emphasizing the seriousness of the situation and the discipline that would be required. Their suggestion that he could be most valuable as an ambassador to the family's foreign properties—Donald Trump on a permanent golfing tour—hardly sat well with him.

There were rumblings about legal threats he might face. All the more reason to keep his head down and not provoke the new sheriff in town.

The state of his mental health was a whispered concern. He really did not seem to appreciate, or grasp, the reality of what had occurred.

His chief adviser in the White House, the aide with real authority and influence, the conduit of normalcy to the extent that any existed, was his son-in-law, Jared Kushner. Trump expected Kushner to continue in Mar-a-Lago as his right hand. But Kushner's own clear and immediate post–White House plan was to put distance between himself and his father-in-law. Asked about his father-in-law's future by a friend, Kushner replied, "What was Nixon's future?" Kushner and his wife, Ivanka, for social and tax reasons, were themselves moving to Florida—but to Miami instead of Palm Beach, using new schools for their children as an explanation. Replacing himself, Kushner staffed up his father-in-law's new exile office. But it wasn't much of a staff: Susie Wiles, a local Florida political operative at retirement age (in a young person's profession), took on the job more out of duty than ambition; Nick Luna, a young man married to one of Kushner's assistants, would commute several days a week to Palm Beach from Miami; Jason Miller, a comms person in the campaign, would be on call for a few months in Washington; and Molly Michael, another of his look-alike assistants, would step in as the designated young woman attending to him (notably, Hope Hicks, his favorite young woman retainer, had fled during his effort to overthrow the election).

His wife, Melania, was straightforward about how she saw her husband's future—or the future she did not see. She had not enjoyed a single day in the White House. To the extent that they had had a marriage (even on a negotiated footing), it was further disrupted by her husband's mood swings and constant sense of offense and injury while in the White House. It had all been bad, in her view, for their son, Barron, and had only increased tensions between her and the rest of the Trump family. So, good riddance. She was young, her husband was old, and she had her own life to make—she felt nothing but relief that he was finished with politics (or it was finished with him).

Trump, however, simply did not acknowledge his defeat and exile. There was not the slightest indication, not the smallest opening of self-awareness, that he even sensed the enormity and finality of what had occurred since Election Day, November 3. He showed no inclination to look for meaning in the events, or to sift the experience. Nor was anyone aware of a friend or confidant with whom he might be considering the recent past and unknown future. He was not, as many defeated politicians have described themselves, consumed by a period of self-doubt and reflection. Rather, he was still, for all intents and purposes, and never breaking character, the president.

You might believe such an ongoing fantasy of, say, a despot of some minor country exiled to the South of France, surrounded by a retinue of sycophantic loyalists, seeing himself in a displaced but unchanged world. Perhaps this was similar. Most of the people around the former president in Mar-a-Lago—family, his political and Mar-a-Lago staff, the Mar-a-Lago members—were certainly humoring him. But, really, this was transparent stuff, politesse—at least in the beginning.

The central facet of his exile—alarming pretty much to all and prompting a necessary lack of eye contact among the people around him—was his continuing and obsessive focus on the stolen election. He would bring it up no matter the topic at hand. There was virtually no conversation in which he did not return to the victory that he maintained, full of outrage and certainty, had been corruptly taken from him.

Yes, the arc of history may seem since then to have bent to his delusion, but in the spring of 2021, and perhaps for most of the year after, there were very few, if any, reasonable, professional, establishment (whatever you might want to call people who live in the empirical world) voices of any political stripe who did not entirely appreciate that Donald Trump had lost the election. From his staff to his lawyers, to his family, to his cabinet, to the entirety of the Republican leadership in Washington, even to Tucker Carlson and Steve Bannon—there was no way *not* to accept the facts of his defeat. Even extending the benefit of the doubt and granting instances of possible dispute, virtually everyone but the former president and his small support group of nutters understood that the result would not meaningfully have been changed. It was simple math.

Trump, though, was in a loop of numbers—the individual numbers in his rendition often changing, supplemented by weird "fact" sheets that he'd had his staff assemble and by articles from the right-wing press that he kept at hand, which he would spin out in conversations—a monologue, really, one that might end only when whomever he was talking to made polite and desperate excuses or from which Trump was dragged away. You could not listen to him and believe he had any understanding of even the most basic facts. Or, alternatively, you might reasonably conclude he was purposely and, in the face of all evidence to the contrary, stubbornly trying to disguise the basic facts in layers of nonsense.

He believed it, or he convinced himself he believed it, or it was a bravura performance, with no possibility that he would ever let on that he was in fact performing: There had been a conspiracy that subverted the true result, and therefore, he was still president. "A group of people within the Democrat Party working along with Big Tech and the media" had stolen it from him, he explained to a Mar-a-Lago visitor. It was "a coordinated effort." He promised: "Names are going to be revealed." Of course, they never were.

For a while, there was pathos here. There is hardly anyone, at least not with something better to do, who did not recognize the quixotic nature of this. But certainty has power. Unwavering certainty. Psychotic certainty, even. Perhaps disgrace, too, has special power—if you refuse to accept your disgrace, it becomes righteousness. And perhaps delusion has power. And the larger the delusion is, the more power it may have.

• • •

Given that he had not changed, that, in his mind, he was still the president, there was never a natural progression to refer to him as the former president, nor even a segue to understanding "president" as just a polite honorific—the correct title for a former president is "Mr."—and never back to his first name. He remained what he was. Hence, he may not ever have considered *not* running again. He may not have looked at it as a decision to make. Rather, simply, 2020 had never ended.

But did he really want to go on being president? Weren't there other things in life for an older man?

His wife lived at a curated distance, his growing son with her. His older children more employees than family. There was no domestic life to return to. (Indeed, he lived in a country club.) He wasn't going to write a book, or organize a presidential library, or raise money for a foundation, or do good works to burnish his reputation, or return with any cheer to his real estate business, such as it was. Nothing but golf tempted him.

Arguably, there were just no alternatives to running again. What would he do? Who would he be? To be Donald Trump, he had to be president; otherwise, he was into the existential abyss.

Given his great baggage—an unpopular president with a dubious record who had staged a failed coup—it, of course, made no sense that he should run. That would have been the assessment of most political professionals in both parties. Who, *reasonably*, would have thought this was a good idea?

All potential presidential candidates have a yearslong discussion about should they or shouldn't they. This is a way to build allies: "Yes, you should run"—okay, that's an increment of support. "Well, yes, interesting, but these are the impediments"—okay, less than support. Or, "Let's look at this realistically"—a wet blanket. Trump never once had such a discussion. Nobody came to Mar-a-Lago and outlined the hard realities of his dismal popularity, his lack of support among the party leadership, his legal problems, or the difficulties of facing an incumbent president.

Nobody was logically triangulating the known world for him.

Mar-a-Lago is not truly in the Cartesian universe.

Even beyond its deferential membership, inclined to treat their host as something like a beloved but aged rock-and-roll act (Elvis, in so many ways), Mar-a-Lago became the setting for a particularly extreme cast of

bootlickers, opportunists, and grifters. In the months after his defeat:
the actor Jon Voight, fetishistic in his patriotic ardor for Trump, on one
day; Mike Lindell, the My Pillow CEO, who would sacrifice his business and fortune for Trump, on another; Sean Hannity, whose Trump-
led television ratings had transformed him into one of the most powerful
political figures in the nation; Kurt Olson, part of Trump's legal retinue
and a deep-state conspiracy theorist. Yes, Kevin McCarthy, the House
Speaker, appeared at Mar-a-Lago, but only in a kiss-the-ring effort to
head off plotters on his right flank. A trail of people of no standing or
purpose, save access to him, made their way to Mar-a-Lago, offering
flattery and get-rich-quick schemes—among them a set of no-account
would-be entrepreneurs whom no other former president would have
entertained, who proposed he front a media company start-up (which,
as preposterous as Trump's own return, would one day be worth ten billion dollars).

Mar-a-Lago, as one Trump intimate put it, was less Camelot than
Jonestown.

. . .

The feet-on-the-ground, putting-two-and-two-together, cause-and-effect
world is where American politics, in its historic accomplishment, has
always lived. Politics, the art of the possible, is an enforced rationality. It
exists in a narrow space of fixed rules and reactions. The system—that
nexus of guardrail process and bureaucracy, institutional weight, reputa-
tional standing, and legal lines and tangles—deals with irrational actors
who try to break it. And no one really has.

It was hard to see Mar-a-Lago and its prince as anything other than
an unnatural exception to that.

Trump, beyond reason and practicality, in the months and years
after his defeat, continued to see himself as the rightful and deserving
president. His steadfastness in this role was so implacable and logic defying that, certainly as performance, it became convincing to many. Meanwhile, no one truly rose to replace him or challenge him, not least of all

because others logically shrank from a man who seemed unfettered by ordinary gain-and-loss calculations, who, in that sense, was a crazy man.

Politics is also the art of losing—democracy is premised on it. Even winners lose, so you must always hedge your bets. Have your retreat prepared. Your good face ready. Even—indeed, necessarily—if you plan to try again. (In America, helping to maintain an ultimate equanimity, there are the spoils of both victory and defeat.) The logic of the system fails, though, if you don't acknowledge or accept your loss, if you don't allow for it. That is a vastly different kind of politics—the man on the tightrope without a net. Who can take their eyes off him? As Trump's third presidential campaign came to life—or, unaccountably, did not die—and as the stakes for him became crystal clear, his proposition as a candidate playing both hero and martyr became utterly straightforward: Elect me or destroy me.

PART ONE

The Law

CHAPTER 1

New York—Bragg

Boris Epshteyn, Donald Trump's forty-year-old Russian-born legal adviser, came on to the Microsoft Teams call with his video off. Then his screen came to life in a sudden reveal.

Bearish, balding, and overweight, a man at the center of potentially the most profound constitutional conflict in American history short of the Civil War, Boris, confounding all Trump's other lawyers, was Trump's most recent candidate to replace Roy Cohn, the lawyer who had once represented him and whom Trump had elevated into the diabolical magician who could get him out of any jam, were he only still alive.

Here, in his home office, in his onscreen box, was a bare-chested Boris, showing off his massive torso and dense pelt to quite a collective gross-out that resounded through Trumpworld and the ever-growing case of distaste for Epshteyn.

Susie Wiles, the sixty-five-year-old Florida political op and the closest thing Trump had to a campaign manager, recoiled. "Oh, God, Boris. Oh, God, Jesus. Oh, my God—put on a shirt!"

Everybody else on the call guffawed, groaning and shielding their eyes.

This was something close to the four-hundred-pound hacker in his parents' basement whom Trump often conjured as an all-purpose modern bugaboo. Or, on a slightly different theme, Boris was a *Jersey Shore* guy, a reality show figure of exaggerated vulgarity and attention-seeking neediness, a familiar type in Trumpworld.

Trump's political and legal staff had had its heart in its mouth for several weeks now, anticipating an inconceivable blow to the campaign, the first criminal indictment of an American president in history. Worse news: They needed to rely on Boris—everybody in Trumpworld needed to rely on Boris—the architect of the entire Trump defense and the effective legal team manager, to keep them informed enough to deal with the mess.

Boris had been in the Trump orbit since 2016. And often—and not least of all for his social impairments—pushed out of it. But he'd always clawed his way back. Now, generally confounding to all, here he was, the key man in Trump's vast legal woes.

Mock him—and he was aware that everyone did—but today Boris was taking a victory lap.

With no firm information, Trump had jumped the gun and announced his own coming indictment in New York. He was pre-empting the New York DA if he did indict, and highlighting the DA's weakness if he didn't. Win, win. In the days after, when there was no immediate indictment—with the political and media world brought by Trump to the edge of its seat—the former president directed his various stand-ins to say it looked like the DA was dropping the case. And that was the news that a delighted Boris now brought: The grand jury sitting in New York, threatening the first indictment of a former U.S. president, had announced that it was taking a month off, and *that*, according to Boris, was as good an indication as any that it was a dead-duck case.

Boris hadn't practiced law in more than a decade. He wasn't in fact one of Trump's lawyers in New York. His lawyers in the New York case were Joe Tacopina, a frequent figure in Manhattan tabloid trials, and Susan Necheles, whose claim to fame was that she had defended the mobster "Benny Eggs." But Boris had personally chosen the lawyers on each case and then had wedged himself between them and Trump and between the lawyers and the campaign staff. Because the lawyers in Trumpworld were always shifting, Boris, even as the persistent antagonist to all the other lawyers, represented some level of stability, which, given how many times he'd been bounced out of Trumpworld, said quite a bit about how stability was measured.

Nothing would happen, Boris was assuring his boss. They had made it—safe for now. Possibly safe forever. "Literally there's nothing that's going to happen," he said, and, as well, to virtually everyone in Trumpworld, "at least until the grand jury returns." That was a month off. "And there's a really good chance an indictment doesn't happen at all," he said. "Delays are bad for them"—that is, for the New York City prosecutors. "It means they're trying to come up with a new theory of the case. They don't have a case, in other words."

The Manhattan district attorney, Alvin Bragg, in Boris's telling, was truly fucked.

"He's already celebrating," Boris reported. *He*—that is, the president (former).

Trump had been celebrating on the phone with friends and on the Mar-a-Lago patio almost since he'd had the brilliant idea of announcing his own indictment—precisely because, as Boris had promised him, he *wasn't* going to be indicted. He had announced his coming indictment on the golf course through posts on his social media network, Truth Social. "Will be arrested on Tuesday!" The date was Trump's inspiration alone—and the product of his itchy social media trigger finger. Within seconds, the news blew up.

The campaign team immediately reached him on the golf course, trying to figure out where "Tuesday" had come from.

"From all the fake news," he said confidently.

Lawyers and staff dutifully composed a formal announcement—which basically took back Trump's announcement: "There has been no notification, other than illegal leaks from the Justice Dept. and the DA's office, to NBC and other fake news carriers, that the George Soros–funded Radical Left Democrat prosecutor in Manhattan has decided to take his Witch-Hunt to the next level. President Trump is rightfully highlighting his innocence and the weaponization of our injustice system. He will be in Texas next weekend for a giant rally."

But Trump wanted more: Put it in, he instructed the lawyers, that everybody should go protest.

"That could be a problem," one of his lawyers chimed in, Trump still on the golf course. It could be supporting evidence in the January 6 case, under continuing investigation, of him having urged supporters to act in his name to storm the Capitol, Trump was told.

"Fuck it. Put it in there," said Trump.

The statement went out without a call for mass protests. But simultaneously, Trump was putting out social media posts calling for "PROTEST, PROTEST, PROTEST." His defense for his role in the January 6, 2021, attack on the Capitol continued to be that he had been a passive and, indeed, bewildered bystander—at the same time, his most consistent fantasy was of great numbers of people, unprecedented numbers, gathering to defend him.

The indictment he was predicting became, overnight, a political inflection point: What would ordinarily have killed a political candidate was suddenly earning him a wave of support. There was a rush of Republicans (including House Speaker Kevin McCarthy and two of Trump's declared primary opponents, Vivek Ramaswamy and Mike Pence, along with the party congressional leadership and other might-be Republican presidential candidates) to defend him and attack the Manhattan DA—except for Florida governor Ron DeSantis, debating whether to run against Trump in the primaries, who didn't, and then *that* became the story. Why wasn't Ron DeSantis defending "the president"?

Trump's announcement of the indictment came just before the first big rally of his campaign, and it gave the rally special meaning. The indictment (even an indictment that Trump was now convinced wasn't going to come) *was* the reason for the campaign—and the campaign, this demonstration of Trump shock and awe, was the reason the indictment was not going to happen! Who would dare? And if it did happen, it was only because he was running for president—and the Democrats were therefore trying to stop him!

He was, as he believed—and as, helpfully, Boris most persistently kept telling him—invulnerable. Returning from the rally, Trump was flipping around post-rally coverage on the conservative news channels. Even he, in front of his spread of Quarter Pounders and Chicken

McNuggets, found the adulation over-the-top: "It's like *Saturday Night Live*," he said, mimicking: "Trump is great. No, Trump is really great! No, actually, Trump's really, really, really great!" Here was a story, a joke on himself—sort of—he repeated (and repeated) through the week.

Except that while Trump's invulnerability was always the working thesis, elsewhere another of the lawyers was saying that no matter what Boris said, they really did have it on good information that the indictment was coming.

"Have you told him?" asked a surprised colleague.

"Are you kidding?"

Trump's weekend golf plans were on, Boris announced to the group. Mar-a-Lago could relax. "Easy weekend. Nothing's going to happen. POTUS is happy. Don't worry."

Ending the call (now with his shirt on), Boris said he, too, was taking the weekend off.

• • •

Boris was born in Moscow in 1982 and was part of the great migration of Russian Jews to the United States in the 1990s. He grew up in suburban New Jersey. After law school and his brief stint in a New York law firm, he shifted into the emerging field of conservative media, a new political front line and career opportunity, which included, none too successfully, helping to prep Sarah Palin in 2008 for campaign interviews. In 2016, he became involved with the Trump campaign as a television defender, a surrogate when it was still difficult to find people to front for Trump, when, basically, any willing body would do.

A measure of the distaste and suspicion Boris aroused—not least, as the Russian mess unfolded, because of his Russian connections—was that he lasted in a White House job for a matter of weeks before being bounced for "security concerns." He continued in Trumpworld as a talking head, briefly joining Sinclair Television, an upstart conservative outlet, and marketing in private venues the influence he had with the White House (often with the many people he had so frequently irritated and confounded).

His perennial outsider status perfectly positioned him in the days after the 2020 election. Taking it upon himself, and to most everyone's surprise, he was among the first Trump representatives (albeit self-appointed) to fly into Arizona to help contest the state's vote count and then to try to overturn it. As the ensuing election dispute hurtled forward, Boris aligned himself with Rudy Giuliani, traveling with the former New York City mayor on his mission to secure new electors in various states and to seek legislative overthrow of the official votes. In the days leading up to January 6, Boris was holed up with Giuliani in the Willard Hotel in Washington, a key focus of prosecutors' interest in the January 6 case.

After January 6, Giuliani, demanding payment for his fruitless efforts, was cast out of the Trump circle, even deprived of Trump's new cell phone number when he left the White House. But Boris continued. His bona fides with Trump were his foot soldier loyalty in the election fight. As almost everyone else in Trumpworld tried to distract Trump from his election obsession, Boris, ever on the phone, diligently fed it.

Meanwhile, he became a semi-official Trump middleman, and began to bill an array of clients for his services. If you wanted the endorsement of the guy in Mar-a-Lago, then perhaps you should hire Boris Epshteyn as your political adviser. Boris was selling Trump's possible endorsements, even though Trump often snubbed Boris's clients.

It was not just the general grift, the inept legal advice, the hoarding of information, and the worming himself in as *always* the last voice in Trump's ear that rankled the legal and political staff about Boris, but also the likelihood that Boris himself might be a target in various of the cases. Trump, however, was unmoved. Boris was his guy.

As Trump made his announcement of the forthcoming indictment—the indictment he'd convinced himself would never come—he had one of his usual gatherings of petitioners, golf partners, and hangers-on in the Grill Room of the Trump International Golf Club in West Palm Beach, fifteen minutes from Mar-a-Lago.

A weird mash-up of patriotic songs sung by the "J6" prisoners had inexplicably gone to number one on Apple's charts and was now cranked up to what felt like a hundred decibels. Trump, in a moment that even sycophantic members of his entourage would report as "a bit chilling," suddenly rose and faced the screen and the fluttering video flag, with his hand on his heart—meaning everybody else jumped up, too. The real flags were behind him, which is where everybody else, confused, suddenly turned. The effect was of a group pledging allegiance directly to Trump, a tableau broken only by Trump's starting to dance a little jig and singing, "Number one, number one, number one." Then, as he sat with his golf foursome, Boris called. Trump held up the phone with Boris blabbing on about how great things were looking for the former president.

"Ah, everyone, this is Boris, my Boris. Calls me like twenty times a day." And, indeed, such calls did happen every few hours. "Always has good news. He's like, 'Sir, you're ahead by ninety points in the poll, sir. Sir, you're going to be indicted next week, sir, but don't worry, it's good news for you.'"

Here was both self-awareness and cruelty—aware that he liked having yes-men around and, too, enjoyed mocking them for it. It was, too, a story that Boris would repeat, as though proudly.

• • •

A defining characteristic of Trump's political life has been who has slipped into it. From 2015, Trumpworld had been a rolling show of unlikely figures entering it and, too late, being expelled from it, many whom Trump would fall out with and fire, many who would blindly do his bidding and face their own legal messes: among these, Roger Stone, his first political adviser; Michael Cohen, his personal lawyer; Corey Lewandowski, his first campaign manager; Paul Manafort, his second campaign manager; Steve Bannon, his third campaign chief; Brad Parscale, the head of his 2020 campaign; Rudy Giuliani, also a personal lawyer; and the extraordinary cast of election deniers.

By the spring of 2023, the surprising thing was the seeming levelheadedness around Trump. Here was Susie Wiles, daughter of Pat Summerall, the former football player and, for two decades, among the most prominent sports broadcast voices; indeed, a sporting institution. Wiles had run Rick Scott's successful campaign for governor of Florida in 2010, and Ron DeSantis's gubernatorial campaign in 2018. In 2016, Trump, finding her running his campaign in Florida, and unhappy with Wiles's age and failure to look the part, directed that she be fired. This, though, was ignored, and in both 2016 and 2020 she ran the Trump campaign Florida operation and was a crucial player in flipping Florida for him. On hand at Mar-a-Lago, in Trump's exile, Wiles gradually took over his out-of-office political operations. Not unimportant: Her long history with Ron DeSantis, Trump's only real possible Republican challenger, meant she understood his peculiarities and weaknesses—what's more, DeSantis had fired her in what was now quite a famous Florida political feud, leaving her with a score to settle.

Then, as Wiles's slightly less than co-equal, there was Chris LaCivita, a marine wounded in the First Gulf War and a well-tried Republican political operative with a host of important Republican races behind him and a long career on the back end of politics with the RNC; various political consultancies supporting (and profiting from) political campaigns, and the super PACs that support them, including the main 2020 Trump PAC. In 2004, LaCivita had led the Swift Boat Veterans for Truth campaign, with its devastating attack ads against John Kerry. He was now running the primary ground campaign and delegate operation.

It was important to note the subtle scramble *not* to hold the title of campaign manager—Trump was invariably dissatisfied with his "campaign manager."

Wiles and LaCivita were the professional leadership team tasked with handling the mercurial former president. The press had noticed this—the two had cordial and professional relationships throughout the political media, even as Trump made it his favorite enemy—and had begun to see this as the reason for Trump's buoyancy and better and better numbers. The new narrative even had Trump learning from the past.

· · ·

So far, it had been a campaign of inevitability rather than plan. Did he even, truly, want to run? While he had left the White House, he did not really transition out of the role he had played as president. (Many argued that he had never really transitioned out of the role of Trump Organization head in Trump Tower.) Mar-a-Lago was a fine substitute White House, and Trump filled his days, as he had in the West Wing, and before that in Trump Tower, with meetings with fans, acolytes, sycophants, and Trump opportunists—and with golf. And everyone continued to call him, and not merely as an honorific, "Mr. President."

Being the king in Mar-a-Lago might have been *better* than being president—every night, he came onto the dinner terrace where two hundred members and their guests stood and applauded (a long applause) and then sought him out for a personal greeting and moments of private bootlicking. Wherever he went, he was held in awed regard by his base, the MAGA crowd. He had his Secret Service detail, as many as eighty agents at various times. And he was the heavyweight in the Republican Party; his clout overruled everybody else's clout. It was West Wing life, but he didn't have to do anything and was responsible for nothing. It was nearly ideal—save only for the fact that another Republican might replace him as standard-bearer. And he could not live with that.

The campaign sputtered into gear over the summer of 2022 with Trump, furious about Ron DeSantis's apparent willingness to be the Trump alternative and incensed that there might be more "witch hunt shit," planning to make an early announcement, but first wanting to get in as much golf as possible. "I might not have too many summers like this left," he told friends, causing speculation about whether he was talking about the demands of the campaign and returning to the White House, the possibility of jail, or the most unlikely, his own mortality.

August 8, 2022—the day the FBI, with thirty agents, raided Mar-a-Lago and seized thirty-three boxes of Trump papers, a variety of them classified, which the former president had haphazardly or mendaciously purloined on his way out of the White House—marked the real beginning of the 2024 campaign (although he did not formally announce until November 22). If Trump's signature victimhood and high dudgeon and his counterpuncher's energy had been fading on the golf course, they were all back now. He was in the role. If they were coming after him, what choice did he have but to go after them? (Indeed, this would become his functional legal defense.) Instantaneously, his lackluster money-raising operation came alive with $22 million raised in the third quarter. A presidential campaign was suddenly galvanized with a motivated candidate, a money machine, and an emotional issue: They were coming for him.

• • •

All Trump's relationships with family, wives, staff, friends, are . . . unusual, everybody serving him in roles that he has more or less concocted from his own imagination. Of all these relationships, the strangest and unhappiest is probably with his lawyers, a revolving door of hundreds over the years. At the heart of this relationship is a profound contradiction: He wants his lawyers to be savvy, canny, astute, and aggressive, pulling him from every pickle he gets himself into, but at the same time, he wants them to be abject suck-ups to his every whim and desire—and to reassure him at every turn that he will prevail. In this, he elevated Roy Cohn into a myth of defense lawyer–fixer omnipotence to whom no one might ever measure up (and who, too, he ultimately found fault with and spurned). Also, in seeing lawyers as essentially dramatis personae rather than technicians, he often chose for his ideal models characters of the type that populated 1960s win-every-trial television shows.

Almost every major Washington and New York firm had refused or deflected an inquiry to represent him during Trump's White House years. Being a lawyer who *was* actually willing (professional reputation and accomplishments not particularly relevant) to represent him was a way into Trumpworld, and being a lawyer who could be utterly abject was a way into the inner circle. Boris was a lawyer not just willing and abject but with a further valued attribute: He was ready to confirm the boss's suspicion that his other lawyers were not willing or abject enough; nor sufficiently savvy, canny, astute, and aggressive. The other criterion Boris met, beyond saying what Trump wanted to hear, was to say it with enough conviction and to supply enough suspicion about others— whispering rumors of plots and perfidy—that Trump would want to hear it often. Boris understood that the real power here, the only power, was always to stay in Trump's ear.

Certainly, Trump seemed to be forsaking reliable and competent legal representation in his uphill battle with prosecutors. This seemed obviously true. But the other point—or theory—was that he had some greater intuitive sense of dealing with the mess he was in than anyone else ever could. Hence, his ultimate legal strategy was just not to listen to his lawyers, who would never understand the larger stage he was playing on— or to only listen to Boris, who reliably told him what he wanted to hear.

• • •

On January 1, 2022, Alvin Bragg became the Manhattan DA, the first Black man to hold the office. A career prosecutor, in the state attorney general's office and as an assistant U.S. attorney in New York's Southern District, Bragg was, at forty-eight, a fixture in the New York legal and political system. He inherited on his first day a complicated and controversial probe into the former president's business practices. Reflecting the general establishment view—life is too short to prosecute a former president; and come on, it's real estate in New York—he almost immediately short-circuited the investigation. The two lead prosecutors on the case, Mark F. Pomerantz and Carey R. Dunne, resigned in public protest. They walked their investigation to the U.S. Attorney's Office—that is, into Joe Biden's Justice Department—and there, too, were met by the establishment's reluctance to prosecute a former president.

But with a new Trump campaign stubbornly coming back to life, and with Trump's own continued passionate harping on a stolen election, the establishment was soon to change its view.

A new climate had begun with the FBI raid, Trump's evident obstruction and casual disregard of the investigation, followed by the brazenness of his resulting fundraising bonanza—and the frustration that, as usual, he remained unbowed. Then there followed the 2022 midterm election, with, seemingly, Trump's political weakness as clear as could be with all his proxies defeated—you could even think that Trump fever had broken. There was no red wave to save him. The Republicans were turning against him, finally. Ron DeSantis appeared, in the sweeping margins of his re-election as Florida's governor, to be a ready Trump killer with vast support coming his way from big Republican donors, and as the clear favorite of Fox News. And then, with his infuriating and thoughtless audacity, Trump made his announcement of another campaign. The evolving establishment logic was that he was weak enough to go after and yet still strong enough for this to be necessary.

It was going to happen: The legal system was going to pull down the former president in one or more no-exit white-collar prosecutions. The question now was which, among the many investigations, was going to produce the first criminal indictment. Alvin Bragg, sidestepping his previous doubts, now reversed himself: Prosecuting Trump wasn't problematic; it was righteous.

Given the rage with which Trump continued to damn the "witch hunt" against him, he remained, in fact, fairly sunny about his situation. This was in part because he was, by nature, impervious to the outside world. Or, merely, that his world simply overshadowed the outside world. He lived in a highly controlled universe populated only by lackeys, flunkies, and sycophants. And, too, the vulnerabilities that undermined ordinary mortals—the doubts, shame, and fear—were absent in him. Conflict made him feel alive, ready to go; it was his elixir. He had endured a lifetime of litigation and had invariably, and, he believed, through sheer force of will, prevailed.

But the other thing was that bad news did not easily get through to him. There were no realistic appraisals of the situation he was in. Boris kept all the other lawyers, already a constantly changing cast, at bay. It was *Boris's* legal appraisal that got through to the boss—and that was always rosy. Lawyers who disagreed with Boris soon found themselves out of favor with the client.

As Trump was more and more convinced that he would avoid indictment in New York, David Pecker was reported to have gone before the grand jury Alvin Bragg had convened. Pecker was the old Trump crony who ran the supermarket tabloid the *National Enquirer* and who, in some convoluted relationship of admiration and soft blackmail, had run scandal interference for Trump. Shouldn't it be alarming that Pecker was now before the grand jury? But in Boris's estimation, Pecker was just old news. All the talk was Bragg's PR talk. All bullshit. Bragg's name in the paper. But in the end, they wouldn't move against President Donald Trump.

Preparing to leave for his long weekend after finishing the staff Zoom call, Boris was on the phone with Trump offering a buoyant view: "I think they're delaying this a month so that they can drop it. Mr. President, I promise you this whole thing just goes away." Trump, who might otherwise mock Boris for his constant good cheer, now widely reported Boris's assurance as grail.

• • •

At 5:30 p.m. that same day—April 4—the Manhattan district attorney announced the first-ever criminal indictment of a president of the United States. It was yet unclear what the charges were, whether they were related to Trump's business issues, that long-simmering investigation, or to other matters, of which there could be many.

Trump was just then sitting down with Mark Levin, the right-wing commentator and Trump sycophant, to tape a show. He then planned to have dinner with Levin and Levin's wife on the Mar-a-Lago terrace.

But chaos now intervened. Boris, having left town, was unavailable. The New York lawyers, Joe Tacopina and Susan Necheles, learned about the indictment only from the campaign staff, who in turn had learned about it only through press reports. The political team had, in fact, on its own, sketched out a contingency response, but now there were no lawyers available to approve a statement. Trump, between the Levin taping and the Levin dinner, was looking for whom to blame, choosing now, as he would on many days to come, his lousy lawyers.

"Why do I have such shitty lawyers? How is this happening? How did the lawyers get this so wrong?" (Boris had gotten this wrong, but Boris was not among the lawyers Trump was blaming.) What might have appeared rhetorical on Trump's part was actually a demand: He wanted an answer. *Why* did he have such shitty lawyers? "Where is my Roy Cohn?" He'd uttered this so often that it ought, at this point, to have been ironic. It was not. And, indeed, he continued to utter it, virtually verbatim, through the nonstop calls he continued to make all evening.

But it was amazing how quickly his mood could shift. It was one reason his moods were often compared to the weather. "How is it?" "Storms ahead" or "It's cleared—perfectly sunny."

By that evening, the calls were coming in at a rate he couldn't respond to. More than 50 percent, maybe 60 percent, of the House GOP conference, plus senators, governors, state AGs—many of whom had turned against him after January 6—all were supporting him, everybody tweeting, rushing out statements of support. He was vacillating between great anger—scary fury—and lapping it up. He kept getting back on the phone with the most passionate of his defenders, looking for indignation even greater than his own.

The worst thing that might befall a candidate for office, a criminal indictment, had now happened. In any understanding of the nature of U.S. politics, this was a disqualifying event. But immediately, the campaign put out an online fundraising appeal, which almost instantly began to reflect a wholly different reality: the fastest minute-to-minute fundraising hours of the campaign so far.

The campaign, grasping to explain this reality, not least of all to itself, started at that moment to talk about the "split screen." On one side, what you saw could not be worse: an inescapable legal quagmire, threatening and perhaps mortal—yes, *likely* to be mortal. But here on the other side, an entirely positive political outlook: overwhelming support in his party, ever-rising polling numbers, lackluster opposition. In the first twenty-four hours after the indictment, they'd raised four million dollars, with a remarkable 25 percent representing new donors.

• • •

Behind his desk, Trump's mood is buoyant. He yells, "Bring me the poison." His basket of Starbursts, Hershey's Miniatures, Laffy Taffy, and Tootsie Rolls instantly appears. "Okay, get the poison out of here," he says, taking two handfuls.

"This is big. This is very big," he now analyzes—he's simultaneously on the phone and talking to people in and out of his office. "They're only doing this because they're afraid of us. This puts us in front of every camera in the world."

His lawyers are suggesting an incremental and procedural response, which Trump waves away. As he has told his staff, repeatedly, he now instructs his lawyers: "Our legal strategy is our media strategy; our media strategy is our legal strategy." This is the premise uttered so often that no one can remember the first time they heard this foundational belief.

Trump's people, many of them, anyway, don't think of him all that differently from how the rest of the world does: He's mercurial, capricious, lazy, ill-informed, inattentive . . . The difference is, having been around him, having seen him survive what other mortal politicians never could, they've come to believe he knows something, sees something, gets to the heart of something—some new reality—that the rest of us don't.

"Our legal strategy is our media strategy; our media strategy is our legal strategy."

•   •   •

Still, nobody knows what to expect—what exactly does being a criminal defendant involve? There's a reach-out to Steve Bannon—who, not that long ago, was arrested and processed in New York on a fraud charge—about what jail might be like: "They put those cuffs on, and they put them on tight. You can't even move, and you're sitting in that cell by yourself. I had to sit there for six hours with cuffs that are so tight you can't even scratch yourself."

In conventional political staging, a politician in such public trouble needs his wife beside him. Jason Miller is one of the few staffers who's been with Trump for all three campaigns, and, taking one for the team (or, in versions of this story, thrown under the bus), he's sent in to talk to Melania. In December 2016, slated to be the communications director in the new administration, Miller got another Trump staffer pregnant, simultaneously with his wife's pregnancy. He lost his prospective White House job in the ensuing mini-scandal, but he remained a Trump favorite, coming back to help manage the 2020 campaign. His conversation with the former First Lady prior to the first court appearance will become an oft-shared cautionary tale of managing the Trumps' relationship. "Nice try," she says, after Miller makes his stand-by-your-man pitch.

It's Justin Caporale who takes over the physical management of the indictment. Caporale, a Florida political op whom Wiles recruited into the campaign, is the logistics guy—by which is meant not just making the trains run on time, but staging the entire look and feel of Trump's movement, presence, and message. Caporale's central mandate is to make the former president continue to look like he is still president—and running for re-election. He isn't a private citizen being hauled into court. He's President Trump.

The motorcade leaves Mar-a-Lago on Monday. Several helicopters follow the train of SUVs overhead to the airport in West Palm, beginning a continual broadcast.

Every day in Trumpworld aspires to be a white Bronco day, recalling the world's cameras focused on O.J. Simpson more than a quarter century ago—an event that, arguably, changed the nature of news and television.

On the tarmac at LaGuardia on Monday afternoon, Trump holds everyone on the plane. He, too, along with much of the world, is watching his aircraft, the Trump name plastered on it, on television. The longer he waits to disembark, the longer he holds the attention of the cameras.

Then the motorcade makes its way into the city.

On Tuesday morning, before the trip downtown to court, Trump gathers with his lawyers—Boris, Joe Tacopina, Susan Necheles—on the sixtieth floor of Trump Tower, in his living room.

"How's it playing?" he asks the group, the same question he's been asking on the phone with friends all morning, although he's been following the news and television coverage as closely as anyone.

"The whole country has your back," Boris offers, which seems like the right response.

Outside, Fifth Avenue is packed—more, perhaps, with the curious than with his overt supporters. (Still, it's not a protest.) He emerges, implacable, indomitable, from Trump Tower and enters the ten-car con-voy. They turn right onto Fifty-Seventh Street and head to the FDR Drive. There are three helicopters overhead as they near the East River, and the networks are cutting into their broadcasts. On the FDR, only one person can be seen giving the finger.

It's a circus atmosphere across from New York's criminal court at 100 Centre Street, a few hundred protestors for and against Trump mugging for the media, a sense of event but not of animosity. Scores of interna-tional camera setups, possibly a hundred or more. Helicopters (police and press) overhead. The Trump motorcade arrives around the back.

Trump, on the phone, now has a new question: "Do you think in-dictment is bigger than impeachment?"

Steven Cheung, who has worked his way through the ranks of the Trump campaigns and the Trump White House to become the 2024 spokesman, endearing himself to Trump with his flamethrower rejoin-ders to the press, makes the mistake of trying to respond literally: im-peachment has just purely political ramifications; this has political and legal ramifications.

But everyone understands that by "bigger," Trump means is it *play-ing* bigger—more drama, more attention? That's the answer he wants: It's bigger because it's *bigger*! And yet Cheung is clearly right. This is a different world. Trump is being *arraigned*. And they don't even know yet what for.

Boris is on the fifteenth floor of the courthouse with Tacopina and Necheles, waiting for the indictment to be unsealed. Trump is in the fingerprint room. To the merriment of the Trump lawyers, in a story that becomes part of the day's lore, the printer that spits out processing forms jams. "Sorry, Mr. President," one of the court officers nervously jokes. "You'll have to come back tomorrow."

Other prisoners have been re-routed from the hallway, now filled only with policemen. The former president, sitting on a wooden chair, waits for what no one is sure, just for the process to go forward. No mat-ter who he is, no matter what standing he has that the ordinary man does not, no matter what great powers of denial he possesses, he is in "the system."

CHAPTER 2

E. Jean and the Boxes

MAY–JUNE 2023

Alina Habba furiously resents the suggestion by various of the other Trump lawyers that she got her job as a Trump defender by hanging out in a bikini by the pool at Trump's Bedminster club, which she and her husband, a parking garage owner, joined in 2019, threatening to sue anyone, if she knew who they were, who says as much. But she does hang out by the pool and, proudly so, in a bikini. The 2010 graduate of Widener University Commonwealth Law School practicing with a small firm in New Jersey did actually get her job representing "the President" because of her membership at Bedminster, and getting recommended, she takes pains to explain, by other Bedminster members and thereby offering her services to the Trump family. Trump, in 2021, had her file several more or less frivolous lawsuits on his behalf, including against his niece Mary Trump, who had written a negative book about him; that suit, like others, would be dismissed. As his legal troubles mounted, he kept suggesting bringing Alina in. Although she had little experience germane to the issues he was facing, he seemed satisfied, pleased to be able to show her picture on his phone—along with that of Lindsey Halligan, another comely lawyer he had hired in Palm Beach—whenever the subject of his legal talent came up, which it did often. "I may not have the best legal team," he took to saying with pride, "but I have the hottest."

The spring in Mar-a-Lago had brought a flood of subpoenas into all

corners, delivered to everyone ranging from Trump lawyers and lieuten-
ants, to the guy who walked around and offered you a Diet Coke at
Mar-a-Lago, to the cabinetmaker who installed the club's storage area
doors. Jack Smith, the dead-eyed prosecutor in Washington, was the
personification of the government's decision, after nearly two years of
ambivalence, to proceed against Trump before the 2024 election—
political concerns or establishment hand-wringing be damned. The
prosecutor in Georgia, Fani Willis, was staking her career on her
willingness—eagerness!—to move against him. New York State and its
ambitious avenging liberal prosecutor, Letitia James, were determined to
wreak havoc with his businesses. If ever the liberal political and legal establishment had focused its might on a singular goal, getting Trump was
it. If there was ever a legal team less prepared to handle such an onslaught, it was Trump's.

· · ·

And then, suddenly, the E. Jean Carroll case was coming to trial. This
was a case that Trump had avoided, and mocked, for many years, and
now here it was.

It was a #MeToo-age anomaly. In a magazine story and a book that
followed, E. Jean Carroll, a magazine writer, described Trump's raping
her nearly thirty years before in a Manhattan department store. This
charge, together with the list of other women who had come forward
since 2016—and his own famous admission of "grabbing women by the
pussy"—was, to put it mildly, much more damning than what had sunk
virtually all the public men who had been accused of abuses in recent
years. Trump, arguably, was the only public figure to have survived sexual opprobrium.

Not only had *nothing* of the sort ever happened, but he did not even
know these women—*any of them*! The charges, every single one of them,
were just lies, Carroll's being among the most preposterous.

That was his defense: incredulity. *Come on, the most famous guy in*
New York is just going to randomly grab some old lady and pull her into a
dressing room in a Fifth Avenue department store?

Trump was optimistic. He thought he finally had a lawyer who could handle things: Joe Tacopina, a Boris choice—though later Boris would adeptly cast Tacopina aside. Tacopina was a New York lawyer whom the tabloids (that is, the *New York Post*) seemed to love. And you couldn't keep him off television. Perfect. He had been all over the news talking about the Bragg case, and that now had rolled seamlessly into his showboating on the Carroll case, making him, to Trump, "the man."

The two-week trial began on April 25. But from the beginning, inside the courtroom, it was Carroll's show. In person, she was an elegant and petite older woman, almost eighty years old, hidden behind big, dark glasses. But she easily summoned an image of her plucky younger self—even as the Trump side kept unsuccessfully trying to emphasize that she was not that young, not young the way Trump liked them young—when Trump, in her claim, attacked her in the Bergdorf Goodman changing room in 1996 (or thereabouts). Trump's hope, even his assumption, that the story would be treated skeptically—Carroll couldn't remember the date, basically not even the year, of the attack—was dashed almost from the first moment she took the stand. Rather, she instantly became a New York City hero, this small woman, alone against the world, taking down the biggest man, the *worst* biggest man. Carroll killed it. As the headlines got worse and worse, Trump blamed Tacopina more and more—why wasn't he being more aggressive? "I thought that's what he was, aggressive, but he's like a kitty cat." And why didn't Tacopina want him to testify?

On the golf course in Ireland, where he went for a few days off from playing golf in Palm Beach, Trump took a rogue question from a reporter: "Why are you playing golf while you're on trial for rape?" And he said, off-the-cuff, "I'm going to go back, and I'm going to confront this woman." Given that this was already an unprecedented calamity, a presidential candidate on trial for rape—a case he seemed destined to lose—any logical reading would say that calling more attention to it, maximal attention by having him show up for it, was a bad idea. Everybody was opposed to his showing up, Tacopina most of all. Meanwhile, Boris, attuned to Trump, was all in: "You need to show up, Mr. President; it could turn everything around. These other people don't have your back. I'm the one guy who's with you here."

Except Trump waffled and didn't show up, and the jury found him liable for sexual abuse, with a penalty of five million dollars.

He blamed Tacopina—and, accordingly, Boris blamed Tacopina, too.

"I listened to the lawyers. That was stupid. I'll never make that mistake again," Trump huffed.

Three themes emerged from the Carroll trial that seemed relevant to all the legal difficulties to come: First, it was always the fault of his bad lawyers—and they were always failing him, his lawyers; and every lawyer that signed on with him would always bear the brunt of his view that they had failed him. Second, he could do it better; staying away from the Carroll trial and *not* making himself its public face had been a profoundly lost opportunity. But the third theme was undoubtedly the most important: Good attention, bad attention—it didn't make any difference; he'd broken the attention paradigm. All attention was equal and positive (the adage of a simpler time was restored: all publicity was good publicity); the number of Trump headlines (of any kind) was the consistent predictor of rising poll numbers.

A judgment against him for hauling a woman into a dressing room, raising her skirt, ripping her pantyhose . . . but the campaign happily went on.

On May 10, the day after the verdict, the most famous sex abuser in the country was given an hour by CNN to make his case to be president and, not incidentally, to further besmirch E. Jean Carroll. He was deplatformed by Twitter—Elon Musk, its new owner, had invited him back, but Trump was now a captive on his own ghost town social media site—with even Fox severely curtailing his airtime. CNN was now replatforming him. What's more, CNN largely turned the production details over to the Trump team. Or Justin Caporale and his people jumped in to take them over, holding a large bloc of seats for security and then, at the last moment, filling them with Trump supporters. There was an uprising of leftish opprobrium—the immediate result of which was to cost Chris Licht, the CNN chief, his job. Licht was out, but the twice-

impeached, recently indicted Trump, whom a jury had just found guilty
of sexual assault, was back in.

And, indeed, every other network, noting the CNN ratings, now
rushed to offer him time. Over the following weeks, the Trump team
arrived in New York to entertain proposals.

• • •

Along with Boris in the top tier of the Trump bubble—ever reinforcing
the bubble—was thirty-year-old Natalie Harp.

She was a Fox News–type blonde, although not on Fox. She had
been a "host" on OAN, the distant-third conservative news channel behind Fox and well behind even the lagging Newsmax. Trump had seen
her on television at the same time that she was lobbying almost anyone
in his circle whose email she could get. Natalie Harp, the 2012 Point
Loma Nazarene University graduate and 2015 Liberty University MBA,
had a story: She had recovered from bone cancer because of Trump's
"Right to Try" law, which, she said, allowed her to get the experimental
medication she needed. While there were holes in this tale, she nevertheless earned herself a speaking role at the 2020 Republican convention:
President Donald Trump had saved her life. In 2022, she came into the
nascent campaign as a fetch-it girl, hovering around Trump in anticipation of whatever needs or desires could be instantly satisfied. This settled
into a more specific function: She would accompany Trump during his
three to four hours a day on the golf course and, riding in her own golf
cart, keep him abreast of events by printing out emails and news stories
on the wireless mini printer in her charge.

In doing this, she became a significant gatekeeper. Trump was frequently seen with a cache of papers. He would often demand time in his
schedule to go over "my papers." (In the past, he had militantly eschewed
papers.) His workload—"my papers"—was almost entirely what Natalie
had printed out. The curation was largely her own. Hers was solely a
good-news printer—and she, a worshipful acolyte.

This was one of Trump's set pieces: always to be surrounded by attractive women who worked for him. It was an inverted feminist creden-

tial: In another outdated culture pin, he referred to them as "Charlie's Angels." His relationship with them was avuncular and flirtatious. Alina Habba and Lindsey Halligan and Natalie Harp were part of the great entourage that accompanied him to the spring NCAA wrestling championship. Trump's subject of discourse at the NCAA event was which wrestlers the "ladies" found most attractive. Everyone seemed happy to play along, critiquing the various bodies, rating them as their type or not. But Natalie couldn't be moved. Trump kept pressing her, trying to make her obvious point even more obvious to everyone listening in with disbelief and embarrassment: "Oh, none of them, none of them, sir. I didn't find any of them attractive or anything worth looking at"—which was to say, *I only have eyes for you.*

"I mean, this is how it is. He just likes people who are, you know, entirely in the sycophant territory," one entourage member explained.

Every effort by the staff to create distance between Natalie and the boss was met by redoubled efforts on her part to remain close, her doggedness amusing and impressing Trump. The weirdness of it all only belied the comfort Trump felt around her—not least because she was literally there all the time, at his beck and call, utterly attentive, hovering and interrupting when others sought his attention—and her growing importance.

What's the new chief of staff say? Ha ha.

● ● ●

He was as strong as any non-incumbent had ever been at this point in his party's primary cycle, consistently twenty-five or thirty points ahead of his nearest rival, and now often beating Biden in current polls. And he was only getting stronger. Yet he was hardly campaigning at all, playing eighteen holes of golf almost every morning.

At the same time, the full force of the justice system was coming down upon him with arguably a greater fury than had ever attended any American political figure.

In the spring of 2022, Alex Cannon, a normie Trump lawyer from the 2020 campaign, had been dealing, none too happily, with the National

Archives and Records Administration, which was increasingly irate over records and papers that had disappeared in Trump's abrupt (and, for him, unexpected) departure from the White House. Almost everybody in Trumpworld credited this to disorganization and to Trump's own constant casual disregard for regulations. With NARA pressing him, he had returned some papers, but begrudgingly—more annoyed with the demands than with losing the papers. But, even here, noncompliance, even as he complied, was his MO. When a subpoena finally arrived, it only increased his ire.

Cannon, who, after the 2020 election, had tried to come down firmly on the side of standard election procedures and rules (i.e., accepting his loss), thereby incurring Trump's continuing displeasure, tried to spell out the situation as it stood after months of wrangling and now with a subpoena in hand.

"If we don't return all of the papers, the FBI will come and take them," he counseled.

Trump replied, "Let them try."

The boxes indictment came a year later, on June 8. Unexpectedly, it came in Miami. On Trump turf. And in front of a Trump judge, Aileen Cannon, whom Trump had nominated for a seat on the federal district court in 2020.

Here was another indictment on what the legal team characterized as a technicality. They were now going after him for not following some bullshit rules about government papers. Just the kind of behavior that his people—the base—have never held against him. Who's been hurt? Where's the crime? Show me the money.

It was another sort of split screen: For half the country or more, this was slam-dunk stuff—he'd been caught on tape: ". . . as president I could have declassified it," Trump was heard on an audio recording while waving a document in front of visitors to Bedminster. "Now I can't, you know, but this is still a secret." But for much of the rest of the country, it was feeble—chickenshit stuff just to try to bring him down.

The arraignment was scheduled for June 13, 2023, in Miami.

If the New York indictment had been stepping into the unknown, the financial, media, and polling success of what the Trump team blindly accomplished after his first indictment was now the model. They knew how to do indictments. They returned to Florida from Bedminster. The coverage was door-to-door. The Trump team was in contact with every major media outlet on a moment-by-moment basis, directing the cameras from Bedminster to the airport, from the plane landing in Miami to the motorcade en route to the courthouse.

As though saying it for the first time, he once again pronounced to the legal team trailing behind him: "Legal and media are the same thing, the exact same thing to me."

Trump was hoping for a hundred thousand supporters in the streets, but in fact it was just, optimistically, a few thousand. (He blamed this on the Secret Service's blocking off the area.) The far-right conspiracy theorist and self-described white nationalist Laura Loomer, whom Trump had previously praised, was outside with a bullhorn. Alina Habba, whom Trump had declared the most camera-ready lawyer he had, was sent out to make a statement.

Trump had resisted the plan to go from the courthouse to Versailles, the vast restaurant on Calle Ocho in Little Havana. Even Trump thought the place was a little hokey. (What's more, he hated Cuban food.) But if there was any community that understood political prosecution, it was the Miami Cubans. What's more, they had flipped Miami-Dade in two elections, making it over in Trump's image. This was coming home.

He was greeted by a mass, and as though spontaneous, rally. As far as the eye could see, it was streets of people chanting, *USA!* and *TRUMP! TRUMP! TRUMP!* Along with U.S. cable and networks, it was every Spanish-language TV camera in the Western Hemisphere.

Inside Versailles, Trump was at the center of a prayer circle with a group of prominent Cuban clergy. He delivered the stem-winder: "the grievances," as the Trump team had taken to calling the litany forming the backbone of his most outraged and angriest speeches and his most menacing cadences.

"Fuck Jack Smith," he said, coming outside to cheers, whoops, and passionate applause, a happy and satisfied man.

CHAPTER 3

January 6

JULY–AUGUST 2023

Letters had started to surface from Natalie to Trump, passed around by his political and legal teams with bewilderment and concern . . . and incredulity, portraying a relationship of an imagined alarming intimacy or one of genuinely strange submissiveness. She slipped them into the stack of papers with which she was constantly supplying him.

> . . . I want things always to be right between us. I also know I've been distracted all week (forgetting to eat through the days, and even forgetting to sleep, and only catching a couple of hours at a time). I haven't been myself, dwelling on the Past, and the pain of losing my Dad, and I started letting the remarks of people who haven't bothered me before, get to me—not because I care what others think, but because I see myself being lowered in your eyes and good opinion. That is the fear you see, because I never want to bring you anything but joy. I'm sorry I lost my focus. You are all that matters to me. I don't want to ever let you down. Thank you for being my Guardian and Protector in this life . . .

> With all my heart, Natalie

Now this is the Note I wanted to write (But the apology needed to come first.) . . . After going through all this self-analysis, my conclusion? I need to reunite my past self with my current into a better version who will make you proud. And please, when I fail, will you tell me? You have the absolute right to cuss me out, if need be, when I deserve it, because no one knows or cares about me more. Thank you for always being there for me—I'll never forget when you made that promise to me after losing my Dad, and I know how happy he is right now that I did get to go to Scotland and Ireland, as he always wanted for me. To modify a classic, "I could not have parted with you, to anyone less worthy"—and, I will add, it is I who is unworthy. Always, Natalie.

P.S. My hands looked worse in Scotland and Ireland because the Cold turns the old "scars" purple. Still on the road to recovery!

Since the start of his presidency, Trump had nearly always had a young woman to buffer and boost him and act as his aide-de-camp, body girl, gatekeeper, and, often, interpreter ("what he means . . ."). This included Hope Hicks, his most senior body girl; Madeleine Westerhout, who would be fired for gossiping about the Trump family; and Margo Martin, his current assistant. All looked the part: thin, tall, with long straight hair, short skirts (in winter, high boots). The fact that these women without political backgrounds, relevant educations, or even long histories with Trump—and each with a clear devotion to or infatuation with him—came to assume outsize influence at the highest levels of government was written off as just one more Trump characteristic. But Natalie Harp now pushed this to a further extreme.

Her fixation was an open secret. This was schoolgirlish and eye-rolling—and discomfiting for all. But it existed side by side with her better-than-anyone proximity to Trump, the deference and authority he accorded her, and her remarkable persistence in overcoming every effort to short-circuit her access.

Her golf cart had become the literal mechanism for shadowing him. In his three or four hours on the golf course every morning, Natalie—close behind in her designated cart with her printer, and holding his phone—was his connection to the world. At every hole, she supplied him with what she thought he might need or want to know. Equally, he told her whom to call for him, and what to post, with her composing many of his outbursts. Political teams often need to deftly and tactically deal with a candidate's bad habits. Natalie's golf cart became conveniently unavailable. Undaunted, and with a thirty-pound printer on her back, she yet pursued, running madly after Trump's golf cart on his spring golfing trip to Scotland.

The summer move to Bedminster became another opportunity to deal with what was now deemed officially "the Natalie situation." In Bedminster, she needed housing—so none was allotted. Out of sight, for Trump, was out of mind. And even Natalie would not presume to speak to Trump about her accommodation. (Who got what room at what Trump property was hard-fought politics, largely unbeknownst to Trump.) And yet, in Bedminster, suddenly there she was. She had reached out to the grounds staff at the country club and gotten herself a maid's room. And when that proved too far from the main house to respond quickly enough to Trump's calls, she relocated herself to the much closer women's locker room, where, with undiminished proximity to Trump, she would spend the summer.

The earlier joking about Natalie being the true chief of staff took on a darker meaning. The more peculiar she seemed to be, the more obvious her obsession with Trump and her lovestruck adulation, the more integral she became. She was taking over the social media accounts; she was communicating, sometimes on a daily basis, with Trump's coteries in Congress—a daily texting relationship with as many as two hundred members of the House and Senate, most more and more confused: Why were they hearing from this person, and why were they hearing so often? The body girl was, in effect, a chief spokesperson.

Trump's girls had always existed in relative harmony with his principal body man, Dan Scavino. Scavino had risen up from a caddie at Trump's Westchester golf club to its manager, then on to the campaign;

and in the White House, he got the title of deputy chief of staff. But principally, he was an integral part of Trump's comfort circle, his particular function being to type up Trump's social media posts. Natalie had become the first of the body girls to seem to have superseded Scavino. In late spring, Trump posted accusations that President Biden had been personally paid five billion dollars in the Hunter Biden affair. This was, in fact, a Natalie post. She had promoted a right-wing accusation about five *million* dollars to an absurd five *billion*. "Did you fucking say five billion? Five *billion*?" screamed an uncomprehending Scavino. The "five billion" error, and apoplexy of the usually mild Scavino, became the much-repeated shorthand for the scope of her misjudgments.

Natalie was now foremost among those unexploded bombs that a candidate's staff needs to keep aware of: More and more of Trump's moods and outbursts seemed directly connected to the clippings and reports she brought him; and more and more reliably, she was there to interpose herself in meetings with the political team, using her printer to re-direct or override their concerns. The aggressiveness of her attention, and her fury when she was denied bestowing that attention on Trump, was also of increasing concern to the security team. The Secret Service, with her letters in their possession, was now noting the strangeness of her behavior.

Nonsense, declared Trump. "She just loves her president."

• • •

For Democrats, one saving secret of 2020 was that the Trump campaign was a mess: Jared Kushner had ultimate charge, but he was, other than when it suited him, MIA; Brad Parscale, the campaign manager—the website designer in 2016 whom Kushner had promoted to the top, until he was relieved a few months before the election (subsequently having a public breakdown in the street and waving a gun)—had integrated his own business with the campaign in such a way that tracking the campaign's income and expenditures became increasingly opaque, with Parscale making millions and the campaign finding itself with a two-hundred-million-dollar deficit ten weeks before the election.

This time around, Wiles and LaCivita were not family nor family proxies; neither were they strictly Trump toadies. They were pros whose sole measure of success was winning, rather than—at least at the moment—gaining Trump's favor or working their percentage of the campaign's expenditures (a factor in all campaigns, but one that in the past had seemed to be an overriding interest among many of the figures around Trump). But another aspect of their professionalism was that they were aware of how prone a Trump campaign was to going off the rails.

For them, the media reports of the campaign's great focus were viewed as another split-screen version of reality. Ever-rising poll numbers, the so far merciless DeSantis takedown, and the competence of the leadership team had created this new sense of juggernaut and inevitability. It was an unexpectedly un-Trumpian, efficient, capable, and tactical group: Wiles and LaCivita, the generals; Jason Miller and Dan Scavino, the loyalists; Justin Caporale, the stage director; and Steven Cheung, the redoubtable spokesperson at its center.

And yet . . . their candidate was Donald Trump, the greatest variable in American politics or, likely, politics ever. What might seem stable at this very moment could go haywire the next. Indeed, part of the current strength of the campaign was Trump's pursuit of his golf game at the expense of his day-to-day interest in the campaign; his attention was somewhere else.

But as the campaign displayed its un-Trump-like competence, the legal team began to remind older Trump hands of his past political campaigns: no clear leadership or consensus; the constant entrance of new players and abrupt exit of old ones; shoddy information and no way to share it even if it was good; rumors and leaks; personal enmity; unpaid bills; a general lack of expertise (and contempt for it), with the overriding imperative to satisfy the mostly misguided and uninformed views of the man at the center of it all.

The prosecutor in Georgia, Fani Willis, had all but announced that her indictment was coming in August. How much clearer could it be? But Boris didn't think so. Boris reported that the Democrats in Washington didn't want Willis to bring her case; they were worried she would fuck it up and overly politicize it. As in New York with the Alvin Bragg case, here was another Black liberal prosecutor campaigning against Trump—not a good look. Boris's theory held that Jack Smith was going to take the case over. That was better for Trump because it was federal, and there were so many constitutional issues that appeals would easily run down the clock to after the election—and then they'd just blow it all off (when they won). So . . . surveying: The Alvin Bragg indictment was just bullshit, and if then there were just two federal indictments, which they could deal with in the White House, it was looking, as Boris reported, hardly that bad at all. Here was Boris at his booster best, waving it all away. Nothing will happen . . . until it does.

But Boris, too, was a split screen. His cheeriness and confidence with Trump belied how jittery and sweaty he seemed at other times. In part, he always seemed sweaty because he was invariably dressed in a three-piece suit (always too small for him), even in hot-weather Florida and not-so-much-cooler-weather Bedminster. Just wipe your head, and everyone knew you were imitating Boris.

Almost every week a new rumor, usually sparked by a media inquiry, and promoted by other lawyers, swept through the team about Boris himself being indicted. Have the feds seized Boris's phone? was one mid-July press query. And in close confines, Boris was often on the phone heatedly talking in Russian.

It was a shared joke (even Trump shared it): "Hey, Boris, are you setting up your exfil order for the Russian sub to get you back to the homeland?"

Among the Trump hands, quite a list of current and former aides, who had been called for Jack Smith interviews and who had analyzed among one another the nature of the inquiry by the questions they had been asked, all noted one thing: There were lots of questions about the lawyers involved in the election denial and the lead-up to January 6 (Giuliani, Jenna Ellis, Kenneth Chesebro, and John Eastman), but no questions about Boris, arguably the one guy in the middle of all the lawyers, the key connector. Why weren't the Smith prosecutors asking about

Boris? Trump aides and lawyers were asking. Could it be he'd already told them everything?

On Tuesday, July 18, Trump posted that he had received a "target letter" from federal prosecutors—all but certainly meaning an imminent indictment. The legal and political teams were in the dark—another Boris fuckup or weird effort to exclude them, with the Trump post being the first time they had heard anything about the target letter.

The grand jury was scheduled to meet on Thursday. This meant the indictment might come immediately after. Or not. Nobody knew. Right away would be good, because Congress was still in session. An indictment in D.C. would turn out a legion of conservative House members, an instant rapid-response team defending Trump on the steps of the Capitol. But the summer recess began on July 31. After that, the town would be empty.

At any rate, after thinking that the January 6 case would somehow die because of political indecision; or because they had the boxes case in Miami; or because it would get bogged down in a wrangle with Georgia; or because Boris kept saying it was all bullshit; or because, even if it went forward, each lawyer seemed to have a grand theory about how it would be thrown out or about the endless delays that would push it into a distant future—suddenly everyone woke up with the understanding this could be the big one: the *United States of America v. Donald J. Trump.*

It could be the biggest case there ever was—and a defendant with among the most sad-sack lawyers there ever were.

· · ·

Steve Bannon, whose life's work had become getting the attention or even the fleeting favor of the man who fired him six years before—a rarely successful effort—had an idea of how to distract Trump, and the Trump bubble, from his legal troubles. (It had become a litany: Bragg, Boxes, E. Jean, New York AG, Jan. 6, Georgia.)

Bannon was working off a good moment. Trump was opening doors to many of his old crew, who had fallen into various states of disfavor. Roger Stone had been occasionally invited onto the plane. The oft-banished Corey Lewandowski was getting his calls returned. Kellyanne Conway (long out of favor because of her now-estranged husband George's social media onslaught against Trump) was back and soliciting work. Even Rudy Giuliani got an occasional shout-out at a rally. (Though that's as far as it went: Giuliani was still demanding his millions in legal fees from Trump.)

Bannon, never too far from every right-wing huckster opportunity, had become a promoter of the surprise summer hit movie *Sound of Freedom*. It was about child trafficking, a current of horror and weird titillation that runs through the far-right view of elite corruption and perversion, presented now in a slick production and with a heartstring-pulling plot. It was a MAGA smash, grossing over $100 million since its release in the spring (ultimately $250 million worldwide), a counter-culture must-see—the counterculture being the Trump base—and wholly ignored by the mainstream media. Bannon hectored the staff to get Trump to host a screening of it at Bedminster—a chance for Trump (and the film's promoters) to claim the movie as a Trumpworld hit and for Bannon to brag about his Trump influence and proximity. In fact, Trump knew nothing about the film, regarded its premise as icky, and was irritated by the suggestion of the screening, suspecting that Bannon was, once again, trying to make a buck off him. But told about the $100 million number, Trump quickly came on board. A small screening inside the club expanded to a large one outside at Bedminster, on a big screen in front of 250 members, guests, right-wing media, and, to boot, Jared and Ivanka, following a buffet dinner at the club. Trump, who had yet to see the film, introduced it (adding a digression for his stump speech list of grievances) and its director, writer, and stars (none of whom he'd ever heard of), butchering all their names. And then, as a measure of his good feeling about the evening, he brought Bannon up to the stage—their first face-to-face in nearly six years—and Bannon returned the compliment: "We've got to get Donald J. Trump back. He's the one who was putting the hurt on the human traffickers, and he's the one who can stop it. It's getting so much worse under Biden—more children suffering every day. This movie is so important that it's brought together me, Jared, and Ivanka, all in support of this movie." This last comment, given the public animosity between Bannon and the couple, provoked some nervous twitters. But here was the secret message: The Trump band was ready to get back together (despite their mortal enmities) and get their jobs back.

The audience of mostly Bedminster members consisted largely of people in their sixties and seventies, all dressed to their demographic version of the nines for a night at the club: pearl necklaces and chiffon, madras sports jackets and pastel slacks. The screening had been sprung on them at the last minute, with Trump leading them to the impromptu alfresco theater, and with puzzlement among many members. But in no time at all, the shock and horror of child trafficking captivated the Bedminster members, with loud weeping coming from the audience, streaked mascara everywhere.

Trump himself was dabbing at his eyes.

After crying at the horrors of child trafficking, the audience got to go for a soft-serve cone—from an old-fashioned ice-cream truck brought in for summer events—dipped in sprinkles or in chocolate coating.

• • •

Trump was starting to take personally the case against him for the January 6 Capitol attack, and he had elevated Jack Smith to his number one enemy. This was mano a mano in the way Trump saw conflict, and it produced a steady stream, sometimes multiple times in a day, of rants against Smith. Smith was deranged. He was on cocaine. He was gay. The least discussion on the part of any of Trump's lawyers about the January 6 indictment—and the discussion often involved how important it was not to antagonize Smith or make it personal—teed him up. Early in the morning and late at night, he publicly fulminated against Smith.

"They're trying to put me away forever. Throw away the key."

He kept asking everyone around him what they thought would happen. But by this, he wasn't saying, what do you think will happen *to me*? Not even—like every other person facing indictment on criminal charges that could put them in prison for the rest of their life—what do I *do*, how do I *get out* of this? *Can* I get out of this? That's not what he meant when he asked what was going to happen. He meant what was going to happen to his *numbers.* Were they going to go up? And by how much? How much of a bounce on this one? In any group, he literally went around the room asking each person for their best guess.

The actual indictment in the January 6 case came on August 1. It stoked Trump in the way that the other two indictments had not. This is Nazi stuff. Yes, the Nazis, Trump insisted. The entire political team, along with panicky lawyers, tried to talk him out of the Nazi references, but Trump was adamant. It was like the Nazis! Just like the Nazis, what they were doing to him.

January 6 had, for many Democrats, become the defining moment of Trump's presidency, a moment Democrats hoped would seal his fate. But he had become as unshakable in seeing it as his defining moment, his finest one. Many of the people around him at the time believed that of all the things he might be guilty of, *not* truly believing the election was stolen from him, an apparently central premise of the prosecution, wasn't one. And even if you did grant a flicker of doubt on his part in the weeks after the election—and many don't grant the possibility of such a flicker—ever since then, the feedback loop had been constant (even among people who quite believed otherwise): *The election was stolen, yessir, yessir, it was. Oh, this is just a witch hunt, a total witch hunt. Yessir, yessir.* And January 6 had been a great day. And he had delivered a great speech. There'd been a million people there—in reality, a moderate guess of 60,000 and an outside guess of 120,000—and it was maybe the best speech he'd ever given, to maybe the biggest crowd. Trying to stress his righteousness, he doubled down on exactly the incendiary language and disruptive fury for which they were trying to convict him.

• • •

In an irony that took the split screen into real life, Fox News was, at the exact moment Trump was being indicted on federal charges for trying to overthrow an election, appearing on his doorstep in Bedminster—he made them come to him—to beg him to participate in its candidate showcase, the first debate of the primary season.

Trump demands and expects to be courted. It's a ritual; you come to him. This has defined his professional life. It is part of the ecosystem of being around him, of him being who he is and you being who you are. Everybody is a petitioner. He's a salesman, but he expects you to be selling him, too. There's a handful of people he might actually travel to, but that only further defined his sense of the people on top—and now, while he had always been near the top, having been the president put him indisputably at the absolute top.

His plan was to get the Fox brass to Bedminster—Suzanne Scott, the CEO of the network; and Jay Wallace, the president—and then dump all over them. But first, as part of the ritual and the noblesse oblige of their coming to him, he had Natalie give them the special guest tour of the club and grounds. This was all done in a manner of great courtliness. A special tour, and given by a special tour guide—"Natalie, the best. I'm giving you the best. You're not being shown around this beautiful club by just anyone!"

Scott and Wallace, both struck by Trump's obvious delight in having them there as helpless petitioners, were then seated out on the Bedminster dining patio for dinner at the Trump table. The Fox duo's desperate pitch for Trump to participate in the debate, an open acknowledgment that no Republican candidate much mattered but for him, was, if Trump needed it, quite an out-of-body counterpoint to that day's declaration by the U.S. government that it would focus all its legal wherewithal on his personal and political destruction. But as further demonstration of his dominance, regardless of the criminal justice system, Trump dismissed Scott and Wallace practically in mid-sentence—he didn't need them. He was uninterested in their offer and blandishments, and cheerfully, with double barrels, he began to blast them for every Fox sin of commission and omission, for their terrible coverage of him—and so little of it! For how soft they were on DeSantis. "And my daughter-in-law, Lara, she could have been a senator from North Carolina. She gave that up so she'd be a Fox contributor. And then you fire her, and you know that's very fucked up."

Meanwhile, if Trump was living sanguinely in his utterly dominant, lord-of-the-manor, king-of-the-hill side of the split screen, quite a few others around him were freaking out. Along with him, the Smith indictment cited six unindicted (as of yet), unnamed co-conspirators. This appeared to transparently include Rudy Giuliani; John Eastman, who had concocted the scheme to get Mike Pence to disqualify electors; Sidney Powell, with her claims of massive voting machine fraud; and Jeffrey Clark and Kenneth Chesebro, who had aggressively inserted themselves into the election legal melee.

The identity of "co-conspirator number six," "a political consultant who had helped implement a plan to submit fraudulent slates of presidential electors to obstruct the certification proceeding," remained unclear and might have pointed to any of the political hands who were around Trump in the two months after the election.

But the inside money was certain that number six had to be Boris.

As Trump was entertaining (and torturing) the Fox execs, the media had started to focus on Boris. And if the media hadn't focused on Boris, other Trump lawyers were telling the media to focus on Boris.

Boris was on the phone screaming back—the full *You have no basis, no basis at all, and if you do, I will fuck you so bad.* "If you write that I'm number six, I'm gonna sue you, and it's going to be the worst thing that's ever happened to you!" This was both a frothing-at-the-mouth and yet also boilerplate response to a list of reporters. (Trump lawyers, like their boss, had a penchant for threatening personal lawsuits.)

At the same time, among insiders at Bedminster, this now naturally devolved into trying to figure out why number six had not been made obvious. Were they, the feds, encouraging people to look for number six or encouraging any possible number six to be covering his tracks? Uncertainty and fear prompts people to make phone calls and send emails and texts and to say, over devices now closely being monitored by the government, what should not be said. Follow the trail of loose lips saying dumb shit.

The next day, Boris was on the plane with Trump—proximity was Boris's go-to move whenever he was in hot water. And somehow that news was immediately out there—Boris accompanying the president. The president would not be traveling with number six, would he? But he *was* traveling with Boris. Therefore, don't be stupid. Boris could not possibly be number six (according to Boris).

That evening, Boris reached out to a friend for some PR help. "So, just, hypothetically, if it were to be me. It's not, but hypothetically, if it were to be me, how would it be handled from the press side?"

• • •

In more innocent days, indicted politicians, as well as mobsters, literally pulled their coats over their heads. But the Trump campaign had vans waiting to take reporters to the Washington courthouse and then back to the airport. Alina Habba was again out on the courthouse steps as chief spokesperson and TV defender. This was Trump at his reality show–casting best.

Although the stagecraft for this third indictment was firmly in place—the existential facets of a criminal indictment reduced by Justin Caporale and his team to camera setups and the images that the Trump camp delivered—Trump, in the staff view, appeared this time to be a lot tenser. As much as he or Boris could rationalize the other indictments and legal threats, January 6 clearly went to the heart of Trumpness. It was a challenge to everything he'd come to stand for in the last two years—here was the issue he was most clearly running on, the one dearest to his heart and pride: that the election had been stolen from him.

At the arraignment, Judge Tanya Chutkan kept him waiting for twenty minutes; his fury mounted at this display of scorn for him. Then she addressed him merely as "Mr. Trump." And then she instructed him about what he could and could not say. *Unbelievable.*

It was his unchallenged grail that they would not have been charging him with anything if he hadn't been running for president. And, likewise, in his mind, running and being prosecuted had become part of the same thing: They were prosecuting him because he was running for president. He was running for president because they were prosecuting him.

As the team returned to New Jersey, Alina Habba, going through the Twitter (X) commentary, noted her place in the sun: "The only thing anyone is talking about is my tits. It's all about my tits. Oh my God. I guess I should have worn something else. My mom is going to kill me."

CHAPTER 4

Atlanta

AUGUST–SEPTEMBER 2023

It suddenly surfaced that the linchpin of Trump's legal defense had himself been arrested not long before.

And there was video.

In early August, *The Arizona Republic* released police body cam footage it had been tipped off about. In 2021, Boris, on a night out alone crawling bars in Scottsdale, Arizona, in an establishment called the Bottled Blonde, and well past drunkenness, had pestered two young women to the point of the police being called—at which point the body cam picked it up. To the police, the girls, captured on video, described in vivid detail Boris's insistent, unrelenting, and handsy drunken approach, rebuffed and repeated. Meanwhile, on video, Boris is reeling, dazed, sloppy, pitiful, and then handcuffed and forced helplessly to sit in the gutter—the Scottsdale nightlife happily and tawdrily playing on about him.

There were two immediate questions: How could Boris survive this, and who had tipped off *The Arizona Republic*? These were probably not mutually exclusive questions.

Internally in Trumpworld, nearly everyone's view of the Boris threat to Trump, highlighted in flashing neon, was in inverse proportion to Trump's seeming lack of concern over it. Boris was a threat most of all precisely *because* Trump would hear nothing against him. He was, in this interpretation, like an unruly little dog: annoying and disruptive to everyone but its owner. Because of Trump's affection for him, there was no restraining Boris, and certainly no getting rid of Boris. Trump was hardly put off by suggestions that Boris delivered to him only an optimistic view of things because Trump valued Boris for precisely that reason. The suggestion, delivered at best obliquely, that Boris might be a turncoat was dismissed by Trump because Trump's measure of loyalty was binary: Boris was loyal; therefore, he could not be disloyal. So, insiders judged the leak about Boris's arrest and drunken humiliation as having such a clear and obvious purpose that it was surely the work of other Trumpworld insiders: Killing Boris was necessary to save Trump (from himself).

In any other campaign, Boris would have been finished. But not so much in Trump's. Here was a heightened *lack* of a double standard. If Trump's own bad behavior did not, in his mind—or apparently in the mind of his voters—reflect badly on him, then the bad behavior of his staff ought not reflect badly on him, either. And if they were personally humiliated—well, that was their problem, not his.

"They're only coming after you because you work for me," Trump reassured Boris. That was, with a little critical interpretation, quite true, but it was also true, of course, that Boris, one evening in Scottsdale, had gotten drunk, pestered and pawed two women, refused to go away, and had to be subdued by police, his humiliation caught on video.

Boris, circumventing staff efforts to keep him out of press-observed proximity to Trump, once again made sure to get himself on the next plane trip—and then leaked it. Whoever was responsible for the original Scottsdale video leak had not helped separate Boris from Trump, but instead had compounded the problem of the Boris–Trump attachment. Boris protected himself by his abject proximity to Trump; the more abject he was, the more Trump was willing to protect him—and take it out on his other lawyers.

"You guys need to get tougher, way tougher," Trump lectured the group in the aftermath of the Boris story. "Republicans never fight, Democrats always fight. You're not fighting. You gotta fight." And as long as he was at it, he pointed the finger at how "stupid" his lawyers had been in the E. Jean case. He wanted to testify, he should have testified, he knew he should have testified. "You guys aren't going to make the same mistake, right?" Meaning, it would seem, that he was determined to testify in the cases going forward—which was terrifying to his lawyers.

. . .

He was, by all reports, going to be charged in Georgia under the state's RICO statute—the Racketeer Influenced and Corrupt Organizations Act. This was a law enacted by the federal government in 1970 to fight organized crime, and that included offenses like gambling, murder, kidnapping, arson, drug dealing, and bribery. RICO had been the downfall of a generation of New York mafiosi. Many states had followed suit with their own RICO versions.

Trump couldn't get New York's tabloid gallery of fallen mobsters out of his mind. "I mean, racketeering, RICO racketeering, like, what the fuck? This is for mob bosses. I went to the Wharton School of Finance. And they're trying to say that I'm Gotti?"

RICO cases are most often based on establishing a conspiracy—you don't actually have to have committed the crimes, but as one of a larger group, you can be part of the *cause* of the crimes—and hence rely on flipping co-defendants. Eighteen others, it appeared, were going to be charged in the Georgia case, among them Rudy Giuliani, Sidney Powell, Mike Roman, Harrison Floyd, John Eastman, Mark Meadows, Ken Chesebro, and a list of other people whom Trump in fact wouldn't have known if he'd run them over with his motorcade—people who had little or no familiarity with him or loyalty to him.

In the Georgia system, there can be two grand juries, one, a special purpose grand jury, to recommend indictments and one to indict. The special purposes jury, convened in this case, recommended the indictment of Trump lawyer Cleta Mitchell, but in the final indictment list, she wasn't there—likely meaning a plea deal, the Trump lawyers assumed, understanding the grim consequences. Even more alarming, the grand jury recommended Boris's indictment—an indictment that never came.

The formal indictment was released on August 15. Trump filed his not guilty plea on August 31. As the date of the arraignment approached, September 6, he was more and more agitated and without a political or media comfort strategy. He increasingly defaulted to the belief—his operative January 6 belief—that an army of Trumpers would come to his rescue.

"We need to tell people to get out there and protest. We can tell people to exercise their First Amendment right and make their voice heard. That's a First Amendment right," he fumed/instructed in a call with his legal team, who tried to demur and deflect. "We have to. I mean, this is insane. We have to call for protests."

Then, in a burst of inspiration, he instructed: "Get the Liz Harrington report out there."

A state-by-state catalogue of how everything to do with the 2020 election had been stolen and rigged, the report, largely sourced from far-right media and almost all of it long discredited, had been surfaced from the greater Trump brain trust, such as it was, by Natalie Harp. Its author, Liz Harrington, living in relative seclusion in rural Maryland, was a sometime Bannon acolyte who had briefly, after the return to Mar-a-Lago, been the official Trump spokesperson. Now, unbidden, she had written a memo and sent it to various people in the campaign and on the legal team, where it had made its way to Natalie and then to Trump and now to official status—becoming, as if by notable provenance, "The Harrington Report"—with instructions to build it out with colorful graphs and charts and to go wide with it to media and supporters.

The report consisted of seventy rambling pages written at the maximum pitch of post-2020 election denialism—the same pitch of acrimony and delusion and desperate lies for which Trump would now be prosecuted. Trump immediately announced a press conference where he would showcase its findings.

The Georgia indictment built much of its RICO case around a wide group of people, all of whom had knowingly pursued and advocated and spread and encouraged others to act on fraudulent election claims. How was touting this report now any different from that?

Continuing to fulminate about how RICO was for mobsters, Trump had gotten it into his head that as long as he was able to convince people that he thought it was true, that the election had indeed been stolen from him, he had an out. "Mens rea," a refrain he was particularly fond of repeating to staff and friends as well as to random Bedminster members, was his workaround—he didn't have criminal intent; he believed in the steal. This, then, was his defense: to dig himself into a deeper hole, ratcheting up his talk about "rigged" and "stolen." In every interview, he became more and more aggressive: computer chips and hacked machines and dead people.

In the days before the scheduled press conference, Susie Wiles pressed the lawyers—which meant pressing Boris to press the lawyers—to be the bad cops on this and tell Trump it couldn't happen. The Georgia lawyers, however, refusing to speak to Boris, were threatening to walk. The research team was feverishly going through the Harrington Report in an effort to wash the most obviously ludicrous sections. This was not just against the immediate clock, but also in the face of the fear that at any minute, Trump would post it all anyway.

"It's Jack Smith's and Fani Willis's wet dream," said one member of the legal team of such a scenario.

It was certainly not the first time the Trump team had looked on in uncertainty and incredulity: "Will he push forward in front of the whole press corps and say something that he can't take back and that will help ensure his conviction, and then hand out a document that will get chopped apart in thirty seconds and serve as a smoking gun? He might . . . or he might not."

Distraction, however, was a faithful Trump friend.

He was absorbed by the upcoming first Republican primary debate, which he was yet refusing to be part of—all the more so for Fox's begging him to do it. This was a test of who was bigger, Trump or Fox. He needed a counter-programming event.

He was having a flirtation with Tucker Carlson, who, just months before, had fallen into Trump disrepute for his leaked emails describing his passionate hatred of the former president. What's more, Trump, on

occasion, eyed Carlson, with his television fame, as a plausible opponent. But Fox had become Carlson's enemy, too, having fired him, and
on that, he and Trump had allied.

Trump would give Carlson a one-on-one interview, no matter that
Carlson's "show" was now untethered and free-floating in the new social
media ether.

"He's getting huge numbers. Bigger than anything," an enthusiastic
Trump assured anyone who might have wondered about the decision to
forgo a cable network audience.

The idea was to spring this major media event, Trump and Tucker,
on an unsuspecting world. But in a reverse distraction, word of the interview leaked. Trump's rage at Fani Willis and his determination to
double down on his accusations of a stolen election with the Harrington
Report was all of a sudden replaced by new ire—he was "ripped, totally
ripped" over his supposedly top-secret counter-interview being out of
the bag: "It's gonna kill the value of the thing, completely kill it,"
stormed Trump, ever his own producer. The result was that neither the
coming press conference nor the release of the Harrington Report was
mentioned again (well, until it was—but that would be a later day). The
leak, which now wholly occupied him, and for which he was demanding
that heads roll—for which, in fact, someone should be "executed"—
seemed easy to explain: Carlson, after the taping of the interview, had
eaten lunch on the Bedminster terrace and posed for various selfies,
which were shortly posted on social media.

The Tucker interview, airing alongside the cable debate, shortly
turned to Trump's delight. The Twitter (X) view meter spun into the tens
of millions, then the hundreds of millions, a ratings measure of largely
illusory meaning, but one that allowed Trump to confidently claim he
had easily bested Fox's audience of 12 million (actual) viewers for its
debate.

• • •

The day after the debate, the Trump team headed to Atlanta for his processing as a Georgia criminal defendant. Trump was buoyed by the ever-

growing Tucker tally: 250 million views. *Is this getting out? Is this the story? This is so big it's got to be the story!* And then, in short order, he was angry because it wasn't the story. There was no explaining to him, and no one wanted to try to explain to him, that 250 million Twitter (X) views basically didn't mean much at all. His new bad humor returned to Fani Willis and her pursuit of him rather than of murders and drug dealers in Atlanta, and then on to the long list of his co-defendants. He methodically went down the list. He wanted Boris to tell him who could and could not be trusted. And he demanded to know from Boris what he'd done to make sure everybody was on the same page, that everybody got it.

Boris—his own loyalty a question to everyone other than Trump—was ginger in his response: "You know, sir, we're not allowed to talk with anyone who has been indicted. If there are conversations, they can only take place between counsels. I mean, that's what we have to do."

Trump's monologue teetered back and forth among his seething contempt for Willis and his wanting to rehash the ratings reports and his sheer amazement over his numbers. And then he turned to the possibility of a mug shot: He'd been practicing it for days—on the golf course, in the mirror, in front of the legal team, and among Bedminster members. It was a detail that had been left hanging, whether there would be or wouldn't be one. The Secret Service might yet have adamantly inserted itself. But Trump had been toying with the idea: A mug shot would make this indictment different from the others.

Arriving in Atlanta, the motorcade passed through Black neighborhoods that Trump judged, by the scale of crowds on the street and the absence of negative signs, as for him. "Did you see all the Black people. Everybody was Black. And everybody for Trump." Caesar coming home.

Processing in Atlanta was not even in the courthouse, but in the jail. Trump entered with his lawyers. And that was a twist—Boris, engendering more intra-legal world antipathy, had successfully ousted Trump's well-respected Georgia lawyers, and only as they arrived at the jail was Trump meeting his new one.

"It's, like, oh fuck, now we have a new lawyer," said an aide, narrating the scene.

He was in and out in no time—with the mug shot taken in an instant. But he was over the moon: He loved the picture. "This looks so cool, this is a classic, this is iconic," he kept pronouncing.

Now what to do with it, how to use it, how to retail what would shortly become a worldwide image?

"What's the caption?" he asked.

"Election interference," offered one aide.

"Never surrender!" Trump added.

Accordingly, on every newscast, and at the top of every paper in the world, and shortly, on T-shirts, coffee mugs, and Koozies and licensed to anyone who had anything else they wanted to put it on, was the mug shot heard 'round the world—and always (a licensing requirement) with the legend "NEVER SURRENDER," exclamation mark.

CHAPTER 5

The "Fifth" Indictment

SEPTEMBER–OCTOBER 2023

By early September, the Trump campaign was a reliable fifty points ahead of its nearest primary opponent; it had survived four criminal indictments—indeed, had prospered from them. What's more, it was an easy campaign, certainly the easiest campaign any primary contender had had since open primaries became a two-year slog. As their opponents were enduring the fast food, long days, and bad accommodations in Iowa, Trump and his team, looking toward virtually certain victory, were—shortly to make the snowbird relocation back to Palm Beach—largely relaxing in Bedminster.

And yet, almost the entire top echelon of Trump advisers and functionaries found themselves having to consider their standing and future in the campaign. Even Wiles and LaCivita were confiding that they had lost effective control of the campaign and needed to consider their options.

All political campaigns—most often as a function of failure, but sometimes, too, of success—are susceptible to bruising infighting. But this was not that. If anything, what was happening had united the campaign.

It was Natalie or, as Trump idly entertained the team (or himself), "Maybe it should be Nathalie. *Nathalie.* That's how the English say it.

'*Nathalie,* would you please come here?' Don't you think there's a ring to that, *Nathalie*? Do you like it?" (For a period, he repeated this constantly in his phone calls—his particular piece of cleverness.)

"Do *you* like it, Mr. President?"

This was more of the yucky theater, open flirtation, at once simpering and mocking, but which, Natalie proudly repeated, had brought everyone to the point of screaming, *Enough!* But it was also just the can't-miss-it fact that something here was terribly wrong.

Trump's son Eric, hearing often from a weirdly authoritative and demanding Natalie giving her opinion on legal developments, took a turn at trying to tackle the situation in a set of annoyed queries to the legal team: *Who is she? Who's letting her do this? Who gave her the authority? Why is she briefing on legal matters?*

This was meant to put the problem onto staff to solve. But it ignored, of course—because you had to ignore this aspect—the fact that she was a figure wholly of Trump's own making. The closer she positioned herself to Trump, the more instructions he would give her. Where her efforts to speak for Trump had so far been mostly relegated to the right of the right-wing media—even for the Trump camp, the wing-nut press—she was suddenly, perplexing various brand-name reporters, expanding into mainstream media. She would bring him good news she uncovered from some far-flung, right-of-right sources (often out-of-date), and he would direct her to get it out to everyone, putting her in direct touch with national political reporters and Trump family members as well as with Republican members of Congress. What is this, they were demanding of Wiles and LaCivita and other staffers: Who was this Natalie person, who was she speaking for, and what was this crazy spamming?

Even the Secret Service had now weighed in: Natalie was a security consideration. But no one was going to tell Trump that.

Hence, a time bomb.

And it was hardly just the personal weirdness. Once, earlier in the summer, on the plane, becoming a cautionary tale whenever Natalie's name came up, an abrupt takeoff had sent the pages Natalie constantly fed Trump from the printer—carefully assembled with Trump's signature gold paper clips, faithfully carried by him in a beige Lululemon bag—flying off his table, and everyone had to suddenly scurry to collect them, seeing, dumbfounded, the contents. What everyone saw was a random collection of out-of-date articles and printouts from obscure websites and fan artwork downloaded from strange Trump-adoring places on the internet—all of which he was hoarding like these were national secrets.

She had, too, become the keeper of the "Truth" phone. That is, she was wholly in charge of the Trump posts—that is, they were *her* posts. Sometimes as many as a hundred a day. Old articles, things not remotely relevant or germane, replies to comments from random people, re-postings of out-of-date polls. Here was a public window into the true oddness and chaos of the Trump campaign—and mind. Fortunately, no one in the press, or anywhere else, was looking too closely at Truth—again, the daily collective sigh of relief that Trump was no longer on Twitter (X), that his posts went largely unseen.

Natalie was both rogue and yet official—with constant confusion over whether it was her voice or his; more and more, it was one voice.

Earlier in the summer, it was Natalie who, taking offense on behalf of Trump that House Speaker Kevin McCarthy, in a fumbled interview, had suggested that Trump might not be the best general election candidate, funneled article after article on McCarthy's slip to reporters in the right-wing echo chamber, who began the drumbeat that would end in the defenestration of McCarthy, otherwise a Trump ally.

She was, too, the reliable nutter conduit: Anyone who wanted to get to Trump could just text her. In late summer, at one of the Bedminster golf tournaments, Laura Loomer, dismissed as a hopeless liar and fabulist by even Marjorie Taylor Greene and a subject of constant effort by the Trump political team to keep her as far away as possible, was brought in by Natalie at the tournament to, in even Fox News' characterization, "pal around with Trump."

"Natalie's so quick, she's great, you guys just don't like her because she's so fast and so good" was a Trump rebut to questions raised about her.

It was not that he was necessarily deluded about Natalie. Beyond how obvious it was that he made wide exceptions for anyone abject in their awe of and devotion to him—men and women alike, loyal troupers who would go running off a cliff—and, too, that he liked young women joined to his hip, there was another aspect that was judged by normie aides to be characteristic Trump: Keeping people around him who were largely inexplicable to others, unsuitable and unseemly—wackos, even— was a way of reminding the people who believed themselves to be officially and appropriately in charge that he was, as demonstrated by how daft his preferences and impulses could be, the absolute boss, unregulated by anybody else's expectations or measures.

If you forgot that, Natalie was there to remind you.

• • •

The Georgia indictment was behind him, and the looming, unknown implications of his civil fraud trial in New York were ahead—now known as "the fifth indictment." The New York case was scheduled to start in a few weeks' time, on October 2. But meanwhile, cosseted by his fifty points, he was in a fine, commanding mood.

Against all advice, he agreed to do the debut show for the new host of *Meet the Press,* Kristen Welker. This was part of his general Fox diss: Where before, loyal-most Fox got all his major interviews, now, with Fox in its disloyal Ron-DeSantis-or-anyone-but-Trump phase, he was determined to give "my ratings" to the competition. But there was something else. This was *Meet the Press*—he would say "It's *Meet the Press!*" with awed respect, as it might have been said in 1975 (he continued to treat *60 Minutes* and *Time* magazine similarly)—and it was getting a new host. This was historic. It would be a historic note that he would be the first guest.

It was a meandering and sour interview. "I had such high hopes for you, but you're not getting off to a good start," he told Welker. But he was pleased with his appearance. "It's *Meet the Press!*"

His good media mood, his fifty-points-up mood, now extended to an unlikely Megyn Kelly interview. He had sworn quite a specific sort of blood oath against Kelly after she attacked him in the first Republican debate in 2015. ("She had blood coming out of her eyes. Or blood coming out of her wherever.") And he had watched with pleasure her departure from Fox, and then as she was blown up at NBC, and then as she was reduced to a podcast. But over the last few months, Kelly had been effusively praising Trump on her podcast; his many flatterers were bringing him frequent reports about great things she had said. (He himself had never listened to her or anyone else's podcast.) Then Kelly pressed for a meeting with him and in response to her full-court press of blandishments and honey, he agreed here, too, ignoring doubtful staff—to do an interview with her.

"She loves me," he was convinced. She'd said as much. Told him it would be an entirely friendly interview. He was going to be president again, and the country needed him, and bygones were bygones.

And it was just, whatever, a podcast. He blew off any sort of prep— and walked into it: striding into the Club Room, most often a lunch venue with bar and tables, on the second floor of the Bedminster clubhouse, in red tie and blue suit, with Megyn Kelly, amid her audio and video setup, in a bodycon all-black outfit. ("She's still hot," he'd been telling friends.)

It's an affable, up-tempo chat until thirteen minutes in—her face changes from cheerful/flirty to pouncing/sadistic—when she goes in for a direct hit on one of his most vulnerable spots: "That is one thing that your critics say would have helped keep some of these migrants out: a wall. Whatever happened with that, because what Border Patrol says is we only added forty-six miles."

He pushes back: "I built almost five hundred."

Whiplash style, she pivots to immigration birthright citizenship, another soft spot—would he get rid of that?

"I would, I would do that by executive order," he says.

She responds, "But you didn't do that in your first term. You said you were going to, and you didn't." He fumbles and she badgers: You gave Fauci an award . . . You said Caitlyn Jenner could use any bathroom. Kelly won't let up. "How do you run a campaign when you're spending these tens of millions on legal fees defending yourself from these criminal attacks?"

And then she asks about Melania.

In some sense, this is the darkest Trump hole. Nobody knows the answer to the what-about-Melania question. Not even the people closest to him. What is the nature of the marriage? Nobody can tell you. Nobody can tell you where Melania even actually lives. It may be, on its own peculiar terms, the most successful marriage in America. Or, it may be ready to blow up at any moment.

Still, it ought to be easy to answer—easy sentiment and cliché. But it goes seriously weird.

MEGYN KELLY: Melania is so mysterious to so many. What do people misunderstand about her?

DONALD TRUMP: I think part of the beauty is that mystery. I was with Barbara Walters. She was a great friend of mine. And she was an amazing person. She interviewed me many, many times, and I was on her show *The Most Fascinating People of the Year*, I think, more than anybody else. I was on there a lot. This was even before politics. But Barbara was unique, and I said, 'You've interviewed everybody, who was the one that you would like to interview more than anybody else? She said, 'That's easy, Greta Garbo.' . . . She was a great actress . . . But she was very reclusive, never did an interview. I don't see Melania as like that, but she's introspective, and she's confident . . . She doesn't need to be out there. She has confidence. She has a lot of self-confidence.

There is a collective *What the fuck is he talking about?* from his staff.

· · ·

As with every single court action against him so far, "the fifth indictment," now days away from trial, appeared as though unexpectedly—so, whatever planning, preparations, messaging, and, in general, consistent and coordinated approach was needed had to happen on the fly.

A civil trial on business issues might have appeared as the least of his problems next to four criminal indictments and a civil trial for rape. The fifth indictment—or, sometimes, the "sixth," if you included E. Jean; or the "seventh," if you included the next scheduled E. Jean case—was largely a matter of what New York State alleged to be the inflated values Trump had put on his real estate holdings. This was not going to put him in jail; it was just going to cost him, a billionaire (theoretically), some money.

But in some sense, he was suddenly taking this even more personally than all the other legal threats, those possibly mortal threats, against him.

This wasn't simply politics, which he still saw as something of his late-in-life adventure; this was his actual life. Here was the fifty-year story of him becoming who he was: He was synonymous with Manhattan and its buildings. Attacking that was attacking, well, his essence. It seemed just plain old unfair, bitterly unfair, that because of his political life, they were attacking his real life. After all, if he hadn't been elected president—something that, he never tired of pointing out, had cost him money—of course they wouldn't be suing him and his business now. This was personal. Well, everything was personal, but this was even *more* personal.

And particularly galling was the bullshit they were suing him for. This was the New York real estate business. *Inflated values? Come on!* They were suing him for being in the New York real estate business.

If he lost this, he could lose conceivably hundreds of millions as well as his ability to do business in New York—and despite what his fellow New Yorkers might think of him, it was *his* New York—and even Trump Tower, a greater symbol of his power than even the White House. (Plus, it was where he was truly comfortable—Mar-a-Lago was a great property, but after all, it was a country club.)

In fact, he had already lost this trial. In a summary judgment, Judge Arthur F. Engoron had ruled against him: Trump had lied. He had committed fraud. The only thing really at issue now was how extreme the penalty would be.

His lawyers had kept him from showing up at the E. Jean Carroll trial. He wasn't going to make that mistake again, even in evident defeat.

His lawyers, he was convinced, simply performed better when he was there. What's more, he repeated (over and over), his legal strategy was his media strategy; his media strategy was his legal strategy. And *he* was his media strategy.

More specifically, he had no actual legal strategy and, practically speaking, little legal competence on his side. Alina Habba, his golf club lawyer, had neglected to check the box on the appropriate form asking for a jury trial, a procedural misstep that had virtually guaranteed the judgment against him (or at least his other lawyers were dumping the blame on her). There was simply no recourse, except, of course, a media one: "Everybody's saying that my legal team screwed up, that we didn't request a jury trial, that we didn't check some box. That's not a good look. We'll just say what some people are actually saying. There's some rule that you're not allowed a jury trial in this kind of case."

The debate about showing up for a trial—a trial he had already lost—became fully engaged. Trump was game, his lawyers aghast. If he were present in the courtroom, the judge could call him to testify at any time. It was a civil trial; there weren't Fifth Amendment protections. (This had to be explained to him.) You're not required to be there; you're not going to change the outcome by being there—so why risk being put on the spot?

But the E. Jean case continued to rankle him: "I would have won that if I showed up. I had that stupid lawyer who said, no, no, no, don't testify. I have the worst lawyers. I didn't go, and I lost. I need to be there."

If his lawyers in E. Jean screwed him, now he was looking at more incompetent lawyers. His annoyance was focused on Susie Wiles—and not, Boris was taking pains to point out, on him—who was responsible for hiring Chris Kise, his lead lawyer in the fraud case, and he constantly repeated his belief that Kise had cheated him by demanding his fee, three million dollars, up front, for which Wiles was now getting the direct blame. "This guy's just no good." This became the refrain: "The guy has got the yips."

He repeated this now constantly: "You know, the yips, like someone who's, like, lining up for a putt, like a three-foot putt, and they're like,

Ah, people are watching me. Ah, then they, like, choke. This guy just doesn't have it. He has the yips. He can't go and deliver. I have this friend of mine at Mar-a-Lago who lines up for the putt, but he gets the yips and he can't hit it—it's like it's three feet from the hole, and he hits it like thirty yards. Some people just get the yips when they go to putt."

· · ·

The court day begins in the living room at Trump Tower—it's a theatrical set piece of bile and recrimination that will figure large in all his New York proceedings. *Who's Afraid of Donald Trump?* Somehow the living room feels as close as you can get to him—closer than anyone wants to be. He's wearing a blue shirt, distinguished from his regulation white, and he wants a compliment. He says how surprised people are that he's wearing a blue shirt and that they've all been asking him what it means that he has on a blue shirt—with those in the room with him at 8 A.M. wondering just who exactly might have seen him in his blue shirt earlier that morning.

Trump is in the Trump chair, and everyone else is in a semicircle around him.

"You, lawyer," Trump starts in on Kise, "you can't have the yippers today, I hope. You know, I'm not very impressed so far. You can't choke today. Like, you have to do good. There's got to be, like, we got to go out there and look our best. Our legal strategy is our media strategy. Our media strategy is our legal strategy." He's staring down Kise—and not getting whatever response he's looking for. "You know what, I'm just, I'm just really tired of you. You know, all this time, all this money, we haven't gotten anything done, and here we are. So, that's it, you can't have the yippers today."

The fifty-eight-year-old lawyer is frozen, flushed, taking it, holding on—barely.

And then, with press and cameras notified, the caravan once again leaves for the courthouse at 60 Centre Street.

In the courtroom, it's a tableau that fixes Judge Engoron as a particular figure of Trump's contempt and disdain. Engoron's awkwardness before the press pool cameras that have been given a brief opportunity for stills and video is pitiful to Trump: Engoron takes off his glasses and then freezes, the seconds ticking off, wearing a goofy smile.

Meanwhile, the judge's clerk, Allison Greenfield, hovers over him, whispering in his ear and seeming to direct him. Letitia James, the New York AG, takes a prominent seat. She's the devil here. There's certainly enough of Trump's spleen and bile to go around, but his true blood score is against James: a Black woman, a *fat* Black woman (*another* fat Black woman—they haunt him), who is both personally out to get him and a stand-in for an entire class of Democratic politicians—the radical left.

The prosecution's opening statement is delivered with dispatch.

Then it's Kise: His is a sleepy, boring, meek opening. No fireworks, no punches, no lines to remember.

When he is finished, there's a recess and the Trump team heads to the break room—everybody knows what's coming and is shrinking from it.

It's a glaring six-foot-three, 215-pound (actually, probably 250-pound and probably six-foot-two) Trump hovering over Kise: "That was a shit job. That was terrible," Trump says, spitting it out. "Quite frankly, attorney, I am so sick of you. I am so fucking sick of you. That was such a shit job out there. You didn't go after the judge—you didn't say anything about him at all. You didn't go after the AG—she's just sitting there, like a sitting duck, and you didn't go after her. All right, new plan. Alina, you're going to go back out and have a do-over for the opening statement. And you're gonna rip their motherfucking heads off."

Habba, who is officially the second chair, but, at best—with no pretense otherwise—the Trump signature adornment, seems in disbelief: "Wait a minute—you want me to go and kind of redo opening statements? I'm not prepared."

"Yeah, you're gonna do it. Like, you'll do fine. You're going to get out there, and you're going to do great, okay?"

In Trump's view, Habba scores—she somehow pulls it together without preparation and saves the day. She blasts Judge Engoron, and she blasts Letitia James—it's a political trial, a witch hunt trial, a trial by Democrats; and nobody here knows anything about the real estate business, anyway. The more this registers on both the judge's and the AG's face—and neither seems very good at hiding their personal offense and annoyance—the happier Trump is.

On the next break, Trump's mood has entirely altered. It's "my Alina" and everything's good. Kise is slinking back and trying to stay out of view. But, somehow, he has bumped his head, or has some nervous issue that produces a raised red-blueish spot on his forehead. It's hard to miss.

On the way back in, Trump walks past him and stops. "What's that?" He points, clearly with disgust, at the raised patch. He doesn't wait for an answer: "It doesn't look good. Get rid of it." (He will rehash Kise's red bump with friends, as a point of both mockery and concern, with a digression into various New York dermatologists.)

The afternoon, which features testimony from Trump's accountants, is detailed and painstaking, and Trump is clearly fidgety. He decides he's going to go out and talk to the cameras waiting outside the courtroom. This is unanticipated and ad-libbed—occurring, perhaps most of all, because Trump is bored. Trump rips the judge and rips the AG. There's a complicated and nuanced appellate court ruling finding that some aspects of the case are outside the statute of limitations. Judge Engoron has yet to rule on exactly how this will affect the case. But Trump now, before the cameras, is happily announcing what sounds like the dismissal of the case. "Eighty percent of the case is over." It's another split screen: Trump's bombastic, garrulous, camera-ready interpretation of the legal proceedings versus the actual legal proceedings.

Every break now becomes an impromptu news conference.

After court, the Trump entourage heads back uptown, where there's a debrief in the Trump Tower living room and another opportunity for Trump to crucify Kise: "You know, I have the worst attorneys. Everybody knows that, right? Everybody knows that. I have the worst attorneys. When I had Roy Cohn as my attorney, he knew what to do. He would have known what to do in there today. But now I have the worst attorneys. You know, you guys got to get out there on TV, declare victory on the statute of limitations, that's been decided, anything before 2014 is off-limits. Eighty percent of the case is over. The attorney general should drop the case. How could they have ever brought this case? Letitia James is a monster. She's hurting the state of New York. Violent crime is high. Illegals are pouring into our country; the streets are filthy. And this is election interference—I could have been campaigning in Iowa, but they're making me sit in a courtroom, so I can't campaign. That's definitely election interference."

Partway through the second day, in no small measure because it's as boring as the afternoon before—it's still the same accountant on the stand; the trial is really about the bookkeeping minutiae of the real estate business—Trump starts to pay attention to the judge's clerk, Allison Greenfield, a thirty-seven-year-old lawyer and career court employee, who seems to be often, if not continuously, in the judge's ear. Also, she's texting on her phone during the proceedings. Trump is keenly interested. Is this related to the trial? Is she communicating with the AG's office? Taking instructions from other nefarious New York Democrats? A quick Google search reveals that Greenfield is a Democrat—of course she is. Then there's a back-and-forth with her social media accounts. Somebody has flagged something—but when they return to it, the Trump team finds that it's been taken down. Ahh, but someone finds it—it's been saved, yes. What has surfaced is an Instagram picture of the clerk with Chuck Schumer, Democratic U.S. senator from New York, in which they're "yucking it up."

"Wait, what is that? That's her? The lady with Chuck Schumer is the clerk?" Trump is amazed—thrilled. "All right, here's what we're gonna say—it's Chuck Schumer's girlfriend." He dictates a post to Dan Scavino and waves away everybody's horror here, especially Kise's. "Get it out. I don't give a fuck what the lawyer says."

Trump's post—the picture with the legend "Chuck Schumer's girlfriend"—rolls out in real time with the courtroom able to watch the judge's clerk, sitting by his side, as she realizes that she's just gotten publicly blown up by the world's foremost bully for being the girlfriend of the Senate majority leader, which she most assuredly is not.

Meanwhile, Trump heads out to the cameras to continue to blast virtually everything and everyone associated with the proceedings. At the same time, there's now an emergency meeting in the judge's chambers, with the clerk saying she is already getting threats and with Alina Habba yelling back at her that this is part of the job; she signed up for this. And the clerk firing back, no, she absolutely did not. But the other thing that seems to be on the judge's mind as he obviously struggles with how to proceed is a slow-motion understanding that already, at the rate things are going, the trial will stretch for months, an incredibly boring trial, providing Trump a daily opportunity to do what Trump does, which is to make life miserable for everyone connected to the trial—and for that to be the only thing that's really of any interest here: the Trump Show. The pundit class has consistently said that a courtroom will be a substantially different arena for Trump: In a court, a judge is in charge. It's his rules, it's his power that counts. This, then, is the first test of that theory.

The judge tries vainly to press for a settlement—the number in the ether is one hundred million dollars. But no way Trump is going there. The judge also says he's issuing a "limited gag order," protecting his staff—that is, his clerk. This has the effect of both making the clerk top of the news and focusing all eyes on Trump and what he might say— how close he'll come to violating the gag order. What exactly would that mean? What happens to an insolent Trump?

. . .

The great choler about Boris's lurking presence and general bad juju had suddenly been replaced by his eerie and suspicious absence. Boris, whom no one could get rid of, was now never around. MIA. He was still, many times a day, on the phone with Trump, feeding and seconding Trump's doubts about his lawyers and lauding Trump's own legal instincts and acumen. He was the former president's only consistent legal adviser, his consistently good-news legal adviser. "No joke, on the phone ten times a day at least," by one count. But he seemed clearly to be avoiding the rest of the team. And everyone else.

The most dangerous place had always been between Boris and a camera. Now: sorry, unavailable. *Have you seen Boris? Have you spoken to Boris? Has* anyone *spoken to Boris?* That was the background conversation that was raising more questions about likely unindicted co-conspirator number six than it was answering. As much as Trump continued apparently not to give a shit, it seemed bizarrely clear-cut to everyone else on the legal team: If unindicted co-conspirator number six didn't cooperate, then he was going to be *indicted* co-conspirator number six—and he hadn't yet been indicted. Therefore . . .

In the past few weeks, a disturbing thought had run through Trump's Palm Beach golf course and his staff and lawyers. It may have started with several former Trump lawyers, part of an alumni group that kept close tabs on the ongoing legal mess, whether to confirm their sagacity at staying at arm's length or to be mindful of future opportunities (after all, Trump might very well be the next president), during their conversations on the greens of the Trump International. And then it jumped to his present lawyers and closest staff, where it seemed to sum up the tempting-fate nature of Trump world in the existential question—with Boris hotly denying it and threatening to sue anyone who suggested it: How could anyone be sure Boris wasn't wearing a wire?

PART TWO

The Season

CHAPTER 6

Perry Mason

It was one hundred days before the Iowa caucuses and the opening of the primary season. The goal: to have a clean sweep of every one of the early states, making Donald Trump the de facto Republican nominee for president by, at the latest, South Carolina on February 24, and to finish the sweep on Super Tuesday, March 5, and have a committed delegate majority by mid-March.

The strategy was not the usual slicing of the issue pie, triangulation of the party factions, and ground game door-to-door canvassing—the method of most crowded-field candidates. Rather, it was to keep DJT at the center of attention, letting him do what he did best—Trump as the star. In zero-sum airtime math, this kept any of his opponents from getting their share of coverage and attention. His show was the overwhelming ratings leader, and everything else was just marginal programming.

His was not a strictly political audience; it was a fan base. A Taylor Swift inversion. Trump fed his fans with his ongoing tour. His act was a constant reminder of his character, the Trump persona—the strongman—with the dramatic tension being would he, could he, bear up and keep on, stronger than ever, and more fabulous, even with everything they were throwing at him?

But in early October, the headlines, annoyingly, did not involve him. A MAGA core group—that is, a group more MAGA than other MAGA people straining to be unquestionably MAGA—had decided to take on the lack of absolute MAGA commitment on the part of the congressional leadership and take down Kevin McCarthy, the Speaker of the House and the highest-ranking official in the party. The immediate cause was a budget agreement opposed by the hard MAGA faction, forcing McCarthy to recruit Democratic votes to continue to fund the government's operation. McCarthy's slim majority could ill afford the blame that would come from a government shutdown; at the same time, making a deal with the Democrats meant facing the wrath and, too, the glee of the bomb-throwing opportunists of his own party.

McCarthy had faced this wrath before, enduring an unprecedented and humiliating fifteen ballots to get the Speaker's job after the Republicans had taken majority control earlier in the year. He'd survived only because Trump, to whom he had largely been abject, had not broken with him. Having managed once, McCarthy seemed to think he could make it again.

Curiously, Trump, not a man of soft spots, had one for "my Kevin." At Trump's lowest moment, after January 6, when nearly every leadership figure in the Republican Party had condemned him; when, ignominiously, and uncelebrated, he had left the White House; and as his second impeachment began, with the real possibility this time of conviction, McCarthy had come to pay court to him at Mar-a-Lago. This arguably began the Trump redemption—a swift one at that—whose rewards Trump seemed now to be amply reaping.

But as Trump had created a new, populist, and performative right wing, and sucked most workaday Republican legislators, intent on holding their jobs, into it, he had also spawned a faction that, while loyal to him, was even further to his right and, emulating him, at least as performative as he was.

Two of the principal figures here were Steven Bannon, that self-appointed Trump consigliere without portfolio, and Matt Gaetz, the congressman from Florida whose MAGA stature had somehow saved him from sexual scandal and political death.

Arguably the main architect of Trump's 2016 win, Bannon had nevertheless faced myriad setbacks and humiliations at Trump's hands. Still, he had only ever continued to double down on his original Trump bet, turning himself, if not into the powerful political mastermind (a MAGA Karl Rove) or right-wing media mogul (à la Roger Ailes) he aspired to be, then into quite an effective gadfly and eminence among the disruptor set.

Gaetz was a rich kid with a politically connected father. A low-rent Florida party boy, handsome enough and audacious enough for prime time, he was elected to Congress on the back of Trump's 2016 victory and tipping of the state. Financial, drug-related, and sexual allegations followed him and broke into headlines in 2021, putting him at the center of sex trafficking allegations in South Florida. Bannon, among other Trumpers, came to his rescue. The House opened an ethics investigation into Gaetz that Speaker McCarthy refused to quash, which had led directly to Gaetz's current attack on him.

Trump was suddenly flooded with calls both to save McCarthy and to support the Trump-rump clusterfuck determined to bring him down. Trump demurred. For the first time since he'd come on the political scene, here was an internal Republican shit show that he wasn't at the center of. Trump, hands off, posted that Republicans shouldn't be fighting one another; they should be fighting the Democrats.

Bannon leveled a fire hose of outrage, slurs, and obscenities at everyone in Trumpworld, including friends and family, threatening to turn the MAGA movement on anybody who stood in the way of the McCarthy takedown—and it freaked Trump out.

McCarthy was unable to hold the Gaetz-led and Bannon-backed faction, and with Trump failing to weigh in—"standing with his dick in his hand," as a McCarthy supporter noted with surprise—he was deposed as Speaker.

This, in fact, left Trump pissed at everybody—perhaps even himself—for how Matt Gaetz had claimed the headlines: "Matt fucking Gaetz."

It soon became clear that there was not an obvious person to replace McCarthy. The Bannon-Gaetz cadre, unable to agree on a compromise candidate with the less-right-wing House faction, declared, deus ex machina–like, Trump for Speaker. (Trump was not a House member, but technically, a Speaker doesn't have to be—though they have always been.)

This was, from the Trump staff's view, bonkers.

Bannon pressed for Trump to become Speaker for one hundred days, while the Trump staff was trying urgently to remind everyone that the Iowa primary was in *one hundred days*.

Trump as Speaker was a ridiculous and implausible notion proposed by an extremely small group—the far-right Gaetz, Marjorie Taylor Greene, and Troy Nehls among them—the high-media, low-numbers set. In fact, they didn't remotely have the votes to give Trump this unlikely job. Nor did he want it—a job of keeping track of daily minutiae, listening to people's issues and complaints, and, as Trump understood, "taking a mountain of shit." And Trump, certainly, was not going to risk having himself voted down in Congress, which, other members were warning him, could very well happen.

Still.

"Why don't we just let them go and say it," he said, as the staff suggested he cut short any further discussion. "Let it percolate for a while."

And he directed: "Just put it out there," that there might be a plan for him, Trump, to show up in Washington and appear before the Republican caucus. "Put it out there," against the backdrop of virtually everyone in the Republican Party, save the Gaetz–Bannon group, across the board saying, "No, don't do this. No, don't come to D.C." And suddenly, giddily, pundits and cable news were looking forward, once again, to American politics being stood on its head—a former president and current presidential candidate stepping in as Speaker of the House—although, in fact, there was no sense, logic, wherewithal, or possibility for this to happen.

"The media is going nuts," Trump happily observed.

By this point, he'd distracted the media from his trial in New York, overshadowed the congressional meltdown that threatened to overshadow him, and incidentally, taken whatever airtime might have been left for his opponents in Iowa. He was the story.

• • •

Trump doesn't go to D.C. because, of course, he's not going to run for Speaker. Instead, he calls Brooke Singman, a low-level Fox reporter, whom he finds attractive, and tells her that, yeah, he would expect to hold the speakership for a short amount of time. (It's not the first time he has called Singman, and aides start to strategize about when they can next get his phone and delete her contact info.) This is wholly at odds with anyone's ability to manage any of this because, in essence, he is just pretending he is going to do something (and no one can entirely say that he understands he is *just* pretending). He is wholly managing the pretend reality while, at the same time, his staff, reaching out to friends, donors, and congressional allies for support, has to manage the actual reality but not contradict the pretend one. What's more, in the middle of this pretense, there are House members who are legitimately trying to run for Speaker, including Jim Jordan, among Trump's strongest supporters in the House.

It's unclear at Mar-a-Lago what in fact are Trump's actual or pretend intentions, with House members calling Trump staff in a panic to report that the Secret Service is coming to do a walk-through to plan for a Trump visit. The staff and congressional allies are left to manage a media hungry for details about what he'll say to the party caucus at a meeting that is, they well understand, *not going to happen.* Plus, they are having to deal with their ally Jordan, who is confused and furious about his own plans being disrupted; and, as well, having to plan the complicated security and visual logistics of an unprecedented visit by the former president and effective leader of the party to the House Chamber; and, at the same time, planning the logistics of this not happening; and, equally, indulging the clear desires of the boss to continue to pour gasoline on the roaring fire. Meanwhile, the Trump camp and its congressional supporters understand that were any of this to actually happen, they would need a strategy of whipping and member targeting in order to win over the moderate group, who would surely have serious reservations about selecting an outsider and, at that, a presidential candidate on the campaign trail for their leader, not to mention reservations about Trump himself—all the while understanding that in fact none of this *was* going to happen, nor should it.

Jim Jordan finally gets through to Trump on the phone. Jordan's desperate plea is for Trump *not* to come to D.C.: It would hurt any chance Jordon might have to get the job. Jordan also gently points out that it takes only twenty members to shift the meeting to a closed executive session that could exclude Trump and that there were enough moderate members who would like nothing better than to embarrass him.

Jordan is pleading for something not to happen that was never going to happen anyway, but this pisses Trump off and will keep him from delivering the full support Jordan will need—and Jordan will fail to go over the top.

• • •

And then, on Saturday morning, October 7, the world, and Donald Trump, wakes up to the news of the Hamas attack on Israel, overrunning miles of towns on the Gaza border and killing yet-untold numbers of Israelis. Amid the bad news, there is good news out of this for Trump: His legal problems, including his present fraud trial, will fall off the media radar; whatever ambiguous place he ended up in with the congressional leadership race is now of no interest; and most important, his primary opponents are completely locked out of the news. He, however, has a voice here as leader of Trumpworld and as, in one of his convenient designations, "the best friend Israel ever had."

But, in fact, he's petulant. Other than his stated all-in support for Israel, he's always been bored with Israeli-Palestinian dynamics, pleased to farm out the issue to others, including Jared Kushner, his Jewish son-in-law (with whom, at this moment, with Kushner and his daughter keeping their distance, he has a cold front going). Now it's a bigger story than he is.

He has a rally in Waterloo, Iowa, that day—previously scheduled flyby campaigning. It's a perfect setup to deliver a forceful defense of Israel and to go even further than Biden in backing Israel's military plans. The evangelical base in Iowa (where there are indications that he's not as strong as he might be) is, with their biblical Last Days obsession, overwhelmingly pro-Israel. A Trumpian show of fire and fury toward the Palestinians will surely play big.

It's not a teleprompter speech composed by his speechwriters. He's riffing. (Standard line: "Who wants me to read a speech? No, I have the best speechwriters. But, you know, it's more fun when we do it this way.") When he gets to the subject of Israel, finally, in a ramble of more than sixty minutes, he is half-hearted on the burning topic of the day. He seems absent a Trumpian point of view.

The next speech of the day is in Cedar Rapids, Iowa. Among the many issues that have festered from his lost 2020 election, and one that he has clung to with particular rancor—well, he had clung to many with outsize rancor—has been Netanyahu's early phone call to congratulate Joe Biden. The man for whom, in his mind, he had done more—not just in his defense of Israel, but in helping Netanyahu stay in office and out of jail—than any other American president ever would, had contributed a major voice to the international consensus that Biden, rather than Trump, had won the election. If he was unclear about his feelings on the Hamas attack before, now, in calls he's been making all day, he has sharpened his view: *None* of this would have happened if we didn't have Biden—and one of the reasons we have Biden is because of Netanyahu.

So, five hundred, or six hundred, or seven hundred (the count was still growing and would reach twelve hundred) Israelis were dead, and it was Netanyahu's fault! If Netanyahu had supported him, and condemned Biden for stealing the election, then Trump might now be president, and if he were president, obviously, Hamas would never have had the temerity to attack Israel. Blame Bibi!

There is a further festering issue—Jews and their disloyalty to him. One of the many reasons he's mad at his son-in-law, Jared Kushner—Jewish Jared—to whom he gave carte blanche in a Mideast portfolio, is that he doesn't understand why, after he did everything he did—with the embassy, with the Golan Heights, and with getting (well, with Jared getting) other Arab countries to go along with Israel—he still gets shitty support from Jewish voters.

At this moment, shaping up to be the worst day in Israel's history, he's full of annoyance at Israel and the Jews.

But this *is* a teleprompter speech. In the end, by the time he gets to Cedar Rapids and through his speech, to his staff's relief, he's largely forgotten about what's going on in Israel and seems content with the tempered teleprompter remarks—though he will shortly post much of his anti-Netanyahu spleen on Truth Social.

Meanwhile, Trump has been consistently at least thirty points ahead of any other Republican's best case, and there he will stay. His total domination of the race and of his party has failed to be as staggering a story as it should be, Trumpers complain, because the media's own function diminishes without a plausible horse race.

Gallingly, with DeSantis hopelessly struggling, the media is now inventing Nikki Haley as the fallback contender. In October, Trump's lifelong friend Andy Stein (their fathers were friends!)—a former New York City politico and Rat Pack buddy who in 2016 and 2020 led the self-created Democrats for Trump (for which Trump dangled many impressive jobs in front of Stein) and who now, in retirement, is a habitual opinion contributor to *The Wall Street Journal* and *New York Post*—declared his support for Haley. Trump responded with a personal note to Stein of vituperation and denunciation—he was done with him; they would never speak again; this was the worst disloyalty he had ever seen. And on and on.

• • •

He's pissed about not just Israel and Haley.

At this very moment, there's the overwhelming likelihood that he will be fined hundreds of millions of dollars and that he and his children will lose the ability to do business in the state where most of their business takes place. It's another gift of the Israel-Hamas war that people fail to notice he's slipped his bonds. But it is there for anyone to see, spelled out in minute-by-minute nutty invective and furious onslaughts on Truth Social posts and, behind closed doors, in trigger-happy raging at everybody near him.

Even his senior people are cowed and unsure how to proceed. Susie Wiles, a woman of enormous composure and discipline, becomes a pointed subject of Trump's wrath. Unreported, she just leaves: She goes effectively off the grid for two weeks. The senior manager of a presidential campaign heading directly into primary season says *Fuck it* and disappears.

Natalie Harp is once more fingered as a hidden hand behind Trump's moods, alternatively feeding him "uppers" in the form of right-wing hagiography (stoking his sense of omnipotence) and "downers" in the form of any signs of disloyalty (stoking his rage).

Forget the media's write-ups of new campaign discipline—he's firmly back to his old ways: freaking out about legal problems, creating fires to put out other fires, emboldened to do what he wants whenever he wants.

And, so far, it is all to Trump's advantage, not least of all because much of his fury is directed at Ron DeSantis.

He rises, in his own mind as well as in the polls, as a function of how much he can trash an opponent. In this, the mission—elevating him now to his feelings of omnipotence—is not just to oppose DeSantis, but to utterly rubbish him.

Trumpian politics is an act of cruelty—he's a deranged comic with a rapt audience. Previously, it was a one-man sally of insults; now, in his image, it's backed by an organized, though largely invisible, activist troupe. The internet's sophomoric humor, sneering derision, and body-shaming jokes are harnessed on a fusillade basis against Ron DeSantis. These are Trump hobbyists waging this new kind of political destruction. You don't need war rooms or op research teams, just manic glee. It's guerrilla stuff. You don't know where it's coming from nor whom you're fighting. It isn't politics. It's some other weird strain of personal entertainment and empowerment—again, it's fandom.

. . .

He is back in New York for his fraud trial—it will run from October to January—and he can't affect its outcome. The verdict, with pre-trial rulings, is effectively already in. So far, in his court appearances, he has only seemed to make things worse for himself, much worse. But he can't keep from believing that he can somehow will this to his advantage. Trump force has to prevail. What's more—and perhaps what's foremost—is the bank of cameras that is always there for him at court. There is literally nothing between him and broadcast. Even in the White House, there were layers of intermediaries before he could speak directly to the press (or he had to personally put reporters on his schedule). But here, by merely stepping outside the courtroom, he's in front of the camera. His lawyers of course try to discourage him. But that's the other thing: By being here in court, he is his own lawyer. Or, very much more to the point, he's found a workaround to the apparently impossible dream of finding a replacement for his ultimate advocate-fixer-promoter Roy Cohn: It's he himself. He'll be his own Roy Cohn.

He's come to believe that lawyers don't know how to speak anymore. Courtroom speech is a lost art. This is the new obsession he is sharing widely: Courtroom *performance* is gone. *Where did it go?* He frequently launches into rousing disquisitions on how the great lawyers could hold the courtroom in the palm of their hand—television lawyers, in other words.

In addition to Chris Kise as an object of his disgust, Cliff Robert, the lawyer for his sons, who are defendants with him in the case, has slowly begun to get under his skin. Robert is a shambolic sort, quite the opposite of the lawyer Trump clearly has in mind, slow in his movements as well as in getting out his thoughts.

Before the court day, Trump can't get his focus off Robert and begins to pick at him. Robert speaks too slowly. He's not reacting fast enough. He's not direct. He's not ready.

"Roy Cohn could speak. You guys"—meaning all his lawyers, but he's looking at Robert—"can't speak. Do you even know how you're supposed to speak in court? This is what I want to ask," he goes in with his heaviest scorn. "Have you ever heard of Perry Mason?" He wants an answer, too. "Have you ever heard of Perry Mason? Do you think what you do in court is in any way like what Perry would do? I need you to be like Perry Mason. Do you understand that? Do you understand what that is?" Trump is not making fun of himself here. No, he wants Perry Mason!

(Proudly so! He will repeat this to his call list as his incisive solution to all his legal problems, reciting his lecture to the beleaguered Robert.)

At the lunch break, none of his furor or focus has abated. His lawyers don't know how to stand up in court. They don't know how to be lawyers. The lunchroom is narrow, unventilated, with only a table and chairs, and at the end of it is an open bathroom, with Trump sitting at the end.

He's shortly on Robert again—a widely repeated, there-but-for-the-grace-of-God warning to all his other lawyers: "Why can't you guys get organized? When you're up there, you're so damn slow with the papers. That's, like, your job, just to be organized with your papers—like how hard is it? 'I'm gonna have a trial today, so let's get my papers organized.' But you're, like, standing there: 'Where are my papers? I can't find my papers.' Every time you're up there, all you do is 'Where are my papers? I can't find my papers.'" And then he goes into his derisive, spaz mode—convulsive, twitchy, flailing. It's a go-to move reserved for anyone who can't seem to talk, or act, or perform, to whatever ideal he has; or, in general, for anyone whom he perceives as weak and annoying. The poor, lumbering Cliff Robert, far from Trump's Roy Cohn or, for that matter, Perry Mason ideal, fatally in his sights.

• • •

And then, on October 19, Sidney Powell, one of the 2020 election denial lawyers who'd been indicted with Trump in Georgia, flipped. Powell had long seemed to have departed ordinary reality and come to inhabit an exclusive Trump sphere of devotion and conspiracy. To the extent that everyone in Trumpworld might doubt, if not their own grounding, certainly everyone else's, Powell was a good baseline measure: You might be out there, but not as far out as Sidney Powell.

After the 2020 election, Powell had wiggled into the close Trump orbit with a finely layered unified field theory of how the election had been stolen, tying in machines produced by Dominion Voting Systems, the dead Venezuelan despot Hugo Chávez, the U.S. intelligence community, George Soros, and the Clintons, to the plot to steal the election.

Now, suddenly, without warning, she was fleeing in the opposite direction from the outer edge and meekly repenting. She hadn't really meant any of it, she apologized in her plea. There were, in fact, many ardent Trump justifiers who didn't really mean any of it, but Powell had always seemed safely to be a true believer. If Trump had others in the Georgia indictment to worry about, Powell had not seemed like one of them.

But then again, if her original beeline for the outer edge of conspiracy was an opportunistic bid for the president's attention, a convenient intersection of nuttiness and opportunism, her retreat now might also be as opportunistic. She was able to trade herself out of massive and expensive legal difficulty for just a misdemeanor conviction, probation, and an $8,700 fine. Beyond the obvious uh-oh of a co-defendant pleading out in a RICO conspiracy case, what Trump lawyers and staff noted with both horror and dawning appreciation was that the networks immediately went to Georgia and this legal development, overriding the Israel-Hamas war and the soap opera of the Speaker's race.

"Man, if this Sidney Powell thing can make people forget about the war in Israel," said one lawyer, "just imagine what the actual real criminal trials are going to be like." Again, the drama, whatever the drama was, seemed always to redound to Trump's great benefit, a logic so perverse that his antagonists could never grasp it.

And then Ken Chesebro flipped, getting off with probation, a five-thousand-dollar fine, community service, and an agreement to testify against Donald Trump. A jury might easily be convinced that Sidney Powell was a fantasist and a paranoid. But Chesebro, one of the primary legal architects of the plot to replace Biden electors with Trump electors, did seem like a more or less credible voice. If Chesebro was flipping here—essentially admitting to knowingly trying to defraud voters—he would certainly be called to testify in the federal case. Again, everything seemed connected in the legal mess, a broad, interlocking criminal justice attack that cried out for a brilliant, Machiavellian mind to wage the counterattack.

This made Boris once again the focus of frustration and alarm for the legal team.

He was yet on the phone with Trump, but attempting to stay off the radar of the campaign principals Wiles and LaCivita, who had become his open antagonists. This meant that the campaign had even less of an idea what was going on with the legal side. And more to the point, if there was a sense of no one being in charge when Boris was otherwise maintaining that *he* was in charge, now, truly, with Boris God knew where, it seemed indubitably that nobody was in charge.

There was a constant sense of pivot among the team of lawyers, with each variously trying to represent him- or herself as the lead lawyer or the "president's personal lawyer" or the campaign general counsel when something good had happened and then, when the news turned, each displaying a hands-off affect: "Oh, that's not my case" or "I'm not the lead attorney on that one" and "Isn't so-and-so on top of that?" and "What we need here is someone actually in charge."

In fairness, this was not specifically a dysfunction of the legal team, but a characteristic of Trump organizing principles. He himself was exclusively in charge, and if someone did manage to actually take control (to become, say, the campaign manager), they would invariably be fired. So, survival dictated that you honor the vacuum.

Still, the campaign, absent a campaign manager or anyone with ultimate authority, was functioning fine. It was the legal side that was ever in chaos and, on almost every seismic event, blindsided.

Boris was uncomprehending. "What do you mean? It's all good. It's all going the way it's supposed to. You shouldn't worry about any of this. Powell and Chesebro are much more dangerous to Rudy than to POTUS, and they'll be terrible witnesses anyway. All these cases are going to collapse."

This had become the effective or default legal strategy: Don't let it distress you enough or demand so much of your concentration that you can't move forward with everything else. Trust the broader picture of how the stars will align.

CHAPTER 7

The Buffet

NOVEMBER–DECEMBER 2023

Ron DeSantis had walked dead-on into Trump's ridicule. It was not just that the ridicule was part of the inherent cruelty of a Trump campaign, but that so many Trump staffers had worked for DeSantis and understood his glaring personal weaknesses. This was their revenge.

Wiles; Caporale; James Blair, the political director; Tony Fabrizio, the pollster—all had done time with DeSantis and were left with bad feelings toward him, and all understood his significant weaknesses as a candidate.

It would have been difficult to design a better sitting duck.

The attacks that Trump and Trumpworld delivered were so much more ferocious and performative and imbued with a spirit of joie de guerre, and delivered so much more frequently than anyone else was capable of doing or willing to do—and with no embarrassment over the constant repetition—that everyone else appeared tongue-tied, down-trodden, or weak-willed. They suffered while Trump thrived. No one more so than Ron DeSantis. With particular relish, the Trump meme machine intensely focused on DeSantis's height, a delightful and, for DeSantis, galling inversion, because at five foot eleven (even if that's a slight reach), DeSantis wasn't short. The Trump memes, however, obsessively singled out DeSantis's cowboy boots. Why would someone in Florida wear cowboy boots? Were there lifts in the boots? Lifts! Arguably, all cowboy boots give an incremental boost with their various heel designs and heights—slanted, walking, riding, $1^3/_8$–$1^5/_8$ inches. It was the word *lifts,* constantly repeated, rather than *heels,* that seemed to turn this fashion nuance into a human flaw.

. . .

DeSantis is on Bill Maher's show, and something about the way he is sitting makes his feet look scrunched up in the boots. The Trump meme team highlights this with yellow marker, making it as seeing-what-you-want-to-see as the most egregious Bigfoot/Loch Ness Monster photos. And in no time, this racks up 14 million social media views, and DeSantis is forced to say, haplessly—pleading—that, really, his are "just standard, off-the-rack Lucchese boots." In late October, the Florida podcaster Patrick Bet-David gets DeSantis in for a studio interview, where he plays a viral TikTok about "Liftsgate." "I've got a gift for you. I'd love for you to wear . . ." Bet-David says, handing him a red Ferragamo shoebox . . . One beat, two beats. Certainly DeSantis isn't going to put them on, but . . . but . . . Well, he says, finally, sputter, sputter . . . "I'm not permitted to accept gifts," DeSantis says, leaving the box to sit between them untouched and unopened. After that, it's off to the races.

Even in Florida, where DeSantis's political strength has created the basis for his national credibility, Trump turns him into a weak and crumbling figure and succeeds in quite a stunning effort to recruit endorsements from nearly every significant politician in the state. "How DeSantis Lost Florida to Donald Trump" is the headline in *The Wall Street Journal* on November 4.

Issue attacks, placed in his binder or on the teleprompter, don't really move Trump. He believes they are boring and, as well, might have a sense of his weaknesses on the issues. He does not really want to talk about the economy. Immigration? He is worried about having to answer questions about the Wall. Ukraine? Israel? Rather not. It is a notable advance in his coming campaign against Biden that, in late fall, when onstage talking about Biden, he finds his voice. He starts to pretend to wander around the stage looking for an exit and walks into the

backdrop, looking to the left, looking to the right, looking perplexed . . .
I can't find any stairs. Where are the stairs?

There is no reason, he believes, why such give-no-quarter attacks,
ad hominem, mocking, unrelenting, can't work against his legal opponents, too: Alvin Bragg, Judge Engoron, Jack Smith, Fani Willis . . . Rip
them, too.

Election interference, witch hunt, shoe lifts, senility . . . all as one.

● ● ●

Still.

His lawyers are realistic enough to accept that if they do get to court,
he will be convicted in the January 6 case, on the boxes charge, and perhaps even on the weak criminal case in New York (because it's New
York), and also in the fraud case there, which could cost him his business. No one can say if *he* is realistic enough. The enormity of what he is
facing seems to go in and out but appears finally to have begun to more
heavily weigh on him.

"Can you believe this shit?" he takes to repeating, seemingly slightly
in awe. "You guys are so lucky I'm bringing you along for this ride. They
are literally trying to put me in jail. That's actually pretty cool. I'm like
Nelson Mandela. I'm ready, I'll do fine, and you send me to jail, I'm
guaranteed to be president."

On Monday, November 6, before Judge Engoron, Trump becomes
only the third president to testify in open court (following Ulysses Grant
and Theodore Roosevelt). He has been strongly advised not to testify,
but he goes forward anyway, and is doing so with limited prep, only his
sons, the lawyers Alina Habba and Chris Kise, and his sons' lawyer, Cliff
Robert, with him over the weekend in Trump Tower, because he doesn't
want it to get out that he has been prepped (and, really, he hasn't been).

The courtroom is packed with media eager to learn what Trump is
like on the stand. Is this the moment when he has to answer (as his antagonist Michael Cohen would say) for his dirty deeds and crimes? Considering all the potential courtrooms in front of him, this performance
might reveal the future. Will he sink himself with his helpless untruths

and bile or put on the greatest courtroom show since "If the glove doesn't fit, you must acquit"?

To the welter of questions about financial statements, instead of the standard "I don't recall" answer, which, from him, might actually be true—he himself can't read a balance sheet—he takes the opportunity to disparage Letitia James, the prosecutor; Arthur Engoron, the judge; Joe Biden, the president; and everybody else. He has already lost the trial—the judge finding in pre-trial motions that Trump did indeed commit massive fraud; the only question now is about damages—but is nevertheless turning this into a prime messaging event.

"I think this case is a disgrace. You have an attorney general sitting here all day long watching every little move. I think it is a disgrace. And people are leaving New York. And they are fleeing the city. And it is a shame what is going on. And we sit here all day, and it is election interference, because you want to keep me in this courthouse all day long . . ." James is in the front row, angry and showing it, her expression set in disgust. Trump sets his dead-eye glare on her and then turns around to glare at the judge. ". . . and we have a very hostile judge, extremely hostile judge, and it is sad." And they're just letting him go as he blasts away, leveling everybody with his flamethrower, with the courtroom going from wide-eyed, to WTF, to OMG, to tittering.

Among the answers as to why the judge doesn't step in and stop him is, for one, that he is unstoppable: It's a fire hose of bombast, declaration, digression, and free association, unbothered by logical sequence or coherence—and without any pause for breath on his part for someone else to be able to interject. There is, too, a fearful certainty on his part and contemptuous authority. On top of which, how could you stop him? With what threat? Remove him from court, creating an even greater drama with him at the center? A contempt citation backed up by . . . what? Here is the reality limbo of what to do—physically how to contain a former president with an entourage, militant supporters, and Secret Service protection. The liberal view that he should be treated like anyone else (even rougher, if possible) meets a juggernaut of imponderable real-time power mechanics and metaphysics.

His show of verbal force is not just theatrical; it is also practical. The more he talks, the more the clock runs down. The entire witness examination playbook of yes-or-no questions and yes-or-no answers is out the window. His whole approach is to be on fire, unplugged, Machine Gun Kelly style. If there's airspace, he'll fill it. If he's talking, nobody else is talking. Zero-sum. But most of all, if he is on the stand, if the light is on him, he's going to take full advantage of it and give the Trump show that everyone is expecting.

If you're a Trumper, what you see is Trump coming out like a fighter. If you're a hater, you see unhinged political rants.

At the same time, this is—in any reasonable context—catastrophic to his interests. Prosecutors are now asking for a $250 million fine. This behavior could up the ante. Without a jury, Trump's fate is with the judge, whom he is antagonizing and alienating. He is hardly even playing the game at hand. He, and perhaps only he, is seeing a much larger game: The legal strategy is the media strategy; the media strategy is the legal strategy.

The goal is not to hide or minimize the legal peril, but to bring it on. Combine everything: It's all part of one big witch hunt. It's all part of one big election interference. The goal is to hammer DAs, judges, Jack Smith, and primary opponents—it's the system against him.

• • •

Trump returned from the Manhattan courtroom, where he held the headlines, to Florida for the third debate, where, by not debating, he would keep the headlines from those who were.

The first two debates he snubbed because they were Fox debates. But the effect—Trump in a different universe than his desperate opponents—was an entirely pleasing one. The third debate, hosted by NBC in Miami in mid-November, which he had been thinking he'd attend, he snubbed now, too. The attention he got for not debating was at least as good as, and arguably much better and much lower risk than, the attention he'd get for debating. For drama, his courtroom appearances were serving as a better debate replacement.

The curious, or ironic, or fortuitous fact of the third debate being in

Florida, if the point needed to be made—and Trump and his team liked nothing better than to make a point that had been made over and over again—was that Florida was Donald Trump's state, and it was perfectly willing to turn a cold shoulder to the governor it had re-elected in a landslide little more than a year before.

Eleven miles up the road, in Hialeah, at his "alternative event"—another instance of masterful Justin Caporale stagecraft—the strategy was not just to one-up the debate, but to debate the debate. While the debate was in progress—and the Trump rally going—the campaign had a real-time spin room running, feeding the cameras and press that had come out for the Trump event. It was a minute-by-minute live breaking down and ripping apart of the debating candidates as the coverage of the Trump event proceeded, accompanied by relentless social media posts—"far more exciting than the actual debate," noted one reporter. By the time the debate was done, it had already been mocked, dismissed, and thrown onto the ash heap. The message was the all-important one: Ron DeSantis, Florida's governor, had been upstaged in his own state. Once again.

Capping off the point, the next night, at Mar-a-Lago, there was a Trump dinner for 250 Florida politicians, including most of the Florida Republican delegation to Congress, making the simple point that DeSantis was isolated in his own party in his own state. And not yet to be finished with DeSantis, the following night the campaign had a sit-down dinner with selected reporters, with Trump scheduled for a pass-through—the dessert: a cowboy boot with lifted heels made out of chocolate and filled with pudding, as in the pudding that the meme team had had Ron DeSantis eating with his fingers.

* * *

There yet existed the faith, the liberal faith, that somehow, given the enormous and unprecedented—you really could not quantify this in any normal historical terms—legal pile-on against him, and indeed, with all the opportunities his own actions endlessly provided, he would be stopped. Something would stop him.

As most of the Trump legal attention, such as it was, focused on New York and his fraud trial, that week, on Friday, November 10, a few members of the team finally focused on a trial in Colorado, where there would be final arguments over forcing Trump off the ballot. Here was the Fourteenth Amendment thesis that he was ineligible for office because of the part he played in the January 6 attack on the U.S. Capitol, an act of insurrection.

The Colorado action, the trial already a week in progress, was barely on the radar screen. Nothing organized, no thought given, hardly any sense of who even the lawyers arguing the case were—someone, yes, but who? And now, suddenly, the case was going forward.

"Holy shit," said one ranking aide when passed a story in a Colorado paper about the trial.

The on-site lawyer had stressed the increasing urgency of the Colorado action—but neither Boris, whose job this might appear to be, nor anybody else on the ever-burgeoning and chaotic legal team seemed to focus on the case nor to communicate word of the impending showdown to the political team.

Now a set of aides, unbriefed and without strategy—other than a general game plan to besmirch the judge, Sarah B. Wallace, who in a quick Google search was revealed as a Democrat—was hurriedly deployed to Denver for what would shortly shape up to be one of the more existential legal rulings of the campaign (although, in fact, they were all existential).

* * *

But if he *wasn't* stopped . . .

There was suddenly—as scare story and part of the general wake-up—a bewildered scramble among Democrats and punditry to ask the obvious but yet, in so many ways, fathomless question: What would a return presidency actually be like for a man who had been impeached twice and defeated once and who had struggled furiously and, as several current indictments argued, criminally to hold on to his office?

To the exasperation of the Trump team, Trump's own words were being literally applied to evoke, not surprisingly, quite an unholy picture. There were the "vermin" he was going to clean up, which seemed to portend redoubled cruelty in his attack on immigrants, but also a sweep of the Marxists, the communists, the left-wing thugs against him; his promised "retribution" against his political and legal opponents; and the enemies list he had all but announced—all part, it would glaringly seem, of a certain dismantling of democracy.

And yes, these were his words; and yes, in the most general sense, you could infer something from them. And while his words and actions might, in fact, in some instances, be connected, as often (more often) they are not. Once again, the mainstream media, as abnormal as they found Trump, were treating him as a normal candidate and treating a Trump campaign as a normal political organization, in which there were actually people in the candidate's confidence who were thinking about a "transition" and a future application of policies and positions. If so, that would be a secret kept from the campaign team.

Still, precisely because Trump so often had no positions except rhetorical ones, this had allowed an orbit several rings away from Trump and the campaign to begin to attach real-world policies to that rhetoric. There were genuine ideologues who saw an opportunity here to back up Trump's words with extreme and eccentric policies. And there were, too, as a part of the Trump industrial MAGA complex, the sycophants and would-be deputy assistants who believed they, however self-appointed, were saying what Trump wanted to hear or who would, at some point, with no governing policies of his own, find useful to hear.

In a particular unforced error, when *The New York Times*, in mid-November, approached the campaign to look at the question of policies in a new Trump White House, particularly about immigration, Stephen Miller stepped forward. Miller had been a speechwriter, gadfly, and peculiar person in the first Trump White House, with various spectrum-y obsessions, including about immigrants. With Trump having no real position on immigrants except to keep them out, Miller was suddenly providing *The New York Times* a new level of detail to the approach. The

resulting *Times* headline was what sounded like an official announcement of the Trump position: "Sweeping Raids, Giant Camps and Mass
Deportations."

"Well, yes, that was certainly our fault for not having a handle on
Stephen's masturbatory fantasies," said one rueful staffer.

Well, yes, that was bad—exactly the fright stuff the campaign wanted
to avoid.

Yes, it was possible Trump could spend four years rounding up every
immigrant in the country, but as likely, he could spend an easy four
years on the golf course. Why didn't the media understand that?

The campaign was left, weakly, to issue a statement that talk of future policies should be regarded as official only if it came directly from
the Trump staff.

• • •

Along with numbers far better than any challenger had ever had in an
open primary, and now regularly ahead of the incumbent president, the
campaign saw Jared Kushner's sudden appearance on the scene to be
quite a reliable victory barometer.

The second couple of the Trump White House years had aggressively
distanced themselves from the former president and the Mar-a-Lago
court. It was as if they always had been skeptical bystanders to, and
could bear no responsibility for, the peculiar behavior of their screwball
relative. They were, like Trump, largely unwelcome in New York, but
were careful to settle in Miami, at a distance too far from Palm Beach for
casual visits to Mar-a-Lago.

Jared had helped organize the logistics of his father-in-law's exile in
Mar-a-Lago, crucially installing Susie Wiles as Trump's aide-de-camp,
therefore allowing himself and his family to be decorously and conveniently as absent as possible. Meanwhile, Jared had quickly transitioned
from the White House into running an investment business almost entirely funded, without even a pretense otherwise, from financial sources
in the Persian Gulf, one of the key parts of his previous government
portfolio. It was a Trumpworld joke that Jared was a wholly owned en-

tity of the House of Saud. (After October 7, low-profile Jared, heretofore unavailable for any surrogate appearances or even a show of family unity, was suddenly on the air defending not foremost the Israelis, but the Saudis, explaining how much safer it was to be a Jew in Saudi Arabia than on an American college campus.)

If Trump ended up convicted and defeated, Jared would surely be nowhere to be found. But, meanwhile, with Trump on the upswing, Jared had contributed a million dollars to the Trump super PAC.

Jared, arguably the most successful figure, or at least one of the few surviving ones, of the Trump White House, seemed—even though he had so carefully rejected the job—able, at will, to step back into the role of his father-in-law's manager, bypassing the campaign, with his father-in-law's acquiescence. In November, Jared suddenly set up a dinner for Trump—or "Donald," Jared being the only one left who called him by his first name—with the head of Univision, the Mexican American Spanish-language media company. Dinner with the Univision CEO, now bragging about his closeness to the Trump family, then segued, with Jared as go-between, into an exclusive Trump Univision interview.

For the campaign, there were few other audiences as sensitive as the American Spanish-speaking audience. Here was the margin of victory in Florida, without which they could not return to the White House, and a growing advantage in several other swing states, where they were taking crucial points from the Democrats. But this now suddenly became entirely a Jared show, with Jared's assurances that there was nothing to worry about, that—wink-wink—they would be well taken care of. And indeed, Jared, to the fury of the U.S.-based Univision news staff, appeared to deliver, getting the questions in advance; having the anchor, Enrique Acevedo, brought in from Mexico City (rather than using a U.S.-based anchor); and getting particular hot-button issues like DACA and abortion struck from the interview.

Trump and his son-in-law were then on the set, with Jared waving the questions around and openly quizzing Trump from the prep sheet in front of the U.S.-based Univision news crew, who now seemed openly aghast. Even with the questions, Trump fumbled answers about his threats for retribution against his opponents and delivered a weirdly balanced view of the Israelis and Palestinians. Kushner said he'd make sure those answers were cut. And, indeed, they were—but then they were also leaked. "What do you expect?" said Kushner, always handily sidestepping whatever side you might suppose him to be on.

As he kept seeming to be incapable of offering absolute support for Israel in the wake of October 7, Trump, not for the first time, turned to Jared for Jewish cover, explicitly asking him and Ivanka for a public endorsement. As Trump had continued to waffle, *The Washington Post,* the campaign understood, was working on a piece that would recycle all the language Trump had variously used over the years, which, on its face, might certainly sound anti-Semitic. Kushner kept dodging on the formal endorsement of his father-in-law. The campaign then tried to settle for merely a statement from him that his father-in-law was not anti-Semitic.

"No, Ivanka and I aren't going to do that. We're not going to go and put our names on something and get in the middle of things. That's just not what we're going to do this time," Kushner said, finally ending it.

● ● ●

An accomplishment of the 2024 campaign was, so far, to make Trump-world *less* of a family enterprise, and yet there was a nagging hole where a family member ought to have been: Trump's wife.

Since the first indictment in New York, when Melania had simply laughed at the campaign's effort to get her to accompany her husband ("Nice try"), it had been clear that she wasn't going to show up. During the past year, she had yet to make a single campaign appearance. In only one instance in 2023 did she even appear on the plane—and then only hitching a ride. Magically, the Melania issue had not, in the White House years nor the Mar-a-Lago years—with both staffers and press quite aware of the Trumps' nontraditional living arrangements and their careful distance from each other—become an issue.

"She was randomly at the White House and only occasionally at Mar-a-Lago," observed one inner-circle member.

It was so glaring that it would have been too flat-footedly literal to ask about. It was an inexplicable aspect of media behavior: Why on this issue, and this issue alone, would there have been a sense of propriety? (It was an issue that might, as much as exposing his true net worth, have shattered much of his identity.) It was as though the press did not want to know or be forced to acknowledge that they couldn't comprehend the former First Couple's arrangements.

On November 29, Melania did, however, go to Rosalynn Carter's funeral. Trump, distinguishing himself from all other living American presidents, did not. It seemed like an unexpected avowal on his wife's part that she, too, had been a First Lady. Or something else. Trump was worried that Melania wasn't, apparently, going to wear black, and he kept random-sampling friends: *Didn't they think she should?* But she didn't, and then he seemed to make a point of telling everyone how proud he was of that. Again, the Melania mystery: What was her game?

In early December, Trump was scheduled for his second day of testimony in his fraud trial, with all preparations in place for the entourage to travel to New York. And then it was abruptly canceled without explanation. Or the explanation from Boris and Alina was "issues," and then "areas." And then "dicey issues," and then "questions we need to avoid." And then, "It could open him up to some potentially embarrassing questions."

And then: "Melania."

That profound question at the heart of Trumpworld, the answer to which no one quite knew, could get asked under oath: "Where exactly does your wife live?"

This was potentially relevant because it went to representations Trump had made about the size of his personal holdings in Trump Tower. Those in his closest orbit speculated that Melania had a separate apartment in Trump Tower—and not just their official one. That question might also lead to the specifics of where each of them resided now, how much time they spent in various locations, and what might qualify for each as their permanent residence. Who knew? "She's like a special guest or something when they're seen out in public together for dinner or whatever the case might be," described a Mar-a-Lago intimate.

To say the least, that arrangement, an American marriage on a coolly transactional basis, might be difficult to explain in open court and to "family values" America.

Hence, Trump reluctantly gave up his second day in court.

• • •

After January 6, Fox News boss Rupert Murdoch had made it a personal mission to banish Trump from national life. Even after the ninety-two-year-old Murdoch announced in the fall of 2023 that he was stepping back from his active CEO role, that seemed only to give him more time to get on the phone with his own reporters, and with anyone else who could reach him, and vent his views on Trump's mendacity and danger. Trump was brought regular reports about Murdoch's perfidy, along with constant clips of Fox personalities continuing to treat DeSantis or Haley as credible figures. Trump kept swearing off Fox, claiming to banish it from his mind and schedule, but then helplessly creeping back to it.

Most of all, he relished his particularly deep bond with Sean Hannity, certainly as close a bond as any president, former president, or candidate has ever had with a prominent voice in the media. To many in Trump-world observing the Trump-and-Hannity byplay, Trump, in refusing to understand that Fox News was no longer his safe place, was the innocent figure, the big, good-hearted quarterback on the high school team. And Hannity was the kid with all the angles, easily playing the dopey big guy. Two friends, one gullible, the other endlessly fucking him over.

Hannity, traveling from his Palm Beach condo down the road to Mar-a-Lago, made a pitch for Trump to do an on-air town hall hour with Hannity presiding.

A credulous Trump, bragging to friends, reported Hannity's pitch after their meeting: "'The Fox execs don't want me to do it,'" Trump had Hannity saying, "'but I'm gonna force them to do it, and this is going to be great ratings. I'm really here for you. Here's the strategy. This thing's over. I just can't act like it's over. When I'm on TV, that's all fucking bullshit. But we'll make it clear now. This is it. You're it.'"

And Trump readily agreed—and walked into it.

The Hannity town hall opened with a montage of Democrats saying Trump, in a second term, would surely be a dictator. And then Hannity turned to Trump: "You're promising America tonight, you would never abuse power as retribution against anybody?" Tell the audience, in effect, that you don't beat your wife.

Trump, as a smartass, or to play to the moment—and perhaps hitting a fuck-you high note to the pleasure of Trump fans—smirked and said he wouldn't be a dictator "except for day one," a line that would haunt him for the rest of the campaign.

. . .

The inverted reality of life in Trumpworld was that even to the extreme extent that things should not work out—self-inflicted wounds were a common occurrence; lack of discipline was far more the rule than was discipline—they did often, in fact, work out wonderfully. Two thousand sixteen was certainly all the proof you needed of that. But even in 2020, with Covid-19, a stalled economy, and a campaign in such disarray that it had effectively run out of money before the crucial final weeks, they came within 44,000 votes (the cross tally of Arizona, Georgia, and Wisconsin) of winning; in essence, laying the foundation for election denial and the basis for the present campaign.

And, indeed, there seemed nothing, practically speaking, that could derail them from an inevitable and overwhelming Republican primary victory. Still, this was Trump, and you could never ignore the possibility of an imminent catastrophic end.

In the past, Trumpworld had co-existed with this existential sense, disaster on the one hand, Trump magic on the other, but the very purpose of Trump's new professional campaign team was to avoid Trumpian political calamities. And yet, the campaign lived side by side with the most glaring Trump threats. There was Boris, for instance, the hopeless yes-man, a professionally substandard blunderer in a pivotal administrative position, on whom the former president's future and freedom might rest. What's more, on top of being an incompetent, Boris might be a turncoat and, in his person, the potential equivalent of Nixon's tapes: He knew it all and could serve it up. The smoking gun.

And there was Natalie, not only irksome, and threatening in her ever-growing authority and purview—likely the single greatest influence on the candidate; his muse, his whisperer, his security blanket—but inexplicable.

In this, there was the buffet.

The golf club buffet came to symbolize how true power in Trumpworld flowed unevenly, randomly, and far from rationally.

The spoils of the billionaire Sun King's salubrious world had been a touchy subplot since the 2016 campaign and through the White House years. On the one hand, you had the stripped-down, no-frills crap food and bad accommodations of politics (think the DoubleTree in West Palm Beach), and on the other, the contrasting world of Trump luxe (Mar-a-Lago). But for the staff, in jockeying or negotiating for Mar-a-Lago standing, there was also a critical tonal challenge. Trump had a special radar for anyone overstepping his or her place, and worse, he reserved unique ill will and spitefulness for anybody who he thought might be taking something from him, who might be grabbing for something of his they should not get. The DoubleTree, most had concluded, was infinitely safer than aspiring to Mar-a-Lago.

But Natalie subverted all this at the buffet.

The restaurant buffet, all you can eat and piles more, had come of age in the 1960s, at the apogee of American postwar expansion and plenty. It was all in front of you, all for the taking, generations of scarcity wiped entirely away. The buffet concept had, perhaps naturally, descended into vulgarity, kitsch, cheapness, and steam trays, an aspiration of the lower middle class rather than upper middle.

But the boffo buffet yet existed in Trumpworld.

Mar-a-Lago's country club drawback is that there isn't a golf course on the premises. For golf, you have to drive fifteen minutes to Trump

International in West Palm Beach. That's where Trump headed every morning. He regularly had lunch there, which had become, like dinner at Mar-a-Lago, a designated moment for club members, their friends, and the multitudes of political and opportunistic invitees to kiss the ring. On Sunday evenings, there was an old-fashioned family club night with full-service buffet.

"We're not talking about some, you know, shitty hotel buffet. I mean, we're talking, oh yeah, 'Would you like your own lobster?' Boom! 'Here you go,' like holy shit," in one guest's description.

A Trump staffer would not presume, other than by specific invitation, to have privileges to the buffet. But when Natalie was in Palm Beach—that is, when Trump and his entourage were in Palm Beach—she and her mother, under the attentive eye of club members, reliably showed up for their Sunday meal, and put it on the Trump tab.

Curiously, there was little supposition that Natalie might be the "bit on the side." That issue, for a man who had spent most of his adult years in open, proud, undaunted, and, in repeated accusations, predatory pursuit of women, had been largely expunged as a possibility. Since the first year in the White House, when Trump's sex life was a persistent mystery or puzzle, it had drifted off or flatlined. No one said it. No one would ever say it—of all things, you did not tread into personal territory with Donald Trump. But he was, if you had to draw the obvious conclusion, post-sex. "He replaced it with politics. There's a liberal dilemma: Would they rather he preyed on women or on the country?" remarked an amused Steve Bannon in the waning years of the Trump presidency.

Natalie being the bit on the side would have been a reasonable explanation. Beyond that, she fell into the context of the Sun King's court: Insofar as she amused him, or her efficiency with respect to his desires was useful to him, or the way her irritation of everyone else reaffirmed his dominance, she was welcome at the buffet. Her mother, too.

If you were in the circle of relative normies on the campaign, you might have seen the illogic of Trumpworld, but have little or no influence over it. And because the numbers continued to go up, thereby basically protecting your world, you could tolerate it. Well, you had to tolerate it. Because of the numbers, and the prospect of ultimate (if still not-quite-believable) victory. Hence, the normies existed side by side with Boris and Natalie.

But it was far from clear who would be blamed, the normies or the ab-normies, if the numbers faltered or if the legal battle began to present palpable peril. And surely that would happen, wouldn't it?

CHAPTER 8

Victory Number One

DECEMBER 2023–JANUARY 2024

He was spending less time in Iowa than any other non-incumbent winning candidate had ever spent—less even than any serious contender. Ron DeSantis had basically relocated to Iowa, concentrating all his resources there and making the formal bow to the famous Iowa fool's errand, the "full Grassley," following its aged senator, Chuck Grassley, in ritualistically visiting each of Iowa's ninety-nine counties during the campaign.

Trump, when forced to travel, liked to go out and back in the same day. The three-hour flight out to Iowa with several hours on the ground and then back, usually put touchdown in West Palm after midnight. This was harder on the staff, whom Trump liked to have at work at an early hour, than it was on Trump himself, who was golfing most mornings, followed by lunch at the club, and then hitting the road for an after-lunch departure. (If he wasn't traveling, his day, after golf and lunch, was a few hours of calls, then downtime before dinner.)

In effect, DeSantis and Haley were doing his work for him, each battling the other and, decorously, leaving him untouched. He had been taking it easy for the entirety of the campaign—the Iowa trudge was basically the better part of a year for most candidates—and had taken it even easier in the run-up to the holidays, and then he was entirely down in the week between Christmas and New Year's, only two weeks before the caucus vote.

There was another factor besides the fact that he hardly had to campaign: His plane was broken—the windshield was cracked. It would be out of commission for almost a month, right up until caucus day itself. However much it was refurbished and repainted—the Trump brand always being buffed and burnished—it was an old plane, always breaking down. Trump did not take this well. He might have accepted all kinds of chaos around him, but not a malfunctioning plane. "I mean, he just loses his shit every single time it's going on," said a frequent passenger (in addition to staff, the manifest generally included members of Congress and MAGA-world celebrities). To an extent, it was like anyone else's reaction to the breakdown of their car, undermining key aspects of daily order and suddenly exposing a person's vulnerability. Nothing could be relied on. He blamed much of this on the pilot—"Captain John"—whom he didn't like, and on John's wife, who was the lead flight attendant (yet a "stewardess," in the Trump lexicon) and, in Trump's view, "a psycho bitch." Of course, he could just have chartered another plane. But it would hardly have been the same. *His* plane was like someone's particularly notable high-end auto—you wanted to be seen in it; that was the point of it. It wasn't just about getting somewhere. It was about the plane itself—sitting there, announcing his presence on the tarmac. If there was vanity here—there was—there was strategy, too: The plane looked presidential. That was the consistent motif of the 2024 Trump campaign, looking presidential—he was the president (all right, the president-in-exile). His signage (the presidential seal had been rejigged to just this side of infringement) and production values had to be as good as those of any sitting president. Underneath the wing of the plane was a favorite Caporale set, with his team bringing in the portable floodlights, showing off all the Trump Force One branding. Now the staff had to go out of its way to distract the press from a white-label, generic charter plane. *Well, you know, the Trump plane—that big plane—is just too big to land in so many of Iowa's airports.*

Still, Iowa, in the days before the caucus, was going to require *some* attention. Even some sleepover days. If only for show.

• • •

But then planning for Iowa was suddenly interrupted by a legal battle that, like most, the campaign had only been dimly aware was on the horizon—but which now slammed into it and suddenly claimed all Trump's attention. The E. Jean Carroll defamation case, an add-on to the abuse and rape claims—he had defamed her by saying that he hadn't abused her when, well, according to the jury, he had, and called her crazy, to boot—that had earned her a five-million-dollar judgment against him, like some sticky thing they couldn't shake from their fingers, was to begin on January 16. (Yes, this had been on the legal calendar, but so much else was on it, too, and always shifting; and anyway, keeping track of it was someone else's job.) And now Trump, who had on *bad, bad* advice blown off the first E. Jean trial, was damned if he wasn't going to show up at this one and do something about it!

Further, the New York fraud case had wrapped, and that decision—with the prosecutor upping the ask from $250 million to $370 million—was now expected in January. What would it mean—symbolically, practically, personally—if a presidential candidate, one whose very identity was wrapped up in his wealth, suddenly had to beg for a bailout, with his business and possibly even his home in danger of being taken from him? It was too big to consider the implications here, and no one did. It was just another specter hanging over the campaign.

But then there was good news, too—sort of.

The most daunting doom date out there, potentially more existential than all the rest, was March 4, the day before Super Tuesday. The *United States v. Donald Trump* was scheduled to go to trial at the E. Barrett Prettyman United States Courthouse, on Constitution Avenue in downtown Washington D.C., eight minutes from his former White House residence and the scene of numerous political downfalls.

It was part of the political race: for prosecutors to convict him before the nation voted in the 2024 election; for Trump, and his lawyers—all, other than Boris, quite certain of defeat—to do everything possible to push as many of his trials as they could beyond Election Day. Still, for the Trump legal team, this was hardly a plan. The trial(s) of the century were regarded as unpredictable weather that you'd wait until the last possible moment to prepare for. Lawyers? Witnesses? Discovery? Prep? All in the air. All competing against conflicting trial dates, a presidential campaign, and a golf game.

But Judge Tanya Chutkan had now ruled—bending over backward, in the view of the liberal legal establishment—that Trump's motion that presidents and former presidents had effective immunity from all prosecutions had first to be decided by the appeals court and then, possibly, by the Supreme Court, before the case could go to trial. Now, you would think, there was very little possibility (theoretically, none) that the courts would rule that a former president was immune from criminal prosecution for anything whatsoever—murder, wife beating, grand theft auto, treason, you name it—as Trump was asking. But anyway, there was now a likelihood that the March 4 date would be pushed back. The effort here, of course, which Judge Chutkan had clearly decided to overlook, was not a real defense or good-faith effort to resolve pertinent legal issues, but to push the case—all the cases—into a future in which circumstances, those imagined and those yet to be imagined, might throw so many more wrenches into the works, if not entirely absolve him.

Any delay was a victory because it created the circumstance for some other as-yet-to-be-imagined disruption. There was no sense of fate in Trumpworld; rather, it was all about escape.

That was another reason to push as quickly as they could to a general acknowledgment that he was the nominee. Getting over the primaries and the illusion that there were other candidates and other choices might bring the courts and the media to a new psychological state: There were two men running for president. Do you really have the guts to take one out? And what if you tried and failed? What would happen if he *were* convicted and *yet* became president?

On the eve of the quick succession of caucus and primary votes sure to secure him the nomination, it was far from clear if the campaign and election were mere sideshows to the greater historic make-or-break drama of a candidate facing legal (and, too, financial) ruin, or if trial, conviction, and loss of freedom (as well as bankruptcy) were footnotes to his amazing and unprecedented march to political victory.

Anyway, now they had to wrap up the primaries—and face a stumbling Joe Biden.

· · ·

Actually, Trump, if you paid attention to his rambling, was fully confident that Joe Biden would not have the will to run against him, nor that he would be allowed to try, one of his frequent riffs to his phone list and on the Mar-a-Lago patio. They were surely going to swap him out—they had to. It was one of the few matters on which most people seemed to have no hesitation in contradicting him—Biden's bowing out was crazy stuff. In Trump's parallel world of political prognostication and, perhaps, paranoia, too—in many respects, a fantasy world, yet one he regularly willed into life—he knew whom they were going to replace Biden with, for sure: "Mike" Obama.

"People call her 'Mike,' you know. You know that, don't you?" he said, widely repeating far-right QAnon-type chatter, a favorite part of his phone monologues for at least a month. "They think she looks pretty manly. Those very big shoulders. What's that about? That's what people will call her if she runs, 'Mike.' That's the name she'll have: 'Mike.'"

· · ·

With a multimillion-dollar house in Palm Beach, Fox's Bret Baier is an avid golfer. It's a New Year's foursome with Trump, Baier, Baier's son, and a golf pro. Magically, with a wink-wink, Baier and the pro lose to Trump and Baier's son, which Trump proceeds to widely brag about. In the aftermath of Trump's victory glow—"I whipped you"—Baier pitches Trump on doing a town hall on Fox just before the Iowa caucuses. The campaign, with Trump's full agreement, has precisely mapped out its strategy in Iowa for a candidate running a consistent thirty points ahead: "No sit-downs, just kind of clear the board, you know, nothing that could trip us up, since we have this huge lead." But on the golf course, Trump agrees: a town hall in Iowa with Baier and Martha MacCallum on January 10. The campaign team again takes Trump through the strategic view here—there's just no upside at all to a Fox thing. There's only Fox trying to rip him—an ambush, for sure—and possibly setting him up on abortion, which could cost him dearly in Iowa if he voiced any of his new demurrals. A slightly chastened Trump says, "Yeah, let's go and push it off." The campaign tells Baier they're willing to do it, but only after Iowa. Baier then directly calls Trump, and Trump says, "Yeah, no. Let's do it on the tenth, okay."

"So, that's a little roadside grenade waiting for us," says one staffer.

• • •

Trump, though, does commit that he will go from his anticipated victory in Iowa on the fifteenth directly to New Hampshire on the sixteenth, and will, the campaign cannot be more grateful, forgo appearing at the first day of the second E. Jean Carroll trial, the defamation trial, on January 16.

• • •

On January 4, refocusing after the holidays, the lawyers gathered with Trump in Palm Beach—or the lawyers gathered, and Trump dropped into the meeting.

This included Chris Kise, the lawyer whom Trump believed gouged a multimillion-dollar fee from him and who delivered, in Trump's view, a consistently weak performance in his New York fraud case; Todd Blanche, Boris's lawyer, who, despite what seemed like an obvious conflict, is on the January 6 Jack Smith case and is theoretically in charge of all the cases; Steve Sadow, who replaced the first set of lawyers in Atlanta; John Lauro, who is handling the boxes case; Alina Habba, on whom, to the general shock and bewilderment of all the other lawyers, Trump has come to depend more and more; and Boris, whose general coordination and oversight job has now, without much pretense otherwise, become to sanitize and recast whatever bad news the lawyers might otherwise want to give Trump.

The meeting turned out to be not so much about the lawyers' strategy as about Trump's strategy. On January 9, the appeals court would hear the Trump lawyers' argument for absolute presidential immunity—and Trump wanted to be there. Had to be there. Six days before the Iowa primary, the day before the town hall in Iowa with Bret Baier that he'd committed to, Trump was now insisting he had to be in Washington sitting in a courtroom listening to his lawyers' arguments. There would be no jury, nor any witnesses to stare down. There would be no forum in which he could speak. This was federal court, and there would be no cameras. There were no phones. The press wasn't going to be allowed anywhere Trump could provide them with a Trump moment. This was entirely different from New York. That was the argument to keep him away. His presence was unnecessary. The more pointed argument, which was not made to him, was the fear that his presence would only add insult to injury: The case against him was that he had threatened the functions of government and democracy itself, and here he was, again, threatening. There was no neutral Trump, just an intimidating one. It was the key tenet of his fifty years of being a litigant: He did not believe in blind justice; rather, he could stare her down. The other point, and as important, was that he would be there to intimidate his *own* lawyers. There were the decorum and civility they might otherwise want to display in the interest of their own reputations as well as their client's, and then there were the spleen and vituperation and indignation he wanted them to show, unmindful of their reputations or of the consequences to him.

Once again, Trump's lawyers, litigators who ought ordinarily to have been the main players and strategists in the proceedings, and who were all now resigned to having found themselves in an inverted world, were left as satellites to their client, who, in his mind, was more expert than they. He was the counterpuncher, he was the heavyweight, he was the weapon—his lawyers were pussies.

On the ninth, he faced the three-judge panel of the U.S. Court of Appeals for the District of Columbia Circuit on his claim of immunity. He was disgruntled, agitated, and restless, but, sigh of relief, he behaved reasonably in court, as the three justices clearly expressed skepticism, if not incredulity, at the argument his lawyer D. John Sauer was making for a blanket protection against all prosecutions.

The behind-the-scenes issue was finding a location where, after the hearing, Trump could attack prosecutors and the judge and all others in hot pursuit of him—and where Justin Caporale could stage an imposing presidential look. The federal courthouse was inhospitable, other than on the sidewalk. Trump did not want impromptu; he wanted formidable, presidential. Alas, he was not president. He had no base at all in Washington. They might have done a press conference on the tarmac in Virginia, against the backdrop of Trump Force One, except that plane, with its smashed windshield, was still laid up in the shop. His Washington hotel, Trump International, which had been a sort of annex to his White House, had been sold in 2022 and was now the Waldorf Astoria Washington.

Although very much not ideal to have lost the Trump branding, the campaign had to make do and rent a reception room, a hospitality suite, from the Waldorf, né the Trump Hotel (with Trump himself forced to call the hotel manager to make it happen). Caporale's challenge was that any sign of doing without or cheapening out or getting the presidential setting wrong was met with zero-to-sixty fury from Trump. He walked into a room, and his eyes moved about, and everybody held their breath. It couldn't be just perfectly presidential; it had to be *Trump* perfectly presidential—official, formal, and just slightly more over the top than you might be if you were actually president. He would vent if he did not find enough flags. And yet he had some fine sense if there were too many beyond the too many he wanted. Justin Caporale's standing in the campaign continued to rise as he more and more came to be able, in all situations, to marshal the props and accoutrements that satisfied Trump's vision and his taste.

And, indeed, you could see it on his face, the satisfaction, as he came from the federal courthouse and onto the makeshift stage in what, shortly before, had been a bland, depressing, inconsequential reception room in a hotel, but which was now a brazen, somewhat too glitzy, slicker version of the Oval Office. To the cameras, he delivered a report on how well they had done in court, despite, in the courtroom (without cameras), the judges' hostility, and he made his own case for immunity as though its merits and logic would be obvious to everyone.

And every network cut to it live. Days before Iowa, he was once more wholly stealing the news cycle.

• • •

That was on the ninth.

On the tenth, he had to fly back out to Iowa (in his rental plane) to do his Bret Baier town hall.

With four days before the caucus vote, the campaign was sure that here, and probably only here, a shoe could drop on them—a tough question (not the usual questions that might rile liberals, but a question designed to rile conservatives) that Trump, and quite a tired Trump, obsessing over the real trials facing him, couldn't sidestep.

The stakes had gone up, too—revenge stakes for the Fox campaign debates that Trump had snubbed. DeSantis and Haley had scheduled a debate with CNN across town, so Fox was now poised to make Trump part of the debate, to take him on in the place of DeSantis and Haley.

Trump arrives at the Iowa Events Center in Des Moines, where the town hall is being held, about an hour and a half before the scheduled start. It's the usual tenor of a Trump run-through—unfocused, distracted, a waste of Trump's time, and flying clearly in the face of his attention deficit. Wiles, LaCivita, Miller, and Caporale are in the room with him.

"Oh, shit!" Miller suddenly blurts out, looking at his phone in what would shortly become a legendary moment of the campaign, to no one as much as Trump himself.

"What?" Trump says, thinking it's a news break about him.

Miller passes around his phone. "I think it's the interview questions."

It's not just the questions, but the follow-ups, too. And not just the questions from the Fox hosts, but those from the town hall audience, too.

"It was better than something falling off the back of a truck, if you catch my drift," Trump tells friends, spreading the tale of his good fortune far and wide.

• • •

On the eleventh, it was back to New York for final arguments before Judge Engoron in the fraud trial, who, along with Letitia James, now held pride of place among Trump's most galling tormentors.

James had begun the trial asking the court to fine Trump $250 million. Her ask had now gone up to $370 million.

Less than a year before, it could all have gone away for $100 million, a figure that was then preposterous and infuriating to him; it could not even be discussed.

Here was another view of the Trump legal strategy: to dig himself deeper into a hole; to raise the stakes; to assume his mettle was greater than anyone else's; to trust that some development or event yet to occur, a deus ex machina, would on its own change the field of play, or that he could invariably create one. But now his fury at James and Engoron seemed to be intensified by the fury he felt toward himself for not having paid the $100 million—and he was now looking down the barrel of what more and more seemed like an inevitable $370 million. But whatever those divided feelings might be, the effect was for him only to go deeper yet, ever stiffening the righteousness of his victimology. He had ordered that Kise, his detested lawyer—no better, at this point, than a donkey with a Kick Me sign—find a way, any way (and don't mess it up), to let him speak in open court. Kise seemed almost plaintive in his plea to Engoron to give Trump two to three minutes to speak. The judge, equivocating—two to three minutes for Trump being, for all intents and purposes, an open-ended invitation—seemed finally moved by Kise's desperation.

Engoron asked Trump if he would stick to the facts. "I think this case goes outside just the facts," said Trump, not pausing for debate and launching into a critique that otherwise had no bearing and would have no effect on the issues in court, continuing for six minutes before En-goron cut in.

Leaving the courtroom, Trump repeated much the same for the media.

Meanwhile, he had been so happy with the impromptu Oval Office–like stage set that Caporale assembled in the hospitality suite at the former Trump International, now Waldorf Astoria Washington, that he had ordered the set to be transported to New York and reinstalled in the building he owned at 40 Wall Street, a short way from the courthouse. All morning, the media had been fed a nearly constant ticktock of where Trump was and where he would be, with the limited space offered to outlets that would go live with his performance. By the time he was in his car on the way, Fox was already teasing the waiting microphone. That was the report relayed to Trump as he came through traffic: Fox was holding on an empty lectern shot, just as it would have in the West Wing waiting for the president to appear before the press.

And then it was back to Iowa again.

• • •

In Iowa, the cold persisted. It was nothing-functioning cold. Silent-streets cold. Face-blistering cold. How-does-anyone-possibly-live-in-Iowa cold. The weekend before the Monday vote was essentially canceled. Roseanne Barr, the former sitcom star—who, in hindsight, might seem now to have been a weirdly prescient Trump pilot fish in her old role of pissed-off, fuck-you, no-hope, working-class matriarch—planning to fly in to pump for Trump, had her appearance scrapped due to weather.

Trump was irritated by the cold. And he was irritated that the plane was still out of commission. And he was irritated by the hotel and volu-bly expressing his irritation to almost everyone on his call list. The Hotel Fort Des Moines occupied a place in Iowa caucus lore: Candidates and top-level press stayed there. While it had been recently renovated, it was, to Trump, run-down and crummy. He berated his entourage: *Why are we staying here? This place is no good. Who picked this place? Who put us here?* Trump was always unhappy when he wasn't in his own bed, between his own sheets. He was preoccupied or obsessed with who might have been there before him. If he had to stay overnight, he had strict requirements: the newest hotel possible, preferably a chain hotel. And, specifically, he didn't like the Fort's slippers. They were just out there, for anyone to use. He liked the ones with sterile wrappers—so, someone had to be sent to Walmart. The anxiety always mounted over Trump's creature comforts, staff scurrying to get him his strawberry vanilla ice cream, two quarts of it. His own churn seemed to increase the general sense of low-level panic and disarray.

Disgruntled and unsettled, he was at the center of his own mess in his room at the Fort: clothes dropped at will, papers discarded—he ripped them in half and let them fall to the floor—plus candy wrappers, Starbursts and Milky Ways, left in a trail.

He was over fucking Iowa.

Early on caucus night, Trump and entourage went out to one of the big caucus sites. All the candidates were there to address the crowd—one of the few big crowds assembled in the cold.

Trump was petulant about having to wait as Asa Hutchinson, the former governor of Arkansas, an unlikely contender, seldom rising above a percentage point in any polling, rambled on: "Why the fuck am I waiting for Ada Hutchinson?" And as an aside to at least three people whom he called on the spot: "Do you know why I call him Ada? Because that's a woman's name."

But then, whatever pretense of this being *an election* with competing candidates blew away as soon as Trump started to speak. Instantly, it became a Trump rally, with a *USA!* chant taking over the place. Then, minutes after the caucus vote closed, the AP called it for Trump—with CNN and Fox almost immediately following—leaving even Trump confused. "Fucking already? Can they do that?"

On to the Iowa Events Center, where it was all kiss the ring and selfie ops, and a procession of Trump job seekers and hangers-on, as every single Iowa county save one—the point person in that county would be fired—went for him. He was heading for a thirty-point victory, the highest in the history of contested Iowa caucuses. Better yet, dead-issue Ron DeSantis would squeak by Nikki Haley, her surge done. Here it was, Trump nailing the nomination, surely, if there was any doubt—which, other than among the very wishful and those in utter denial, there was not.

There were big screens tuned to Fox, but Trump wanted to see CNN, too, and there was a rush to locate the remote, which was found by a junior staffer, whereupon Natalie snatched it from his hands—but it switched every screen, so it was all CNN now. But that's not what Trump wanted. And then it went back, with Natalie insistently pointing and pounding the remote, to exclusively Fox, and then again the other way, prompting a general meltdown and a tussle to pry the remote from Natalie's hands as dozens of other staffers lined up to have their individual photos taken with the boss.

Trump was prepared to spend another night at the detested Hotel Fort. But no reason now. And he decided he was not going directly to New Hampshire, as he had promised. Prompted by a series of articles Natalie had collected for him about E. Jean Carroll, just as he should be celebrating his Iowa victory, he slipped into a raging, Lear-like fury, with almost nonstop vitriolic, scabrous, nearly incoherent posts about Carroll—he was damn well going to show up on the first day of the trial.

"Let's get out of here," he said at nine thirty.

He could sleep in Trump Tower.

CHAPTER 9

Robbed!

JANUARY—FEBRUARY 2024

The E. Jean Carroll trial started on the sixteenth of January. The New Hampshire primary was on the twenty-third. He'd be commuting back and forth between his march to the Republican nomination and the obloquy of his status as a sexual abuser. In both places, there was a woman who had become a persistent irritant, if not a menace. E. Jean, suing him for rape, getting a jury verdict on sex abuse and a five-million-dollar judgment, had hardly brought him down. But now she was back, suing him for defamation, and what would she get now, another five million? This was not slowing him—Iowa's thirty-point victory, hello!—but it was infuriating to him. In New Hampshire, Nikki Haley—who could not win, who was little more than a marginal figure in the Republican Party, who existed only because he had made her—continued to harp. E. Jean Carroll he had made, too. What would she be without him?

He was still crazy mad—his rage continuing to be directed at Joe Tacopina—that he had lost the first E. Jean trial. If he didn't truly believe he was utterly innocent, totally pilloried, accused by a complete fraudster, the victim of #MeToo run amok and of a New York jury and corrupted justice system, there certainly wasn't anyone around him who ever saw him break character.

It was all because of the weak defense Tacopina had put on in the first E. Jean trial and, he repeated for the thousandth time, people saying he should have testified (the Greek chorus of "people say . . ." that existed in his head). Tacopina, for his trouble, in addition to being a constant subject of Trump's derision and anger, was left with unpaid bills.

This was now one of those examples of the Trump bipolar reality in which everybody around him had to exist: his absolute certainty that he could have held the courtroom in his hands and everyone's clear understanding, including poor Tacopina's, that, as a close Trump crony noted, "This was just one of those things that couldn't happen. I mean, who thinks that he would have behaved and been a normal person and not been out of control in front of a jury?"

He was being sued by Carroll for defamation and yet, in a seemingly uncontrolled torrent, could not help continuing to defame her. On Truth Social, virtually every night, sometimes appearing not to sleep, in splenetic and sputtering fashion, he smeared every aspect of her motives and character. It was a furious, helpless internal monologue, except it was public (though, perhaps, even he could be forgiven for forgetting this, given the quiet of Truth Social). It was also a measure of how ready for combat he was and how little rationality he was bringing to this fight.

With Tacopina out, he had promoted Alina Habba to his lead lawyer—a lawyer with little relevant experience and hopelessly mismatched by Carroll's team, which had been at work on this case for more than five years. But to the degree that any lawyer would have been in the way of Trump's irrational fury and worst instincts, Habba would be much less so—she would take his orders.

Habba seemed stricken, if not terrified, to find herself the default lawyer. It was such an evident train wreck. It was going to be bad; the guess was that it could even be $15 million bad (the Tacopina camp was already reminding reporters that the Tacopino-led trial had cost Trump only $5 million). She gingerly approached the obvious idea—that they should settle. She tried to explain reasonably, "We've already lost." Trump had accused Carroll of lying about things the last trial had found to be true: He had hauled her into a dressing room in 1996 and stuck his fingers inside her. A jury had declared that to be a fact, not now to be disputed.

Trump, though, was in a bubble of it's all good, it's great, he would prevail. The bubble was fortified by Boris, continuing in the care and feeding of Trump's legal illusions, whipping Trump's rage, along with goading him on with the prospect and the pleasure of destroying Carroll. Even Trump's just-this-side-of-demented posts were, in the Boris version, an effective way of influencing the jury—putting aside, once more, that Truth Social influenced no one. Natalie, too, had become complicit in this, researching to the darkest corners of the internet to find anything negative or anyone's outlandish speculation about Carroll and her true motives and putting this in front of him in gold paper clips.

During a break on the first day of the trial, Boris worked the hallway, chatting with a handful of reporters. "I really think that we're getting through to them. I really think we're starting to get some movement." He pointed out a particular juror he thought was *actually* on their side. "I think this is going in our direction. I think things are going really good for us."

"Oh, my God, is Boris really saying this shit?" muttered one reporter at the trial.

Habba understood that the trial could have only a dismal outcome. Quite simply, the facts had already been confirmed by another jury, and they were against Trump. But he proceeded to grievously compound the situation. At a witching hour every night, usually beginning at eleven or twelve, he began to dump upward of twenty-five or thirty anti–E. Jean Carroll posts in a single hour, a stream of rumors and bile and, well, libel about Carroll—a kind of fury, or sexual vituperation. He was frothing about vaginas and penises and anal sex—in the middle of a trial that was principally about punitive damages; that is, punishment for the behavior he was, each night, still exhibiting. "Crazy, whacked-out shit," in one aide's description. And while no one else may have seen Trump's Truth Social posts, E. Jean Carroll's lawyers certainly did: Every single morning of this trial, her attorney, Roberta Kaplan, and team came in and went: *Look, here are the new posts from last night. He's doing it again—he is not only a defamer, but a compulsive one.* A serial defamer screaming to be stopped.

And if there was any doubt about how the trial was going, by the third or fourth day in, as an indication of the certain doom facing them, Boris was telling reporters all the credit for the case should go to Alina: "It's Alina's case; she's trying it; it's completely her case; she's handling it."

From the trial, Trump made three trips to New Hampshire, growing more and more irritated with this other woman, Nikki Haley, who was gaining attention and preparing to make money off his name. She was in this not to win, but just to be the last person against him! He was furious that she was harping on his blunder of mixing up her name with Nancy Pelosi's. (His mix-ups had started to become something of a subtext; his team, so far, was treating this as merely amusing: *Pelosi, Haley: It's a distinction without a difference! Ha ha!*) E. Jean and Nikki had just put him in a foul mood about everything.

· · ·

Election night in New Hampshire with his certain victory isn't a happy one. For the longest stretch, CNN and Fox keep showing him with a single-digit lead, whereas the statewide election tracker has him up at eleven, twelve, at some point thirteen. He's yelling at the TV: *How come I'm not winning by more? You know, why are CNN and Fox saying I'm only ahead by single digits? You know, what the hell's going on there?* And even into double digits—and it would settle at an eleven- to twelve-point victory—he had expected twenty. Twenty he would have gotten, but for the flood of independents and Democrats into the Republican primary for Haley.

But it's a victory turnout at the Nashua Sheraton, a coronation pandemonium of sycophants and job seekers verging into chaos. Even George Santos, the Republican congressman expelled from the House by his own party for his whopper lies and criminal fraud, is in the crowd—with a scramble not to let him near Trump. (Nor does anyone else want to be in a photo op with Santos.) Vivek Ramaswamy, who had run a long-shot wannabe-Trump campaign, and for whom Trump has conceived a clear aversion, won't leave Trump's side. Just absolutely badgering in his grille—literally, hardly an inch from his ear and, by some remarkable dexterity, staying there—trying to give him talking points: "You have to say it's double digits, you need to make it double digits, you gotta say it's double digits," with Trump vainly trying to pull away.

And then, suddenly, Haley is on the air and declaring something close to victory—and Trump is near to losing it: "Why aren't we speaking? Who fucked this up?" Then he starts yelling, petulantly: "Why is she doing this? Why didn't we go first? We should be out there. Why are we sitting here?" He's yelling at the television: "Fuck her, fuck her, I'm done with her. She'll never be VP. She's not gonna be a part of anything. Fuck her. I'm done with her."

When he finally does get up on the stage, he goes off on Haley. It isn't a celebration of his "double-digit" victory; it's just fury over Nikki, over the dress she's wearing and the way she's talking—she's under his skin, in his head.

It's a doom loop: "Why didn't we win bigger? Why did she speak first? Why is she even still in the race? Why didn't the networks give me double digits?" Court has been canceled in New York for the day, and dismally, Trump heads back to Palm Beach.

• • •

A day later, he returned to New York to testify. This was when he was expected to blow the roof off the courtroom. Whatever spectacle this trial was, it would now be *his* spectacle, a Trump spectacle. The plan was to introduce a raft of what he believed were damaging tweets from Carroll suggesting that she was a gold digger, a Democrat, and an anti-Trump litigant.

But before this testimony, and with the jury out, the judge wanted a preview. Almost all of it he ruled out, reducing Trump's testimony to practically nothing.

He was on the stand for four minutes.

. . .

Days apart, RealClearPolitics put his lead over Biden at the greatest it had ever been, and on January 26, the E. Jean jury came back with an award of $83 million to Carroll. (Plus, there was the $5 million she had already received in the first trial.) It was one of the largest defamation awards against an individual on record, dwarfing any of the worst-case scenarios the Trump side might have imagined—almost $70 million more than their worst case! Here was the collusion of terrible legal advice and Trump's own unrestrained behavior, the two fixed realities of his legal woes.

Alina Habba openly wondered how much Boris would contribute to paying this award, for his miserable legal strategy, and, likewise, what Natalie would chip in for egging on Trump's venom every night. (The Alina camp would in turn say that she had taken one for the team.)

There was suddenly a corollary to Trump's famous dictum that he could shoot someone on Fifth Avenue and not lose any voters: A Manhattan jury would be delighted to convict him of anything.

How could he sustain this? Whatever this was—witch hunt, vengeance, accountability, justice—it was all on his head, as great a weight as it was possible to imagine. It wasn't possible! Had anyone ever, in the face of such systematic vilification and depredation by the powers of the land, merely shaken it off and continued? Napoleon, perhaps.

On the one hand, Trump seemed to be a man with a wholly limited perspective, focused only on the moment he was in. On the other, he yet, somehow, seemed to have an appreciation of the entire field of play, that the race was long—nearly endless, in his case—and that there was always another day.

. . .

Meanwhile, the immunity defense, the wholly preposterous immunity defense—quite the product of lawyers so bad that they had no real reputations to protect and, hence, were willing to serve up such embarrassing balderdash—was in D.C. District Court, effectively gumming up the works for the trial Trumpworld feared most.

Yes, going on trial in New York for paying off a porn star was surely bad, and being convicted of a felony—and there were thirty-four counts he could be convicted on in New York—could not be good. But the Washington trial fed right into the issue the Democrats believed they could run on: Trump as a threat to democracy (that and abortion seemed the Democrats' only clear issues). If they were right, if 2 or 3 percent of the electorate wavered on this issue, then this might be a bumpier threat than all the other threats. But with more luck than the Trump campaign thought they would have, or deserved, the January 6 trial was moving very slowly. And might the Supreme Court punt, too, and push it out further yet, possibly beyond the election?

Anyway, March 4 for the January 6 trial was going to slip. March 5 was Super Tuesday. And March 13 was now the day the campaign was tracking to wrap up its delegate count for the nomination. On the one hand, so much could get in their way, so much real pain, true existential stuff; but on the other hand, nothing could.

• • •

And Fani Willis. Always put your faith in shit happening. And you don't even have to make it happen; it just does.

It suddenly came out: Willis had hired an outside lawyer, Nathan Wade, to lead her case against Trump. At some point—*after* she hired him, she said, not too credibly—she began an affair with the married Wade. Vacations abounded. Lots of money was spent, as Willis paid Wade nearly three-quarters of a million dollars in public funds. None of this had been uncovered by Trump's beleaguered team. One of his co-defendants, Mike Roman, the Philadelphia Republican who'd gotten on board the Trump post-election bus and then been indicted with him in Georgia, had proper lawyers, and they'd gotten wind of filings in Wade's wife's divorce case against him.

Pure dumb luck.

Too great!

Even Trump couldn't believe it: "This is so amazing. Is this for real? I was afraid she might be smart. She's a fucking idiot."

Trump had never so much disputed the Georgia case as merely lambasted it as an opportunistic grab by corrupt Georgia Democrats, and he had characterized Willis, in full sexist and racist fury, as a figure out of gangland Atlanta. Now, through no fault of his own, he was getting the exact narrative he wanted—no, better. Indeed, Roman's lawyers leveled their charges against Willis on January 8, and for twenty-five days she didn't respond. They just hung out there. Undenied. Unexplained. Imploding in real time.

And while none of this refuted any of Trump's actual charges, it perfectly buttressed what he was charging them, his pursuers, with: These low-down people, with secret agendas, were engaged in a dirty cabal of self-interest and political skulduggery to get him. And because all four trials, and additional civil cases, were hopelessly running together, each one, if it was sullied, sullied the others. And, too, he was being prosecuted by Black people (Alvin Bragg, Letitia James, Fani Willis), and they were particularly vengeful and unscrupulous—as anyone could now see!

• • •

Days after the E. Jean verdict, he's at Teamsters headquarters in Washington, in the penthouse suite, in a wholly engaged, upbeat, relaxed mood. It's only the third time a president (or former president) has visited Teamsters HQ—and he's the first Republican. It is a pleasing diss at Joe Biden's supposed working-man street cred—and the Teamsters leadership seems proud to have arranged the diss. Trump is at a conference table with Sean O'Brien, the Teamsters president—who is showing surprising courtliness to him—and the union leadership. They are surrounded by a dozen or so rank-and-file members in the room—and whatever the distractions of an $83 million judgment, Trump seems wholly focused now, quite an un-Trump-like laser. His message is immigration: *It's going to completely undercut everything you do and undercut the entire labor movement.* He hammers on steadily about it. While the rank-and-file in the room seemed standoffish in the beginning, now the group is nodding and murmuring in assent. And then his personal experience: "I've been building buildings with Teamsters my whole career. I never built any buildings in New York that were non-union. I know I could have done that. I could have gone that way, but I never did."

There's a lineup then, for everybody to get a selfie with him.

And then a televised press conference in the marble lobby, a half hour of questions.

He's asked a question, a wise guy's question, about his red hands. For the past week, he's had lobster hands: raw, puffed up. What is going on there? Among all questions, as hostile as they can go, personal questions, the most personal being about that most glaring anomaly, the oddness of his corporeal self, seem to puzzle him most—as though he is unaware of his own corpulence, preposterous hair, orange skin coloring, or dangling ties and out-of-date suits. A "paper cut" was his unlikely explanation.

Trump now holds up his hands, bewildered, and goes, *What?* As though for the first time, he's looking at his hands, too.

"Look, they're fine," Trump says, holding up his hands again.

But the question is pressed: What *was* the matter?

"I don't know," Trump says, seeming to avoid an answer, and then finding a satisfying, near-genius riposte: "Maybe it was AI."

• • •

He bounces back, keeps bouncing back. All politicians compartmentalize, but this seems like something different. First, there's the enormity of what he has to box up. No one in public life has ever been able to merely set aside a criminal prosecution—no less four, in a concerted state and federal attack, plus grievous civil penalties—and just go on whipping and entertaining and selling himself to his public. Huey Long, maybe—but even that was a less bumpy trail than Trump's. And certainly this wasn't disciplined emotional control. It was more . . . Jekyll and Hyde.

Truth Social is less a social media platform than just naked Trump. Every other politician is finely repressed, carefully circumscribed, hidden behind protectors, full of secrets, a construct of public acceptability, but there on Truth Social every night, Trump is an open wound. What terrible turmoil one might assume he is internalizing—he isn't.

"He's posting these screeds in all caps, and we're like, well, nobody actually reads Truth, and the reporters who do cover [it] are kind of numb to it at this point," says a staffer trying to fine-tune the nature of the Truth Social threat. "But if you don't normally track him, and you look to Truth Social on just any kind of given random day, your mind would explode. I mean, these rants are completely unhinged. I mean, he can be in the best of moods all day, and then in the dark night of the Mar-a-Lago soul, he's face-to-face with them trying to wipe him out and lock him up for the rest of his life. And he loses it, and publicly so, if anyone wanted to look."

. . .

On Thursday, February 8, they would be in the Supreme Court for the hearing on Colorado's efforts, now being mimicked by a catchall of other states, to keep him off the ballot based on the Fourteenth Amendment's proscription against anyone holding office who has participated in an insurrection against the United States.

Here again was the wide gulf between one view, in which Trump was the worst you could possibly imagine him to be, having executed a failed coup against his own government and worthy of the (never-invoked) *only* constitutional definition of unfitness for office; and the view in which Trump, ever misunderstood, was wholly a victim of the machinations and plotting of an entrenched guard and ancien régime.

And here was Trump ready to lead his own courtroom charge—because having the candidate in court had, to date, worked out so well.

But the Nevada primary was on February 6—in a Nevada anomaly, there was also a caucus on the eighth—and although he was running unopposed, Nevada was a key state for the general election and part of the clean-sweep, maximum-margin primary strategy. Anyway, it was a good enough argument to help dissuade him from showing up before the Supreme Court.

More and more, he had taken up an antagonistic position to the justices—Kavanaugh and Barrett and Gorsuch—whom he considered to be his own. In 2020, they had rebuffed him on the election issues. And then, their throwing out *Roe v. Wade* he regarded as somehow a direct hit on his 2024 prospects—what were they thinking? His own antagonism might now, with him inside, staring down the Court, easily spread to antagonizing them. While nobody was seriously worried about the Fourteenth Amendment case, there were other cases to come, including his most-dreamed-of bid for universal presidential immunity, and what fights might come to the Court after the election.

Best, obviously, to keep him out of their court (which he often called "my court").

• • •

"J6," the Trump legal team's term for the Jack Smith storm-the-Capitol election interference trial, was now formally moved off the docket. Yet, they still couldn't actually believe they would be lucky enough to have the Supreme Court push it beyond the pre-election calendar. But for the moment, it could slip out of mind. Atlanta was all fucked up, so that wasn't going to happen. And it seemed like they could count on a delay in the boxes case from Judge Aileen Cannon, who seemed to rule consistently in their favor and whom Trump cronies were now calling "future Supreme Court justice Aileen Cannon." This left New York, tentatively on the calendar for March 25, and there was no reason, beyond specious motions by the Trump side, anyone could reasonably see for delay. Still, six weeks out, no one had yet to focus on the case.

• • •

With Trump safely in Mar-a-Lago—he would fly to Nevada later in the day—instead of facing down *his* justices, the Supreme Court took up the arguments for Colorado's bid to exclude him from the ballot.

There wasn't a lot of frisson about which way this would go, but there was a subtle tension about tone and about generally reading the

Court's demeanor toward Trump. It was the subtext of history in the making—might Trump's court be getting tired of Trump?

Curiously, the case had largely been prepared out of Trump's view and that of his personal lawyers. Jon Mitchell—only Trump seemed old enough to think it might be bad luck that one of his lawyers had the same name as Nixon's ill-fated attorney general (though Nixon's was John Mitchell)—the lawyer who was arguing the case before the Supreme Court (with, behind him, a respectable lineup of cases he had previously argued before the Court), had not only *not* met Trump, but had preferred not to, recognizing that a client's desires were not really relevant to a Supreme Court argument, and wanting to avoid them.

Trump would later say that he had "watched" the arguments, but, in fact, only the real-time audio was broadcast—aides explained that he had "watched" the static picture on the screen while listening to the audio—and he had not actually *seen* Mitchell. That was fortunate, because Mitchell seemed inauspicious—small, nervous, church-mousey, a dweeby nerd—far, far from Trump's central casting ideal. Nobody seemed too impressed by Mitchell's initial argument. That is, until the other side, led by attorney Jason Murray, gave its opener and then took questions. Clarence Thomas, as the longest-serving justice, got the first question. Leaning back in his chair so far that all you saw were his glasses, he asked for other examples contemporaneous with the Fourteenth Amendment's adoption in 1868 of someone disqualified from the ballot—and Murray flubbed the answer, because, basically, no one ever had been. But it was not only the conservative justices who seemed skeptical. Murray was challenged in a tone bordering on disbelief by the first liberal-bloc justice to get a question, and not only a liberal-bloc justice but Elena Kagan, for whom Murray had clerked: Why should a single state get to decide who runs for president? Instantly, the air came out of the room. For a moment, too, there even seemed to be light at the end of the partisan tunnel. Here, beyond ideological motives, was just a matter-of-fact deconstruction of faulty logic and unthought-out conclusions, rendered trenchantly, swiftly, and without rancor.

It was over by twelve thirty—with Trump immediately out in front

of the cameras at Mar-a-Lago claiming a sweeping victory. He had taken
to noting that Mar-a-Lago had really become just like the White
House—the press was always there, just waiting for him.

The legal team repaired to an Alexandria steakhouse that evening for
a long dinner, drinks, and self-congratulatory photos. Mitchell, shaking
his head in some wonder, as though something were amiss, said the justices "were way too nice."

* * *

With Trump on his way to Las Vegas, Robert Hur, the special counsel
appointed to investigate the government documents Joe Biden had removed from the White House after his term as vice president, issued his
report. There would be no prosecution or further action against Biden.
But, the report said, Biden had willfully retained these documents and
shown them to outsiders—hardly that different, at least to a layman,
from what Trump was being accused of. Still, the former vice president
would not be prosecuted because . . . he was out of it, the report said,
offering, as a gift to Trump, a critique of Biden's sentience: "Mr. Biden
would likely present himself to a jury, as he did during our interview of
him, as a sympathetic, well-meaning, elderly man with a poor memory."
Gone. Creeping dementia at the very least.

Trump at seventy-seven, with the contempt, and relish, of an old
man who sees the faltering of a contemporary, now had confirmation of
his most visceral and powerful issue.

* * *

On February 15, Trump was in Manhattan Criminal Court again, facing
District Attorney Alvin Bragg and Justice Juan M. Merchan, on the subject of his first indictment—his payments to the former porn star and
his former lover (although he still contested this) Stormy Daniels. With
his first attorney, Joe Tacopina, disappeared from the case, and Boris,
too, far from the defense table this time—out of sight from a losing enterprise, others on the legal team inferred—Todd Blanche, yet in Trump's

good graces, was now up front. He would be either hero or goat. The first appearance in front of Justice Merchan, ten months before, had been of moment—the only ever criminal indictment of a U.S. president. Now, today, same place, same issues, it seemed like, eh, Thursday: business as usual.

Denied, denied, denied, went the litany from Merchan, as he turned down each defense motion to further delay the trial. It was set in stone: March 25, as they knew it would be, twelve days after Trump, in current calculations, would have captured his party's nomination for the presidency. The trial would last a minimum of four weeks, with, for his lawyers, the horrifying possibility that he would surely want to take the stand—where, under oath, he might finally be forced into a reckoning with Stormy Daniels.

The next day, February 16, after three months of trial in front of Judge Arthur Engoron—and at this point, everyone, including Trump's staff and lawyers, would need to be forgiven for mixing up courtrooms and court dates and the various judges—judgment was rendered in the fraud trial: the first, and presumably far from the last, game-changing judgment for Trump.

He was in Mar-a-Lago, having flown back from yesterday's New York court appearance on the hush money felony. The first word was from a press report—$100 million. Trump's fury was zero to sixty, while his legal team, at that moment, was full of wonder and relief that it was *only* $100 million. But that first report reflected just the top line of the decision and not the complete, itemized list of penalties. The actual total was $354.8 million. And with interest that had accrued, and continued to accrue, the total was $454 million. A massacre. For the staff, legal team, and, in a sense, the nation itself, it was the first-ever real glimpse of Trump in definitive defeat. Here was physical deflation and internal collapse—hit by a ton of bricks. And, most ominously, silence. For the first time ever, Trump seemed not to want to face the press. It wasn't until 6 P.M., three hours after the first news, that he got himself out in front of the Mar-a-Lago entrance with a small group of assembled reporters for a four-minute statement: witch hunt, corrupt New York State, election interference, a Biden White House plot against him.

. . .

The next morning, he flew out to Michigan—its primary would be held on February 27—where he seamlessly added the $454 million to his list of grievances and made it another reason the presidency was the revenge that had to be wreaked on his behalf.

On the plane, Trump was going over points in his speech. Natalie eagerly presented a brainstorm: It should be made clear that the New York judgment, together with all the other legal battles against him, would make it, if they lost in November, a stolen election. "Let's put it in that all of this legal stuff, if the other side wins, which they won't, it will make the election illegitimate."

"Good line," Trump agreed.

By general agreement of the campaign team—and rising panic that, once again, he was announcing a stolen election—the line was deftly lost in the final notes Trump took with him.

Later that day, Trump flew into Philadelphia to address, of all things, Sneaker Con—his appearance there as confusing to Trump as it would be to almost everyone else—a mass gathering of sneaker fans and connoisseurs and a launchpad for new sneaker lines and models.

This had somehow been organized outside Trump's attention by Bill Zanker, the founder of the Learning Annex, a 1980s storefront phenomenon offering how-to courses on virtually any subject it could, for the most part, find teachers (or people who claimed they could teach) to teach for free; it went bankrupt in 1991 (although Trump himself was paid amply for lending his name as a Learning Annex "teacher"). Zanker became a co-writer on one of Trump's various self-aggrandizing business books and then a Trump merchandiser, most recently as the impresario behind Trump's NFTs—and now a Trump sneaker line at $399.

As they landed in Philly, Trump, a man who had never worn a sport or leisure shoe beyond the golf course, kept asking for a greater explanation. "What is this?" he demanded with more puzzlement. "Why are we doing this?" Apolitical independent men, youth voters, minorities, a good group for you, was the strained answer, beyond the more obvious promotional scheme. And perhaps it was. Trump came onto the stage at

3:30 P.M.—"God Bless the USA" blaring—and Sneaker Con did suddenly seem like a Trump rally: *USA! USA! USA!* chants filling the big room, joined by a *FUCK JOE BIDEN!* chorus drowning out the weaker boos. Onstage, Trump called up a middle-aged woman with a "Trump 2024" hoodie, who grabbed him tightly and began to weep—with the panic evident in Trump's eyes, and Secret Service moving in around him. Afterward, he singled out from the charged-up crowd a young man with a tattoo in the middle of his face. Trump seemed unable to ignore it, looking away, then looking back.

"Interesting thing," he said.

"Thanks, Mr. President." The young man beamed.

"But let me ask you, how much would it cost to get it removed?"

• • •

In Nashville, on February 23, one day before the South Carolina primary, for a fundraiser and speech before the National Religious Broadcasters, the plane, up and running for a month, broke down again. A mechanic (who was fired on the spot) had mistakenly deployed the inflatable chute. Nearly a dozen and a half people were traveling in the entourage, so not only did the campaign have to scrounge up a plane before Trump found out and went into a spiral of recrimination and wrath, but likely they would need at least two Gulfstream IVs or Vs. A scramble ensued among the entourage, with a frantic tapping of everybody's immediate call list. In an hour, Justin Caporale produced two Falcons.

• • •

CPAC, the Conservative Political Action Conference—scheduled in the days before the South Carolina primary, with an invitation to Trump to speak the day of the primary—had become one of the most important events on the MAGA calendar. It had first hosted Trump in 2011, introducing him as a plausible right-wing personality; then had dissed him as he rose against other, more established right-of-right-of-center Republi cans; and then had embraced him again, after his victory, and transformed itself into Trump Con, with a Trump appearance always its main event. But this year, CPAC had been mysteriously cut from his calendar.

Or not so mysteriously.

"Who's the dummy who said yes to this?" Chris LaCivita demanded.

This seemed suddenly meaningful and like some serious flexing. LaCivita seemed to recognize, too, that CPAC particularly brought out the demon Trump: The more MAGA maximal he went, the more the CPAC crowd responded. If, as the campaign believed, the general election was starting now—with Nikki Haley to be dead and buried in her home state—then why walk into it waving a bloody shirt?

But Wiles, in fact, had pushed back hard on CPAC, and had prevailed. She knew what the Trump fallout would be. *They're throwing a party for me. It's a four-day conference to celebrate how great I am, and I'm not even going?*

Yet, LaCivita was probably right—no good came from Trump at CPAC.

. . .

On the way to the conference, Natalie shows Trump a clip from Newsmax. The news network has agreed to make certain statements to settle lawsuits against it over the 2020 election, and to state its belief in the results of the election despite Trump's persistent claims otherwise (including in a speech carried by Newsmax the day before). So, the morning begins with a steaming, pissed-off Trump declaring Newsmax and its CEO, Chris Ruddy, Trump enemies.

Landing at Dulles and then heading to CPAC, in Oxon Hill, Maryland, Trump takes a call from the pollster John McLaughlin, who pitches Trump on supporting a senate candidate from New York who has hired McLaughlin. Trump asks, offhandedly, what McLaughlin thinks the margin in South Carolina will be that evening, and McLaughlin, as offhandedly, says maybe fifteen to twenty points, where previously, at least as Trump reports, McLaughlin had told him he could count on twenty to thirty points. This, now, becomes a "What the fuck?" moment. A ranting one. "If that number doesn't have a two in front of it, that will be so fucking fucked up. Fucking, what happened?"

Then Natalie informs him that she's seeing chatter on social media about low turnout at the polling stations in South Carolina. (There will in fact be a record turnout.) The Trump volatility index reaches red, and he is sent into CPAC in the darkest mood anyone has seen since the last darkest mood, the $454 million one.

Trump stays on script for the first quarter of the speech and then puts aside the rest and goes on for another hour and a half in a next-level shit-show fury, declaring that "judgment day" is coming for his opponents and that he is the victim of "Stalinist show trials" and promising the biggest deportation in history—oh, and that he is a "total genius."

"Our country is being destroyed, and the only thing standing between you and its obliteration is me."

And, too, as he meanders, with a high unlikelihood, it appears, that he will ever give up the stage, he slips in that Kellyanne Conway, persistently trying to work her way back into the tight Trump circle, might be joining the RNC, which LaCivita is in the process of taking control of—which comes as a complete surprise to the campaign staff in the room: "What did he say? Did he just say that? Kellyanne? *Kellyanne!*"

Or was DJT just breaking LaCivita's balls?

• • •

In Columbia, South Carolina, that evening for the primary results, Trump's overriding concern—a fixation, at this point—was that Nikki Haley not speak before he did and thus upstage him, which would allow her to put a positive spin on defeat, as she had in New Hampshire. Justin Caporale's production team had placed pieces of tape on the stage, indicating where the two dozen or so guests and local VIPs should stand, each piece of tape with a name—and at 6:50, the South Carolina MAGA good and great were all lined up like a squadron of Canada geese, waiting for the polls to close. The AP called the race for Trump exactly as the polls closed at 7 P.M.—and Trump, flanked by his South Carolina MAGA retinue, began his speech at 7:06.

Trump got his "two," with a 20 percent margin. But after he swept the first four primaries with a double-digit advantage in each one—Nevada was uncontested—effectively wiping out his media-inflated competition, first Ron, then Nikki, a good part of the mainstream coverage now turned on a dime, speculating as to why his unprecedented victories were fundamentally flawed. In this view, the "independent" voters whom Haley had pitched herself to, those middle-of-the-road, no-party types (or old-fashioned Republicans) who had not become infected by Trump, were not just cool to him but resisting him hotly. And he would surely need a portion of them if he was to win in November. Here was the math problem: a deficit that might be made up by a convincing move by Trump toward the middle (which seemed unlikely); or by Democrats staying home because Biden seemed too old and embarrassing to vote for; or by an increasing, and perhaps magical, belief in the Black vote.

In this, there had been a recent resurgence of the odd-man, deeply suspect, Whac-A-Mole political consultant Dick Morris. Most famous for having helped Bill Clinton emerge from his 1994 midterm defeat by tacking rightward and for a sex scandal involving toe sucking, Morris had re-emerged holding Trump's cell phone number in the 2020 campaign. He was an apt example of the hucksters who succeeded with Trump: You just pitched him, relentlessly, until you wore him down or found an idea he liked. Now Morris had polling he claimed showed that Black men were unenthusiastic about Biden. Trump claimed he was taking only one in ten of Morris's calls, but he was obviously tantalized by Morris's promise of a Black Trump surge. It had suddenly become a reasonable theory in the campaign that an additional five to ten points of Black male voters might be up for grabs—and, for Trump, somehow a silver lining of his pursuit by law enforcement was that, in his view, he was gaining street cred.

• • •

Super Tuesday, on March 5, will wrap the primary season with fifteen states voting and delivering their delegates. It will be a massive victory day for Trump. His sweep strategy has been entirely successful. No candidate in any contested primary race has wrapped up the nomination as handily and as quickly.

But he has gone into Super Tuesday in a bitter mood. It's Nikki Haley. *Why is she still in the race? Why hasn't she gotten out? What is her deal? What is she trying to prove? Why is she doing this? What is the matter with her? What does she want? What is really behind this? Who is really backing her?*

The evening will destroy any pretense that Haley has a 2024 future. She will get out of the race. She will have no more money and no more resources. He will crush her. She will be history. Already forgotten. And yet, he is obsessed. For him, *she* is the centerpiece of the night—not him. She is the ugly spoiler, although she spoils nothing. And certainly, as predicted, every state comes in for him with an unprecedented margin.

Save one: Vermont. Liberal Vermont. Inconsequential Vermont. It goes for Haley.

What the fuck! He dwells. His balance, his precarious balance, teeters. He demands of everybody that they explain this. *Is this true?* It couldn't be true. *What happened? What the fuck happened? I was robbed!*

His night is ruined.

PART THREE

The Nominee

CHAPTER 10

Coming Together— or Coming Apart

MARCH 2024

"I don't think the cocaine they found in the White House was Hunter's; I think it was for Joe," remarked an amused Trump, as Joe Biden began his State of the Union address on March 7 and seemed to rouse himself to a new effort at outrage and energy. (Trump would turn his cocaine banter into a bona fide conspiracy theory in subsequent interviews and speeches.) Trump watched the speech from a war room set up in the library bar at Mar-a-Lago, poised to supply moment-by-moment rejoinders to the Biden speech—Natalie at his side, ready to post.

Trumpworld was struck, not for the first time, by Biden's appearance during the speech. For all Trump's physical absurdities, Biden's untouched gray on gray, trending toward invisibility, made the harsher point. Trump's clownish appearance distracted from his age. Biden's effort to be dignified magnified his. The point was once more reiterated with both confidence and worry: Trump wasn't running against Joe Biden, who seemed unable to do anything to affect his own fate, but against Trump himself and when he might run out of luck or, as ever, shoot himself in both feet.

In the days after Biden's State of the Union, a cogent enough condemnation of Trump's policies and the dangers he'd present in a dangerous world, there was no real measurable improvement in the sitting president's numbers. And, his general good fortune continuing, on March 14, two days after Trump's delegate count formally locked in his nomination, Alvin Bragg, the Manhattan DA whom Trump had been raging on for his perfidy and partisanship, now seemed to have extended to Trump a gift of shoddy preparation.

Trump regarded Bragg as "fat and dumb," the Manhattan District Attorney's Office as "total hacks—where you go when you can't get a job," and the case as the "total bullshit one," much more bullshit than even the other bullshit ones. (Trump aimed a separate especially venomous and frequent attack at Matthew Colangelo, the former DOJ lawyer, and, to Trump, deep-state agent, who had joined the prosecution team.) This was echoed by Boris into a general legal view that if you were doubling down on New York, you were wasting your time and the boss's money—"it was chicken shit." And now, as it happened, Bragg's office had somehow failed to review and turn over the results of the investigation into the Stormy Daniels hush money payments that the feds had begun in 2019 and then had decided not to pursue, as the law required. The prosecution was forced to agree to at least a thirty-day delay in the trial. Once more, Trump, through no fault of his own, had benefited from shit happening, lucky shit. And who knew what would happen in thirty days?

And with more luck, Fani Willis, having cast a *Real Housewives of Atlanta* aura over her proceedings, was now directed by the judge leading the inquiry into her alleged corruption to fire her lead lawyer, also her lover, if she wanted to pursue the case. This all but guaranteed a long delay, almost certainly past the election. (Trump, ever obsessed with the comparison between him and O.J. Simpson, suggested, only half facetiously, that Willis should have used the example of the O.J. prosecutors Marcia Clark and Christopher Darden to excuse her affair.)

The Supreme Court, too, was sending an unexpected signal. Surprising nobody as much as the Trump campaign itself, the Court announced that it would hear arguments on Trump's immunity defense, thereby delaying the January 6 trial—the "kill shot" case, as some on the legal team saw it—certainly well into the general election campaign and likely until after the election.

What's more, the smart money, or at least the big money, seemed to be rushing back to Trump. Not long after claiming the nomination, Trump got off the phone and came out of his office at Mar-a-Lago with a quizzical look and said to his waiting aides, "Now, that was an interesting phone call . . . Rupert!"

"Murdoch?" said one of the aides with involuntary surprise.

The two men had not spoken since the November 2020 election—the night Murdoch himself had approved the early call of a Biden victory in Arizona, setting in motion, Trump believed, the stealing of the election. After January 6, 2021, Murdoch had utterly washed his hands of Trump and become an implacable foe. He had personally encouraged Ron DeSantis to oppose Trump and then directed Fox News to both support DeSantis and keep Trump off the air. Even in the weeks before Murdoch's call to Trump, he had continued to revile Trump to virtually anyone who would listen.

Now, according to Trump, Murdoch was calling him to say that this election was the most important in history and that the country was lucky to have a man like him.

This, of course, was the conversation *as reported by Trump*. Trump also credibly reported that Murdoch had strongly lobbied for Mike Pompeo as VP, Trump's former stoic secretary of state and CIA chief, quite a Republican Party stalwart; a reliable, old-fashioned interventionist neocon type of Murdoch's liking; and someone else whom Murdoch had tried to encourage to oppose Trump in the primary race. (There was almost no earthly possibility Trump would choose Pompeo as his VP.)

Bets were being made; money was being put down—even for policy positions, as with Murdoch's effort, far outside the MAGA circle. Now was the time.

Trump's old friend Andy Stein—who, in a moment of new-day optimism, had publicly endorsed Nikki Haley in an op-ed in *The Wall Street Journal,* only to be personally vilified by Trump and cast out of Trumpworld—now hastily threw together a groveling homage: "I was one of those who doubted he could pull off a second presidential victory and backed Nikki Haley. I was wrong—Trump is ready to be president again, and the country needs him," he said in an apology in the *New*

York Post, adding a few pointed digs at Haley. And shortly, Stein was back in Trump's good graces.

In Palm Beach, Nelson Peltz and Ike Perlmutter, two octogenarian many-times-over debt market billionaires, were arranging come-to-Jesus-style dinners with Trump and their fellow billionaire machers, including Elon Musk, who met with Trump at Peltz's Palm Beach house on March 3 with Musk immediately leaking the story. Given Trump's stout opposition to environmental rules and incentives that favored electric vehicles, the Tesla chief's interest might have seemed counterintuitive. But everybody appeared to know on which side the bread might soon be buttered. Jeff Yass, among the largest American investors in Tik-Tok, with a secretive fortune that some said rivaled Musk's, was communing with Trump—this new friendliness hand in hand with Trump's dramatic flip-flop in his support for TikTok. The Peltz–Perlmutter list also included Oracle founder Larry Ellison and Uber founder Travis Kalanick (kicked out of Uber, but still with a fortune to dispense).

This new oligarch class of American businessmen, largely untethered to corporate respectability, shady figures in Palm Beach's sunny clime, many who had once resisted Trump as a somewhat embarrassing parody of their own will to glamour and power—they knew "Donald"—were finally accepting him as one of their own. It was a particularly propitious moment for a billionaire to make himself available to Trump, not just because success seemed once more in Trump's grasp—Elon Musk had been telling people that "history was a series of unlikely events," Trump foremost among them—but because now more than ever, he needed money. He had already at great cost posted a bond for the $91 million, with interest, he owed E. Jean Carroll, as he appealed that decision; in a matter of days, he had to come up with a way to guarantee the $454 million he owed the State of New York.

He was, incontrovertibly, his party's nominee, crushing the opposition—if you could even consider him having had any opposition. He was up against the least popular incumbent in modern history, one seemingly unable to capture attention, articulate a message, or walk a straight line. And most confoundingly, with menace and confusion, he seemed to have fought a legal system bent on his destruction to something like a draw, at least a temporary one.

• • •

But the pitfalls of success can be as great as those of failure.

It was one of his key characteristics that Trump was never prepared for success (or, for that matter, failure). In 2016, he had not believed he was going to win—in some sense, he had never even considered the possibility. And even if he had, he had always been of the view that planning ahead was bad luck. He had even resented the money Congress had authorized for major-party candidates to begin the transition process—and the Trump team efforts that were made to prepare for a transition to the White House were chaotic and mostly useless.

His calling card was as the consummate businessman, but in fact, he was in almost every sense anti-organization. He often seemed incapable of appreciating, or at least of being in any way interested in, everything that occurred outside the reach of his own voice or that he did not see on television. He ignored rather than delegated. He almost entirely lacked the ability to listen—sourly looking at anyone who tried to talk to him, before reflexively grabbing back the floor and resuming his own discursive stream of consciousness. He was neither cowed nor impressed by nor appreciative or even comprehending of anyone else's expertise. One result here was that there was no vetting and no basic standards or discernment, nor, often, even a reasonable explanation for the kind and the caliber of people who crowded into his orbit—a democracy of opportunists, grifters, and dunces. The cacophony around him of people trying to get his attention seemed to register, if he heard it all, as a low murmur. Everybody's voice was equal to the extent that they were mostly unheard. And when a particular voice did become clear, that was the point at which it usually started to annoy him.

In some sense, this had worked to his political advantage: The outsiders around him, often with scant professional or educational credentials, burnished his status as an outsider bucking the hierarchical system, with its doctrinaire expertise. At the same time, what came to assemble around him was more voluble town square riffraff than team.

Now, with the growing belief that he might actually—even, in the minds of many, possibly likely *would*—pull this off, there was an ever-increasing number of voices in his orbit drowning one another out, all of them struggling up to the decibel level that would finally capture his attention, and his annoyance.

The Wiles-LaCivita campaign group that had brought him this far, from ignominy through indictments to this current penultimate political pinnacle—and which had operated in a parallel and often-overlooked world to his golf game and legal problems—understood that from here on, it would likely be competing with other power centers in Trump-world and dealing with efforts of one or more among them to emerge as the person closest to Trump's ear (putting aside that this was almost invariably an unhappy, if not dangerous, place to be).

Super PACs, with their unrestricted giving rules—after the Supreme Court made them a workaround to otherwise strict donor limitations—had become a central part of any campaign's operation. The catch, the workaround, is that the super PAC can't formally coordinate with the campaign. Hence, a smooth and efficient campaign–super PAC relationship demands a mind-meld familiarity between the super PAC director and the campaign's needs and intentions. The person running a candidate's key super PAC has the job—has been put into the job—precisely because of this shadow ability, and as an incentive to that subservient willingness and loyalty, they can look forward to being duly rewarded by the spoils of victory. In other words, the independence of a super PAC is fiction, and its real role is as a powerful entity in the operation of a campaign.

The key Trump super PAC was Make America Great Again Inc. It was formed in 2022 after Trump returned to Mar-a-Lago and was run by twenty-seven-year-old Taylor Budowich, a junior communications staffer in the 2020 campaign whom Trump had become fond of and whom Wiles helped put into the super PAC job. Budowich, in turn, now worked closely with the pollster Tony Fabrizio. A longtime Republican operative, Fabrizio, in the 2020 campaign, had been a consistent check against both the chaos and the excesses of the unmanaged Kushner-led side of the campaign and, after the loss, against the election-denial nutters. In other words, the 2024 super PAC was in line with the campaign's goal of avoiding the worst Trumpian influences and focused on locking down the nomination as early and as conclusively as possible with the backing of a united and unquestioning party. Budowich, Fabrizio, and MAGA Inc. deserved significant credit for the systematic dismantling of DeSantis, getting on the air in the early phase of the DeSantis surge and almost singularly driving the message that DeSantis was disconnected, maladroit, and weird.

At the same time, MAGA Inc. had been a consistent target of the Trump orbit—of Bannon and other far-right performers, of some of Trump's donor cronies, and of anyone competing for Trump's attention or for MAGA purity. The campaign, because it was winning, could not so easily be directly attacked, but MAGA Inc. was an available proxy for it.

Shortly before Super Tuesday, Axios ran a story that Sergio Gor, a Trump hanger-on and sometime factotum and business partner, was thinking about launching his own Trump super PAC—which, given his proximity to Trump, was a potential existential event for MAGA Inc. and, as well, a red-flag warning for the campaign.

Gor, a scrubbed-faced, Brooks Brothers–wearing, Young Republican type, had been the butt of many jokes among the campaign normies: He was "the Mayor of Mar-a-Lago" for his ubiquity, for the familiarity he had developed with staff and members, and for his inevitable presence at both club and political events; and "the Patio Panhandler," for how he worked the wealthy dinner crowd, cementing relationships with the richest. With Trump's blessing and partnership, Gor launched Winning Team Publishing, which created high-priced Trump-themed coffee-table books and marketed them through MAGA channels—putting money directly into Trump's pocket (a necessary interest of Trumpworld).

"He's a goofball and a charlatan, but the president loves him," another patio regular said of Gor.

This was not just ad hominem strafing, but also an acknowledgment that goofballs, grifters, and charlatans were a distinct part of the Trump constituency—people willing and able to cater to Trump's mercurial, eccentric, and demanding needs. In Trumpworld, there always existed a tension between them and the less shameless.

Meanwhile, Gor, in his patio efforts, had bonded with Trump's Palm Beach friend, Mar-a-Lago member, and patio regular Ike Perlmutter.

Trump's awe of billionaires was both wide and specific. Any billionaire anywhere was an exception to any other feelings or prejudices he might have—anyone who was a billionaire was vastly better than anyone who was not, and worthy of the greatest respect. The billionaire's club was a club in which Trump not only needed to belong but might die if he did not. But the category beyond that, a vastly more rarefied group, and to which special benefits flowed, included any billionaire who felt toward Trump what Trump felt toward them (or any billionaire willing to pretend he did).

Perlmutter, like Trump himself, was a huckster story of indefatigable gumption and inexplicable leaps of fortune. Unlike Trump, Perlmutter, emigrating from Israel as a young man, had started with nothing, rising, without an education, from street vendor to tenacious leveraged takeover specialist, making several of his billions in the takeover and subsequent sale of Marvel Comics to Disney. He had been, throughout his career, press-shy, litigious, and mostly a bane to anyone forced to work with him. In retirement in Palm Beach, after finally being pushed out of Disney—it was an agonizing process over many years to pry Perlmutter, one of the company's largest shareholders, from the various positions he claimed in the company—he had more and more dedicated himself to Donald Trump, as crony, adviser, flatterer (and flattered in return), and foursome member, a latter-day Bebe Rebozo, Nixon's big-money Florida counselor and comforter. In this role, it might even be said, Perlmutter was one of the few people whom Trump listened to. That is, one of the few people whom Trump shut up for. What's more, Perlmutter, as a self-appointed protector of Donald Trump—generally believing everyone everywhere was trying to undermine his friend Trump—had a lot of certain opinions, among them that Trump's people were not loyal enough, at least not loyal like Ike Perlmutter was loyal, or Sergio Gor.

The fundamental lack of loyalty out there was exactly what Gor had sold Perlmutter on—that is, Gor's own loyalty and everyone else's lack thereof. In this view, MAGA Inc., and by extension, the campaign itself, was fundamentally out for its own interests—and that would only become more the case as they came closer to November and victory. Gor and Perlmutter, as true friends of Trump, needed to build a team that would protect the president in the White House as he had not been protected the last time.

The Axios story, supplied by unnamed sources, laid down their marker: Gor would be the CEO of the new super PAC, with its tight relationship to Trump, and Perlmutter would be its sugar daddy.

Other unnamed sources responded in kind, working to supply a portrait to the media of Gor as a grifter, with Perlmutter in tow. Fury ensued, with Sergio blaming Boris—catching Trump in the middle of two people he seemed unswervingly and unaccountably never to question—and the litigious Perlmutter saying he was going to sue the Daily Beast, which had published the attack, and blaming Susie Wiles, directly implicating the campaign and attacking its very foundation. Perlmutter's press-phobic wife, Laura, buttonholed Trump on the Mar-a-Lago patio, demanding that he hunt down and punish the people in his campaign who were defaming them. Trump appeared cowed and helpless.

Meanwhile, Elon Musk, too, was telling people he was going to start his own Trump-supporting super PAC. And Larry Ellison, also, was going to start a super PAC for Trump. (He never did.)

That was what success got you: everybody fighting for a piece of it.

• • •

Chris LaCivita was seeing the Republican National Committee, since the expulsion in February of its chief Ronna McDaniel—who, incurring Trump's wrath, had seemed to wait on the sidelines for an alternative Republican nominee—as a natural expansion of his logistics-focused power base. Here was a state-by-state foot soldier, fundraising, and data-gathering operation that had resisted Trump control. LaCivita seemed cavalier about turning the RNC into his instrument, while Wiles, in a longer view, understood that the campaign was protected as long as it was winning and bringing money in, but the RNC was the shifting border of the party factions, both of the party's entrenched base and of the patronage play of whoever held power at a given moment.

On Monday, March 11, LaCivita spent the day at RNC headquarters with the committee's new chair, Mike Whatley, and co-chair Lara Trump, both front people appointed by the Trump campaign. In a movie-worthy scene of how backroom politics is played, Whatley, theoretically in charge, having tried to defend various staffers, but fooling no one with the reach of his power, was placed in the chairman's office with nothing to do. LaCivita, making this Black Monday, arrived in the office and set up individual meetings with Ronna McDaniel's key aides, firing them, with relish, one by one. "LaCivita always wants to remind you that he was a marine and that tough is his middle name," said one staffer. McDaniel's apparatchiks were promptly replaced by LaCivita's (although in some cases, he fired McDaniel's insiders and, in a quick rejigging of their loyalties, then hired them back). Other than that, they were virtually indistinguishable party bureaucrats—which of course was the nature of the RNC.

Bannon, who had coordinated much of the drumbeat against McDaniel, now, on a dime, refocused his attention on LaCivita, blaming him for replacing one set of RINOs at the RNC with merely a new set of RINOs. Some had wondered why Wiles had so willingly acceded the RNC to LaCivita. At least one answer was that it had immediately put a target on LaCivita's back. He now represented the party bureaucracy rather than the Trump insurgency.

Here was another potential showdown for the future, not Wiles vs. LaCivita, as might have been expected, but a more overt take-no-prisoners match between Bannon and LaCivita, the kamikaze fighter against the field officer strategist.

Meanwhile, Lara Trump, in her role as RNC co-chair, marked the formal return of the family to the Trump campaign. Jared and Ivanka were maintaining their watchful distance. (In March, Kushner announced several major international development deals involving Trump adviser Richard Grenell, which the campaign found an annoyance, if not an affront.) Eric and Don Jr. were tied up in the legal battles and now facing their own costly defenestration in New York in the aftermath of the fraud trial and judgment. Wiles had been able to keep a tight guard on the campaign's management lines, where, in the past, each member of the family had been able to introduce their proxies and allies. Lara now took the family seat. Trump activist and election denier, and possible QAnon adherent Scott Presler was to be her guy in-house at the RNC. But given that he was also a gay Republican with a public chronicle of sexcapades—including, in his past stint at the RNC, having sex on the premises and widely sharing the pictures—he would not last long.

In other turf wars, the competition between the Heritage Foundation and the America First Policy Institute, with its Stephen Miller offshoot, America First Legal, had now become overt. For the Heritage Foundation, the AFPI was the "Jared group," hopelessly tainted by Kushner proxies in its ranks and by Kushner's personal ambitions both in and out of Trumpworld. The Heritage Foundation's Project 2025 manifesto, a far-right wish list, was meant as a tool to out-MAGA the AFPI (and which the Democrats would promptly weaponize as the secret plan for a new Trump administration). For the AFPI, the Heritage Foundation was a bastion of Never Trumpers, but was now trying to paper over its disloyalty to the true cause. For each group, it was a scramble for attention from the press as much as from Trump. Here were the Sharks and the Jets, and the contest between them was to determine which one could get the attention of the mainstream media for its version of Trump's revanchist world—the darkest version wins. As the campaign saw it, just at the moment when they needed to focus on that small sliver of independent voters, greater Trumpworld was intent on undermining the best-laid plans.

• • •

The campaign, at moments, actually believed in Trump's impulse to moderation.

The central tell that somewhere in all his instincts for grandstanding and fire-and-fury pronouncements and reflexive bids for attention there was an understanding, however uneven, of the importance of the political center: his wiggling on abortion.

"Don't talk weeks. Nobody talk weeks. Weeks get you in trouble. No weeks" was his new position. There were either not enough weeks or too many weeks—whatever the number was, it was a losing number, so no number. The more unspecific he got, in effect, the clearer his position became: He was looking for a sweet spot in which everyone could think he was partial to their position. He could, in other words, accommodate.

He had, curiously, taken to circumnavigating the word *conservative*. Apparently, he wasn't one. He was, suddenly, even non-ideological. No labels. What he was, what his thinking was, was "just common sense."

"What I would do is what anybody would do if it wasn't about politics."

"You're apolitical?" said a skeptical friend sharing a steak with him on the Mar-a-Lago patio.

"Yeah. I'm apolitical."

The reflexive fear that the billionaires traipsing across the country to Mar-a-Lago (if they weren't already in Palm Beach) undermined the most basic populist message was balanced by a sense that, helped along by their interests, he might be leavening those impulses—he was back to being the responsible businessman. (Pay no attention to his recent fraud judgment!) His new patter, in the face of Heritage and AFPI issuing scorched-earth anti-elites policy papers, now went back to how he had attracted some of the most respected people in business and the military to come into his administration. (Pay no attention to the fact that he had fallen out with almost all of them!) Similarly, there was suddenly a sense that Trump, who might speak like an intransigent isolationist, ready to sacrifice Ukraine and, all in all, pretty ambivalent (truth be told) about Israel, was thinking about inviting hawks like Marco Rubio and Tom Cotton into his administration.

This seemed both a clear nod to actually getting elected and the mishmash of aspirations—on the one hand, saying something; on the other hand, generally not doing it—from the first administration. (A lesson: Trump likes to do what he has done before.) A campaign line: Beyond the bombast and chaos, there was less to fear from Trump than virtually everyone would have you believe.

Except there was the bombast and chaos.

• • •

March 16, in Dayton, Ohio, is arguably the first Trump rally of the general election. The rally opens with a Voice of God announcer: "Please rise for the horribly and unfairly treated January 6 hostages." Trump, in white shirt but uncharacteristically without a tie, as close as he comes to informality, salutes the audience, which salutes him back, while "Justice for All," aka the "J6 Hostage Song"—sung by the J6 Prison Choir, with the voice of Trump reciting the Pledge of Allegiance—blares at a frightening volume. He has been playing this song before rallies and before dinners at Mar-a-Lago for the better part of the year. At dinner, he would be brought the iPad, and then from Spotify, he'd bring up what he called "the Song," and everyone, facing him, would have to rise and put their hand on their heart. "Weird as shit," as one Trump club member put it. And for a year, the campaign has feared that the song's video, in all its kitschy menace, will go viral. Almost everyone around him, except the nutters, flinches when it comes on, and they breathe a continual sigh of relief that somehow, even as it has risen up the hit parade charts, it had not spread and poisoned the wider independent pool. The best of a few good rationalizations about the events of January 6 has been that it was a demonstration that went out of control and certainly did not involve him directly—but here now, in this panegyric, he's owning it.

And it is finally about to go officially viral.

The video is coupled in Dayton with particularly concentrated hortatory language from Trump of the most malevolent kind. He heaps praise on the January 6 rioters and on the 1,265 people who have been criminally indicted for their actions on that day (Trump among them), now characterizing them as hostages and then, with a malfunctioning teleprompter, charging further than even usual into repetition and incoherence, and hitting the "bloodbath" line for which the speech will be most remembered: "Now, if I don't get elected, it's gonna be a bloodbath. That's going to be the least of it. It's going to be a bloodbath for the country."

The Biden team, trying to play the meme game, puts out a mash-up of "the Song" and the "bloodbath," and the story leads each of the network morning shows on Monday. (The story has lasted from Saturday until Monday.) The campaign, in turn, rushes into damage control: Trump's "bloodbath" is not about a bloodbath per se; certainly not a literal bloodbath. *C'mon guys, it's about*—and here the campaign is trying to cut and paste the disjoined context and references in the speech—*what will happen in the auto industry if Biden continues to press his support for electric cars!* This then becomes a second- and third-day news cycle question: Whose bloodbath is it, anyway?

What does Trump mean, if anything? How to parse it?

Trump sometimes tells a story about a friend, or a famous actor, or, sometimes in the telling, a "genius producer—one of the greats"—pitching a television show and losing the attention of the network honcho. Looking into the honcho's eyes and seeing that they've wandered off, the person giving the pitch jumps up on the desk and drops his pants. (Warren Beatty is said to tell a similar story about pitching movies.)

In this understanding, Trump is always looking into the eyes of his audience, measuring their interest, aware of when he's losing it, always trying to redouble it, an endless series of attention-grabbing gambits. His technique is vivid language, the kind of hyperbole a politician would never ordinarily use: hence, "bloodbath." In Trump's telling, "headline words."

But the other understanding is that Trump is often just a raw nerve, his own rage, resentments, and personal grievances churning in him and, at any given moment, expressed in his public performances—which is exactly what makes them so compelling and, for the campaign, unpredictable.

At that moment, in Ohio, what is churning and ready to blow—and giving the media its "bloodbath" headlines—is the pressure he is under because of the money he owes and the foreclosure he is facing that could devastate his holdings and possibly his political identity.

· · ·

Letitia James had extended him thirty days to pay up or secure a bond for his $454 million judgment while he appealed—with the deadline shortly upon him.

"I guess we're going to finally see what the brother is worth," said one Trump crony, nailing the universal skepticism, even among his inner circle, about the black box and sleight of hand of his personal finances.

Boris continued to wave away the concerns of a worried campaign and legal team: "There is no fucking problem here at all. It's covered. I don't know why anyone would doubt that. We are in great shape."

In addition to the $454 million, there was (with interest) the $91 million he owed E. Jean Carroll.

His cash on hand, fortified by the sale in 2022 of the Trump International Hotel in Washington and the refinancing of a property in San Francisco, he avowed in a separate filing, was approximately $500 million. In other words, he was, if not bankrupt, then looking at a liquidity crisis that could easily precipitate a distress sale of much of his business—an existential threat to his brand and livelihood. The alternative to using his own cash was to arrange for a bank or an insurer to underwrite a bond, but a mad dash through the most likely sources showed that the universal requirement seemed to be more than 100 percent, with an unwillingness to take a pledge of real estate—not least of all because so much of his real estate was either not actually his or already encumbered.

The Trump legal team managed to secure a bond, with 100-plus percent cash collateral, for the E. Jean judgment.

Without the campaign's knowledge, his lawyers filed a motion acknowledging that no bonding company was willing to provide the $454 million against the resources he had (once again, wholly seeming to contradict the Boris version of legal reality), challenging the foundational myth of the Trump media and political persona, his multibillion-dollar fortune.

Ten billion was always the round-number, double-digit net worth baseline he liked. His generous critics usually put his real net worth at $2 to $3 billion. The more hard-hearted, at hundreds of millions (after you subtracted all the liabilities). Whatever the actual number, he had created a construct in which both assets and liabilities were always in a state of flux and where perception was the fundamental currency (part of the reason for his perpetual stonewalling about releasing his tax returns). His situation now was coming perilously close to unmasking the true state of his finances, certainly closer to real-world hundreds of millions than to billions—and, stripped of $537 million of those hundreds of millions, functionally down to extremis.

One way out was for him to declare bankruptcy, which would prevent New York State from enforcing its judgment. His lawyers were urging him to consider this. The campaign was adamantly against it. (Of course, several of his businesses had declared bankruptcy before without him wavering in his billionaire identity.)

There was often, not unfairly, the sense of Trump as the truly consummate huckster, unafraid that his misrepresentations might be revealed because he had, up his sleeve, endlessly more of them. Without humility, and with a taste—even a need—for constant battle, he never relented, never even came close to an admission, and hence a true, no less final reckoning always rolled into the future. Here was a part of his appeal—and charm: the artful dodger. Caught red-handed, as Trump so often was, who wouldn't like to be able to talk his way out by stumping his accusers with a trick bag of diversions and sleights of hand? Who doesn't, at least secretly, admire the man who can turn his accusers into flat-footed bullies, and himself into a hero?

And yet the reality was that he was so often less Robin Hood than he was the petty, spiteful, raging, aggrieved King John—nothing ever going his way. Since the judgment was rendered, he had been able to talk of almost nothing else. He was up for a good part of the night posting on Truth Social. Everybody was steering clear of him. If he wasn't flaming mad, he was self-pitying and plaintive: "Can you believe they're doing this to me?"

March 25, a Monday, was the day he was supposed to pay up.

Letitia James had let it be known that she was focusing on his West-chester golf club and the office tower at 40 Wall Street, among his other properties. In fact, while she had the judgment in her hand, her next move was less than clear-cut. Did she want to become a property man-ager? Did she want to untangle complex debt structures—perhaps only to find that, in the end, she held nothing at all? For Trump lawyers, there was the mischievous, even subversive idea of just handing her the keys to 40 Wall Street—give her an office building during the greatest downturn in the commercial rental market in several generations.

In the days prior to March 25, an entourage of uber-billionaires, led by Wilbur Ross, Trump's former secretary of commerce (in fact, only a minor billionaire), was said to have formed a consortium to underwrite the bond. At least one foreign government (speculation: the Saudis) had offered to step up. Whether this was actually possible, given cam-paign finance regulations, or politically tenable—the billionaire populist being bailed out by even richer billionaires, not to mention Gulf state sheikhs—was subsumed into the alternative reality of Mar-a-Lago.

But that alternative reality was suddenly buttressed by *another* alter-native reality. In the week before his money was due, the Securities and Exchange Commission, after an almost two-year period of review, ap-proved the merger of Trump Media & Technology Group, the parent of Truth Social, with Digital World Acquisition Corp., the special purpose acquisition company (SPAC), or publicly traded financial vehicle, that would instantly turn Truth Social into a public company, worth ten bil-lion dollars, of which Trump held more than a 60 percent stake. An outpouring of individual investors enamored by the prospect of being in business with Donald Trump (plus at least one secretive mega-billionaire, Jeff Yass, the maybe-richer-than-Elon major TikTok investor) bought up the shares of a company whose only asset would be a social network that had scant revenues or users other than Trump himself. These were fans, buying Trump stock as they would Trump sneakers or, in the case of

Yass, looking to protect TikTok—influence buyers, rather than investors. (Theoretically, Trump could, with the permission of a board of di-
rectors he controlled, immediately sell his 60 percent, though that, of
course, would likely crash the stock.) What's more, there was nothing
stopping others in his entourage of super uber-billionaires, including
foreign entities, from stepping in and buying the stock to prop it up
merely to benefit the possible next president. If he did become president, investing in TMTG or even buying ads on a social network that
no one used would become a perfectly legal way to put money directly
into Trump's pocket. (If he did not become president, of course, Truth
Social would likely become dust.)

Over the weekend, lawyers were full of assurances that Trump had
secured a bond or he was close—or, alternatively, that the case to lower
the bond amount was a solid one. And, really, the date, March 25, was
not actually a drop-dead one. It was more complicated than that, more
a floating, moving target. And yet he was raging, over-the-top raging,
constant in his anger or panic. "It's worse than the steal. They want
everything. Everything! They want to take everything. They want to
leave me with nothing," he fumed, unprompted, to a Mar-a-Lago member who greeted him after dinner (notably, this member had approached
him on behalf of Rudy Giuliani, who, in fact, was being reduced to
nothing).

"This is an around-the-clock thing," said one Trump intimate, uncertain where Trump or the campaign stood. "The lawyers keep saying
everything's going to be okay, but man, you wouldn't get that by looking
at his social media posts or talking to him."

CHAPTER 11

Limbo

APRIL 2024

A key incumbent advantage is in having a long runway in which to build and stabilize a campaign organization. Second only to that, in considering political fortunes, is the advantage of an early finish of the primary race, securing certain nomination and having a reasonable amount of time to put in place the complex management and fundraising structure of a national campaign. Trump, in other words, could hardly be in a better position for the battle ahead.

But with rages, threats, and something near to weeping (well, a kind of sad clown face), as he found himself caught between financial crises and a looming trial date, it was impossible to keep him on political course and personally dangerous for anyone to try. The campaign had been virtually dark since he clinched the nomination—no events and little planning. Here was another part of the problem, some insiders judged: He had peaked too early. He had accomplished what he set out to do. Now he just wanted to play golf.

Meanwhile, Biden, in the aviator glasses that infuriated Trump—"Who does he think he is, Steve McQueen? C'mon. Steve McQueen?"—was out on the stump. And for the first time in a year, he was moving the needle—not by much, but still, by a point or two. Enough so that Trump was demanding other polls that said this wasn't true.

• • •

On March 24, Trump and his legal team left Palm Beach for New York and his 10 A.M. court appointment the next morning to officially and finally set the date when his hush money Stormy Daniels criminal trial would begin. This was the day when the actual trial was supposed to begin: March 25, a "date certain," according to the judge. But not so certain, it turned out, and instead, Trump's March 25 court date would *really, truly* set the ultimate date. Trump, however, was hardly about to give up his faith in the essential lightness of the trial calendar—Boris was full of assurances of new contingencies—and few on the team seemed yet to grasp that the showdown might truly be upon them.

But the filled-to-capacity courtroom—the worldwide press corps descending on this ground zero event (even just its prelude)—might have been a tip-off, as he entered, that history was seeing it otherwise and that it was ready for what might be the main event of the 2024 campaign (although there seemed to be plenty of main events).

Trump arrived with his courtroom face—glowering, grim, ready for blood. He compared this moment to that of a fighter entering the ring; notably, he was more of a sulking Floyd Patterson than an animated Ali.

A year before, Joe Tacopina had anchored the defense table when the hush money indictment came down. Tacopina was now gone (without his fee) and replaced by Todd Blanche. Much had come to depend on Blanche: the first criminal trial of a U.S. president and, quite possibly, the second. If the January 6 trial happened, Blanche was scheduled to lead it, too.

• • •

This morning, up at bat for the first time, Blanche whiffs. In private, Trump liked Blanche's certainty and forcefulness. But now, in open court, with sudden humility, unaccountably weak and deferential, Blanche seems to stumble and suck his words and fill his hesitations with "ums." ("POTUS really hates ums," says a reproving aide.) He is suddenly melting before the judge, Juan M. Merchan.

A nervous Blanche, introducing himself and his colleagues to the court, fails to flip on the microphone—just the kind of human error that infuriates Trump.

The judge then recounts the cause of the most recent delay, principally the Trump side's allegations of extreme malfeasance in the prosecution's failure to produce a wide variety of documents and its motion to dismiss the case because of it. This is what is being argued today.

Blanche goes first. But before he can build up a head of steam, Judge Merchan interrupts and asks why the documents issue wasn't raised earlier, when the defense first became aware of it. Blanche, for a moment appearing unsteady on his feet, has no clear answer.

Focusing on the large volume of documents, the judge tries to zero in on what might actually be relevant.

The prosecution claims it's under three hundred documents.

"We very much disagree," says Blanche, seemingly prodded back into the fight by a look from Trump, and cites the sheer vastness of material, too much to quantify.

But the judge presses for a specific number.

"Thousands and thousands" of documents, says Blanche, indicating a hopeless netherworld, but it appears he's talking specifically about the large cache of records in the government's possession from the Mueller investigation, which have little bearing on the hush money allegations.

The judge dismisses this as not relevant, takes Blanche to irritated task for even suggesting that Mueller documents are related to this case, and continues to press Blanche for a number for the *relevant* documents. Blanche, hesitating and ruffling through papers, cites thousands of emails—but then admits they haven't been read. The judge seems to find it an affront that unknown emails could be cited as relevant. Again, Merchan wants a specific number, and Blanche can't give it.

"How many *relevant* docs?"

"I think probably—let me look for one minute," mumbles Blanche. Finally, he says, "Your Honor, I mean"—clearly at a loss—"thousands."

"Two thousand? Twenty thousand?"

It's a continuing assault by the judge on the Trump claims and arguments. The judge is skeptical about the material the defense thinks it might find (and clearly hasn't found yet), incensed as to allegations being made of misconduct on the part of both the district attorney and the court itself, and incredulous at the defense's seeming contention that the Manhattan DA must take responsibility for actions, faulty or otherwise, of the U.S. Attorney's Office and the FBI.

"Can you give me a single case—one case—that stands for the proposition that the U.S. Attorney's Office is under the prosecution's discretion or control?"

"I don't have a case that says that exactly," Blanche stammers.

The judge delivers a tongue-lashing, suggesting that if there is perfidiousness, it is on the part of the defense—or, otherwise, it is incompetence, Blanche's incompetence.

"You're a former AUSA, right?" the judge grills Blanche, an assistant U.S. attorney. "In that office?" The Southern District.

"Yes," says Blanche.

"How many years?"

Blanche explains that he was there for four years as a paralegal and nine as a prosecutor.

"So, you were there for thirteen years. So, you know the defense . . . has the same ability as the prosecution to obtain these documents . . ."

The judge continues brutally, scoring again and again against Blanche's knowledge, motivations, intent, and honesty. While perhaps it would be unseemly to attack Trump personally, Blanche is the clear proxy. But as the proxy, he is unable to punch back in Trumpian fashion—and by the break, he is rocking back and forth, ready to go down.

The Trump side is holding its breath. So much depends on Blanche, and he is near to being destroyed. The larger implications are not even the issue: It's what Trump's going to do to him right now. Tacopina fired; Kise kicked to the ground like a dog; Alina slapped silly. *What happens now?*

Just after eleven—Blanche has been pounded steadily for an hour—they leave the courtroom for a forty-five-minute recess.

On the way to the break room, Trump and the team suddenly get the news from another court with Trump's fate in its hands. An appeals court judge has reduced the amount of the bond Trump will be required to post while appealing his fraud judgment, from $454 million to $175 million. They've clawed back from the brink. This, rather than the hush money trial, will be the headline of the day.

It was again a split screen: the bad morning in court now upended by a good morning in another court, distracting Trump from the Blanche performance. In the break room, as relief sweeps the Trump team, Trump seems to take a conscious breath and, with a wave of relief washing over the other lawyers, offer encouragement to a stunned Blanche instead of savagery: "You're so smart, you're so good, when you tell me what you're going to do, I want you to do it in court like you do it when we're together."

It could really begin to seem that Trump and the legal team around him know what they are doing, that they are crafty and gifted tacticians. Whatever the legal system serves up, they can hit back. But . . . *obviously* . . . it is *not* the *brilliant* legal team, unless brilliance has been inverted to on-the-fly, never-clear-who-is-showing-up chaos. Then perhaps it is Trump's own basic thesis (that is, if he could actually frame a thesis): The mighty system, a process-oriented, top-down, institutional superstructure, is not in fact so mighty. It is vulnerable, as so many institutions are, to anyone not in awe of it, not wanting the respect of it; to anyone willing to upend its processes. Here is an advantage to having bad lawyers: Without white-shoe reputations to protect, they can shamelessly file the motions, an endless dilatory stream of them, over-the-top and baseless, that would embarrass respectable lawyers. Then, too, the system, it turns out, like everybody else, is afraid of the media: Constant press attention is as daunting to prosecutors, judges, courts—the system—as to anyone unaccustomed to fighting daily battles in it. Trump's media strategy *is* his legal strategy, and seemingly a good one. And then, too, perhaps, however hard to imagine, he isn't *all* wrong. Everybody in the Trump age—Trump and his MAGA cohorts; anti-Trumpers and their political and bureaucratic support structure—exists in a state of hyperbole. On the one hand, there is Trump and his invective and threats against liberal society; on the other, anti-Trumpers in their efforts to do *anything* to stop him. Who blinks first? Liberal society being liberal society, it now seems to have offered up at least one appeals court panel that appears to feel guilty about a tenuous prosecution of a New York real estate guy for doing what New York real estate guys do, and, to boot, bankrupting him before he might even appeal.

The celebration is muted by Trump himself: "Don't get too excited. I still have to pay a hundred seventy-five fucking million dollars."

Court resumes at noon. The judge appears shortly thereafter and briefly summarizes the issues at hand: Who bears the responsibility for the withheld documents? Has the defense suffered? Finding the district attorney not at fault and that the defendant will not be harmed, the judge sets the trial date for April 15, three weeks hence . . .

Trump, though, is hardly willing to resign himself to the date, and Blanche, with quite some cheek, asks to file a motion for further adjournment because of the pre-trial publicity surrounding the case.

"See you all on the fifteenth," the judge says, with quite some certainty.

The Trump entourage repairs after court to 40 Wall Street and Trump's mock Oval Office set, where he ritually eviscerates prosecutor and judge—only, the names are different from the last time he was here eviscerating prosecutor and judge.

. . .

On Tuesday, the day after getting back to Palm Beach from the New York court date, Natalie informed the team they'd be returning to New York again on Thursday, to attend the wake at a Long Island funeral home for New York City police officer Jonathan Diller, who had been shot and killed during a routine traffic stop.

This visit had been conceived and coordinated by Trump on the phone with whoever had his number or whoever passed his number to someone else. Here was a further danger of this post-primary moment, a lack of daily structure that allowed him to revert to being his own freelance campaign manager. The stop in Long Island certainly wasn't out of character for Trump's law-and-order message (though the campaign was queasy about just how to hit this message, considering his imminent New York criminal trial). But the real reason for it was Trump's perturbation—growing into grievance—about the concurrent Biden fundraising event in New York, a Democratic trifecta with Obama and Clinton onstage with Biden at Radio City Music Hall.

The line from the Trump side was that contrary to a show of strength for Biden, this was the Democratic establishment getting in close to take the measure of Biden's weakness: Was he really up to it? How big a problem did they actually have? Did Joe know who the president was? The Obama–Clinton turnout was a sign of desperation, not strength. But for Trump himself, as he saw it, here were three presidents "ganging up on me." Here were insult and injury: Clinton and Obama, and their lackey Biden, putting their contempt for him on display. And raising money doing it! So, he counter-programmed with the dead cop.

The campaign was further unsettled by Trump's freelancing when, on Tuesday night, he had dinner at Mar-a-Lago, on the terrace, in full view, with Kellyanne Conway. A particular way to Trump's heart was for his enemies to become yours. He couldn't get enough of the details of Kellyanne's divorce from George Conway, who had backslid from conservative lawyer into anti-Trump gadfly and now open Biden proselytizer—indeed, now a social figure and man on the New York liberal scene, with a new diet and new John Varvatos–like wardrobe. (Trump especially enjoyed mocking the fashion transformation.) Almost immediately, there was a report of the possibility of Kellyanne's coming back into Trumpworld in an "undefined role." The campaign quickly put out that no actual offer had been made to her and—sotto voce— that actually, she was widely disliked in MAGA circles; plus, she was always inflating her influence and prospects.

Still. "Undefined role" could be the signal of an extremely powerful role. In a surmise of the role she might agree to take, there wasn't much else but for her to replace one or the other of Wiles and LaCivita, or both. Or, only slightly less bad, this was a warning shot. Conway probably did not want to give up her lucrative Fox pundit payday or the six figures flowing to her through the RNC—"Everyone else has been able to monetize the Trump relationship, now I need to," she was unabashedly and petulantly declaring—but at some propitious moment, she might want to. And Trump, in this new, uncertain phase of the campaign—and the Conway leak was judged as clearly Trump-approved—might want to trade up.

As another indication of this new phase of the campaign, and the growing reality of an actual new Trump presidency, Rupert Murdoch's *New York Post* had shared drafts of the next morning's front page for the funeral home visit with the campaign staff (upsetting even some of the *Post*'s jaded staffers). Likewise, at the no-photo event, the *Post* photographer had slipped in as a member of the Trump team. There it was, Trump, a soulful man of the people, and the Dems, unfeeling and elitist pricks:

GIVE AND TAKE
Trump attends wake for killed hero NYPD cop . . .
as 3 Dem presidents shut down city for glitzy $25M fundraiser

This was judged as the day's true victory: Ninety-three-year-old Rupert Murdoch was, however much he might continue to disdain Trump, definitely back on board, building his capital for the victory that might well come. (Trump himself seemed to miss the point of the headline, sorely pissed and disbelieving about the $25 million. "How could that fucking be? This is fake. It's gotta be fake. If they're really doing such good business, what does that mean? It means I have shitty people.")

There was a possible element of subconscious strategy in the funeral visit—one that Trump had neither mentioned nor was necessarily aware of: In preparation for his New York trial, he was activating a secret New York base, cops. And with pictures—a cop's wake on a rainy day. Very Hollywood.

Trump's comments at the funeral home curiously represented him as a quick-change political pro of a sort no one would have thought him to be, turning on a dime from campaigner and mass rally performer into a figure of quiet humility, addressing much of his remarks to Jonathan Diller's one-year-old son, the proud legacy he would carry and his hopeful life to come—all the while desperately trying not to look down at the body in the open casket.

• • •

Any sign of bad fortune, minor or cataclysmic—for instance, the slight wrinkle of losing one state, Vermont, in his primary march—could send Trump into a perilous mental slide. So, don't go there. Yes, they were imminently facing a criminal trial in Manhattan. But delay was truly working for them, as few had thought it actually would—and, of course, the nomination was theirs. So, this had somehow become internalized in an it's-not-that-bad, could-be-a-lot-worse, we're-really-ahead-of-the-game sense of winning the war.

Perhaps. Or not.

Judge Merchan smacked down the motion to delay the April 15 trial start because of the attendant publicity. And he denied the motion to delay the trial until after the Supreme Court ruled on Trump's presidential immunity claim. And he quashed a subpoena sought by Trump's lawyers for material related to a documentary about Stormy Daniels, which might have formed the pretext for a further delay.

Merchan also extended a partial gag order on extrajudicial statements about court employees to include his own daughter, with a broad condemnation of the defendant's motives and honesty.

It would be hard to imagine how Trump could engender a greater level of hostility in the man who would shortly hold his fate.

• • •

On April 6, at the $110 million Palm Beach home of the multibillionaire John Paulson, and against the backdrop of Trump's last-minute reprieve from financial extremis and now a countdown to his first criminal trial, Trump insiders kicked off the general election with a dinner. Million-dollar donations got you top-tier status (which included "seating at President Trump's table, reception and photo opportunity, personalized 'Our Journey Together' coffee table book by President Donald J. Trump"), and the back of the tent filled out with $250,000 bodies (mere "VIP seating," but with photo ops and the book).

Actually, it was not *all* the insiders. Presaging other internal contre-
temps to come, Ike Perlmutter, who considered himself, in his Bebe Rebozo status, the ultimate Trump insider and the most powerful duke in
the Mar-a-Lago court, was boycotting the dinner. Perlmutter saw this as
a campaign/RNC fundraising event—that is, an event of his personal
bête noire, Susie Wiles. Indeed, at this very moment, he was trying to
siphon contributions from the campaign/RNC into his new Right for
America super PAC, which, under Gor and Perlmutter, would be truer
to Trump. Perlmutter was just a more extreme example of the general
frisson of the evening, which was that billionaires want what billionaires
want (and, in the end, as one aide noted, they never put up all the money
they say they'll put up).

The official evening's hosts (at a much, much higher ticket price)
were Paulson, the hedge funder short-seller who had emerged from relative obscurity to make four billion dollars in 2007 in a bet against the
subprime real estate market; and his girlfriend, Alina de Almeida, a nu-
tritionist and Instagram fitness personality thirty-three years his junior.
(Not long into the evening, Paulson's personal situation precipitated a
crisis. Before the dinner, at a red carpet–type moment, a photo was
taken of his girlfriend, Alina, whom Getty Images mistakenly identified
as Paulson's first, and still current, wife, Jenny, prompting a real-time
shitstorm. Paulson, until recently, had been lukewarm if not cool toward
Trump, and the campaign was doing everything possible to accommodate him—that now meant a panicked, Whac-A-Mole effort to recall
the photograph and the offending caption.)

The million-dollar circle (actually, within precise giving rules,
$824,600, but double that with a wife or date) included shale billionaire
Harold Hamm; Robert Bigelow, a UFO-obsessed Las Vegas real estate
guy (who had previously made a $1 million contribution to Trump's
legal fund); John Catsimatidis, the New York supermarket mogul, frequently unsuccessful political candidate, and radio talk show host on
WABC, the New York AM station he'd bought for himself; José "Pepe"
Fanjul, one of a set of Cuban-born Palm Beach brothers who had mo-
nopolized the U.S. sugar market with its massive government price sub-

sidies (another brother gives lavishly to Democrats); Mike Hodges, the payday lender whose business exploded with his early Trump support; Woody Johnson, the Johnson & Johnson heir, New York Jets owner, and Trump's ambassador to the United Kingdom; Howard Lutnick, the CEO of Cantor Fitzgerald and a New York media personality; Linda McMahon, who, with her husband, Vince, built a wrestling empire; Robert Mercer, hedge fund quant investor; Mercer's daughter, Rebekah, a right-wing hobbyist and eccentric (both father and daughter formerly Steve Bannon's key patrons); Steve Wynn, the gambling king who lost his empire over sex abuse charges, but kept his billions . . . and quite a long list of others.

What was represented here was a Trump-type ethos separate from red meat rally headlines and MAGA true cause policies. Here was entrepreneurial pluck and audacity—and more than a little show-off, wear-it-proud, I'm-rich-and-fuck-you vulgarity. If you had to parse which was the true Trump ethos, it might be here. His was a simple, practical, political, and even moral equation: If you made a billion dollars, you were doing something right. And further, if you gave some of it to Trump—his taste, his vig—you deserved added respect and protection.

The Democrats' wealthy supporters may have coughed up $25 million at Radio City Music Hall, but Trump's people were good for $50 million! (The Democrats, however, outraised him by $94 million in the quarter.)

Still, it was not that easy to ignore that many of Trump's billionaires were here begrudgingly, some, perhaps most, having hoped another billionaire-friendly political face would have emerged, some having even, however briefly, flirted with DeSantis. All of them certainly—over endive and frisee salad, filet au poivre, and pavlova with fresh berries—were aware of the fundamental Donald Trump.

But then again, they were here, and paying up. (Well, they said they were going to write the check.)

Trump's mood seemed to vacillate between vast satisfaction in having, no matter what they might truly feel, corralled these beasts into the room and worry over events beyond Mar-a-Lago. Had anyone heard

from Hope Hicks? he asked one group, who seemed mystified that he
thought they might have reason to hear from her, his most intimate
White House aide, who had fled amid his election denial campaign.
Hicks had recently shown up on the prosecution's witness list in New
York. "Is she still with us?" he wondered.

And yet . . .

He had his audience. Under a large tent, among rich men and their
young wives, an achievement he invariably noted (though many of the
once-young wives, with their now-octogenarian husbands, were not so
young anymore), Trump spoke extemporaneously for forty-five minutes, in high Trump form. It was Friars Club tummler form (here with a
high population of Jews, instead of stadiums full of anti-Semites)—
digressive, incoherent, with no one to drag him from the lectern. He was
in love with the microphone, each word, for better or worse, a characteristic pearl—here in a tape secreted out by a donor, who would play it for
the amusement and incredulity of family and friends:

Don and Eric and Laura and Kimberly . . . and Tiffany is here
someplace . . . great Tiffany . . . We love Tiffany. When I go
around the room, and 'cause I know so many of you, and when I
talk about what incredible people you are . . . I have a man who
owns the New York Stock Exchange and every other exchange . . .
so smart, and his wife is even smarter than he is. I have many
people . . . great real estate developers, Steve . . . We have some
great friends that are no longer with us, right, like Stanley Chera.
Sort of reminds me of John Paulson a little bit, except for the
weight. Stanley was slightly heavy. Stanley had the three curses,
right, Howard? . . . You know Stanley . . . great real estate man,
one of the best, and he couldn't care less about politics. Actually,
I would say he didn't hate it or love it; he just didn't care about it.
He liked buying buildings all the time . . . "Let's syndicate, let's
syndicate" . . . But he was great and big and smart. And one day
he called me and said he wasn't feeling well . . . and I said, "You'll
be better, you'll be good" . . . and he was just amazing. He became a political junky . . . He went from not caring about it to

he didn't care about real estate anymore . . . He used to call me and say, "We should do this about this . . . do this this this" . . . "Stanley," I said, "you've become a wild political lunatic" . . . Well, he calls me and says, "I'm going into the hospital. I have Covid." I said, "Oh good, you're not feeling well." "I'll be out tomorrow," he said. "I'll call you." He had three curses, I say: He was old, slightly chubby—I'm saying that because it's a nicer word than saying anybody is very heavy; you can't mention fat today. You do that, you're out of business. He was slightly cherubic . . . he was cherubic, and he was—wealthy . . . Covid hates all three of those . . . When I call and say how is he doing, they say he's in a coma . . . He's in a coma . . . like one day later . . . He was an incredible guy. But it makes me think of John . . . and Alina . . . You guys make a fantastic couple . . . and you have to hear her play the piano . . . In fact, we don't need entertainment . . . Would you please play the piano? . . . But I've known John . . . and John has never been a political guy . . . and he likes betting against the market . . . He does things that nobody ever heard of . . . things that nobody thinks of . . . and now he's political and wants to take Madison Square Garden . . . and have a rally . . . and wants to do this and wants to do that . . . and he has fifty, fifty-one people . . . and that's such a stupid law, eight hundred twenty-four thousand, and if you go one penny over that, you're in trouble . . . Zuckerberg could give five hundred million . . . You know they have some in the lock box . . . One lock box had four thousand votes in it in a fairly good area for me . . . and not one Trump vote . . . this lock box . . . Four of them with no votes for Trump . . . and seven of them . . . and four thousand votes for Biden because he's such a great, dynamic person . . . And the Black vote . . . He did horribly everywhere across the country but the four swing states . . . He beat Biden in a slaughter, because they hate him . . . We're doing great with the Black, the Hispanic, the Asian, the women . . . Word came out that we're leading by fourteen . . . which actually doesn't sound that great . . . A friend of mine says, "How is it possible, President?" . . .

I say, "Call me Donald" . . . he says, "Okay, President . . ." because he can't . . . I've known this guy forty or fifty years . . . I
can't say that because I have a young wife . . . "Can I ask you a
stupid question? You're leading by eight . . ." Eight is a lot for a
Republican, because it usually means more than eight . . . "How
come I saw a poll where you're leading by twelve points? . . .
These guys can't talk, can't put two sentences together . . . How
come you're only leading by twelve?" . . . I said, "It's hard to explain . . . but they have certain groups of people, like unions . . .
They have others; I won't mention them, but you probably have
a pretty good idea of who they are" . . . They get those votes . . .
You see this fork here? . . . If this fork was running, it would start
at forty . . . Now he has thirty-three . . . which is hard to do . . .
Harold Hamm is here . . . the great Harold Hamm . . . They say
he puts a straw into the ground and oil comes out . . . These
companies spend billions looking for oil . . . Right, Woody? You
know Harold . . . He puts a straw into the ground and oil comes
out . . . and he freaking makes another billion dollars . . .

I could go down every one of you, and it's amazing the people who are here . . . amazing the people . . . and I really appreciate it . . . Woody, you were a great ambassador. I have a lot of
ambassadors here—and they want to be an ambassador again . . .
and they maybe want a different country next time. They want
to step up. I think they want Woody's place. They want that one.
But you like that one, too—I have a feeling you'd go back . . . in
about two seconds. Woody said, "Well, I don't know" . . . Suzanne says, "We're going back!"

So, I just want to thank everybody. We have a lot of work to
do. We have borders that nobody believed was possible. We
have . . . there are things that are happening . . . women being
attacked . . . women in sports . . . Do you see what's happening
in volleyball play? . . . A woman got hit so hard on the head, she's
never going to be able to play again. I didn't know a volleyball
could do that, but it can when it's hit by a man. Men in women's
sports. Who would think that? Who would think that? It's em-

barrassing. You know when I give a speech, I mention different things . . . How stupid is this? . . . We're going to stop men from playing in women's sports . . . It's not the biggest thing but . . . and we're going to stop the electric vehicle mandate. You know, in Iowa we won in a landslide. In every single state, we were up against the competition, Ron DeSanctimonious and Nikki Haley. We won in a record . . . In New Hampshire, we got more votes in the history of the primaries, which is a great honor . . . Kennedy was third . . . John F. Kennedy was third . . . In either party, we got more votes . . . That's a great honor . . . New Hampshire, we won, and it was forty degrees below zero . . . It was the coldest . . . If I walked from here to halfway through the tables, and I was frozen by the time I got . . . [*He's mixed up Iowa and New Hampshire.*] . . . I was supposed to make a speech, and they dropped me off there. Harold, he doesn't go in for the corn stuff; he's the actual oil, I walk here, and I have to walk for thirty feet. I go inside and I say, "I'm freezing my ass off" . . . But what happened is that on the way over, the Secret Service— Thank you, fellows; you're the greatest. The only thing I don't like about the Secret Service is that they are all over the golf balls, so when I play in the club championship . . . I got guys all over the place, I can't move a ball . . . I hit a ball down the fairway and it's a little rough, and there's a guy standing behind a tree . . .

The problem we have here is that we have a man who has no idea what's going on . . . I don't believe he's running the government. I think the maniacs, the communists around him, his beautiful Resolute desk, the most beautiful thing I've ever seen, it's the desk of twenty-two presidents. If you become president, they give you a choice of seven desks; one was the Resolute. You've seen it, Woody, many times. Ronald Reagan used it; many others used it that I respect used it, so beautiful, and he's using it. I might not use it the next time, because it's been soiled, and I mean that literally . . . which is sad . . . And what's happened is that he's surrounded by communists, fascists, and crazy people . . . people who have no idea . . . people who actually hate

our country. I would never say that . . . but I believe these are
people who actually hate our country . . . and we have to stop
it . . . So, they are coming in from jails and prisons, and there's a
slight difference, too . . . And they're coming in from mental institutions . . . and insane asylums . . . and someone said, "What's
an insane asylum?" . . . And I said, "Did you ever see *Silence of
the Lambs?*" . . . The late great Hannibal Lecter . . . Did anyone
see that movie? Not a nice movie . . . not if you want to sleep
well . . . But there was a gentleman named Hannibal Lecter . . .
That's what's coming into our country . . .

And then on top of it all, we have the nuclear problem . . .
You don't know about nuclear, but I do . . . and I have seen the
power of the weaponry . . . where you can hit New York and take
out Miami . . . It's just so big . . . so powerful . . . so destruc-
tive . . . And I said, "Never mention the word *nuclear*" . . . I had
scientists come down from MIT . . . My uncle was a professor at
MIT for years and years and years, the longest-serving professor
in the history of MIT . . . and he used to tell me many years ago,
"Someday somebody is going to have, like, a bag for your office
and walk into a building and blow up the entire city of New
York." He told me that fifty years ago. He said it's the most powerful thing anybody has ever seen . . . and now bring it back fifty
years, and you look at Nagasaki and Hiroshima and multiply it
by six hundred twenty-three, six hundred twenty-three times . . .
And you see where the granite was melted flat. You can't melt
granite with a blowtorch. If you kept it there for two weeks, the
granite wouldn't even be affected . . . The entire island of granite
is melted like an ice-skating rink. That was seventy-five years ago,
so if you multiply that by many, many times . . . And we have a
man negotiating for us who can't speak, has no mind, who
doesn't know what's happening . . . and he's dealing with Putin,
with President Xi, with Kim Jong Young [*sic*], who I have a great
relationship with. So we have to get our country back, we're losing our country . . .

I believe there is a chance this will be the last election we ever have . . . if we don't win this . . . This could be the last election this country ever has . . . if we don't win this . . . People say that. And I'm thinking about it and thinking this could be the last election this country ever has . . . So, we have to get out and we have to vote; and November 5, I believe, is going to be the most important day in the history of our country, and somebody says, "What about July fourth?" and I say, "It's not as important [as] this . . ." July fourth is not as important as this . . . This is going to be the single most important day in the history of our country. I said in 2016 this election is the most important we ever had, and I meant it . . . but this blows 2016 away.

CHAPTER 12

Trump Time

APRIL 2024

Todd Blanche had a long tenure as an assistant U.S. attorney in the Southern District of New York, a prestige posting for a career as a prosecutor or white-collar defense attorney or for a future in politics. After the SDNY, the forty-nine-year-old Blanche spent time at several top New York firms before landing a partnership at Cadwalader, Wickersham & Taft, one of the oldest firms in Manhattan. A Wall Street fixture, generally representing major public companies in commercial and financial disputes (and families of great wealth: the Rockefellers!), the firm was considered a leading example of the "white-shoe" establishment, a closed world of WASP social circles and Ivy League universities.

But in the struggle for billings and profits, the firm had had to compromise its snobbery.

Blanche's criminal defense and white-collar work—white collar being the opposite of white shoe—was a deviation, a profitable one, from the firm's traditional corporate and trust and estates work. Blanche's practice in recent years had included figures from the Trump administration caught in the Trump-related legal churn, among them Paul Manafort, Trump's former campaign manager; Boris Epshteyn, in the ongoing January 6 case; and Igor Fruman, the Rudy Giuliani crony, hoisted on campaign finance violations. This was much less an indication of an ideological position for Blanche, officially a Democrat, than it was that the Trump circle was producing a lot of lucrative clients. Still, firms like Cadwalader, as much as they liked the money, held their noses at this sort of practice. What's more, Blanche was very much not their sort. Noted *The New York Times* archly, "Mr. Blanche joined the Southern District in 1999, not as a prosecutor, but as a paralegal. He worked days and went to Brooklyn Law School at night, commuting from Long Island. Mr. Blanche, who was married at 20 and a grandfather in his 40s, conveyed a decidedly middle-class vibe at an office known for its Ivy League pedigree."

At this class intersection, Blanche formed an increasingly close bond with his client Boris Epshteyn, who introduced him to Trump.

The two lawyers were both ambitious, *hungry*, suburban, backyard barbecue kind of guys; resentful of their supposed betters and uncomfortable around them, too; smart enough but not smooth enough, looking for both opportunity and a place to shine—they got along.

It was Boris who painted a sky's-the-limit picture of the opportunities for Blanche. Boris billed this as an effective legal partnership between them, with their sole client being Donald Trump. Boris had the relationship and, he assured Blanche, Trump's absolute trust, and Blanche had a top-of-the-profession reputation, a scarce commodity in Trump's circle.

While much of Trumpworld's lawyers saw this as sketchy, if not incomprehensible—Blanche's defending two men whose interests might radically diverge, each with a defense that might require the sacrifice of the other—Boris saw Blanche as one of the keys to keeping those interests aligned. If Trump were elected, and if Blanche led the legal team and kept him out of jail, then Boris and Blanche would be positioned to control the White House legal portfolio.

Blanche, in this view, was on a plausible trajectory to the top of the Justice Department (put aside that, at least until recently, he was a Democrat, and probably a pro-choice one), and Boris to control of the White House legal portfolio (put aside that he was a named co-conspirator, ever on the verge of indictment himself, and always a prime candidate to flip on his boss).

This was enough of a sell for Blanche to walk out on his partner-ship when Cadwalader balked at representing the former president. Similarly—and Blanche did not seem to draw the obvious conclusion—Rudy Giuliani's big-name law firm had declined to represent the then president, and Giuliani set out, fatefully, on his own.

It was a life-overhaul, brass-ring plan. In this plan, Boris encouraged, and helped choreograph, Blanche's personal relationship with Trump. Blanche set up his one-man firm and moved himself and his family to Palm Beach. Blanche, in Boris's picture, would become Trump's guy—or at least move into the kind of proximity, and offer the kind of positive reinforcement, that gave Trump comfort. With Boris as both the Trump whisperer and Blanche whisperer, Blanche first took over the boxes case, then the January 6 case, then the New York case—all Trump's eggs in the Blanche-and-Boris basket.

Blanche, though, was far from the Trump ideal. Trump had a fixed view of what he wanted in a lawyer—a sharp, fast-talking, silver-tongued performer (Roy Cohn, F. Lee Bailey, Melvin Belli, Louis Nizer, Gerry Spence, Johnnie Cochran, Perry Mason . . . Clarence Darrow!)—but what he tended to get, to his furious frustration, was whoever walked in the door. Blanche, with a separated-at-birth resemblance to Ron DeSan-tis, was mild-mannered, mousy, hesitant, and without swagger—indeed, traits shared by most lawyers. And, shortly, he would be in front of judge, jury, and his client, caught between the nuances of getting the best result possible from judge and jury and his client's desire for theatrical spectacle.

• • •

There were three more efforts in quick succession to delay the New York trial.

After Judge Merchan rejected the Trump side's move to have him recuse himself, Trump lawyers asked for a stay in the trial so an appeals court could rule on the motion. This was denied.

The Trump lawyers then sought to sue the judge himself over several rulings and to halt the trial while this was considered. This was immedi-ately denied.

Then the lawyers sought to challenge the gag order and asked for a delay. Denied.

Each of these moves had such a remote chance of succeeding that, in any normal proceeding, the risk of antagonizing the court would have far outweighed the potential benefits of making the motion.

Few lawyers who had to function within the system, having to hold their heads up in the legal community, would ever have gone down this relentlessly fruitless road, making enemies of not just the system itself, but of anyone working in it. But Trump's lawyers needed to keep bringing him new, outlandish possibilities. Because someone else, eager to indulge him, would be asking why this or that implausible thing hadn't yet been done. And because Trump had no analytic facility here to weigh risk and reward or cause and effect, why wouldn't his lawyers make a motion, no matter how far-fetched, if they could make it?

Again, this was asymmetric: Instead of seeing the trial and, in general, the legal system as a needle to be threaded or a complicated game to play or an ultimate negotiation, it was *attack with anything you've got.*

While many of his own people assumed he would lose, Trump himself did not. He might be casting this as us versus them, and challenging the legitimacy of the court, and going out of his way to reach total hostility in the proceedings, and still—effectively doing everything possible to stack the deck against himself—he saw this as a winning strategy.

As another misalignment, putting his legal team at a singular disadvantage, he would yet expect them to win, ever limiting that possibility by his own actions and then holding it against them, often mortally so, when they did not.

Chris Kise, who had been forced to defend Trump in the fraud case in a non-jury trial, before a judge whom Trump taunted, insulted, ridiculed, and threatened, was now held solely responsible for Trump's loss in that case, with Kise vilified by Trump on a daily basis for not winning a trial that, literally, no one could have won. (Indeed, the judge, without a jury, had decided the key facts against Trump before Kise even entered the case.)

While Trump still looked forward to winning against all odds otherwise, he also continued to believe his trial date in the New York case,

now days hence, could—even as his team's increasingly desperate, if not
harebrained, efforts were denied—be delayed. With the countdown on,
instead of his team focusing on his defense, they were in a frenzy, working on yet more tenuous if not risible gambits to subvert what now
seemed surely to be an immutable trial date.

• • •

Another courtroom, this one in Arizona, was now, too, suddenly, toying
with his fate, he believed.

On April 9, Arizona's state supreme court had restored the 1864 law
from before Arizona was a state, banning all forms of abortion. This immediately threatened Trump's prospects in Arizona, a swing state he lost
in 2020 (though he continued to dispute that loss) by little more than
10,000 votes. A raft of other swing states were putting abortion rights
on the ballot, sure (at least the Democrats hoped) to help bring out an
anti-Trump vote in November, as red states were imposing new draconian abortion restrictions: 2024 could be the abortion election. Even
IVF and other fertility treatments were now in danger in states with
powerful evangelical and pro-life lobbies.

"This is so fucked up if this kills me," a dolorous Trump had been saying, and variations thereof, since the U.S. Supreme Court tossed out *Roe
v. Wade*. It was the irony that got him. His judges on the Court had put
him in this position. But, also, here he was, after the life he'd led, finding
himself as the poster boy for not being able to get an abortion! Him!

There were many ironies about Donald Trump, and who he was,
and the way his supporters chose to perceive him (or excuse him), but
this was one of the greater jokes among his friends, especially that circle
that had known him long enough to be fully familiar with his escapades
and views.

Indeed . . . he had for many years volubly and freely voiced his views
about condoms (hated them) and boasted that he had held a personal
celebration in 1970, when abortion became legal in New York State. The
"Trump Law," he said, was what it should have been called, for how
often he would use it.

When he had first recognized that if there were to be a political opportunity for him, it would more likely be as part of the new Tea Party current, he understood that the abortion stuff was just one peculiarity he'd need to swallow. And why not? It rallied people, but there was no chance of changing the law. His perfect issue: He could run on it without having to do anything about it, and simply by professing his new position, he could be absolved of a lifetime of loucheness.

As much as his critics wondered how on God's earth evangelical, rural, lower-middle-class America could embrace him, his friends often wondered how he could embrace *them*. A mass rally was one thing, his up-close distaste and incomprehension another. But that was of course part of his genius, as he saw it—that they loved him without his having to be remotely like them. He, because of who he was, gave them power. They did not want someone like them. They wanted someone like *him*.

He saw the pitifulness of pro-life politics vividly reflected in his former vice president, Mike Pence—who had lost in his pathetic primary efforts and was now saying he would not support him. Pence, a devout anti-abortion Christian, was exactly the kind of person nobody would vote for. "He doesn't get it," Trump would say. Nobody really wanted to vote for someone who was *actually* that way, *truly* that kind of religious freak.

Anyway, he had mostly succeeded in holding his fire, beyond a constant low level of grumbling, toward the absolutist pro-life Republican wing throughout the primaries. But with the general election beginning, he, the certain nominee, had started to roll out his new position: He was against a federal ban. Leave it to the states. That was essentially the position the Court had taken in its *Dobbs* decision vacating *Roe*—it was a state matter.

But now the State of Arizona had gone too far. Kari Lake, a former local news host and his Senate campaign pick (who would have had a good shot at his VP slot, if she hadn't lost her race for Arizona governor in 2022), had slavishly followed the Trumpian and MAGA line, including an uncompromising anti-abortion view, and she now pivoted with him, immediately calling for a repeal of the Arizona law.

It raised a new question: How far out was Trump from the true pro-life heart? How far from the deeply God-fearing, old-fashioned, conservative heart? Or was he simply *the* heart, and was abortion another Republican verity for him to bend, reverse, or disregard?

Shortly after the Arizona decision, a reporter asked him for his views on mifepristone, part of the medicated abortion formula. Blanking on what mifepristone was, if he had ever known, he said he would be making an announcement about it in two weeks—that standard Trump diversion in a world where no one could remember back two weeks. (No announcement would come.)

But as much as Trump had been able to get away with being Trump for so many in the "family values" American heartland—in fact, even turning himself into an evangelical hero!—it was on the minds of some aides that his revisionism on abortion was coming at the same time as his soon-to-start trial, which would feature what promised to be a detailed reciting of his evening with a porn star.

. . .

When the trial began on April 15, he would need to be in his seat in the Manhattan courtroom for four days a week for at least four weeks and possibly six. Wednesdays, the court would be closed, and then there were weekends, when he might campaign. But this was a sorely restricted schedule for a candidate in key months of an election.

The Republican convention would begin on July 15 in Milwaukee. Now was the time to unite and energize the party and lay the groundwork for the themes that would then make for a vivid coronation. But the campaign would be largely stuck in place. Hence, in the days before, there was a rush to cram a month into a week, to keep him on the road.

But he stopped everything to fit in *Time* magazine.

There were many puzzling questions about the world (and era!) Trump lived in. There was the Mar-a-Lago bubble, a country club setting with its kitschy (though not kitschy for Mar-a-Lago) "Italian night" and "Hawaiian Luau Saturday"; his all-box-suit wardrobe, out of step with pretty much every current fashion trend and deviation; his office in Trump Tower, a preserved-in-amber late-eighties moment (framed and autographed pictures of 1980s athletes); his frequent references to old television shows and movies as though they were playing today.

For many decades, the cover of *Time* magazine was arguably the single most powerful piece of media in the nation, a true measure of the influence and the celebrity of the person on it. Trump often offered his various appearances on the cover (exact number a matter of dispute, including a cover he had produced himself that he was not above passing off as genuine) as proof of his unique standing.

But *Time* magazine had not been that kind of arbiter in two generations. The media disruption that began in the 1990s was particularly devastating to magazines, and particularly to weekly newsmagazines. Time Inc.'s parent company, Time Warner, after going through several destabilizing combinations of its own, finally sold all its magazines, including *Time,* in 2013 (those magazines would go through several more ownership changes), with *Time* itself, now owned and funded by tech billionaire Marc Benioff, largely disappearing from newsstands and discontinuing its weekly frequency. One might reasonably be excused for not knowing that it was still in business.

But Trump, as though unaware of any alteration in the media firmament or of *Time* magazine's place in American life, was delighted—there could be no question otherwise—to sacrifice a campaign day for a visit from a vestigial *Time.*

A modest effort by the staff to fine-tune his priorities was met by incomprehension on his part. Of course he would do the *Time* interview!

Running for president and a *Time* cover story remained, in his mind, part and parcel—and, as well, a perk of the job that he would never pass up. This was, too, surprising to the people at *Time,* quite aware of their own diminished status in the media and cultural world.

He was—another in the split-screen gallery—the most current figure in American life, dominating every aspect of conversation and media, for better or worse—the one, true shared cultural moment. And yet he lived in a time warp: the Rat Pack, network television, octogenarian billionaires, Perry Mason.

His own team had long since given up on trying to understand what might be his naivete, or his stubborn need to hold on to what he knew

best, his time capsule worldview, and at the same time, his ability to oc-
cupy the lion's share of everybody's mind space in the present.

Roger Ailes, who created Fox News and led it for twenty years, had a
theory in which there was a modern nation, striving to live up to the
minute, and then another nation, the Fox audience, that lived happily
and unaware in 1965—a cultural anomaly to which the modern nation,
in its need to deny the past, took personal offense.

Time was given the royal treatment at Mar-a-Lago.

• • •

As his Stormy Daniels hush money trial approached, with him unable to
understand why it could not somehow be stopped, his incomprehension
about the entire nature of what he was being charged with grew.

In the playboy lifestyle in which he had proudly dwelled for most of
his adult decades, the advantage of money, and a leading reason to make
it, was the ability to pursue sexual desire beyond middle-class restraints.
Among the like-minded, there was a shared understanding that having
women—many women, who were paid in direct or indirect ways—was
a marker of success. In this currency, Stormy Daniels was small change.
Sometime model, sometime stripper, sometime porn performer and entrepreneur . . . whatever. In the Trump world of casinos, beauty pageant
deals, modeling agencies, and every-night nightlife, he was the impresario, and Stormy, along with unlimited numbers of women seeking
money and spotlight, a fungible character. Vast numbers of interchange-
able women, B-roll in his public life, were not a moral or even a worri-
some issue, because everybody knew the score; they were in the life (or
wanted to be). What happens in Vegas stays in Vegas (or, in the case of
Stormy, Lake Tahoe). When complications arose, they were dealt with.
You paid.

This was a way of life. There was a code.

By the evidence, a good part of the country accepted that Trump had
a morality pass of the kind that larger-than-life stars were traditionally
given—pre-internet, pre–social media, pre–the new market for bringing

down the rich and celebrated, pre–Trump's political ambitions. And, indeed, even as the facts of the Stormy Daniels case (along with quite a few other examples of Trump's incorrigible sexual behavior) became well known, there was little outcry or even apparent consternation from his supporters. They got it, apparently. Even got why he would have tried to pay her off. Nothing unexpected here.

Now his liberal enemies had concocted this flimsy pretext to try to turn the life he led into a crime . . . Well, where was the crime?

To have paid off a woman? Who hasn't?

While so many others had been caught and humiliated in the headlights of a new age and climate, Trump staunchly took the view that there had been no change. His way—having women, lots of them; lying about them; paying them off, if necessary; and covering your tracks— was a life people understood. *Obviously.* The liberals might believe there was a new world, and new rules, but he was proof there wasn't.

So, how could he be put on trial?

. . .

Five days before his trial—as he saw it, a trial of the century—was to begin, O.J. Simpson died. His, of course, was the trial of the last century, and he a Trump hero. Trump, in 1995, had been mesmerized by the O.J. trial and had actively tried to inject himself into the story as a commentator, an expert on sports figures and on media reaction. And if decent and sophisticated opinion had long ago consigned O.J. to the far margins of the human experience, Trump could easily slip back into 1995, impressed by the "Dream Team" of O.J. lawyers and yet offering various pretexts for how Nicole Brown Simpson and Ron Goldman might have been murdered. The O.J. connection to Trump's legal battles had been a subtext since the first indictment.

Every day in Trumpworld aspires to be a white Bronco day . . .

In Simpson's obituary in the *L.A. Times*, making the Freudian connection, the name "Trump" somehow replaced "O.J." in a description of Simpson's release from prison after his armed robbery conviction: "Long

before the city woke up on a fall morning in 2017, Trump walked out of
Lovelock Correctional Center outside Reno, a free man for the first time
in nine years," wrote the paper.

But the real point and real connection was that the O.J. Simson trial
had been a media event so large that it turned assumptions about the
media, about race, and about jurisprudence on their head. O.J. rose as a
character in this courtroom drama rather than being diminished by it.
O.J. was a victim of law enforcement, as was Trump!

O.J.'s victimization by the police, in some extraordinary convolution
of context and culture, became of a piece with Trump's victimization,
and similarly inspiring. More and more, to Trump, the silver lining of
his legal travails was that, as he saw it, Black men understood what he
was going through.

Trump was aiming to be bigger than justice—like O.J. (Pay no attention to what happened to O.J. later.)

· · ·

In the twinkle of yesteryear, there was also RFK Jr.

The second son of Robert F. Kennedy, Bobby Jr.—still "Junior" at
seventy—had been recruited to run in the Democratic primary to embarrass Joe Biden. Among his key promoters were Steve Bannon, Tucker
Carlson, and Roger Stone, who opened up right-wing media channels
for this liberal apostate with his famous name and history of vaccine
denial. Their plan seemed to backfire for Trump when Kennedy announced that he would run in the general election as an independent,
positioned to take votes from Trump as well as Biden. Hence, there was
suddenly a panicky Trump team reverse effort to paint RFK Jr., underneath his MAGA-like views, as actually a left-wing Democrat, even
though that was less and less convincing with Kennedy's every utterance.

At the same time, Trump was swooning, upending his own politics
by extolling the great Kennedy days. Here seemed to be the American
greatness he wanted to restore—glamorous and muscular Kennedy lib-
eralism (and don't forget all of those Kennedy women). So, why not

RFK Jr. for VP? "What about Kennedy?" he kept asking people. A Trump–Kennedy ticket. What a brand! He made people say it: "TRUMP–KENNEDY!—Just tell me how that sounds. Can you do better than that?"

In this, the past was better than the present. In a sense, he just didn't like anybody he could actually have as vice president; he didn't like anybody who wanted it.

The week before the trial started, the unofficial Trump feelers to Kennedy were unofficially turned down. Kennedy seemed happy continuing his spoiler race.

. . .

In a spasm of discipline nearly a year before, Trump had decided that he would not return in the summer of 2024 to Bedminster, his hot-weather encampment forty-five miles from Manhattan, where the Trump set gathered and where his New York "guys" could drive out to golf. In 2016 and 2020, there had been summer lulls in his campaigns, with one diagnosis being that he just liked the Bedminster golf course too much. But now, he vowed, he'd stay at Mar-a-Lago, focused on the campaign. It would be too hot to play much golf, and his people and the campaign infrastructure were there (actually in low-rent space in West Palm).

But he was getting restless, and the reconsiderations were starting, what with his having to be in New York for a trial that could stretch into June. And the golf course at Bedminster being so close . . .

The Mar-a-Lago season ended every year on Mother's Day, May 12 this year—a blowout affair at the club of families, carnations, and chiffon. And by then, the weather was already nearly unbearable, and a few weeks later it would be Death Valley stuff, with only crickets on the deserted patio.

Here was another existential variable: Yes, there was the efficiency of everybody in Palm Beach, but what would he be like in an empty club? It was an eerie, *Sunset Boulevard* Gloria Swanson idea of him eating by himself on the terrace looking out at the Intracoastal.

His mood, his identity, was maintained by his being the belle of the ball in Palm Beach and at Mar-a-Lago. The inverted reality of Mar-a-Lago was central to the inverted reality of being Donald Trump.

It was his true Camelot.

"Well," said a Trump intimate, quite aware of Mar-a-Lago's unique atmosphere, considering, "perhaps more Jonestown."

The court here waiting on his every breath, feeding off his presence, believing, too, in the centrality of Mar-a-Lago, of billionaires kissing his ass, was the illusion of power he required.

What would it do to him when the snowbirds left?

• • •

With the uncertainty of the New York trial date, there was an idle-hands sense of drift and troublemaking—part of the effective suspension of normal activities with the approaching trial and, too, a nameless dread at the unknown outcome and effect of the trial. How would voters react to Stormy Daniels's recall of their night together? (She seemed to have a vivid and unimpressed recollection of it.) How would he react? And Melania, that Sphinx-faced mystery?

Without the forward movement of the campaign and a clear daily schedule, Trump was spending more time with Ike Perlmutter. The eighty-one-year-old billionaire with little to do but offer billionaire advice to his would-be-billionaire friend, the potential next president, was continuing his own personal campaign, quite a determined one, against Susie Wiles and whatever it was that had, now a half dozen years ago, during the DeSantis gubernatorial campaign, offended him. *She* was the problem in the campaign—even though there was, arguably, no problem at all.

Meanwhile, Wiles, who had seemed like a figure of great stability and fortitude, now became a figure of great insecurity. More and more, she was assembling around herself a praetorian guard of her own loyalists, her cadre from the 2018 DeSantis campaign, with her daughter on the payroll at five figures a month—causing Perlmutter further ire.

Axios, the political tip sheet, went out with a report of an argument between Wiles and LaCivita at campaign headquarters in West Palm Beach. The report offered no sense of the substance of the argument; nor did it in any way reflect on or undermine the candidate—and, indeed, a minor leak in Axios was hardly a news cycle event. But this now up-ended Wiles and, therefore, the campaign. There was a leak hunt. Plane manifests were searched and cross-referenced. Meeting schedules triangulated. Expense accounts compared. Email and phone records reviewed. Everyone looking over everybody else's shoulder. Paranoia.

Steven Cheung, the steady-eddy spokesperson whom everyone liked, was downgraded to a spokesperson only for legal issues. Wiles loyalists were now elevated to central communications roles.

The campaign's estimable and unflappable mother figure was now depressed, agitated, wrathful.

More important, the campaign was losing its candidate. All efforts otherwise having failed (desperate, wholly wishful last-minute efforts still going on), he would be an effective prisoner—indeed, formally under arrest, he was an *actual* prisoner—in a New York courtroom, held in his seat for the next four to six weeks.

PART FOUR

The Trial

CHAPTER 13

100 Centre Street

APRIL–MAY 2024

On trial day, April 15, Natalie passed Trump another of her heartfelt and besotted letters. There were Bible verses and her deep hope that everything would work out and her assurance that, in any event, she was there for him—indeed, would be at his side, supplying him with feel-good news coverage, throughout the trial. (In her backpack, she carried her printer, a ream of paper, extra ink cartridges, and an auxiliary charger.) Natalie's real purpose, in addition to comfort and reassurance, was to help Trump circumvent (or, in the prosecution's view, violate) his gag order; she assembled right-wing articles that damned judge and prosecutor, which Trump or designated others could repost. She had a direct line—here she represented herself as speaking for Trump—to right-wing media, every prime-time anchor at Fox News, and the loudest far-right MAGA people, Steve Bannon and Laura Loomer among them.

• • •

Todd Blanche, for all he had to look forward to if he won this case, was, however, also looking at the worst kind of humiliation if he lost.

And now, with no more trial delays, Trump had begun to mete out humiliations to those around him, especially lighting into Blanche—a chewing out that echoed through the legal team:

"I don't even know what we're doing here. I told you to stop this. You should have been able to get this killed. It's a bullshit case. Everybody says it's a bullshit case. What the fuck were you doing? Huh? I'd like to know. I'd really like to know. This is a witch hunt. They're doing this to embarrass me. There's nothing here, but they're going to embarrass me. That's all they want to do. You need to deal with that. I paid you to handle this. But you're blowing it."

And while other lawyers in the room might single out Blanche for the brunt of Trump's mistreatment, when he was finished, he went on to Gedalia Stern and Susan Necheles, who, with Emil Bove, were part of the second-chair team. Stern and Necheles had been the attorneys for Allen Weisselberg, the Trump CFO who had been convicted on tax and perjury charges, an outcome Trump now, in a takedown that echoed through the Trump legal world, took out on them: "How could you lose that? You were terrible. Now I get stuck with you. And"—focusing on Stern with horror—"what's that you're doing?" Stern was sniffling. "What's wrong with you? Are you sick? Are you *sick*?"

Those in the room held their breath, trying to will Stern to say, "Allergies."

"I'm just a little sick," Stern admitted.

"A little sick! Just a little sick! Just what I need now! Get away. Get a-way!" he shouted, holding his hands out, as though to block Stern and to push him as far away as he could be pushed.

• • •

The media, during the first week of the trial, was seated in an overflow room, an unused courtroom even more dilapidated than the actual courtroom, with a feed from video cameras head-on to the defendant and lawyers and another head-on to the judge. Trump himself seemed initially unaware that he could be seen face on, instead of, as otherwise would be the case, with his back to the courtroom and cameras.

The morning of the first day, *The New York Times* reported, in quite a dramatic rendering that became that day's biggest news, that Trump had fallen into a stupor, head lolling, mouth slack. Somewhat more accurately . . . he had evidently zoned out and was, as he would be throughout the trial, heavy-lidded and motionless, in more a pose of "I'm bored, why am I here?" than humiliating public zzzz.

Trump had once styled himself as the quintessential Manhattan son—eighties style—brash, moneyed, in the news. In a more chastened era, he had become the most shocking and reprehensible apostate of Manhattan's virtue-signaling ethos. Now he was here in criminal court, at 100 Centre Street, getting ready to face a jury of his Manhattan peers—and his legal team rightly feared their revenge on him.

Almost exactly a year after Manhattan DA Alvin Bragg indicted him on what then seemed to be a kludgy collection of charges that, squinting your eyes, turned this into a felony case, Trump was back in Bragg's court. This trial would follow his three catastrophic civil losses this year in New York. The liberal view, previously skeptical about Bragg's charges, with the other Trump criminal indictments seemingly more righteous, had now, in default, come to see the New York hush money case as a just and principled stand.

In the opening days of jury selection, the assistant district attorney leading the prosecution, Joshua Steinglass, was adept, precise, forceful, and unfaltering on his feet—and rather struggling to keep a straight face at a juror pool so aptly representing the new, clean-living, urban-professional, Manhattan demographic. Blanche, for his part, perhaps cowed by the hegemony of the jury pool and its likely judgment and, as well, by a difficult client, often grasped for words, let his sentences trail off, and appeared rattled by the judge's admonishments.

The goal was to select twelve jurors and six alternates acceptable to both sides. There was a forty-two-question sheet meant to give a basic profile of each juror and to surface any overt bias. Then, in the voir dire, each side could specifically question individual jurors. But even before this, half the jurors—ninety-six were in the pool—voluntarily disqualified themselves by declaring they were too biased to fairly judge Donald Trump.

• • •

The jury pool represents a litany of some of the world's most expensive addresses: the Upper West Side, Chelsea, Greenwich Village, the East Village, the Upper East Side, Gramercy Park, Sutton Place. Most in the jury pool are *New York Times* readers, and many are NPR listeners. Many are single women who live with their dogs. They hike and read and enjoy the theater and eating out and doing yoga and meditating and are all evidently part of a cultural stereotype that once seemed comically rarefied (cue the Woody Allen films) but that now appears to include everyone on the island. (Manhattan Criminal Court draws its jurors only from Manhattan.)

The judge keeps asking the jurors to weigh whether they can be fair and impartial. But it also seems as much that he's urging them (winkwink) to *believe* they can be fair and impartial, however they might, even obviously do, abhor Donald Trump.

There is an old newsreel quality to what is being promised in the courtroom: Trump characters once prominently in the news, but long since left in his wake, coming back again. The potential narrative here might seem to be designed to reanimate all the feelings of rage and incomprehension provoked by the 2016 election (particularly in Manhattan), that national day of liberal mourning. The defense gets this with foot-stamping frustration. Their boiled-down view, unfortunately not technically a legal one, is that whatever happened, American voters elected him and might appear to be on their way to electing him again, so get over it.

The prosecution, in turn, is counting on not just a mountain of evidence of a conspiracy to cover up Trump's affairs and falsify his records, but also the inability of a Manhattan jury to get over his election in the first place.

Trump is under glass. At the outset of the trial day, photographers are allowed to scurry in for sixty seconds of up-close photographs—cameras stuck inches from his face, as though he were inanimate.

There is no television in New York Criminal Court, but there are video monitors. Some in the audience are using opera glasses for an upclose of the video. Trump has a practiced face—glowering, tough, immobile. There's an ongoing watch among the press for any deviation here—grimace, pointed look, raised eyebrow, or the least sign of drift.

But what is he thinking? That's opaque, except for his venting in social media posts and in his vituperative appearances before the cameras in the courthouse hall every time the judge allows a break. He's playing a part—victim of a grievous injustice. For him, this is a kangaroo court—manufactured charges in front of a judicial system (indeed, an entire political system, from the president down) that has set out to prevent him from becoming the president again. This is not a trial in which the primary outcome will be guilt or innocence, one in which the jury gets the final decision. In this regard, Trump may well understand the stakes better than anyone else in this courtroom: He wins this trial, whatever its outcome, if he wins this election.

• • •

Monday, April 22.

The prosecution's opening argument was a methodical forty-five minutes of laying out a cogent case of cause and effect. In 2016, Donald Trump was facing embarrassment and humiliation, and possibly even disqualification as a candidate, in a variety of potential scandals and, so, he had set out in an underhanded conspiracy to keep this information from coming to light and, in one instance, covered up this effort to suppress information by cooking his books, all in the hope of keeping his presidential campaign on track.

Blanche, in a stumbling thirty minutes, failed to disrupt this narrative. The best he could do was argue that a main witness here, Michael Cohen, was unreliable. One problem with this argument was that if the prosecution could bolster Cohen's reliability with other corroborating evidence, Blanche had no defense at all. He did not attempt the larger argument, that the case was a collection of mismatched fabric making a very strange-looking outfit. Curiously, he argued the facts, which seemed glaringly against Trump. Trump, of course, no matter how obvious the facts were, believed in the power of adamantly denying them. (He was continuing to insist he had never had any relationship with either Karen McDougal or Stormy Daniels.)

The tongue-tied Blanche was certainly going to be blasted to smithereens. On the way to the break, a nettled Trump, in passing, asked Blanche, "Why can't you make words come out of your mouth normally?"

But then Alina Habba and Chris Kise (both very much on Trump's shitty-lawyers list) showed up. In a nearby courtroom, the New York State attorney general, Letitia James, had argued that allowing Trump to post a bond for $175 million in the fraud case, instead of for the full $584 million owed, was a flawed decision and should be reversed. But that morning, James's motion had been rejected, and Habba and Kise were now on the scene to claim credit. Whatever dissatisfaction Trump might have felt toward Blanche was now focused on his victory against James, with him back on the phone bragging about his win. Habba was ordered to get outside the courtroom and announce their great victory to the press. "Doing Marisa Tomei in *My Cousin Vinny*," in the characterization of one member of the legal team.

Trump, over pizza in the small break room, was suddenly in a very good mood.

It would be a rotating menu, vexing to the lawyers with dietary concerns and adult eating habits, during the trial and, sportingly, noted by various court watchers: pizza one day, McDonald's, always Trump's favorite, the next, followed by Chick-fil-A, and then Jimmy John's.

• • •

The first witness was David Pecker, the nexus of the case. Pecker was the CEO, along with holding all other top titles, at the odd-lot publishing company American Media, which owned the *National Enquirer*, the supermarket celebrity tabloid. Pecker was a linchpin in the prosecutor's narrative of Trump's conspiring with his lawyer-fixer Michael Cohen both to cover up reports of his sexual affairs and to besmirch his 2016 political enemies, including Hillary Clinton, Ted Cruz, and Marco Rubio, in order to influence the 2016 election. Pecker had been forced to testify under an immunity deal. But from the start, his testimony seemed the opposite of begrudging—his relationship with Trump had destroyed his career.

Pecker, seventy-two and retired—or, really, after years of dubious management as well as his Trump perfidy, forced out of the industry—had been a curious figure in the New York publishing world for more than forty years. As magazines came under increasing cost pressures in the 1990s, Pecker had used his training as an accountant to rise to senior positions in the business, even though he lacked the faintest editorial sensibility or taste, or any inclination to acquire them or even to pretend he had them. He was the ultimate sleazeball vulgarian, proud of it and with contempt for anyone who might not think he represented the true reality of the business—money. He was neither bright nor charming nor good-looking (sporting a decades-out-of-date 1970s porn star look) nor, with various bankruptcies to come, even particularly good at his business. But he was cockroach-like, and indefatigable, and shameless, and always ready with another angle—blatantly in the business of selling anything that could be sold, even if it should not be sold. He was the low-rent discount store you might not want to do business with but sometimes had to anyway.

Transactional, without airs, and with a lowlife's desire to yet consort with his betters—rather more a familiar figure from, say, the wrestling and boxing promotion world than the publishing world—Pecker was an easy Trump mark. The *National Enquirer* was his flagship. It had a long and robust history as an immensely profitable, big-circulation, down-market, even underclass title, with Martian landings and Siamese twins among its special interests. But by the time Pecker acquired the *Enquirer,* it had lost most of its circulation and most of its profits. With private equity money, Pecker repositioned the paper into the low end of the still-thriving, pre-internet celebrity magazine market. Reality television stars, a growth business, provided much of the *Enquirer*'s new subject matter, including the star of NBC's hit series *The Apprentice,* Donald Trump. (The *Enquirer*'s research showed it to have a particular audience of Trump fans, a commercial marketing point that would shortly become one of the most significant political insights of the age.)

Still . . . business was not all that good, especially when you had to pay down private equity debt and produce private equity returns for your investors. You had to find more things to sell. As it happened, you could sell not just coverage of celebrities to your readers, but also *how* you covered the celebrities to the celebrities themselves. In fairness, many respectable magazines were in complicated, "soft," quid pro quo arrangements with celebrities and their handlers—cooperation and access for positive coverage. Pecker advanced this to hard deals. He was running both a protection racket and a set of backroom partnerships—conspiracies, if you will—in which his businesses profited by carrying out the press dictates of his partners: stories killed, things promoted, people attacked (among his partners: Arnold Schwarzenegger, Tiger Woods, and Harvey Weinstein).

A meeting in Trump Tower in August 2015 with Pecker, Trump, and Cohen that prosecutors had elicited from Pecker in the early minutes of his testimony as a key moment in the conspiracy was neither unnatural nor unusual for Pecker. It was standard business—except for the fact that Trump wasn't just a celebrity but a presidential candidate. For access to Trump and, no doubt, for a sense that he was crucially in the mix, and hence might be able to broker and otherwise monetize his relationship with Trump, Pecker agreed to be Trump's "eyes and ears" in the tawdry precincts where rumors and stories and photos and videos about celebrities were retailed. Further, Pecker and the *National Enquirer* and its editors would act—here in specific conjunction with Michael Cohen's direction—as Trump's attack dog toward his political opponents.

Pecker, with his editor Dylan Howard (an Australian who, apparently, had fled the jurisdiction back to Oz), was a soldier in the world of dishing out and covering up scandal. The two double agents, in a sense. Pecker and his editor paid for dirt—sometimes as much as ten grand, but generally no more than a few thousand and frequently no more than a small tip. Low-value dirt came to them; they were market makers in it. Among the immediate favors for Trump after the 2015 agreement was dealing with the story of a Trump Tower doorman who claimed to have evidence of a Trump love child with one of his regular maids ("house-keeper," in courtroom parlance). There ensued a lie detector test taken by the willing doorman and a deeper investigation by Howard and Cohen—with Trump kept abreast on the sidelines. Trump denied the story, and Howard concluded that it was not remotely true. But Pecker was yet pressed to handle it. He did, putting the doorman's story on ice for thirty thousand dollars (perhaps not unreasonably suggesting that, if not this one, then there were other Trump love children or Trump pregnancies out there and best not to get people wondering).

The next get for Pecker and Howard was the *Playboy* "model" Karen McDougal, who said she'd had a ten-month affair with Trump. She preferred, she said, not to go public—she did not want to become Monica Lewinsky, Pecker testified that she said—and was satisfied to be paid off (though, of course, the implication was that she would go public, if necessary). Her price tag was $150,000.

Simultaneous with catching and killing these stories was a constant back-and-forth between Pecker and Cohen about payment and how it was made and who was picking up the tab. This remained mostly unresolved, with none of the parties being satisfied. There was little honor among thieves. Predictably, Pecker felt cheated. Cohen, ultimately, felt cheated, too. And, of course, the cheater, Trump, felt cheated.

The crux here, the legal crux, was to understand why exactly they were making these payoffs. Was it because that's simply what powerful men do? They indulged, then covered up. People might want to embarrass them because they were rich, but because they were rich, they could pay not to be embarrassed. It was the dirty blackmail circle. And that's what lowlifes like Pecker were for, to do the dirty work of men richer and more powerful than they. Or was it more specific? And this specificity would then define Trump's criminal enterprise. Did Trump want the doorman's rumors and Karen McDougal's and Stormy Daniels's tattles covered up because scandal would directly impact his run for the presidency—which, reasonably, it would? Was it a calculated effort to deprive the people of the State of New York of vital information in the presidential campaign? Or was it simply rich-guy business as usual, as the defense seemed to maintain (though, at the same time, denying anything untoward had happened at all)?

There were several problems here for the defense. First, the amount of money far exceeded business-as-usual supermarket tabloid scandal payments. Second, the co-conspirators were up front about the immediate urgency of getting this taken care of—with specific links to the revelation of the *Access Hollywood* tape, which itself had threatened to derail the Trump campaign. Another problem here was that there was a defense available to Trump—except, he couldn't use it. First, he might show this was business as usual by detailing the times—and the people close to him didn't doubt that there were many times—he had paid off women over the years. Nothing exceptional here! Second, he could also easily produce evidence that neither he nor anyone who worked for him had believed he had a chance in hell of being elected president in 2016. Everything he was doing was related to Trump brand building, not to the expectation of winning an election. But none of that, of course, could now be said.

There was, too, a fundamental problem for the prosecution: Paying off women was not illegal, and more to the point, paying off women in order to help your chances to get elected was not illegal, either. But here was where the gang that couldn't shoot straight, with its stumblebum thieves and double-crossers, gave the prosecution its case. Pecker arranged the doorman and the McDougal payments, but Trump didn't pay him back, or make Pecker feel he'd gotten value for his contribution. (His testimony here was part of a plea bargain not to be prosecuted for the illegal campaign contributions represented by the payoffs.) Hence, Pecker refused to make the Stormy Daniels payoff. Therefore, Michael Cohen made it himself, quickly setting up a bogus company through which to do it; and Trump paid Cohen back, disguising the payments as for legal services. Hence, falsified business records, the misdemeanor charge that becomes a felony if it's tied to larger criminal intent—in this case, a cover-up that could affect the election. It remained for prosecutors to explain why the cover-up was not being charged here as a crime. So far, what they had was Trump doing sleazy things with business records to cover up more sleazy stuff in his generally sleazy life, which had become part and parcel, if not the calling card, of Trump's (in the fall of 2016) still-ridiculous run for president.

• • •

On Wednesday, April 24—court was dark on Wednesdays because, in this same courtroom, Judge Merchan took time off from his regular trial calendar to hear mental health–related cases, an unacknowledged irony—the Arizona grand jury, which a few months before had sent out a blanket of subpoenas across Trumpworld in its election interference investigation, indicted, among others, Rudy Giuliani and Boris Epshteyn, naming Donald Trump as an unindicted co-conspirator.

Is Boris still on the team? Has he been fired, given this indictment? the press immediately inquired.

The next morning, Thursday, the otherwise-absent Boris packed into a three-piece suit took his seat in court, publicly asserting his proximity and favor to Trump.

In the courtroom, Boris and Natalie sat side by side—favorite son and daughter (and full of sibling rivalry).

At the same time, Trump's recent favorite, Alina Habba, ever trying to climb back into his good graces, seemed now to have been voted off the island. The night before, she had gone on Greg Kelly's Newsmax show and said she didn't have "hopes really that high" for this trial—with Natalie bringing this to Trump's attention. Trump now dictated a furious text message to Habba: *What the fuck are you saying? This is not even your case. We're going to win this thing!* And insisted that there was no way he was going to pay her most recent bill.

Trump had a few personal staffers with him, primarily Natalie; Walt Nauta, his body man (indicted with him in the boxes case); Steven Cheung, his spokesman; and now Boris. Jason Miller was in court regularly, too, sitting in a back row. This was Trump's primary yes-man coterie, with everyone here reliably programmed to offer fulsome, over-the-top, ever-flowing words of the most bootlicking support. But the campaign itself, strangely, seemed to be remote from the central stage, as though this trial were part of some other business.

Chris LaCivita was spending most of his time on RNC concerns, as if that, rather than this, were the beating heart of the campaign. Susie Wiles was in West Palm Beach.

"Where's Melania?" had become a question regularly shouted at Trump by the press poolers hanging in the courtroom hallway waiting for any statements Trump might give during the various court breaks. (On Friday, April 26, Trump told the poolers it was Melania's birthday and that he wished he could be with her . . . alas.) Was it perhaps that she was shunning him?

• • •

The small break room for the defense team had a long table and, at the end, the bathroom, with a single toilet. In the cramped room, Trump took a seat at the head of the table, inches from the bathroom door. Given that Trump necessarily had to use this bathroom, every other lawyer understood that they needed to find other bathrooms elsewhere in the court building—except for the second-string lawyer Gedalia Stern, the one who had annoyed Trump with his sniffling. To all the other lawyers' notice, and silent incredulity, and in a story that swept Trumpworld, Stern kept using the bathroom—Trump's bathroom. He was the only one who, densely, used it, with even Trump trying to ignore his denseness, until he ignored it no longer:

"Who the fuck is this guy? Does he just show up to use my bathroom?"

• • •

Pecker had been a strong and purposeful witness against Trump—he'd been there, seen it all, and wasn't remotely beating around the bush about the sleazy world he occupied, where Trump was pleased to have him act as his agent, his "eyes and ears." The cross-examination by Trump's lawyer Emil Bove ("E-mil," "E-meel," or "You" to Trump) wasn't much focused on arguing the facts. Instead, Bove was trying to hit the seventy-two-year-old over his recall and memory. It was a long setup to what the defense saw as its possible kill shot. Pecker had testified that he went to a meeting in Trump Tower and there encountered Mike Pompeo (whom Bove incorrectly identified as about to become secretary of state; in fact, Pompeo's first position in the Trump administration was as CIA director); Reince Priebus, who would become chief of staff; Sean Spicer, slated to be press secretary; and James Comey, the FBI director. The rub was that Comey had testified in other investigations that he was the only one in the room with Trump at the meeting. On the verge of Bove coming to the reveal of this discrepancy, Steinglass, the prosecutor, objected, and Merchan sustained.

But whatever was going wrong—Alina, abortion, the weakness of his lawyers, the judge's help to the prosecution, someone using his bathroom—was swept away for Trump as reports started to come into the New York courtroom of what was transpiring simultaneously in the Supreme Court hearing that morning.

There had been no hope whatsoever among anyone on the Trump political or legal team (save for Trump himself) that his claim of a blanket legal immunity for what a president might do, *anything* a president might do—murder, mayhem, robbery, coups, or otherwise—would succeed in any fashion. "Brazen and cynical," said *The New York Times*.

"Don't forget ludicrous," a Trump lawyer added.

The best result of this preposterous gambit was delay. The fact that the Court had even agreed to hear this claim might push the January 6 case to after the election. Maybe. Though many on the Trump team still thought the Court would facilitate things for Trump only so far and that Trump would still have to struggle against a September trial—meaning his efforts at election subversion might still hang over 2024's November election date.

And yet . . . inconceivably . . . on this Thursday morning, the Court's conservative majority seemed quite favorably disposed to granting at least some sort of immunity to Donald Trump (and all other presidents).

The case had come before the Court as a result of Trump's exceptional behavior—the Justice Department's accusation that he had violated the law in order to vitiate an election and stay in office. But, in a jaw-dropping inversion, the Court's conservative majority seemed to be proposing that without immunity, presidents might well cling to office, to avoid prosecution as private citizens. The justices had leaped past the reality at hand and into considerations of another reality not remotely present in the case or before the Court—and were on the verge now, it seemed, of upending that most basic no-one-is-above-the-law civics lesson.

"If an incumbent who loses a very close, hotly contested election knows that a real possibility after leaving office is not that the president is going to be able to go off into a peaceful retirement but that the president may be criminally prosecuted by a bitter political opponent, will that not lead us into a cycle that destabilizes the functioning of our country as a democracy?" asked Justice Alito, in fun-house-mirror style.

The decision that now seemed likely to be forthcoming potentially undermined all the criminal cases against him. "This could be the luckiest day of Donald Trump's life since the day he became Fred Trump's son," said a Trump insider.

More immediately—well, at least for the day—it took the pressure off his lawyers in New York and their flailing case.

Except that, to him, his lawyers *were* to blame. He would not be in any of these bad situations if his lawyers had done their job and kept him out of court. Publicly, he placed the blame on prosecutors and judges and on Joe Biden; privately, he placed the blame on his own lawyers. "Todd is weak. Very weak. He's losing this case," Trump told Wiles and, in what was now standard monologue, almost anybody who inquired—his "talking-shit phone calls," in campaign team parlance. "Do you think I should fire him?" he asked Wiles. "I think I might have to fire him. They would have to give us a thirty-day delay, at least."

CHAPTER 14

Contempt

MAY 2024

Would the trial make a difference? Trump seemed less agitated—though this was far from saying he was at peace—with this trial than with the rape or fraud trials, which had cost him so much money. That was money; here the stake could be prison . . . but only theoretical prison, so theoretical that he could not help returning to Nelson Mandela. The only universe in which he and Mandela might be joined was that of world-wide celebrity. Mandela, and the fame his years in prison had brought to him, was Trump's fantasy of going to jail and, no doubt as well, the only example of political martyrdom that came easily to his mind.

Still, the campaign received a media query about a meeting with prosecution, court officials, and Secret Service to discuss arrangements for, in actuality, locking him up, at least on a contempt citation, if that became necessary. This caused brief concern—as though no one in Trumpworld had quite considered this—and a sudden reality check: "If Trump's just a total asshole during the trial, if his behavior is just totally unhinged, like it was with Engoron, and he's constantly attacking the judge on a daily basis, well, sure, the judge could be like, fuck you, you're in the slammer," acknowledged one insider. But that quickly passed to the vast difficulties, if not the absurdity, if they did lock him up, and the huge advantage it could be to the campaign.

So, what was the downside of the trial? Well, yes, a felony conviction. There was no model to imagine that effect, except that the three
trials that he had now lost in ignominious fashion—civil, yes, but ignominious all the same—had apparently not dented his electoral standing.
And yet, there was Stormy Daniels (and in the background, Karen Mc-
Dougal) and a talented prosecution that surely would, in the most
straight-faced way, elicit a mother lode of salacious details. Affecting his
own mental balance, there was the lineup of witnesses whose loyalty to
him he would measure to the slightest deviation, with the prosecution
undoubtedly hoping they could provoke him, as in his other trials, into
a courtroom meltdown. Already, that was his continual question: Can
we count on them?

Pecker was curiously forgiven by Trump, because he was being forced
to testify. Trump wanted his lawyers to press the point that the prosecutors and FBI had really screwed poor Pecker over and were responsible
for making his life miserable. He was discreetly steered away from this
gambit because the logical inference the jury might make was that
Trump, really, was the one who had screwed Pecker over and made his
life miserable.

Rhona Graff, his career-long assistant in Trump Tower—whom,
hurtfully to her, he had left behind when he went to the White House
and who now, walking haltingly with a cane, had come to the stand as a
prosecution witness to confirm both Trump's office procedures and
Stormy Daniels's access to him—"held," in his estimation. This wasn't
a flip.

Hope Hicks, his White House factotum and closest confidante, had
left him even before January 6, turning on him over the election denial;
they had hardly spoken since. He kept inquiring about who knew what
about her and about where she stood, but at the same time, he assured
everyone that Hope would be with them, though immediately asking
people if they thought she would be with him. Madeleine Westerhout,
his personal assistant in the White House who had been summarily fired
for indiscreet gossiping about the Trump family, had been to a few recent Trump events, and he had been "nice" to her—and so, he felt she
was maybe fine.

Notably, he yet seemed to feel warmly toward Karen McDougal. She was "a good girl," he had told David Pecker when he was arranging the catch-and-kill payoff, and he was still repeating this now, wanting to know what she looked like, if she still looked good—indeed, suggesting they bring up how good she looked (mitigating circumstances!). Stormy Daniels, forget about—she was trash and a liar. But Karen—and both women, he continued to insist, he had done nothing whatsoever with—he still seemed to believe he had bonded with her and that she would not help sink him if she were called to testify (though they would fight it if she were).

• • •

Meanwhile, on the other end of Manhattan from criminal court, Columbia University was engulfed in a bitter protest against Israel's war in Gaza and, on the part of many, against Israel itself, if not Jews in general. It was the largest political demonstration at Columbia since 1968, when the campus was the site of one of the bitterest college uprisings. As in 1968, when the university, disastrously, invited the police on campus to clear the students, on April 18, 2024, they did similarly, with the result that the encampment-style protests, with pup tents populating university grounds, spread virally to universities around the country.

The protests might have seemed to be bad news for the Democrats, clearly defining the polarized sides of the party: Biden, on the one hand, continuing his few-questions-asked defense of Israel, and a younger, left-leading Democratic cohort wholly rejecting Israel's moral claims. The Democrats' uncertain response to the protests was in marked contrast to the Republicans' absolutist position not only against Hamas and the Palestinians, but also that all protests on the subject were necessarily anti-Semitic (and that, therefore, the party historically hostile to the Jews, and to which the Jews were hostile, was somehow the party reliable in its defense of Israel). Here, then, was a beautiful opportunity for Republicans both to make their moral case and, as important, to bait protestors who might be counted on to fuel national antipathy to the privileged young acting out.

Mike Johnson, the House Speaker, made the trip to Columbia and got his media moment.

Trump was urged by Johnson and others to do the same. He had visited a Harlem bodega and a construction site in his off moments from the trial. Why not take the thirty-minute trip uptown to Columbia and, in and out quickly, score his obvious and easy points? The certain hecklers would cement his case.

"No students! No students!" he shouted down the idea.

But—

"No students!"

That is, to note the not-insignificant political point, he appeared only before admiring audiences. As much as he might seem pugilistic, he was never really engaging in a debate. He played a role, and that was confirmed by the outpouring of adoring fans. A fan thing, not a political thing.

"Stupid of me, really stupid," said one of the people who had enthusiastically made the campus-visit suggestion.

• • •

Midway through the trial, Trump was awarded a further $1.8 billion in Truth Social stock on top of the billions in shares he already owned. Here was another example of his magical, reality-denying capacity— that weird disconnect that was never to be discounted. The business was preposterous. Few knew this as well as the people who actually followed Truth Social—that is, who followed, practically speaking, its single user. The stock had climbed as high as seven billion dollars and now had fallen back to four—but four billion, *four billion,* for what? A social network with no users, poor tech, no-nothing management? Trump had been encouraged over and over again to get back on Twitter (X) or to join with one or more of the other none-too-successful right-wing social networks. But he saw inevitable value, quite unimaginable value, in his network of one, even as it dragged through one of the longest IPO approval periods in corporate history. Even now, with a gyrating stock, he seemed to have no worries. "Hot as a pistol," he continued to repeat to friends, never changing his script.

He frequently complained that he had lost money on his political pursuits, and with the legal judgments against him, and the controversy that now surrounded his brand, perhaps he had—and yet, here now he had magically monetized his vanity enterprise at a level of great autocrats with unnatural sway over their nation's laws and economy.

· · ·

Arriving in court, Trump stopped to address the hallway cameras, ranging over many current and past insults:

> Thank you very much. So we begin again. This is a case that should never have been brought. Every single major legal scholar—Jonathan Turley, Gregg Jarrett, Andy McCarthy, Dershowitz—every single scholar. Mark Levin, the great Mark Levin, had a whole show on it last night. He said that this is a disgraceful case. It's a disgrace to the New York State and City court system. And all of the cases are, frankly. All of them are.
>
> You probably saw last night that Jack Smith got caught with his hand in the cookie jar. It was released late last night, and it's a big story. The documents case is a hoax created by them for election interference purposes. And so that one looks like it's going asunder. A brilliant judge [Aileen Cannon] saw some facts, and I haven't read what was revealed yet; it just came out. But the document hoax is indeed, it is indeed a hoax. The whole thing is a hoax. All of them are hoaxes, including the civil cases. They're controlled by the White House, they're controlled by Democratic judges and prosecutors that were put there specifically. They hate Trump. And the people are getting it. That's why we just came out—a new Emerson poll just was released about two minutes ago, and I'm leading by a lot in every swing state and leading in the general election. And you saw the CNN poll.

I'm sure they aren't too happy with it, but the CNN poll was fantastic.

So, we're here. This is a hoax. This is a judge who's conflicted. Badly, badly, badly conflicted. I've never seen a judge so conflicted, and giving us virtually no rulings. Here I'm not even allowed to say "advice of counsel." This is a new one to me, "advice of counsel." When you have a lawyer, and the lawyer does something or advises you of something, you say "advice of counsel." He said you're not allowed to say that. And so you'll all figure it out. But I think the public has figured it out, because the poll numbers are the highest they've ever been. And I appreciate you've treated me actually, I thought, quite fairly, at least to the people here, which is a lot of people. And I appreciate that.

The Biden protests that are going on are horrible. It's all caused by him, because he doesn't know how to speak. He can't put two sentences together. He's got to get out and make a statement, because the colleges are being overrun in this country. The anti-Semitism, all of the problems going on, they're being overrun. I've never seen anything like it. He said he ran because of Charlottesville. Well, if the people that know Charlottesville, when you extend the statement, it's a big hoax. What was, what they say was said. And they understand that. And Charlottesville is peanuts compared to what you're looking at now, with this whole country up in arms, breaking into colleges, knocking the hell out of Columbia University. I mean, they took over. I know the building very well. They took over a building. That is a big deal. And I wonder if what's going to happen to them will be anything comparable to what happened to J-six, because they're doing a lot of destruction, a lot of damages, a lot of people getting hurt very badly. I wonder if that's going to be the same kind of treatment they gave J-six. Let's see how that all works out. I think I can give you the answer right now. And that's why people have lost faith in our court system.

So, the Biden protests are a disaster, and he hasn't even made a statement. Because he's not capable of making a statement. I'm still waiting for him to debate, he said on the very lowly rated *Howard Stern Show*, he said very strongly, "No, I want to, I want to debate." Well, we haven't seen it. But we would love to debate anytime. And I think it's a good time to have a debate, even though it's early.

But six months is pretty close. November fifth is going to go down as the most important day in the history of our country, because we're going to turn our country around; the country is going to hell. It's going to hell. It's very sad to see, but November fifth is going to be the most important day in the history of our country.

So, I'm going to go into this trial. I'm going to sit in a freezing-cold icebox for eight hours, nine hours or so. They took me off the campaign trail. But the good news is my poll numbers are the highest they've ever been. So, at least we're getting the word out. And everybody knows this trial is a scam. It's a scam. The judge should be recused, and he should recuse himself today. It's the most recusable judge. I've been told recusal abuse. And he should recuse himself today. And maybe he will. Maybe he will. Maybe he'll do the right thing. But really, more important than the recusal, he should terminate the case today. The judge should terminate the case because they have no case. As Jonathan Turley said, as all of them said, every single one of them—Dershowitz, McCarthy, every one; Gregg Jarrett, Mark Levin—they all said that this case should be ended immediately. This case is over. It should be ended immediately. And many of them are not fans of mine, but they want to do the right thing for the country.

So, I appreciate your being here. Thank you very much. And I'm going to go into the icebox now and sit for about eight hours or nine hours. I'd much rather be in Georgia. I'd much rather be in Florida. I'd much rather be in states that are in play, states that, you know, I'd like to be able to campaign. Biden's out campaigning, if you call it campaigning. He can't campaign, because every time he opens his mouth, he gets in trouble. But Biden is out campaigning very nicely. I think when I start campaigning, he'll stop; he'll go back into his basement. But I want to thank everybody. You've really been treating me very fair. I want to thank *Time* magazine. They did a cover story, which is very nice. And it's actually at least sixty percent, it's at least sixty percent correct, which is about all I can ask for. So, I want to thank you, everybody.

• • •

A spring day in New York, with the temperature expected to hit nearly seventy, the cold courtroom was suddenly starting to feel uncomfortably warm.

Susie Wiles, looking skittish, spent the day in court—a sign that the room, heretofore a campaign sideshow, might, as the case relentlessly proceeded, become the center of gravity. Trump was accompanied, too, by Ken Paxton, the Texas attorney general long mired in his own legal difficulties (his Trump allegiance part of his own continuing defense).

Surprisingly, the judge granted Trump's request to attend his son Barron's high school graduation—Trump had already generated considerable rhetorical outrage by announcing that the judge had denied him this absence from court. As it happened, over the weekend, Barron had told his father he would be willing to sacrifice going to his graduation and, on that day, would accompany his father to court—which Trump thought was sheer brilliance. He turned now to Blanche and ruefully asked if they could get the judge to take back his permission.

Then, at the midmorning break, with Blanche doing a going-nowhere cross-examination of one of the bookkeeping witnesses—the rising temperature in the courtroom and monotony of the testimony taxing everyone—it blew up. You couldn't miss the steaming Trump. Bad weather coming. Nobody was talking or making eye contact. As soon as he was outside the courtroom, he turned face-to-face with Blanche and let it rip, damning him for his weakness and lack of aggressions, and then delivering the ultimate swipe:

"Why are you so weak? You're not being aggressive. I don't know why I'm paying you. All you want to do is be nice to this judge. You're going to lose this case. You have no fucking chance of winning this case. I see the jurors. You keep saying we're doing well. We're not doing well. All I have is PR. That's the only thing that's saving me. And this fucking gag order. You let them have this fucking gag order."

Blanche tried to push back, but he was as weak as he was in the courtroom, helpless here to keep Trump from running again and again through the loop of his diatribe. Only briefly did Trump deviate, and this was just to include the other lawyers in his fury.

The full entourage returned for more bookkeeping-related testimony, everybody's eyes again getting heavy until Keith Davidson, the lawyer who had negotiated the payoffs to McDougal and Daniels (while at the same time in cahoots with Pecker and Cohen), brought Stormy Daniels, both her relationship with Trump and her importance to the case, into focus. As much as Davidson was there to confirm the cause-and-effect ticktock of key events, he, too, brought the spotlight back to the two-bit-hustler world from which this entire tangle had sprung. There was the crime and, as the prosecution clearly understood, the smell.

Davidson also became the way to introduce the *Access Hollywood* tape.

• • •

The *Access Hollywood* tape was central to the prosecution's case. Here was the moment that, beyond all other Trump political blasphemies in 2016—accusing John McCain of cowardice and insulting Gold Star families, among them—was surely and finally, in the view of almost everyone around Trump, going to sink the campaign. "Wave the white flag. It's over people," had noted the *Enquirer's* editor, Dylan Howard, about the Trump campaign, according to Davidson. Reince Priebus, then the head of the RNC, who would become Trump's first chief of staff, had shown up at Trump Tower and, in so many words, asked Trump to withdraw from the race. Not just political defeat, but personal ignominy—erasure!

This, then, had been the motivation to bury any further scandal, to save the campaign and Trump himself, according to the prosecution.

Conversely, though—again highly unlikely that the defense would make this case—*Access Hollywood* showed not his political vulnerability, but his sui generis *in*vulnerability. The *Access Hollywood* revelation was accompanied by a procession of women coming forward to graphically detail allegations of how he had abused them or, in Trump terminology, how he had "moved on them." His voters seemed at best unruffled by any of this. His wife, however, by many reports, was deeply embarrassed—and livid. And that was his fundamental argument—none of this was about election interference, but just family stuff. Of course, if so, wasn't his concern about placating his wife a political consideration, too? Then, and now, the Jackie O, give-no-quarter presence from which Melania, apparently, took some solace—her issues with her husband were perhaps not that different from Jackie's—seemed a key part of his personal insouciance and Teflon advantage. His Rat Pack behavior may not have been a political issue, but the same might not be said of the effect of Melania's walking out on him.

But *Access Hollywood,* if it had apparently left Trump voters unbothered, was resurfacing here now as a fathomless part of Trump lore: How, even as the #MeToo movement was taking flight, had Trump survived his bold declaration about celebrities such as he freely manhandling women? The prosecution was arguing that he had survived it by fraud. But that, as the defense was hotly aware, was pretext to revisit the scandal and to take the opportunity to punish him now for surviving it. The voters in 2016 had litigated this, and Trump had been found not guilty. Eight years later, a jury, presumably not one of Trump voters, had the opportunity to come to a different judgment. (Unfair!)

The defense had of course done everything possible to exclude the *Access Hollywood* tape, prejudicial as it certainly was. They had kiboshed a dramatic playing of the tape, but not a verbal recital of the tape's words, some of Trump's best known; nor would there be a limit to how much or how often the jury could be brought back to that moment in 2016 that, in a better world (at least a better world from the Manhattan view), should have finished Trump off.

Here again Blanche had miserably failed him. Trump had every basis to believe he had put *Access Hollywood* behind him. An electoral majority of Americans didn't care at all about it. How could Todd not have gotten this excluded? Its only purpose was to embarrass him. The only thing this trial was about was embarrassment. The judge was party to this—obviously. What did he even have lawyers for if they couldn't get rid of this? Why weren't they making the trial about this, this witch hunt to embarrass him? He wanted Blanche to stand up and give an angry and rousing speech as soon as *Access Hollywood* was mentioned. Hit them hard. But Blanche was weak. Once again, Trump repeated in his constant phone calls, he was being fucked by bad lawyers.

• • •

The day had begun with a story in the *Times* by its two top Trump reporters, Maggie Haberman and Jonathan Swan, based on unidentified sources, spelling out Todd Blanche's precarious position. The story itself was most certainly a purposeful leak—the familiar sound of a fateful Trump drumbeat. The day ended now with Haberman and the press-shy Susie Wiles spotted by another reporter, heads together, at a restaurant on the Upper East Side.

Wiles had carefully kept herself far from the press. This could be more about Blanche—more threatening messages from the boss to Blanche through the *Times*. But equally, even the reticent Wiles—working for a candidate both capricious and malevolent, who might turn against anyone at any moment—might want an escape hatch for her story.

CHAPTER 15

Get Shorty

MAY 2024

Each morning, Trump arrived in the courtroom hallway and, separated by an impromptu police barrier that created a caged effect, delivered a statement to the hall press pool, captive, too, in a different police cage, to catch these words. They were, pretty much, the same words every day. He was being gagged. He was being deprived of his rights. These experts—and here he carried a sheaf of papers printed out by Natalie—the greatest legal minds in the land, agreed with him. (He also continued to complain to Natalie that he didn't have time to read all these experts.) Trump tread the line of the gag order by quoting them rather than saying it himself or, when called on that, by virtually quoting them by saying he could not quote them. The prosecution was monitoring him closely.

The looming problem for Judge Merchan of Trump's reflexive-seeming disregard of the gag order and of the prosecution's calls for new contempt charges against him was how to enforce a contempt ruling. Merchan could continue to fine Trump the thousand dollars per instance, and Trump could continue to go on in his merry, vituperative manner, making quite a mockery of the court and of Merchan. Or there was jail. In this regard, there could be—probably would be—insurmountable logistical problems, certainly a complex negotiation with the Secret Service, which would likely result in one of the most expensive and cosseted incarcerations on record. Nelson Mandela in silk chains and an all-you-can-eat fast-food buffet. It was likely, too, to instantly become the central event of the campaign—the ultimate reality star challenge.

Then, too, there was the actual constitutional dilemma. Donald Trump, after all, *was* running for president. One of the primary arguments of his campaign, whether his opponents liked it or not, was that the legal attacks on him were an effort to keep him from being president. Hence, political speech. His attacks on the court, judge, witnesses, and jury were, he argued, part of the case he was making, and not being able to make that case was directly interfering with his ability to run for president.

In the third week of the trial, lawyers were stunned to hear Natalie—whose provocations were largely responsible for the gag order in the first place—offer a solution: She would post his attacks under her own name.

"I'll go to prison," she announced. A bewildered legal team stared at her as though she had three eyes in her forehead.

. . .

Elmore Leonard's *Get Shorty* is about a savvy mafioso loan shark who decides he'd like to be a film producer, not all that dissimilar from the real estate developer/reality TV star who decides he'd like to become president. Each of the characters in *Get Shorty* functions in an ecosystem of workaday self-interest and casual betrayal. To the extent possible, everybody is comfortable with their role as the bigger or lesser unscrupulous man in a complicated food chain. Nobody questions their relative morality or values. It's a not entirely unpleasant inverted world of moral cause and effect. Yes, everybody is screwing everybody else, but there is some respect and understanding of the craft of screwing. At some point in the immersion into this often-genial stew of shady operators, it's the outside world, the middle-class world, that starts to seem so much less interesting, sharp, and real.

. . .

Keith Davidson, with brilliantine hair and rosy Irish cheeks, an overage altar boy, seemed glumly resigned to a bright light on his dubious life as he continued on the witness stand.

He was an L.A. fixer or connector or middleman with a law degree—and a bar suspension to prove it—whose sleazy clients had information that could make life difficult for sleazy celebrities if they didn't pay up, with Davidson taking a cut. His targets had included Hulk Hogan, Lindsay Lohan, Charlie Sheen—and Donald Trump.

The question, though, and a not inconsiderable threat to the case, was about how much of Donald Trump's fundamental sleaziness, and extraordinary life on the other side of public morals, had been long figured into the market. His base, for sure—who among them was going to be turned by the tawdry details, many of them the same old tawdry details that had been aired so often before? This jury, this microcosm of disapproving Manhattan, who might well dislike Trump as much for his tawdriness as for his policies, could finally hold him to moral account. But they, too, as likely could have long been inured to Trump exceptionalism. Might the disapproving majority have accepted its defeat? Yeah, Trump is a sleazebucket. All right already, but move on.

· · ·

If you were to write a Trump roman à clef, à la Joe Klein's *Primary Colors* (originally written anonymously), about the 1992 Bill Clinton campaign, with a main protagonist who was both captivated and eventually disillusioned, that protagonist would be former Connecticut gentry girl Hope Hicks. Except Klein's protagonist is a worthy reflection of liberal hopes and doubts. Someone like Hicks would be more confused than conflicted, and perhaps more interesting for it.

Hicks blithely took up duties in the Trump campaign at age twenty-five (reportedly to her mainstream Republican family's horror) because neither she nor anyone else thought it was going to be more than . . . an experience, a product promotion—and that's what she did; she was a PR girl and this was a publicity stunt. Why not? She had yet even to begin her real life. What could go wrong?

Then, when he was elected, she, with so many others disoriented by fate, went down the rabbit hole.

During the early denial phase, after the 2020 election, Hicks, like many in the White House, made herself scarce, and immediately after January 6, she fled altogether. Following a number of disastrous relationships with other staffers in her Trump years, she was now engaged to an older man, Goldman Sachs partner Jim Donovan, and had taken no further part in ongoing Trump fortunes. Indeed, she had since been replaced by various look-alike figures (or would-be look-alikes), including Molly Michael and Margo Martin and Natalie Harp. Hicks herself was a Melania look-alike. Precisely coiffed and made up on the witness stand, she had Melania's ageless former-model look—or, arguably, it was Ivanka whom she recalled, all Trump women blending into the same engineered mold.

Without political interest or expertise when she ascended to the White House—really, without any expertise about anything—Hicks became Trump's factotum and alter ego, pulchritude and an eagerness to please her only qualification and his only requirement. Even with the vaunted title of communications director, she was mostly a deer in the headlights, an agent of Trump's daughter and son-in-law and a nursemaid lackey to the president, her authority coming from her abject obedience.

She was here under subpoena. She surely did not want to be in this seat. Off the political and media grid since 2021, she had carefully disconnected from Donald Trump. And yet she had certainly not, like so many others from the Trump White House, disavowed him in any way. And, curiously, it was quite possible to believe she had personal affection for him. Trump treated the people who worked for him very badly, except if you were very beautiful. Hicks had been lifted out of obscurity and young adulthood and unskilledness and put on the world stage by Donald Trump, valued by him and his family. (And for this, you could have the decency not to publicly criticize him!)

Anyway, here she was, nervous and quaking. She was poised and beautiful, and the media tended to promote her to cool professional. But panic had always surrounded her, with her eyes darting and with a

What am I doing here? bubble hanging over her head. Now this porce-
lain fragility affirmed her credibility, as did the way she looked. Beauty
and vulnerability—this was the look of public Trump women (versus
the private look of his strippers, Playboy bunnies, and beauty pageant
contestants), a Disney princess brushing up against Trump's sordid
world.

Hicks was the person first alerted that the *Access Hollywood* tape was
about to be exposed and aired. A *Washington Post* reporter sent her the
transcript. Here was Trump the misogynist, degenerate, gross guy. It was
a political code red, with she and everybody else equally shocked and
confused. But one did not have to pass judgment, this was politics:
Trump's gross sex life didn't count if it could be managed and handled.
And, however amazingly, it *was* handled. It didn't bring him down.

Shortly after *Access Hollywood*, there was another report of bad stuff,
and Hicks reached out to Michael Cohen. Cohen was the fixer; Hicks
was the handler.

The prosecution was pumping some smoke here. Covering up secret
dalliances, high or low, isn't illegal; it's politics. And that was precisely
the point. A cover-up is a cover-up—you're doing it to fool people. The
beautiful Hicks explained the Trump approach: deny, deny, deny, handle, and fix. In her testimony, she set herself into the greater context that
was key to the prosecution's case—that all this was part of a political
operation, and that operation was to run for president.

There was another subtext here, a lingering pollen in the air. It was
about not only handling and fixing what Trump had done but also handling the fact that he was going to lie openly about it. There wasn't even
the blurry optics of a Bill Clinton threading the needle of contrition
without quite an admission. Through Hicks's stoic—though, do we
sense the faintest exasperation?—resignation to her boss's denial of the
obvious, we get a good sense of what Trump demanded to be accomplished. He drew a line that, no matter how preposterous, had to be
followed: Nothing of any sort had ever happened, none of it, ever.

And then we got to the predicate lie to the specific criminal act, the
conspiracy to falsify the business records. Michael Cohen had paid
Stormy Daniels, Trump told Hicks, "out of the kindness of his heart and

never told anyone about it." To Hicks, who like everyone else around the Trump political operations, found Cohen to be a particularly odious sleazeball character, this was risible and ridiculous. There were no bagmen with hearts of gold, particularly not Michael Cohen.

That's where the prosecution left it: Trump trying to gull, and none too credibly, even the trusting Hicks.

Then, on the stand, when the defense began its cross-examination, Hicks broke down. The beautiful woman cried. How much were tears on the witness stand, that sign of true feeling, worth? The tears read as a dam breaking. Hicks said what the law required her to say about the boss who, no matter what complicated feelings she seemed to have, she had no desire to hurt or betray—and now she felt terrible for it. The tears confirmed that the admissions she had made here were ones she did not want to make, that she would get nothing for making them, and that emotionally and perhaps otherwise, they had cost her heavily.

"Was Hope good for me?" Trump focus-grouped afterward in a phone call to a New York lawyer (one, who, on other occasions he had often asked to take over the case). "Was she good for me?" He was asking the question to get an answer the opposite of the one he very clearly recognized to be the true one.

• • •

Over the weekend, Marco Rubio, Tom Cotton, and Doug Burgum—VP wannabes—turned out for the Sunday morning network public affairs shows to defend Trump.

The point here was twofold. This was an audition for VP. As much as any vetting was going on, Trump was watching and judging. Certainly, if he didn't like you on television, you were out.

But the other point was that this was part of his real defense. Not Blanche, Bove, Stern, and Necheles, but how he was defended on television. Amid the daily rhythm of the trial, and what seemed to be the prosecution's meticulous building of their case, the Trump campaign forced its eyes back on the prize: There was only one final verdict, and that was on November 5.

. . .

As the week began, two longtime Trump accountants took the stand, Jeffrey McConney and Deborah Tarasoff. Everyone knew everyone in the close-knit office of Trump Org, with its flattened hierarchy, where Mr. Trump was the singular boss. And the boss's main management proscription to his accountants seemed to be: Don't pay the bills. Dispute, stall, finagle, screw.

The accountants' evidence was dry—and damning. Michael Cohen would be reimbursed for $130,000 in expenses he had incurred on Trump's behalf. It was not, however, to be paid as an expense reimbursement. Rather, he was to invoice it for legal services. Unlike an expense reimbursement, this would be taxable as income (at an approximately 50 percent rate, given federal, state, and city taxes). Hence, the figure would be "grossed up," in the handwritten marginalia of Allen Weisselberg, the Trump CFO, to double the amount, to compensate Cohen for the tax hit. In sum: falsifying business records, baldly so.

. . .

Risking more contempt, Trump helplessly posted early on the morning of May 7 that he'd just learned who the day's witness would be, and he was ripping mad. He didn't say who, and the post was deleted minutes later, but the cat was out of the bag: Stormy.

Among the many battles of the Trump years, his face-off with Stormy Daniels had been one of the constants. Try as he might to get her to go away—through payoffs, nondisclosure agreements, direct attacks, name-calling, lawsuits, even judgments against her—he hadn't shaken her. The porn star and low-rent playboy president seemed appropriately fused, each defining the other.

Daniels wrote a memoir of her life and her historic encounter, however brief, with Donald Trump. The memoir was arranged by her then lawyer, Michael Avenatti, as another way to monetize her experience, and pay his bills. (Avenatti, one more comet-like character across the Trump universe once discussed as a possible Trump-like presidential

candidate himself, was so visible on television and facile in his performances that Trump, during this period, was openly irritated that Avenatti was not *his* lawyer. He was also even more of an extreme sleazeball
than those already connected to this mess, and indeed, he is now in
federal prison.) The fact that there was a memoir goes to the already
wayback nature of this.

The book affirms that Stormy, head seldom too far above water, had
been hustling all her life—so, no reason not to suspect that she was hustling Trump. And if there were any question, it goes to his character and
judgment that he wouldn't have shown some caution in spending time
with her. Of course, that was in another lifetime, during his life as a
beauty pageant promoter and reality star, when caution was not necessarily required. At any rate, he continued to hotly insist that there wasn't,
that he didn't—absolutely not. But of course, the fact that money was
paid reasonably indicates that she certainly had damaging material, and
the memoir certainly supports, with choice details, the claims that they
were alone together with the intention of having sex. The most famous
story involves Stormy spanking Trump with a rolled-up magazine. But
there are two other brilliant pieces. During one encounter, he takes a
phone call from . . . wait for it . . . Hillary Clinton and then, to Stormy,
extols Hillary's many virtues. In another, he explains the method and
purpose, and admits to the ludicrousness, of his hair: It makes him stand
out, he acknowledges with reasonable self-awareness. Daniels's portrait,
in fact, is of quite a humanized Trump. He's eager to be liked, he's com-
municative, and he doesn't take himself too seriously—given everything,
not such a bad egg.

It didn't matter to the charges at hand if Stormy Daniels and Donald
Trump had had sex, just that he'd wanted to cover up her claim that they
had. Even to the extent that she could be discredited for, in addition to
being a porn star, trying to squeeze her brief encounters with Trump for
as much notoriety and money as possible, that didn't much change the
fact that he *had* paid her off. An apparent view when the Justice Department considered charges (difficult in any event, because this would have
involved indicting a sitting president) was that everyone involved lacked
credibility. But, as with so many of the prior witnesses, the New York

prosecutors seemed to regard the discreditable nature of everybody involved as their friend—they were following the sleaze directly to the
White House. The sleaze of Stormy and friends implicated Trump in his
own sleaze, which if exposed—some imagined tipping point of just too
much sleaze, even for Donald Trump—would have impacted his political prospects and so, by the by, had to be covered up. Indeed, what else
had his sleazy cover-up operation been for?

· · ·

Stormy is all undirected energy on the witness stand, her glasses on top
of her head, her streaked hair askew, mascara and blush not necessarily
hiding her age—forty-five now; twenty-seven when her Trump encounter occurred.

Trump's fury that she is here, confronting him, is not entirely mis-
placed. She doesn't particularly connect any evidentiary dots. Payment
to her has been established. She can offer no facts about the bookkeeping ledger, nor particularly about his real motives for not wanting her
story to come out—beyond "who would?" She is here to embarrass him.
The defense furiously argues this point and does so before a judge who
seems personally squeamish and even offended that such tales might
come into his courtroom. He makes an effort to separate the facts from
the story. But that's futile. Daniels rushes through, unrestrainable. We
are in the Lake Tahoe suite. As memorable as anything to her, and perhaps as damaging as the sordid details, is the size of the suite—certainly
in the movies, a suite of this size would effectively indicate a character
only up to no good. Then there's the silk pajamas; the spanking; Trump
recumbent, expectedly waiting for her, on the bed in his boxer shorts;
and no condom. All there.

Surely, the effort to hush up this evening is among the worst-spent
$130,000 (or "grossed up" $260,000) on record.

Daniels's book spends some delighted details on Trump's genitalia,
and the legal team feared a persnickety back-and-forth about the particulars of Trump's penis, which even a tolerant Trump heartland, along
with late-night shows, might have hee-hawed at. But the judge takes

pains to foreclose genitalia details and, indeed, anything else about the sexual act other than its having happened. He seems as close to anger as he has come when Daniels mentions the missionary position and lack of a condom.

No matter; there are lasting images here. Can a jury remove from its mind the large man on the bed posed invitingly in his boxer shorts waiting for the porn star to emerge from the bathroom?

Daniels somewhat re-shades if not reshapes the story from her book. There, in the book, the seduction is mostly inept, with the implication that she's there for a celebrity experience. Now, on the witness stand, it's darker. She doesn't go so far as feeling threatened, but she goes to a "power imbalance." And for a few seconds, she blacked out, she now says.

If he's picking anything out as the particular focus of his fury, it is this—not so much that they didn't have sex (although, of course, in his version they didn't), but that now he is being cast "like Weinstein," he fumes to his lawyers, naturally blaming them. (In a sense, Trump and Weinstein have always been linked, with one abuser ending up in prison, the other in the White House.)

Trump lays into his lawyers for not objecting. "You're just sitting there. You're taking it. Jump up! Object. Did you ever hear the word *object*? Do you know how to do that? Say it. Say it. 'I object.'"

Among his lawyers—Blanche, Bove, Necheles, Stern, in a line in front of him—there is uncertainty over whether this is rhetorical or if they should actually say it now.

"I object," Trump repeats and once again, the lawyers register that they have never before quite been spoken to this way by a client, even the worst of their clients. "Can you say that? Can anyone say that? You jump up and you say, 'I object.' That's all you have to do."

Blanche explains that the judge has already ruled that her report of being frightened is admissible. But Trump continues: He doesn't care what the judge has said. Object anyway.

A chastened Blanche, voice rising in indignation almost to a squeak, makes a hapless motion for a mistrial. At which point, piling insult on injury, the judge lectures the Trump attorneys on their inexplicable failure to object to Daniels's rapid-fire delivery of salacious details—in the

same way that Trump is unsubdued by decorum and rules, so is the porn
star. (In one instance, the judge enters his own objection.)

Of the various potential holes in Daniels's story, the largest is a detail
that seems to have crept in along the way in the years of her telling this
tale: Shortly after an early conversation about going public, she says, she
was threatened by an unidentified man in a public parking lot. She
didn't tell anyone about it, and no one was ever identified. Trump called
her out here as a liar, and on this point she may well be, and prompted
by Avenatti, she sued Trump for defamation. In what quickly became an
unequal pissing contest, Stormy couldn't mount a case and ended up
stuck with Trump's legal fees.

This is the point where the defense's cross-examination enters.

• • •

Susan Necheles had been the third string of the Trump defense for most
of the year. A lesser string is a better place to be. Her earlier colleague in
this case, Joe Tacopina, had been blamed for the E. Jean Carroll loss and
traduced and abandoned (with bills unpaid) by his client, and was now
busily briefing against Trump to the press. Necheles had hung on, more
or less reluctantly, and on several occasions had refused to put her name
to Trump's more obnoxious motions. Part of Necheles's background was
as a defender of organized crime figures, but even that may not have
prepared her for Trump's rages at her colleagues and at her. Indeed,
Trump returned frequently to how she'd lost the Allen Weisselberg
case—which he'd paid for.

"You really messed that case up, completely winnable, but no, you
lose it." This was virtually an everyday riff, but always as though he were
saying it for the first time.

What was he paying her for, anyway? And whatever it was, it was too
much, he'd regularly announce.

"If you're giving me too much, I certainly haven't seen it," she muttered back at him in a tense moment.

But now, at the apex of the trial, and as the only woman on Trump's
team, she was up, facing Stormy Daniels, womano a womano.

In conventional trial terms, using a woman counsel to question a woman on the stand is meant to engender some perception of mutual understanding, even rapport or the illusion of it. But while Trump may have been persuaded to have the woman lawyer question the woman witness, he still wasn't going to be happy with anything but a kill. Here was, after all, one of the most persistent opponents of his political life.

Necheles, a small, intense figure with something of an unnatural tan, charged forthwith into her cross in contemptuous and accusatory style—and in Trump's television lawyer ideal. Again, Perry Mason. Always Perry Mason. Trump was explicit: He wanted Stormy "taken down"; he wanted her "destroyed"; he wanted her "flattened so she'd never get up again." He wanted to destroy her quite apart from any trial strategy or how this might play to the jury.

He had denied having sex with Stormy for so long that maybe he believed it and had become ever more righteous about it. In fact, some in the Trump circle had always believed there was the possibility of a technical truth here. (He'd denied Karen McDougal, too, but never so vociferously.) Steve Bannon speculated that Trump had "failed to launch." And, therefore, he was telling the truth. It hadn't happened. But, of course, Daniels was wedded to her story of their having had sex, and he wasn't now going to undermine her story by saying they hadn't because he couldn't. The effort in court was to question Daniels's broader credibility and to make Trump the victim of an audacious extortion racket by a money-hungry stripper and her corrupt lawyer.

Coming out of the gate, Necheles went to Daniels's description of Trump's hotel suite—homing in on the black-and-white tiles Daniels recalled. And, suddenly, it felt like a television moment where, in short order, we would learn that they never were black-and-white, that Daniels's description was at dramatic odds with reality—a lie. But, in fact, all that this elicited were further details of the gauchely sized suite. Again and again, Necheles tried to circle back to the encounter, trying to draw contrasts and contradictions with the way Daniels had told the story at various points over eight years. Other than minor quibbles, she managed mostly to draw attention only back to the details of the encounter itself.

And even if Necheles had shaken the fundamental sex story, the $130,000 *had* been paid, presumably for something, and the records had been fudged to pay it. But she didn't shake the basic story. She quite memorialized it. And, too, in her effort at a scornful and dismissive cross-examination, she fortified a perception of the merciless billionaire hammering the feckless sex-worker witness.

After court, Trump lost it—full bulging eyes treatment: "They're try-ing to say I raped her. You're coming back to that and making it sound like I did. You're drawing her out and keeping her on the stand. She's just repeating everything. She's a lying scumbag, and I never had sex with her, and you keep letting her say I did. Why are you going into all this? You keep going into it. Is this your strategy? What kind of strategy is this? You're losing it, completely. You're making *her* look sympathetic. She's a scumbag, and you're making her look good. Do you know that's what you're doing? Do you see that? Everybody else sees that. How can you not see that?"

Nope, not a chance, was the general consensus about whether Nech-eles would ever get paid for this case.

• • •

Shortly following Daniels was Madeleine Westerhout, one of Trump's personal assistants in the White House, offering, along with Hicks, that particular contrast among Trump's women: on the one hand, Stormy Daniels; on the other hand, the classy look, long straight hair worn loose, the good posture, the symmetrical features. (Because all Trump girls looked like this, it could seem less classy and more fetishistic.)

Midway through the Trump presidency, Westerhout had been out one night in Washington, gotten drunk, and publicly dissed the Trump family—and posthaste, she was turned out of the White House. Wester-hout, too, was a figure of Trumpworld speculation: There was the Christ-mas when Trump did not go with his family to Palm Beach, but stayed in the White House and kept Westerhout there.

If you were reading things closely, she was one more reminder that, contrary to the legal line that this was a case fundamentally about business records, it was *actually* a case fundamentally about women, Trump's women. From *Access Hollywood* grabbing them by the pussy, to an outpouring of accusations, to the Karen McDougal and Stormy Daniels cover-up—not to mention, so very recently, to E. Jean Carroll, and to his wife's glaring absence from the campaign trail and from this trial (and her look-alikes on the witness stand).

Indeed, media reaction to the Stormy Daniels testimony, especially to this new version emphasizing her fear, and the possibility that she might have blacked out, had moved this from, bad enough, a one-night stand to in Trump's tantrum: "The R-word! They are using the R-word! This has got to be stopped. We need to stop this! We need to sue!"

Blanche was delegated to write a threatening letter to any outlets threatening to push the rape version of his Stormy Daniels enounter.

· · ·

Part of the on-the-fly planning for the Manhattan trial and Trump's restricted campaign schedule was to do a rally in Madison Square Garden at some point as the trial progressed, with a suggestion of Trump supporters storming Manhattan and bringing their implicit threats to the heart of the elite. This was John Paulson's particular idea and Trump was all in on it. But Trump rallies usually cost between $250,000 and $500,000, and the cost of renting Madison Square Garden turned out to be $3 million. Instead, the main trial rally was moved to Wildwood, New Jersey, a lower-middle-class shore resort—*Jersey Shore* having become part of the Trump aesthetic—which drew north of forty thousand on the weekend before Michael Cohen, the prosecution's star witness, was to appear in court. (Trump was late, the wind on the beach was sharp, and the crowd had dramatically thinned by the time he appeared. The Trump team claimed a hundred thousand and the AP said it would accept that number if a city official confirmed it—the Trump team thereupon produced an agreeable supporter in the Wildwood city government to vouch for one hundred thousand.) Trump spoke, happily retelling a collection of some of his classic ramblings, including his Hannibal Lecter tale. While this might have seemed like a bewildering and misguided gambit when he first happened upon it during his talk at John Paulson's fundraiser, now it had entered the canon. (Was he possibly confusing asylum seekers with people *coming from* asylums?)

CHAPTER 16

What Makes Sammy Run?

MAY 2024

Gedalia Stern, banned for a week for using Trump's bathroom, was back in the entourage, which had been, until now, uncharacteristically thin. In step, too, with Trump were U.S. senator and VP possibility JD Vance, of Ohio; Senator Tommy Tuberville of Alabama; Congresswoman Nicole Malliotakis from New York; Alabama attorney general Steve Marshall; and Iowa AG Brenna Bird. While each was hungry if not desperate in their ambition, here they took on the cast of the Secret Service detail—faceless, waiting, dutiful. The supplicant entourage was followed by Boris Epshteyn, Eric Trump, Jason Miller, Alina Habba, and Natalie Harp. In the hallway cage, Trump stopped to call attention to the *New York Times* poll released that morning. Rather than reflecting the fallout of four weeks of trial and the daily news about his sleazeball life, the poll instead was devastating to Joe Biden, showing him meaningfully trailing Trump in five of six key swing states. *Were the election held today . . .*

• • •

"The people call Michael Cohen . . ."

Along with Stormy Daniels's memoir of her life and her encounter with Donald Trump, as a contribution to Trump literature there is Michael Cohen's published account of his life: growing up on Long Island in the "Five Towns" Jewish enclave; craving nothing more than material wealth; aspiring to a mobster ethos; becoming enthralled by and suborning himself to Donald Trump's whims and orders; subjecting himself to Trump's punishments and rewards; and turning himself into Trump's bagman and enforcer, including handling his payoffs to threatening women and, as well, threatening the women back. Then he was turned out by Trump and prosecuted by the Trump Justice Department, landing in a federal prison. There is no indication of a ghostwriter for the book, but it reads as if it were written by Budd Schulberg, author of *What Makes Sammy Run?*, as a classic American cautionary tale of greed, deception, and betrayal (and of not studying hard in school)—which, of course, might also describe Donald Trump.

Cohen presents himself as wholly repentant. And yet the story he tells in his book—repeating it nearly to the letter on the witness stand—is of a truly and, hard not to discern, proudly loathsome character. Cohen would, he testifies, do anything he had to do, and do it with relish, to get what he (or Trump) wanted—Cohen himself always wanting what Trump wanted. Therefore—and the defense would surely be looking to hammer on this—why would he not repent, too, and with relish, if that were necessary? Indeed, you have the most abject Trump ass-lick and gofer, the worst kind of soulless, groveling movie-script suck-up, who, in the blink of an eye (and a thirteen-month prison stint), becomes Trump's worst nightmare, a rabid dog bent on ripping him to pieces, and also now an avenging angel of anti-Trump Manhattan. (Cohen is a figure reliably spotted wandering near his home on Manhattan's Upper East Side.)

The prosecution has paved the way for Michael Cohen to be, in full, a despicable lowlife. No witness yet has uttered a good word about Michael. Almost everybody seems involuntarily to express their horror at such a creature—actually recoiling on the witness stand. But, as intended, when Cohen comes to the stand, he doesn't seem as bad as all that. He seems ordinary and long-suffering and caught up in circumstances that, if not quite Kafkaesque, are certainly pretty crazy.

Cohen tells his practiced story. From Long Island to Manhattan, a young man in a hurry, a young man on the way up, a lawyer, but not really wanting to be a lawyer, wanting to be . . . cooler, richer. Lawyering is long and hard. Michael Cohen wanted something fast and loose. Michael Cohen wanted to grow up to be . . . a sleazeball.

But more to the point—this is really *the* point—if you think Michael is bad, Trump seems infinitely worse. Trump, as Cohen relates, makes people bad. He turns them. You cannot be good around Donald Trump. You cannot stand up to him. His giving and taking are so constant and extreme that you are forced into a state of fear and obsequiousness. This is whipped-dog stuff—that's Cohen. (Pay no attention to his own sideline as a swaggering bully.) Trump is a groomer—that new word to describe a skilled and heartless manipulator.

What the prosecution might hope for here is for each person on the jury to imagine themselves in proximity to Trump. They might, it is true, say, why didn't Michael Cohen stand up for himself? Why did he take it? But a reasonable bet, too, is that, speaking to everyone's fears—about bad bosses everywhere, really nasty pieces of work, cruelty for the sake of cruelty, sadists, sociopaths—the message is clear: *There but for the grace of God . . .*

And the evidence?

The immediate picture is that Michael Cohen had no independent life from Donald Trump. Again and again, throughout the business day and beyond, he presented himself to Trump with every detail of what he'd accomplished in Trump's name and, often, every humiliation he'd meted out in Trump's name (while he himself was being humiliated by Trump). There is nothing that Michael Cohen did on Donald Trump's behalf that he, Donald Trump, didn't know. Having his fixer fix, having his thug brutalize, was what gave him pleasure.

Therefore, as Michael Cohen engaged in a paroxysm of pursuing and confirming and nailing down payments and documentation, no detail too small in the complicated choreography of arranging payoffs—all documented in the trail of phone calls, texts, emails—Trump was getting a vicarious thrill. He was in the game, too.

Once again—and this might be one of the lasting takeaways for the jury—Trump was hoisted by his own cheapness. If he had not stiffed David Pecker for the payoffs to the doorman with the illegitimate-Trump-child story and then for Pecker's payoffs to Karen McDougal, he might likely have avoided much of the mess he's in. No honor among thieves is a doubly slimy look. And then the thieves all turning on one another . . . Eeech! If Trump is no worse than Michael Cohen, if you want to grant him that, he is certainly no better—Pecker, Davidson, Cohen, Trump.

The bad-guyness of Trump, hardly a secret, is succinctly gathered here in one place. He likes to screw anyone over whom he has an advantage—this is virtually a business model. He belittles his children. He regards his wife (indeed wives) as disposable (really, how long would he remain single if he divorced Melania? he rhetorically wonders). He lies casually, chronically, and gleefully. And, not least of all, he employs someone like Michael Cohen.

The other curious point is that the lawyers currently sitting with Trump are now face-to-face with the lawyer who once sat with him. (A creepy point Cohen makes is that Trump never allowed anyone to come into the space behind his desk.) How can they not put themselves into Cohen's shoes? A lawyer who faithfully works for Trump is utterly ruined by his faithfulness and by Trump's disregard. Indeed, already all of them have been vilified and traduced over and over again by Trump. How do they not recognize at least some of the picture Michael Cohen has drawn of their client? How do they not, even fleetingly, consider Michael Cohen's fate as they consider their own?

Cohen's evidentiary purpose here isn't complicated. It's just to connect the dots.

Unable to get anyone else to pay the Stormy Daniels hush money, and with a deadline looming, and understanding that the fixer would be blamed if he didn't fix things, Michael shelled out the dough himself: $130,000. In this, he credibly establishes that Trump knew and approved. (Hope Hicks has of course testified that Michael Cohen would never have done anything out of the goodness of his heart.) But then Cohen goes through the follow-the-money machinations of getting paid back, which is where the crime occurred: Cohen and Allen Weisselberg went into Trump's office to hash out the reimbursement plan, immortalizing it on a page with notes in their own hand.

"Correct me if I'm wrong," one of the people in the Trump legal team texts to a journalist sitting several rows away in the courtroom. "Was that just the ballgame?"

* * *

Blanche, the weakest trial performer on the Trump team, had reserved the cross-examination of Michael Cohen for himself, a make-or-break moment for him as well as for Trump.

"On April twenty-third . . . you went on TikTok and called me a 'crying little shit,' didn't you?" said Blanche, charging out of the gate.

The jury, reliably impassive, for the first time seemed to come to attention as one, eyes up, pens out, everybody sitting forward.

"Sounds like something I would say," replied a composed Cohen after a moment.

Blanche went for more. A startled prosecution took several more beats before making the obvious objection.

Shortly thereafter, in a sidebar, Justice Merchan upbraided Blanche for putting his own interests front and center at the trial and, with the equivalent of a slap on the side of the head, instructed him not to.

Blanche retreated, deflated. He went from frontal attack to a much slower reframing of the story, poking for holes in the tangle of perfidious relationships and cross-purposes. A problem with the entire narrative of conspiracy, betrayal, counter-betrayal, and not just in the main plot, but in the several subplots—and with the various other prosecutions, pleas, and settlements that spun out of the web of machinations now meeting here, with, to boot, almost everyone involved being, by their very nature, an unreliable narrator—was that it was very hard to follow. You needed Elmore Leonard to guide you. This may be one of the prosecution's main accomplishments. By focusing on the sometimes tedious through line of the business records and the paper trail, this step-by-step connecting of the dots, they had largely avoided the frustrations and the muddle of who had betrayed whom and been done wrong by somebody else.

Blanche almost immediately found himself in this swamp, leading Cohen into it instead of out of it. The best that seemed to be gotten from Blanche's roundabout grilling was to establish that everyone involved had come to mortally hate one another and that, because no one could be remotely cool in the telling, no reliable story could emerge. This may have discredited Cohen, but it discredited Trump, too. Perhaps most of all, it discredited the defense for being unable to extract a clear storyline. When the prosecution led Cohen through his tale, many on the jury were taking notes. Now they sat back, perplexed by or uninterested in a story overshadowed and undermined and jumbled by the certain bile of everyone involved.

Cohen had loved Trump and then hated him. Trump had used Cohen and then had had no use for him. Yuck.

Blanche seemed to wander around among emotions and motives that were out of his affable, nice-guy reach. He had before him a true blood score, a lowlife drama, and he seemed small before it. The fight remained between Cohen and Trump—a pox on both their houses— with Blanche, although he had the floor and held Trump's proxy in the fight, hopelessly on the sidelines.

Cohen was very much still standing before the Wednesday break.

• • •

On Wednesday morning, outflanking whatever Trump might have planned for his day off, Joe Biden announced, in a carefully planned rollout, his willingness to debate: "I've received and accepted an invitation from @CNN for a debate on June 27th. Over to you, Donald. As you said: anywhere, any time, any place." At 8 A.M., both the *Times* and *The Washington Post* published embargoed stories about Biden's decision to debate (i.e., nothing spontaneous here). There was a video, too, from the Biden camp.

Trump, taking the bait and, as well, matters into his own hands, got on the phone with Brooke Singman, the Fox digital reporter whose looks he liked and whom he enjoyed calling direct. Without consulting his team, he was confirming his participation in the CNN debate.

The Biden camp had negotiated the full debate package to its satisfaction with CNN (excluding all the other networks—most notably Fox), and Trump had walked into it, heedless of the anchors (Dana Bash and Jake Tapper, whom he particularly despised) or the ground rules. What's more, Biden would do only two debates, whereas the Trump camp had wanted several more. By agreeing to the CNN debate, Trump had locked himself into the Biden schedule.

Meanwhile, the Biden camp was suddenly accepting ABC's proposal for a September date. On orders from Murdoch himself, Fox was in all-out beseeching and protesting mode to the Trump campaign . . . Don't agree to another debate until you get our proposal. It's coming, minutes away . . . But just at that moment, Trump was back on the phone with Fox's own reporter Singman, who would report that Trump, too, was accepting ABC.

The next hours were a succession of pleading calls . . . Hannity, Bret Baier, Suzanne Scott, with Rupert Murdoch and his son, Lachlan, urging stars and executives to call all their Trump contacts. It was the reverse of Election Night 2020, when the Trump campaign had had its designated entreators calling everyone at Fox to reverse the network's early decision to put Arizona in the Biden column, with the Murdochs snubbing them.

. . .

At eight o'clock on Thursday morning, the second day of Michael Cohen's cross, a dozen members of Congress, the front line of the House Freedom Caucus, the MAGA hard core, showed up at court, reporters googling to put names to faces. Many of them were more party crashers than invited guests.

The courthouse "party" had arguably begun the week before, with Rick Scott, a VP possibility, showing up. This had been portrayed as Scott's selfless and independent effort. But, in fact, Wiles had worked for

Scott's campaign; he was still her client, and she was actively pushing him as a VP possibility. (He was not the only Florida possibility; Marco Rubio was also high on Wiles's list.) Wiles, securing her future base in Florida as well as perhaps the White House, had also recruited House member Byron Donalds of Florida as a trial guest, hoping to run him for governor against her nemesis Ron DeSantis. Then, not to be outdone, there was North Dakota governor Doug Burgum, a VP wannabe; and the former presidential candidate Vivek Ramaswamy—following, in past days, the favored VP possibility JD Vance. Natalie, somewhat to the consternation of a Trump campaign staff still unsure if he was a MAGA friend or foe, reached out to Speaker of the House Mike Johnson, who, too, joined Trump's side. In a dramatic shift in emphasis, the trial had gone from a corrupt Democratic enterprise best ignored and disregarded to a Republican opportunity. Trump's harangues just prior to the nine-thirty start every morning and just after the four-thirty finish meant fifteen to twenty minutes of airtime a day. Now Matt Gaetz, not to be cheated of a press opportunity, organized this Freedom Caucus outing—all of them filling the Trump Tower lobby as they waited for several new vans to be added to the courthouse caravan.

At the criminal court building, a dozen or so guests, the contingent of lawyers, and the traveling staff filled the large exterior holding room until Trump invited everyone into the inner sanctum—he was at the head of the narrow table—creating the kind of bus station jostling around him that Trump particularly liked, twenty bodies inside a room that should have maxed out at a dozen.

There was now a competition to speak up, to offer praise. *We're with you, Mr. President.* Then the Freedom Caucus head, Congressman Bob Good of Virginia, took the official floor, leading the group bow and salutation, repeating much of Trump's own language—phony charges, witch hunt, Joe Biden's trial—with Trump, arms folded, happily having his own words piped back to him.

Trump then said, "Bob"—hesitating just slightly on the first name—"how's your race going?" Good was being primaried, and Trump had not yet endorsed him (and, indeed, would not endorse him!). Good had in fact endorsed DeSantis, which Trump might or might not have remembered. But the Trump campaign—LaCivita's fingerprints were here—in its continuing Florida blood score against DeSantis, had, in the interest of casual retribution or light comedy, inserted Good's opponent, John McGuire, into the group at the courthouse. (LaCivita, hating DeSantis and, too, the Freedom Caucus, had been actively lobbying Trump to give his endorsement to McGuire.)

"Things are going great, Mr. President. We're ahead by twenty-five. Great that you're forcing Biden to debate. My opponent won't debate me."

"That's wrong," piped up McGuire from the back of the crowd. "Totally wrong, Mr. President. I'm ahead by fourteen points. And my opponent has yet to endorse you—unlike myself."

"Oh, jeez, you guys are running against each other? Wow." Trump appeared surprised. "Who's going to win?"

"I'm ahead by twenty-five in the respected polls," Good said tightly.

"I'm ahead by fourteen—and I've always been with you. He's been totally DeSantis," countered McGuire.

The crowded room was frozen. But Trump could not seem to be more content.

"Twenty-five ahead," said Good.

"Fourteen," said McGuire.

"Twenty-five."

"Fourteen!"

$$\bullet \ \bullet \ \bullet$$

What continued to bother Trump most was not Cohen's damning testimony, but the judge's gag order.

Trump was demanding that Blanche once again start the court day by confronting Judge Merchan in another challenge to the gag order. It was the same old, same old: his rights, free speech, the Constitution, unfair . . . unfair. "Michael Cohen is saying these terrible things about me," Trump repeated to virtually everyone. "How come I can't say things about Michael Cohen? Why doesn't he have a gag order, if I have a gag order? This is unfair. This is unfair." The Trump whine was whiplike.

This was, in part, global strategy. Trump's pushback, attacks, slurs, depredations, were his way of politicizing the trial, of extending the drama outside the courtroom and into the media sphere, mano a mano. But it was also a personal need. He was a musician prevented from making music. Helpless in court, his eyes so frequently closed, he wasn't able to be the quick, menacing, audacious, protean, entertaining self he was when out of court.

Again, if he'd said it once, he would say it a thousand times: His legal strategy was his PR strategy; his PR strategy his legal strategy. What happened in court wasn't worth a hill of beans compared to what happened out of court.

He was deputizing the great and good and slavish and ridiculous of the Republican leadership to say what he could not say. And yet, it wasn't the same. They were dutiful but not wholly believable, nor truly threatening. (At the break, the group that day headed across the street for a press conference in the park. As Matt Gaetz spoke, a lone, piercing voice kept shouting, "Pedo, pedo," referring to the continuing investigations of the many allegations of underage girls in Gaetz's Florida lifestyle. When Lauren Boebert came up to the mic, another equally commanding voice kept shouting, *"Beetlejuice, Beetlejuice, Beetlejuice!"* referring to the musical during which Boebert notoriously and noisily groped her date, and was, in turn, groped by him, in a Denver theater, getting them both ejected.) Trump needed his voice back. They needed, once more, to fight the gag order.

Blanche resisted Trump: He wasn't going into court to blast the judge about the gag order that had already blown up in their faces. He wasn't going into his own personal star turn, trying to score with his cross of Cohen, with an angry judge inclined (more inclined than he already was) to knock him back. Blanche, impressing or shocking the other lawyers, faced down the boss.

"Then you fucking better destroy Michael," said Trump. "You better!"

• • •

Blanche's future well-being and livelihood appeared to those around the Trump trial entourage to hang on his ability to pull a rabbit out of a hat and produce a television-ready courtroom moment. The face-off was clear: an exasperated Todd Blanche, an imperturbable Michael Cohen. If Cohen remained cool, a steadfast witness for the prosecution, then . . . well, we were within days of Trump's likely conviction. The justice that so many had been waiting for so long was about to become a reality, barring a Perry Mason reveal.

But would conviction matter? Would the wave of House MAGA members jostling to be near him now desert him?

Clearly, they were here not just to lend their voices to the illegitimacy of this trial, but also to join the show. You could again split the screen: the serious implications of the criminal proceedings versus the get-into-the-picture (elbow-your-way-to-the-front-of-the-picture) political spectacle. Separate realities. A conviction would not likely dim the spectacle, but would instead add new energy and operatic breast-beating to it.

But all the defense needed was a hung jury. Trump had essentially hung the jury on Mueller and two impeachments, each somehow propelling him on. He would again be the man who had faced down the system and won. History could easily hang on a single juror.

That, on the penultimate day of testimony, was the thing Todd Blanche was looking for. Just enough doubt to unsettle one juror, enough to give one disagreeable juror, even a Manhattan juror, a passing cause that might carry him or her through the separate votes on the thirty-four individual counts.

Michael Cohen was, yes, a liar and a scumbag. The problem of emphasizing this—which, really, was the only thing Todd Blanche had to work with—was that it seemed inevitably to call attention to the fact that Trump had so specifically employed Cohen to be a liar and a scumbag. Cohen had been merely the instrument of the greater liar and scumbag. Blanche spent the day hammering at Cohen, threading through Cohen's long liar-scumbag trail, trying to separate the instances where he might have been working less as a liar-scumbag for Trump and more as a liar-scumbag for himself. Blanche scored here and there, splitting liar-scumbag hairs. Was Michael Cohen truly repentant, or was he merely vengeful—and was there a difference?

None of this changed the underlying facts, of course: Cohen had personally paid the money to Stormy Daniels and was repaid the dough in a transaction that involved falsified business records. That was cut-and-dried. An overwhelming circumstantial case, even without Michael Cohen's firsthand testimony, had been built to show that of course Trump had known, understood, encouraged, and approved this book-keeping ruse. Still, technically, in the realm of the infinite there was room—if Michael Cohen's testimony of direct conversations with Trump about the payments could be undermined—to sow at least a hypothetical case for a scintilla of doubt, if not exactly reasonable doubt.

By the end of the day, the scintilla seemed to come down to a single ninety-second phone call. Cohen said he had talked to Trump about the payments. The mostly mousy, stuttering, stammering Blanche, now in accusatory television style, doubted there would have been enough time on a call that began with Trump's bodyguard, Keith Schiller, who then, according to Cohen, passed the phone to Trump. Blanche proposed a theory that the conversation had been entirely about something else—indeed, that Trump had never been handed the phone—and for a second, Cohen hesitated, his certainty faltering. (Would history turn on that moment?)

"Todd, *that* was almost Perry Mason! Almost Perry," pronounced a pleased Trump to the relief of the team—putting Blanche back in the running for a future White House legal career.

. . .

It was closing in, the consensus both that Biden would need quite a miracle to recover—"Seven Theories for Why Biden Is Losing" and "The Dangerous Political Headwind Facing Biden" were two headlines in the *Times* on May 20, as the prosecution closed its case—and that Trump would be convicted.

The line-sitters, who were snagging front-of-the-queue spots by arriving at four or five in the morning, were now arriving the night before as the trial came to its end: Everybody was here.

Andrew Giuliani, Rudy's son, a low-level employee in the Trump White House and, briefly, a pie-in-the-sky gubernatorial candidate in New York, was out in front of the courthouse early in the morning, dressed in a baby-blue suit and matching shoes, speaking into an iPhone set up on a tripod.

Although it was a warm spring morning, the *Times*'s dedicated Trump reporter, Maggie Haberman, at the head of the line, was still in the many-seasons-old winter puffer jacket she had worn throughout the trial.

The Trump entourage, growing larger and more peculiar, arrived behind the courthouse in their van parade, tromping into court single file behind the defendant. On the part of staff and lawyers, it had become quite an effort to disavow having invited this or that particular oddball, which included the former, and long-imprisoned, head of the Hells Angels.

The internal consensus in the campaign and on the legal team was that Blanche had blown away Michael Cohen and, with him, the prosecutor's case.

Blanche, who might have ended on his Perry Mason high note, instead continued, on Trump's prodding, his cross-examination of Cohen into another day—the penultimate day of testimony. Whatever momentum he had established, he lost now. However much Cohen had seemed to falter, he was back in unshakable mode. However much of a sleazebag he was, the defense emphasizing this with every question, the likely lasting impression for the jury was that Trump had *made* him into one. Blanche's one score off Cohen in his final push was an odd one. In getting Cohen to admit that he had inflated the fee for what he had paid out of pocket to a digital firm to falsify (at Trump's instruction) an online poll—this, too, being "grossed up"—confirmed not just that Cohen, like Trump, was open to cheating anyone who could be cheated (in this case, both Trump and the digital firm), but also that, in fact, Trump was reimbursing Cohen, which was the substance of the charge.

The defense might logically have rested here, taking the position that there was no case even to rebut and calling no witnesses—a reasonable cover to Trump's not testifying for himself. Instead, the defense called Robert Costello, a lawyer in Rudy Giuliani's circle of retro tough-guy

New York characters and cigar bar drinkers. On the witness stand, Costello was obstreperous and openly hostile to the judge, muttering audible asides at each of Merchan's rulings. (At one dramatic point, in more of a television court flourish than an actual courtroom move, the judge ordered the courtroom to be cleared—whereupon he privately dressed down the witness.)

During Costello's testimony, a reporter in the court texted a member of the Trump legal team: "Who thought this was a good idea?"

"You have to ask?" was the Trumper's response.

The week before, Costello had appeared before a Republican-controlled House committee and slammed Michael Cohen. Alerted to Costello's passionate and partisan attack, Trump had ordered his team to bring him into court.

The exact purpose of the Costello testimony, other than to continue to besmirch Cohen, was to rebut the claim that Costello had been part of a Trump-and-Giuliani-led effort to pressure Cohen to keep quiet. The result of his testimony was to confirm a general thuggishness very much in keeping with an effort to silence someone.

And there the defense rested.

• • •

On Thursday, the court in recess for the Memorial Day break, the Trump campaign held a rally in the Bronx. Fox teased it throughout the day. Every other network carried it live, too. There were not the forty thousand people the Trump campaign suggested, but plausibly more like ten thousand people, dominated by African Americans, Hispanics, and Orthodox Jews, in a sea of red MAGA hats and under plumes of marijuana smoke; most, according to the campaign, attending their first Trump rally. Sheff G was among the guests. Although the rapper was under a 140-count indictment charging 27 acts of violence, including 12 shootings with 13 victims, 3 of whom were innocent bystanders, Trump invited him up onstage.

"Oh, I like that," said Trump, in a buoyant mood, fixated on Sheff G's diamond-studded teeth. "I wanna get that done."

• • •

Stephen Schwarzman, the founder of the Blackstone Group and worth forty billion or so, was a cautious corporate citizen and mainstream Republican billionaire. He had lent valuable support to Trump in the early days of his administration, a sign of establishment willingness to overlook Trump's rhetoric and behavior. But Schwarzman had eventually retreated from the Trump White House and had come to stand squarely with the establishment's resistance to another Trump go-round. But on Friday, he offered his support again.

Over the weekend, Schwarzman appeared at billionaire art dealer Larry Gagosian's Memorial Day billionaire party in his 11,000-square-foot Charles Gwathmey–designed house on the beach in the Hamptons, kicking off the 2024 summer. Schwarzman's fellow billionaires seemed glum over his endorsement of Trump, but virtually all were in agreement that little, including Trump's imminent felony conviction, could get in the way, five months from Election Day, of Trump's victory over Joe Biden.

• • •

Trump himself seemed to spend much of the holiday weekend rage-posting his own rebuttal to the trial. It was all the fault of Alvin Bragg and of a corrupt judge. And what was the issue, huh? He'd paid a lawyer, and those payments were called legal expenses. Lawyer . . . *legal expenses!*

• • •

The defense, returning from the weekend, went for two and a half hours in its closing argument. Blanche, the weakest on his feet among the defense lawyers, claimed this one anyway. He reprised his basic performance to date—halting, perplexed, not in firm control of his voice, with a dry mouth and stiff movements. His was a scattershot review of the five weeks of testimony. The prosecution had erected quite a fortress; he was trying to assail small pieces of it. He had no edifice of his own to erect, no new and dramatic way to recast the story. He might have told a tale of a man named Trump and of his many weaknesses, and of how he had been relentlessly victimized for it by a collection of grifters. Trump had done what he did—had made the payments, fudged the records—because he had lost control of the situation. There the jury might have found some sympathy for the defendant. But Blanche couldn't tell that story, because he couldn't make that admission. He was between a rock (a client incapable of putting himself or having himself put into any vulnerable position) and a hard place (the prosecution's brick-by-brick case of malfeasance, turpitude, and cover-up). He was left with his client's singular and all-purpose defense—indeed, one that, defying all odds, had continued to regularly work for him: deny, deny, deny even the undeniable. Again and again, Blanche connected Michael Cohen to the word *liar*. He seemed to exhaust himself making the connection. Michael Cohen, liar. Blanche's voice rose and cracked on that note. And he went on, denying every damaging aspect of the prosecution's case. Donald Trump was a virtuous individual doing everything by the book, and everybody else was a vile, lying cheat.

The entire Trump family was in court. Well, almost: Don Jr., Eric (with his wife, Lara, the RNC co-chairman), and Tiffany. But not Ivanka, nor—and by now there was no expectation—Melania (nor Barron, whose mother, reportedly, was intent on keeping him away). The Democrats, a day late and a dollar short, had organized a Biden rally in the park across from the courthouse. For more than six weeks, Trump had been on trial, held captive on their territory, and the Dems were only now getting around to grabbing some airtime out of it. The Trump campaign heard through one of the many cops on Trump duty that Robert De Niro would be the rally speaker. Could they be that lucky? An eighty-year-old man sent out to defend an eighty-year-old whose primary negative was his age. Not possible! But then it was. And this was not just De Niro, good citizen, dropping in; the Dems had put out a press release. This was planned! The Trump campaign quickly moved the several dozen MAGA-ites waiting at the back of the court for Trump's arrivals and departures (that is, there for him to see them) around to the front park just in time for De Niro's arrival . . . *wearing a mask!* The jeers began: *Four years too late, Bob! Covid's over, Bob. Have you heard? Covid, Bob! Four more years. Four more years!* Somehow, this shortly devolved into *De Niro's a pedo! De Niro likes boys!* Then, midway through the actor's remarks, as he made a tough-guy effort at Hollywood liberal fury, a car alarm—an old-style throwback one, from the bad old 1980s, the kind without an automatic-off timer—not ten yards away, a piercing honk alarm, repeating every five seconds, went off, overwhelming De Niro's hoarse screaming. Meanwhile, during the lunch break, the Trump side mobilized the family members on hand to counter the star attack. This all had the effect of an old-fashioned internecine New York neighborhood dispute—De Niro's downtown accent, the accent that had come to define that accent, against that of the uptown Trumps—to be resolved as though in front of a zoning board.

After lunch, the prosecution was up for its last shot, going with Steinglass, its strongest voice. Out of the gate, he hit the most basic and glaring weakness in the defense rebuttal, naming it as chutzpah: that the Trump side could brand Michael Cohen a liar on the basis of the lies he had told for and at the behest of Donald Trump.

This brought the central point back into focus. At the center of this story, you had a web of sleazeballs directly connected to Trump: David Pecker, Keith Davidson, Michael Cohen. (You could, of course, also include Stormy Daniels and Karen McDougal.) Nobody was clean, least of all *Trump*. It took quite some gall to try to establish his virtue up against their treachery.

The prosecution's problem was not that Trump might be guiltless, or that anyone in any universe would think he was, but rather, the fundamental sketchiness of the law. It was a case, after all, about fudged records—a crime, such as it was, that was very hard to care about. Strong case, flimsy law.

The prosecution had to overcome the fact that the fudging—the payments to the porn star for an NDA, characterized as legal expenses instead of, well, hush money (not an accounting category)—had been minor in nature, with no one being harmed. Trump Org was not even a public company. Yes, New York law, in contrast to federal law, was persnickety on this odd point about the particularity of records, and the prosecutors certainly had Trump on the fudge. Together with Michael Cohen's direct testimony, there was the overwhelming circumstantial case that Trump had known about and approved the fudge. But then, in order to convict on a felony, this fudge also needed to be in service to a further crime. Hence, the prosecution argued that Trump, or the people working for him and with his knowledge and assent, had falsified the records in an effort that violated a state election law that made it a crime to help an election by "unlawful means." You get in trouble for falsifying records, but you get into double trouble if, as in this case, it involves an election. In other words, the first small illegal thing gets credited to the bigger illegal thing—even though you haven't been charged with actually messing with the election. But, hell, if you were not convinced that the fudged records actually linked directly to the unlawful means of influencing the election, well, there were several other laws, including tax and election finance (none of them directly charged here), that you could argue had been broken as well. This was tenuous, but it was still important that this—broken law interlaced with another broken law—was the Gordian knot on which the jury focused and which they accepted, rather than seeing it more simply as an effort, of the kind made by so many politicians, to keep a dalliance from coming to light. You didn't want the jury to ask what the difference was between Bill Clinton's sex cover-up and Donald Trump's sex cover-up.

But, anyway, the law, the New York law, was the law—if you created phony records and that helped you in trying to win an election, you were a felon.

Still . . .

· · ·

What the prosecution has clearly hoped will overcome any natural skepticism or sense of the triviality of the actions is the vivid portrayal of corrupt intent—of all the players here engaged in such bad faith, flagrant dishonesty, unscrupulous behavior, and disregard of fair dealings, ultimately to Donald Trump's benefit and, more important, at his behest. And, in summation, the prosecution repeats in glorious detail just about every low move and underhand effort and relentless pattern of large and small screw jobs in the story. The bet is that the jury won't want to give a pass to this kind of behavior—behavior antithetical to every aspect of civil virtue *New York Times* readers and NPR listeners might value—and here, conveniently, they are presented with a law that can punish it.

Steinglass offers a compelling portrait of Donald Trump, one that, without the politics, without the MAGA identity, is immediately recognizable to all New Yorkers even casually acquainted with Trump's local antics and lack of pretense over past decades. He's a small-timer, a chiseler, a flimflam man, a scam artist, a conniver, and an all-around son of a bitch, morally a hollow man—nothing at all good about him except his rank shamelessness. In truth, as much as he has become for so many the moral albatross of our time, his crimes aren't big conspiracies. They are crimes of cutting corners and hiding little shit, loosey-goosey stuff and smoke and mirrors, and of just being good at getting away with it. But finally, here, his two-bitness is being called to account.

Anyway, as it has been for six weeks, it's an eye-opening story—if, over five and a half hours, a wearying one—and told well. Steinglass has a good voice—rising, falling, rolling along; conversational and then aghast; passionate; punctuated by witty or self-effacing asides. Finally, at eight o'clock in the evening, ten and a half hours after the court day began, six weeks after the trial started, a year after the indictment was first made, he wraps it all up and hands it back to the judge.

Judge Merchan spends an hour enumerating the particularities and the demands of the law and then hands the case to the Manhattan jury.

PART FIVE

The Path to Victory

CHAPTER 17

Felon

MAY–JUNE 2024

"How say you to the first count . . ."

"Guilty . . ."

One after the other, to the full thirty-four. His eyes closed.

"It probably didn't last more than a minute, but Jesus, time stopped," says one person in the Trump legal circle.

Each of the heretofore impassive jurors looks supremely satisfied and deserving—like they have seats at the Super Bowl.

Jason Miller, the reliable yes-man who always seemed to appear at Trump's side as soon as he emerged from the courtroom, is now heard pumping him with affirmation and script prompts: "This thing was completely rigged, total BS, sir. We'll be fighting this every step of the way. This is all just part of the fight against Biden—that's what the fight is about . . ."

Trump, flanked by Boris and Natalie as well as Miller, with Blanche behind him, is moving slowly and seems not to quite hear what's being said to him, requiring a gentle touch to steer him in the right direction. But in the cage before the hall press pool, he starts to hit his words, all of them the same as, or only minor variations on, what he has been saying every day for six weeks. But if the verdict has put him in a different place, his lines seem to restore him—certainty, belligerence, fury flooding back, reanimating him.

Meanwhile, Blanche, potentially the real loser here, is shrinking beside him. The small man beside the big man, his Sancho Panza role an unenviable one. Indeed, Blanche falls back, not leaving the courthouse with the entourage.

As they move out of the courthouse and to the motorcade waiting area, Trump's volubility returns. He repeats parts of what he has just said, all his speeches part of his ongoing monologue. To the small group waiting to disperse to the various cars—Trump is riding with Natalie—he says he's already hearing that his hallway speech is the best he's ever given. It's noted by those who have accompanied him from the speech, down through the courthouse, out to the cars, and then spreads in the Trump circle as a particular example of Trump's exclusive conversations with himself that he has not heard from anyone at all.

On the way uptown, he focuses on the "Blanche situation" and where they went now with that. Should we keep him? Trump's felony conviction reduced to a personnel problem. Unspoken here in the Trump circle, his fate front and center but never far from their own, is something of a fearful awe toward Blanche, the innocent who stepped so hopefully into harm's way, the only person who didn't understand his peril.

Uptown, there's a brief regrouping in Trump Tower. TV bookings are in progress. Trump is barking orders. Virtually every potential or would-be vice presidential possibility is put on notice. That is the instant strategy: Flood the zone, everybody repeating Trump's lines: Guilty, my ass. Rigged, rigged, rigged. Joe Biden. And the URL for donations—push it out. It's been ready to rake in dollars whichever way the verdict went. Blanche, who seems to have lost all his bearings, is necessarily drafted into continuing the battle—booking himself immediately with Jesse Watters on Fox and Kaitlan Collins on CNN and the *Today* show in the morning.

Blanche is given his orders: "We don't care what the question is . . . What color is the sky? How many kids do you have? . . . Your first answer is 'The jury just re-elected Donald J. Trump!' "

An instant poll in the *Daily Mail* gives Trump a six-point pop—gratefully delivered to him as proof of concept: The true jury is exonerating him. The URL, right away, starts spinning crazily. (Trump loves

online fundraising: "Like a Jerry Lewis telethon.") Numbers are brought
to him every five minutes. "Guilty" was worth it: In the first six hours,
they raise $34 million, $53 million in twenty-four hours.

Not two hours after his conviction on thirty-four felony counts, he
has time to change his shirt and, in an instance of the grinding nature of
politics and, surely, too, of Trump's own weird indomitability and wholly
external self, he is off to a fundraiser at the Upper East Side home of
Florida's billionaire sugar king, Pepe Fanjul.

At eleven the next morning, the second day of his life as a felon, he's
at the Trump Tower podium with its Justin Caporale bunting and presidential staging. Even for Trump, it is, save for the first few moments of
no-contrition, no-humiliation, no-defeat defiance, a verbal cascade of
incoherence and digression. Still, he largely gets the headlines he wants:
Trump Claims Trial Was Rigged.

On Saturday night, as previously scheduled, he's at the UFC fight at
the Prudential Center in Newark, New Jersey, with 15,000 fight and
Trump fans (largely synonymous) giving him a hero's welcome.

It is all under control—he is under control. For the moment.

The lashing out, though, will surely come, won't it?

● ● ●

The Trump side had continually speculated as to the individual jurors
they might be getting to, who among them they might successfully be
culling from the core Manhattan view—but, in truth, there was none.

Patrick Robson, a civil litigator in Manhattan, "juror number seven,"
had been surprised to find himself picked for the jury. In early summer,
at a media party in the Hamptons—not an inappropriate setting for the
general profile of the Trump jury—he found himself regaling fellow
guests with what he had seen in his unique, even historic, turn in the
jury box. Familiar with a courtroom and specifically Manhattan courts,
he had a particularly objective approach to the performance of the lawyers before him and how they presented their case. The prosecution, he
judged, put on a clear and decisive case, while the defense, a muddled,
tentative, hit-or-miss one, with Todd Blanche the weakest of the defense

lawyers. From the beginning, the prosecution's position grew strong, the defense position weaker. The prosecution methodically built its argument; the defense failed to make much of a dent in it, and did not make its own. The lasting impression was simple: Trump's life was a tawdry one. This case was part and parcel of his distasteful behavior. What's more, Trump, who did not go into the trial as a particularly sympathetic figure, to say the least, before a Manhattan jury, only compounded that handicap under its critical if not disapproving eye. He had dozed and phased out while the jury members struggled to maintain their attention. (The jurors distinguished between two Trump sleep states: eyes closed and head erect and eyes closed and head listing to the side.) The lineup of congressional figures, governors, and other MAGA stalwarts—and Chuck Zito, the former Hells Angels New York chapter president—behind him had been an odd note to a Manhattan jury, and its members read a clear meaning. Jury members saw bully-boy types in lockstep servility, their purpose to intimidate the jury. Matt Gaetz, glaring and smirking during his appearance behind Trump, had particularly seemed to try to stare them down. And the women . . . Hope Hicks and Madeleine Westerhout on the stand; Alina Habba, Natalie Harp, and Margo Martin, Trump's personal assistant, with him in court . . . their look-alike countenances, the impossible-to-miss Stepford Wife–ism and physical requirements a creepy detail that, in a case fundamentally about sexual proclivities, supported the ick factor.

Many commentators had speculated that the unusual presence on the jury of lawyers (there were two) might result in a too-careful nitpicking and, therefore, reasonable doubt about the evidence and the nature of the law. Indeed, the jury, opening deliberations, had immediately turned to Robson, the litigator, for guidance. But his reproving view merely seemed to confirm the unanimity of that of the eleven others—it was a straightforward story of a cover-up and trying to get away with it.

. . .

Trump's rage at the verdict existed—in this new, inverted world where justice was injustice—with the verdict's clear value.

Sheldon Adelson, the billionaire casino king, as mean-minded, unpleasant, bigoted, and casual in his disregard of others as any overt racist or sociopath, had been a mainstay of Trump support. Even Trump, cowed by Adelson's innumerable billions, had to put up with his irascibility and complaints. It got worse after Adelson's death in 2021. Then Trump had to deal with his widow, Miriam, to get access to the Adelson fortune. She was tighter than even her husband and even more suspicious of Trump. She was not so unpleasant as her husband, but she made up for that by being unrelievedly dull. She demanded her due, which was Trump's time and a free airing of her opinions, mostly generalities of no point or end. On top of that, she didn't give the money. Trump had done two private dinners with her, one on the West Coast, one at Mar-a-Lago, both of them endless and painful and without a commitment. "She is so boring. She just goes on and on. I can't do another. She isn't going to give us anything."

But after the conviction, she said she'd go to at least the ninety million dollars her husband had put out in 2020, and would maybe double that.

Crazy money poured in from big donors and small ones alike. Four or five hundred million, Trump was telling everybody in the ten days after the verdict, went to the campaign and to super PACs. The verdict was . . . rigged, corrupt, evil . . . and yet, too, "the best thing that ever happened."

"As though," according to one observer in the Trump circle, *he* had won the Super Bowl.

Days after the Pepe Fanjul event, David Sacks, a B-list type from Silicon Valley—a world where even the B-listers had banked hundreds of millions—and in the Peter Thiel circle, hosted an eight-figure donor party in San Francisco. A Beverly Hills fundraiser followed; then one in Newport Beach; then Vegas.

And at each, Trump's indecision or ambivalence with regard to a VP choice meant a dogged effort of propinquity on the part of a dozen candidates. Vance, Rubio, and Burgum were in the first tier, but lest that seemed set, he would reintroduce Bill Hagerty, Tim Scott, Byron Donalds, Elise Stefanik, Kristi Noem (despite her dog-killer press), and Tom

Cotton. "What do you think of me picking Hagerty for VP?" Trump asked Vance at the Sacks fundraiser, as though it were a serious request for consultation, instead of a taunt.

· · ·

The Supreme Court within the next few weeks—or days!—would decide whether Donald Trump (and yes, all other presidents) was immune from prosecution for whatever he did in office. It yet seemed to be a bridge way too far that the Court would grant him, and the office of president, the absolute immunity he was arguing for. Here was not exactly a legal theory with a lot of proponents—a president *is* above the law! Trump, though, was confident: A president could pardon anything; therefore, he could pardon himself; therefore, he was, practically speaking, immune . . . wasn't he?

But even federal immunity would not clear him of being a New York State felon. These thirty-four counts, fairly low-level stuff in the criminal canon, might not, for any other ordinary miscreant without a prior conviction, mean jail time. Yet, with his ten contempt charges, his efforts to intimidate the jury and witnesses, and his continuing public fury against the court and verdict, in this instance a "custodial sentence" could be a natural recourse for the judge.

Except . . .

Even a symbolic sentence of a few months would mean security arrangements of such vast expense and complication that the New York State Department of Corrections and Community Supervision might never be able to satisfy the requirements—or justify it to taxpayers.

Or, the Secret Service might simply say no—you can't take him. Trump's detail was now the most sought-after assignment in the Secret Service, everybody jockeying for it. The action was around him. That's where you wanted to be. And, too, he liked his "guys" (even if increasing numbers of them were women). After eight years running, they were something like family. Trump, over decades and decades of having his own security, had made his bodyguards his confidants. A man largely without friends or intimates, he defaulted to his paid companions.

His paramilitary entourage, with its sense of personal devotion, functioning under a congressional mandate that probably did supersede local police jurisdiction, was just one more reality show wild card. His muscle.

• • •

There was his unutterable rage at his conviction; and his constant vilification of his enemies with threats of dire reprisals against targeted Republicans as well as Democrats; and his fear of a jail sentence; and yet, at the same time, his eyes on the prize.

Not least of all, there was his understanding that the only way he would stay out of jail was to become the president again and that this could require some political discipline.

He continued to resist the policy proscriptions of the outside groups, Heritage and AFPI particularly, ridiculing their "MAGA fantasies." While Steve Bannon and the core MAGA coterie continued their rejection of all but the most performative Republicans, Trump was using his Republican VP bake-off to showcase a wide, or wider, interest in the Republican family. After his conviction, Maryland's former governor, moderate Republican Larry Hogan, now running for a Senate seat, said there should be respect for the jury's decision. This prompted Chris LaCivita, in his Trump hat, to publicly tell Hogan he had just ended his campaign. Trump, however, immediately took after LaCivita with multiple tongue-lashings. "Are you fucking crazy? What, you want another Chuck Schumer in the Senate instead of Larry Hogan, a good Republican? Tell me how that's going to help anybody? Do you ever think before you open your mouth?"

Perhaps the most telling measure of his political equanimity and discipline was his deference to Ron DeSantis, a man he detested. DeSantis's perceived disloyalty may well have been Trump's single greatest impetus for entering the 2024 race. The campaign against the Florida governor had been one of the most personal onslaughts in modern political history—with attacks on DeSantis's looks, bearing, family, sexuality. Trump's rage at DeSantis had helped discourage any other true opposition from emerging. To boot, his key political handler, Susie Wiles, was locked in her own bitter enmity with DeSantis (which had helped solidify the bond with her boss).

But now DeSantis was brought back to the table by Steve Witkoff. The silver-haired, under-the-radar New York and Florida real estate developer billionaire had continued his early contributions to DeSantis's political career into the latter's presidential run. At the same time, Witkoff had maintained his long friendship with Trump—as golfing buddy, prodigious super PAC contributor, and owner of a backup plane when Trump's went out of commission. Witkoff, a reliable and discreet presence at the New York trial, may have been Trump's closest confidant (vying only with Ike Perlmutter, who had also precisely and successfully calibrated his support between Trump and the Florida governor).

Since DeSantis's defeat, Witkoff had shepherded a calculated campaign of DeSantis's abnegation and, with a developer's patience, slowly convinced Trump of the long-term upside of magnanimity. Whether this was rightly read as Trump enjoying a former opponent's capitulation or as an uncharacteristic broader conception of the advantages of party unity, Trump was now on the phone, nearly on a daily basis (Trump monologizing, DeSantis listening), with his beaten nemesis. It was, in the view of his circle—Witkoff and Perlmutter especially propounding this view—the new Trump, mellowed by success and the coming victory.

CHAPTER 18

"Fuck City"

JUNE–JULY 2024

The constant and ever-intensifying Trump calumny, mockery, and vilification of Joe Biden about his age—not just old, but demented; incapable; the feeble front man for unelected string-pullers; retarded—had caused many Democrats to discount such concerns precisely because they were uttered by a lying Trump. Going into the debate, Trump also feared he'd overplayed his hand. He had long convinced himself—in the way one person of a certain age easily projects aging's depredations onto another (*not me, him!*)—that Biden couldn't make it to the election. (How was it, Trump continued to wonder, that the Dems would not rally Michelle Obama to bury him in a juggernaut landslide?) But all this had lowered the bar for Joe in the debate. With all the senility stuff they had heaped on him, he would seem fine—robust!—if he just stood up straight for ninety minutes.

The Biden team had called this debate, after all. This was their show. This was a trap, it had finally begun to dawn on Trump. All it would take to blunt the constant Republican imputation that Biden was a man in rapid and visible decline (fragile, weak, and uncertain) or the many social media clips of his faltering gait, lost looks, and frequent descents into gibberish was a basic, even ho-hum, performance. Canned answers. Policy paragraphs. Boring would win. Trump was convinced he was going to get State of the Union Joe: a sturdy enough fellow with a set of ready lines. Or, conversely, eating at him, was his other split-screen view that the Democrats were simply looking for an excuse to dump Joe. He had repeated this view so often, that they were never going to let Joe run, and no one had seemed to take it seriously—impossible to replace a sitting president —that he might well have stopped believing it.

Trump's joke, as he watched the State of the Union, about Biden using Hunter's coke was now in formal deployment: They were going to pump Biden full of drugs for the debate; that was the only thing that would keep him going. Trump ridiculed Biden's prep—he needed intensive remedial coaching to get onstage. Trump, for his part, was . . . on the golf course.

In fact, Trump had so psyched himself into imagining a revivified Biden that he had come around to actually prepping. (Just don't call it "prep.") The amazed Trump circle had never seen him so focused. Trump, who otherwise never acknowledged a need to be anything better than he was, now pressed everyone around him for tougher questions, harder stuff, "the real shit." An intense three weeks of prep—in his office in Mar-a-Lago, on the plane, at the RNC, on his trip to D.C., anywhere he was. Susie Wiles, Jason Miller, Stephen Miller, John Coale (former Fox star Greta Van Susteren's tobacco-lawyer husband), the speechwriters Ross Worthington and Vince Haley, Tony Fabrizio in rotation with Stephen Miller, Kellyanne Conway, Marco Rubio, JD Vance, Bill Hagerty, Eric Schmitt, and Matt Gaetz—all were urged to take off the gloves. In fact, Stephen Miller and John Coale came to something near fisticuffs, in their own side debate: Miller demanding the deportation of everyone, Coale defending the Dreamers and DACA programs for young undocumented immigrants—with Trump too suddenly searching for a "compassionate" answer. The stubbornly resistant student was submitting. A man without the humility to acknowledge there might exist a make-or-break moment was accepting this one.

Plus, he had something up his sleeve: During the debate, he was going to announce his VP choice, an idea he widely tested among friends. He had spent two months building up his cast of characters, and now he could upstage the entire debate thing with his reveal. In fact, he had made no choice, or not acknowledged it to anyone. And any choice, anyway, was fluid: In 2016, Mike Pence had been announced, but before the news conference to introduce him, Trump had wondered if he could appear onstage with someone else. (He was reluctantly convinced he really could not.) Anyway, JD Vance was still probably ahead by a thread. But Murdoch, giving up on his first choice, Mike Pompeo, was now heavily backing Doug Burgum, a staunch neocon-type interventionist—"calling me every damn day about it," said a satisfied Trump. Hearing from Murdoch was always cause for a Trump victory walk. (Murdoch put his new wife—his fifth wife—Elena Zhukova, on the phone, telling Trump, as though this might suggest a bond, "She's Russian.") Susie Wiles continued to actively push Marco Rubio (although less so after she was publicly tagged as a Rubio supporter). Before the debate, Trump told his friend Andy Stein that it was definitely Rubio. Or any wild card . . . Glenn Youngkin, which might give Trump Virginia, save for the fact that Youngkin was, unforgivably, taller than Trump.

Announcing his VP would safely blow up the debate and any good headlines for Joe.

• • •

It was one hundred degrees in Atlanta. Georgia Tech's McCamish Pavilion, a professional-size athletic arena where the media would congregate and the spin room was centered, was surrounded by fraternity houses and bare-chested young men with admirable abs and pecs playing non-political drinking games and cranked-up music on the front lawns.

The debate itself, without an audience, was somewhere else. Where? Other than the vast presence of security around a wide perimeter for the two presidents, the location of the actual debate could be any other place in the world. This left the McCamish Pavilion event venue with the feeling of being in search of an event.

A red carpet had been laid on the floor of the arena, but few people were on it. The sense among the meandering press was that they had somewhat been tricked. They had made the trip to Atlanta, *steaming*

Atlanta, for what? This? Was a debate without an audience really a debate? A group of top institutional journalists had banded together to
make a public complaint to CNN to open up the debate proper to at
least a representative pool. After all, what *if* something happened?

If. Mostly nothing happened in debates, of course. But because
nothing happened, and debates were truly the one shared moment of a
campaign, it was important to be as close as possible to find the minor
disambiguations that could be promoted into news. In debates past,
there was the *debate,* a theatrical experience; and then the spin room,
where the individual campaigns could try to convince journalists not to
believe their lying eyes. Now there was only the spin room. Journalists
would be reduced to mere spectators like everyone else in America. That
was a little insulting.

Dave Bossie and Corey Lewandowski, for many years a tag team
in the Trumpworld orbit, were on the arena floor at an early pre-game
hour, making themselves available to . . . whoever wanted to listen to
them. Bossie, with the look of a put-upon and grim-faced high school
wrestling coach whose own training had long since lapsed, was a linchpin in Trump's political history. A key organizer in the *Citizens United*
lawsuit that had brought nearly unlimited corporate and rich people
funds into political campaigns, and an energetic entrepreneur in the
Tea Party era of Republican politics, Bossie, in 2014, had encouraged
Trump's interest as a disruptive stalking horse and signed on as an adviser. When Trump's interest grew beyond his then brain trust of a
not-too-reliable Roger Stone, he turned to Bossie, who, eschewing a
full-time gig in the Trump rabbit hole for himself, recommended the
gadfly and third-tier Republican op Corey Lewandowski, who became
Trump's first serious political hire. Neither Bossie nor Lewandowski had
risen much further since then. Bossie had been edged out of a White
House job; Lewandowski, antagonizing Trump family members, and
having an affair and then a public breakup with Hope Hicks, Trump's
favorite aide, had been replaced later in 2016 by Paul Manafort (who,
in turn, fell to Steve Bannon). If both Bossie and Lewandowski had
failed to move up, they had also failed to move on. Their early support
had helped turn Trump into the only game in town—the era-shaping

only game in town—and they, like so many Republican others, were stuck in place.

Nearly a decade later, here they were, still spinning. Byron Donalds, the Florida congressman and an occasional VP wild card, also appeared in the early hours, indicating a cap on his standing. The Trump campaign was trying to reserve its heavy hitters for the live shots that would come after the debate. Bossie, Lewandowski, Donalds . . . were far from it.

The Democrats might have had something else in mind by getting California governor Gavin Newsom out on the floor during the early proceedings—a glimmer, at least, of a next generation. (Newsom was fifty-six but, in today's politics, a Young Turk.) What you saw in New-som, at Trumpian height, his head above the crowd, were precisely the central casting presidential qualities that might worry Trump. If hair was the name of the game in politics, and it would be naive or, with Trump, impossible to assume it wasn't, then Newsom, with a dark pompadour, soft waves, and light gray streaks, seemingly naturally supported, was the obvious winner.

• • •

Coming in from Mar-a-Lago and landing in Atlanta just after 6 P.M., the Trump flight had been markedly different from the usual hanging out and listening to Trump's shooting-the-shit monologues. He pressed Matt Gaetz, Jason Miller, Stephen Miller, and John Coale on the plane with him, to continue to hit him with questions. They went over the strategy, Coale's advice some of Trump's favorite: It was all about the first half, after which the stories would be written and commentaries composed; the first twenty minutes were key. The format—two-minute an-swers, then one-minute responses—meant the time was wholly yours. If you didn't like the question, answer one you did like! With the other side having a closed mic, there was not just no fear of interruption, but no fear of correction. Likewise, Trump was reminded, hardly for the first time, that he would not be able to interrupt—that making the effort, without a live mic, would make him look ineffectual. Rather, he had to look relaxed and unbothered and utterly confident.

There was another slight wrinkle that had to be discussed . . . ellipti-
cally. Jill Biden was expected to come onstage and embrace her husband
after the close of the debate. What of Melania? Her remove, always obvious, had seemed to become both more distant and more resolute since
the Stormy trial. There was, evidently, no chance of her being there . . .
none. No one had even proposed it. Trump acknowledged the "visual"
of her absence without acknowledgment of any issue.

They were left—after the motorcade into Atlanta, a walk-through on
the stage, and a round of portrait photographs—to chill for almost two
hours in a makeshift greenroom, two dozen or so people crowding in
and milling about. It was dinnertime, but the usually voracious Trump
was turning down CNN's meager offering or a suggestion to send out
for food. (There were many Jimmy John's in Atlanta, one of his favor-
ites.) "Sinatra told me once, 'Never eat before a performance.'"

The monitor in the greenroom was tuned to CNN, naturally. The
network was taking its feed from the set it had built inside the spin room
on the arena floor. Kasie Hunt, Erin Burnett, Abby Phillip, and Kaitlan
Collins were filling the pre-debate air with a steady patter of what-
Trump-has-to-do versus what-Biden-has-to-do, which tilted inevitably
to Trump's public and verbal perfidy and scurrilousness. After fifteen
minutes of Trump growing more and more obviously vexed, focused on
the four women bashing him, there was a hurried effort to switch to
Fox—but the monitor was locked on CNN. Nor could it be turned off.
This was now risking the relaxed, unbothered, and utterly confident
once-and-future-president thing that the team had worked to achieve.
Panicky calls were being made to producers. Justin Caporale, saving the
day, finally located CNN's IT team, getting them to rush in as Trump
now paced—and steamed. This was CNN trying to spook him. Finally,
successfully, with a sign of general relief, Fox was found.

* * *

Joe Biden crept unsteadily, his balance gravely in doubt, up to the lectern. The immediate signal could hardly be misread: Whoever had conceived of this debate as a viable platform had made a woeful gamble.

More than fifty million people were tuned in, and there were few who could not see the trouble ahead—except for Trump; from where he was entering, he couldn't see it. Sauntering in with his usual ready-for-bear face, he yet had no idea that the game was already in radical transition.

He was concentrating on his own opening, and hardly listening to Biden's first catastrophic responses. He thought he had heard Biden claim that he had created 15,000 new jobs, instead of 15 million, but assumed he'd heard wrong. But he yet had little inkling that this was the most bewildering moment that had ever occurred to a presidential debater: This wasn't a mess-up. This wasn't political. This was human pathos. Joe Biden was sundowning before fifty million people.

Within minutes of the start, no one was listening to what Joe Biden was saying or trying to say. It was all just unremitting and excruciating spectacle. And riveting. The most powerful reality television *ever*. Everything that the media, the mainstream media, had so artfully and adroitly *not* shown for the past several years—either engaging in calculated cover-up or disbelieving its own eyes—was now airing in real time.

There was a hush in the spin room. Trump had said it all so many times over, that Joe was senile, mentally incompetent, "a retarded individual," that the government was run by others—a daily cover-up, a conspiracy of silence. But what a shock for Trump's hyperbole, for his disgraceful insults, his sadistic cackling, to be near the truth. Voters, even Democratic ones, had again and again confirmed their concerns about Biden's age, but likely few had imagined this level of physical and mental ebbing. Most Americans, suffice it to say, had personal experience with the ravages and certainty of decline and its warning signals and manifestations—they were face-to-face with what they understood.

Trump had been prepared to defend his largely indefensible positions—on January 6, on *Roe v. Wade,* on Covid-19, on Putin—with a furious, belligerent, double-down defense. Defending the indefensible was the talent he was selling. But he went virtually unchallenged. Nineteen minutes in, perplexed about Biden's bewildering comments about immigration, a mystified Trump openly questioned if Biden himself knew what he was saying, and only then did it hit him that something might actually be wrong. Not watching Biden and having to think ahead to his own next statements, Trump knew significantly less about what was going on than the fifty million people watching the debate.

While yet unaware that this was a catastrophe for Joe, Trump decided it was going well enough for him to abandon his VP gambit. He didn't need it. (He did not really want to make a final choice yet anyway.)

He isn't right, Trump sensed, but he could not be sure if this was what everyone understood. He would later tell people he thought the media was again going to cover up for Joe. And then he started to think he was going to look bad for pounding him too hard. *Do I let up?* he wondered.

But by the commercial break at the fifty-minute mark—he was held backstage with only his Secret Service agent and no opportunity to get his staff's view—he was becoming more and more convinced that it was a setup by the Democrats who wanted Biden to fail so they could get rid of him; that's why they'd gone for this early debate—it *was* a trap, but for Joe. He was right. He had always been right. And now he turned his fury on his staff for getting him into this debate (although, in fact, he had accepted the invitation). Trump was suddenly grasping for a strategy to help save Joe. But there wasn't one. With forty minutes to go, the debate was already over. It was an elaborate plot—to screw Joe and thereby screw him.

"That's it. They're going to swap him out," said Trump, coming off the stage, seconds after energetic Jill Biden bounded out to take her husband to hospice.

• • •

The Trump surrogates spilled out into the spin room—JD Vance, Marco Rubio, Doug Burgum, Lindsey Graham, Tim Scott, Jason Miller, Chris LaCivita, Lewandowski, and Bossie back again. Each was instructed to go strong on Trump's victory and easy on Biden's humiliation.

LaCivita, the dominant Trump voice in the spin room, in his own mind certainly the new Karl Rove, was heatedly and directly making the case to the press gaggle for Biden to stay in the race and against the Democratic desire—already the electricity in the air—to push him out: *They call us anti-democratic. Can you imagine anything more anti-democratic than taking the nomination from someone who actually won it? The Democrats voted for Biden, pure and simple. He is the nominee. It's the Democrats who have no respect for democracy and for what the voters want. That's the scandal!*

But it was the Democrats the media was waiting for—and they weren't showing. A growing circle, almost an encampment, surrounded the spot where the Dem surrogates were expected to come out. Cameras, microphones, tape recorders, notebooks—all poised. But, nothing.

It was nearly half an hour into the spin when a band of Democrats, in lockstep company, finally appeared, Newsom towering above the group. There was a reporter surge nearly emptying the rest of the room. If there was any doubt, the Democrats were the story—if it bleeds, it leads. The stoic answers, delivered largely by Newsom, were to ignore or deflect any questions about Biden and to focus on Trump's Trumpiness. But this was somehow only to reinforce the story: Trump on his game, Biden with no game left.

. . .

In a talk at the Aspen Ideas Festival the day after the debate, the famously profane Ari Emanuel, Hollywood power broker, Democratic Party donor, and the brother of Rahm Emanuel, Obama's former chief of staff (and, to boot, Donald Trump's former Hollywood agent and key figure in Trump's transformation into a television star), pronounced Joe Biden and the Democratic Party to be in "fuck city."

The Trump team's view was as existential. If Biden held, they would win with an undreamed-of margin—every swing state, they were predicting. But if it was anyone else, even Harris, all bets were off—and they were livid at the prospect.

. . .

Most of us live our lives in a low furrow, if not a rut, of uneven or even miserable luck. If your luck breaks for you fifty-fifty, you've certainly done well; chances are it will yield far less than that. Donald Trump, for his part, might seem to have among the highest luck percentages ever recorded, fate, good fortune, or the stars rescuing him from so many nadirs.

In the final days of its term, the Supreme Court first took up a secondary matter in the January 6 prosecutions—including Trump's—challenging the law under which the Justice Department had acted and narrowing or even eliminating several of the charges against Trump (as well as throwing into question many other January 6 cases). Then, finally, in one of its last rulings of the 2023–24 term, with a majority that included the six conservative justices, the Court, doing pretty much the unthinkable—a possibility beyond the comprehension of most constitutional students and, in fact, Trump's own lawyers—granted Trump (and future presidents) broad immunity from criminal prosecution for most actions taken while in office. Thus, the Court ensured that the January 6 prosecution would necessarily slip past the election and might, practically speaking, now be basically moot.

What's more, the Trump legal team immediately argued that his sentencing in the New York hush money case—scheduled for July 11, the next week—should be delayed until the Trump team could make arguments, given that the Supreme Court decision had now called into serious question key aspects of the case. Hope Hicks, for instance, had testified to actions that had taken place in the White House that might no longer be admissible as evidence. For another, the agreement with Michael Cohen had been made when Trump was president—if that agreement was now included under Trump's immunity, there might be no basis on which to prosecute him. Justice Merchan delayed sentencing until at least September.

More "fuck city" for the Democrats.

CHAPTER 19

Yes-men

JULY 2024

So . . . Vance.

But Trump wasn't sure how it had come to this.

There were the Black candidates: Byron Donalds, the congressman from Florida and dedicated Trump suck-up; Tim Scott, who withdrew from the primary race in favor of Trump and dissed Nikki Haley, his South Carolina patron (Trump joked about Scott's willingness to get married to become VP); and Ben Carson, the surgeon and Trump's HUD secretary, who had briefly surged in the 2016 primary race. There were the women: Kristi Noem, the South Dakota governor (but she was suspected of having had an affair with Corey Lewandowski, Trump's former campaign manager, and then further blew up her VP prospects with a proud confession about shooting her dog); Sarah Huckabee Sanders, Trump's former press secretary and now the governor of Arkansas (but she had taken a long time to endorse him); Katie Britt, the U.S. senator from Alabama (but she had flubbed the official Republican response to Biden's 2024 State of the Union); Senator Marsha Blackburn of Tennessee (but at seventy-one, she was too old); and Tulsi Gabbard, who, when she was still a Democrat, Trump had almost picked as UN ambassador (and probably should have—instead, he'd picked Nikki Haley, and look what he got). Then the Hispanics: Marco Rubio and Francis Suarez. And then the central casting people, looking rich and successful (and white): Bill Hagerty, the senator from Tennessee and a private equity guy; Doug Burgum, the governor of North Dakota and a billionaire; and Vance, not a billionaire, but the billionaires' choice.

There was Vivek Ramaswamy, who had run in the primaries as a Trump acolyte (even, at the same time, as he ran against Trump) and then dropped out and prostrated himself as the most Trump person who had ever lived. He'd come in and made a formal presentation to Trump as to why he should be vice president—and was crushed when Trump said maybe Homeland Security (although he seemed to repeat this story widely, and proudly). "You're a brown guy, so when you're tough on immigration, no one is going to get mad."

He was being pitched hard on Burgum. In addition to Murdoch's "daily" calls, the media mogul had delegated top *New York Post* executives and editors to be all over everyone in Trumpworld about Burgum and was himself calling Trump sources on Burgum's behalf (and bragging about his clout and reach). Ken Griffin, the hedge funder, with his forty billion dollars, was strongly, and vocally, behind Burgum. But Burgum, in North Dakota, had supported a six-week abortion ban—contradicting the Trump "No weeks, don't say weeks, never weeks" position—which seemed to have nixed him.

Rubio was out. Rubio lived in Florida, Trump's voting residence—that was constitutionally sticky, so Rubio would have to move his residence to D.C. and leave the Senate. "It's not simple, it's not simple, it's gotta be simple," Trump kept saying. And anyway, Rubio really wasn't out there humping for it—a couple of media appearances, but not many—and was hardly working the phones. Vance and Burgum were hustling and chasing down donors.

So . . . Vance. Peter Thiel, the tech billionaire, had appeared to promise to give $10 million to the Trump super PAC if Trump endorsed Vance among other candidates in the Ohio race for the U.S. Senate in 2022—and then never delivered. Trump was still pissed about that. And Vance was Don Jr.'s crush. (Likewise, Vance seemed to have a crush on the rich man's son.) But when had Trump ever listened to Junior? Still, Vance was central casting—and he was even smart.

Still, Trump would yet bring up Rick Scott—though sometimes

getting him confused with Tim Scott. And while he had told Elise Stefanik it wasn't going to be her, he was telling others he was reconsider-
ing. And Hagerty—he liked Hagerty. All in all, he just wasn't there yet:
"I could win without a VP, and you know, honestly, I'd kind of prefer
not to have one."

• • •

But at least the VP pick would enliven the convention, which Trump,
worried about the ratings, with all eyes and interest on the Dems' meltdown, was now saying he didn't give a shit about. And if, as was looking
more and more likely, they had no candidate to run against, and if *then*
the whole world was going to be focused, with amazing ratings, on the
Dems' own potential reveal . . . what would happen to *his* ratings?

Hardly two weeks before the Republican convention, speakers were
just getting their nods—and now, in a scramble, four days' worth of
speeches would have to be written. This would be overseen by the Trump
team but farmed out to, practically speaking, God knows who, meaning
a lot of crazy stuff would be put into these speeches that would have to
be combed out.

Digging into the disorganized work that had been produced by a
platform committee infiltrated by MAGA activists, Wiles and LaCivita
found a mess of Heritage Foundation, Project 2025, and AFPI
fantasies—and abortion, fuck! Inmates running the asylum. They had to
bump off the more difficult and resistant members of the platform committee and then recast the whole thing themselves. Fabrizio, the pollster,
James Blair, the political director, Vice Haley, the speechwriter, took a
crack at it. The new view was: Why did they even need a platform (not
that dissimilar from Trump's wondering why he needed a vice president)? Why pin policy positions on Trump that he couldn't care less
about? Why get specific? No *"weeks"!* Why not just an overview? A broad
overview: World peace. Great economy. Secure borders. Election integ-
rity. Anything else? In the end, Trump wrote much of it himself—the
tell being the capital letters in the final document.

This was, lest it be missed, an effort by Wiles and LaCivita to win an election. The base would be loyal no matter what the platform said—so don't go out of the way to alienate swing voters and the Nikki Haley leftovers. Then, too, it was Wiles and LaCivita preparing to fight future battles with the MAGA crowd from the White House. (In the run-up to the convention, the media seemed more and more to adopt Project 2025 as something like the official Trump platform—a purposeful diss, the campaign felt, and once more, at the campaign's urging, Trump posted a message snubbing Project 2025.)

There was one convention problem, however, they did not seem able to get around. The candidate's wife had not, in eighteen months, made one campaign appearance. Nor had she ever been at Trump's side in his myriad court dates. Her single political interest seemed to be, in one of her opaque rebukes, to support gay Republicans (in a speech she was paid several hundred thousand dollars to give). She was due, though, to make a centerpiece address at the convention. She was a showstopper, Trump always said. Except, now she was flatly refusing to deliver her speech. She would show up, but that was it—and even showing up seemed iffy. Whatever was going on—and no one had any idea what was going on, at least no more than what was plainly obvious—it had certainly not been helped by the Stormy trial. But that seemed hardly the only thing to explain the colder and colder winter.

Already the campaign had tentatively put out that, in a second Trump administration, the role of First Lady might be adjusted. The usage of "part-time First Lady" had begun. Barron would go to NYU and live at home in Trump Tower—she needed to be near him (just what every college student surely wants to hear).

The Trump circle was decorously and implacably mum on the issue. But, at the same time, if pressed, the obvious was too inescapable to deny: "She fucking hates him," said one Mar-a-Lago patio confidant of Trump and his family, bewildered that this needed saying.

• • •

The campaign had arguably benefited from the parallel power structures that existed in the Trump orbit. There was the campaign doing its thing;

the lawyers quarreling among themselves (and trying to avoid the client); and, much closer to Trump, attending more directly to him, supplying his basic mood drugs, were Boris and Natalie. For the campaign, this was useful—that is, if you could accept the galling nature of his dependence on Boris and Natalie.

Still, there had been a certain expectation within the legal team that Trump's conviction in New York would undermine his relationship with Boris and Boris's agent Blanche and with Natalie, the silent author of so much of Trump's unhelpful vituperation. But that seemed far from happening.

Boris remained—again, to inexplicable wonder—the Trump quarterback. With Boris calling the plays, Trump was down $563 million in judgments, arguably the bulk of his fortune, from a sexual abuse and business fraud adjudication, and saddled with a thirty-four-count criminal conviction, and looking at a possible jail sentence. In every case but those before the specific judges he had appointed—on the Supreme Court and before his federal court pick, Aileen Cannon—Trump had been utterly wiped out. What's more, Boris himself was now looking at jail time—or might need to cut a deal to avoid it—with nine felony charges against him in the Arizona election interference case. But ten times a day, at least—on the golf course, with donors, on the plane, before and after rallies, during meals at Mar-a-Lago—Trump's phone would ring and be answered by the "Yeah, go ahead" reserved for Boris and their nonstop conversation.

Natalie was equally in Trump's ear and by his side. She was both inner face and outer face. He saw the world as he wanted to see it because, in her act of besotted dedication, she presented it to him that way. He heard what he wanted to hear because the world, bypassing his campaign apparatus, called Natalie, who artfully filtered the information—going through Natalie was the smart play!

Yes, it was a troubling state of affairs, his remoteness from reality. This was as damning in its own way as Biden's fragility. And yet . . . in the face of the thousand cuts that would have felled anyone else, he had maintained his extraordinary personal world of certainty and inner-sanctum ease—and was, he mostly felt, cruising to ultimate victory. He had come to regard the campaign itself as a technical operation. They got on with it as he lived in a world where everything went his way, where even bad news was quickly reinterpreted ("here's why another indictment is in your favor"), which, with a little critical interpretation, may be the secret to actually getting things to go your way. "Yes-men" have a bad reputation when, really, these ultimate self-enhancers might be the necessary stuff of dreams.

And yet, on another day, resentment and bitterness pervaded his personal outlook.

"It won't be Harris. It'll never be Harris. They'll get somebody good," said a morose Trump in a patio refrain. If it was Gretchen Whitmer, they were fucked. So fucked that you couldn't really bring it up with him.

This helped explain the appeal and need of his Boris–Natalie yes-man bubble: Everything was so bleak, the world so Hobbesian and nihilistic, that he had to retreat to his place of well-designed and ever-reinforced contentment. Ever deflated, he needed to be ever reinflated. "Whataya think, they're not going to steal it again? They're gonna fix it for themselves. What they always do. They'll figure out how to fuck us." This was now the mantra.

At the same time, even seeing doom and gloom, the campaign made little preparation for a change or even a wobble in fortunes, no less a worst-case scenario. To prepare for the worst, or even a lesser variation of it, was to diss and undermine him. You couldn't prepare for Harris, because clearly it was going to be someone better; but nor could you prepare for someone better, because that would be to admit he could be defeated. The point, he repeated, and it was clear that no one should lose sight of it, was that he had beaten Joe Biden. *He had beaten Joe Biden.* And don't talk about changing the game now.

Such was the fine line you needed to walk between his mania and depressiveness.

• • •

An important focus of the campaign in the weeks before the convention—after the debate and as the Democrats continued their public meltdown—was on a profile of Susie Wiles that *USA Today* was preparing. The panicked planning for the profile appeared to be getting as much attention as convention planning, the VP rollout, and the anticipation of an unknown opponent.

Here were the true colors of a wholly unvarnished not-ready-for-prime-time player whose career mission had been to stay out of the press. Indeed, it was her low profile and nuts-and-bolts attention—not just different from Trump, but different from most of the figures drawn to Trump, and to whom Trump was naturally drawn—that had held the campaign together. But here was, too, Wiles's determination, new determination, to grab for the real power that, more and more, it seemed, might soon be there for the taking. The no-glam, office-manager-type administrator was, more likely than anyone else, on a path to becoming the White House chief of staff and the fail-safe between a working White House and a chaotic, ad hoc, impulsive president moved principally by the sound of his own voice and by the last random person to have gotten his ear.

Wiles had tried to be the adult in Donald Trump's playroom and had so far succeeded. Her run as his campaign chief was singularly the most effective in his three campaigns. In Donald Trump's long history, no organization under him, business or political, had ever run with this degree of standard operating procedure and accountability or been this shielded from the boss's mercurial, and often counterproductive, whims. In Wiles, Trump seemed, exceptionally, to have met his man. In Trump, Wiles—a thoroughly local presence, aging past a political career's natural sell-by date, quite an unlikely figure in Trump's circle of exclusive fawning and fanciable women—saw an unimaginable transformation into ultimate political power and prominence. Many non-Trumpian figures had vied for power under him, but Wiles was, to date, the most successful. She was determined to maintain that position—now and into the White House.

Trump, though, evaluated every public step forward by his staff, every "profile" piece, against his own self-interest and sense of hierarchy. And the proper hierarchy, to be precise, was, on top, the massively inflated figure of Trump and, far below, the invisible balloon-pullers on the ground. At the same time, it was getting harder and harder to avoid the media's interest in who might truly be pulling the strings, and the more you avoided it, the more you lost control of your press. Simultaneously, Trump's view of the world was almost entirely derived from media flash. If you didn't exist in the media, you didn't exist. Then, too, if Wiles was going to become the most pivotal player in the new Trump White House, there were battles to be fought now and public messages to be sent.

Wiles's own kitchen cabinet of advisers gamed every aspect of the *USA Today* profile, carefully vetting the reporter, prepping Wiles's interview, providing sources and scripting their comments, and coaching the narrative with access and attention to the reporter.

The campaign's spelled-out message about Wiles in the profile was, in fact, that it was uncharacteristic for her to appear in one, that she didn't like press at all. She was that rare political bird, a humble one, and a wholly different kind of Trump bird. "Mild-mannered" made the headline. The next note, directly aimed at the Heritage Foundation and at the media giving Project 2025 so much airtime, was that Wiles was non-ideological, a traditional Republican, a RINO by another name. So, possibly, the most significant message yet delivered about a future new Trump administration—or, at least, exceptional fighting words— was: His agenda was *his* agenda; it was far from being set (now or perhaps ever); and possibly, if Wiles had anything to do with it, it was a propitiously more calculated one.

• • •

And it was on to Milwaukee. Most of the staff was already there. A few would go with Trump for a speech in Butler, Pennsylvania, on Saturday.

The coronation lineup, put together largely by Caporale, LaCivita, and Fabrizio, was a mix of strategic messaging and family adulation, with Trump's handpicked addition of various golf buddies.

They were up against the Dems' soap opera and yet uncertain how to quite play this, except to assume that Joe Biden was the opponent and that, whatever happened, the Dems were corrupt, venal, incompetent, and radical. Message set.

Everything was in the best place it could be, but Melania.

Even in the ever-downward spiral of diminishing expectations, every day was still "will she, won't she?" She would not speak. And yet, should they have a speech ready for her in case she would, suddenly, speak? She would attend—wouldn't she? But on every night or . . . what? How could you anticipate, and how could you prepare? And who knew her plans? Did he know?

You couldn't really discuss this. You couldn't actually acknowledge that the most public marriage in the nation was breaking down, even if, by every standard indication, it was breaking down, and doing so in public. He did not acknowledge this. And curiously, by everyone's complicit agreement not to acknowledge anything, the world at large did not yet acknowledge it, either.

CHAPTER 20

Butler

JULY 2024

The twenty-year-old shooter, Thomas Crooks, in neutral-colored cargo shorts and a T-shirt, on July 13, keeping as low as possible, positioning himself on the highest-possible ground and with an unobstructed view, pulls himself across the open roof of a warehouse structure bordering the open field in Butler, Pennsylvania. He has no military training, but a sniper crawling into position is a necessary scene in many action movies and video games he might have committed to heart. As he is pointed out by puzzled bystanders, but somehow glossed over by law enforcement, he sets up his weapon and then begins, inexpertly, to fire.

Trump has a slide he likes to project at the end of a rally speech about immigration. He turns to the image behind him, a graph of immigration trends, and walks his audience through it to the triumphant climax showing record-low immigration during his time as president. But he shakes things up at the Butler rally and calls for the graph at the beginning of his speech, turning his head to the screen at the exact moment the bullet approaches.

His hand goes to his head, he drops, and after long moments of confusion, in which you can yet make out his voice on the live mic, he rises.

The resulting photo is Iwo Jima–like: blood, fist, American flag.

His immediate concern, caught on the still-open mic as he's hustled off the stage, and after he's nailed the picture, is his shoes. He's fallen out of them.

Trump himself, in the aftermath, monologizing through whatever likely PTSD he might have, sounds like Churchill in his descriptions of how he stood up to the Boer bullets and how they always missed him.

He's his own best vivid witness, getting the sound, surprise, and bite of the bullet as it struck him in the single most advantageous place on the body to be struck—the top of his ear (there will be a continuing dispute about whether it was the bullet that struck him or a shard from something else that the bullet struck).

"I will," he says to the small group of staff with him at the event—the rest of the team is already in Milwaukee or due to meet him for the flight out—"look like Evander Holyfield."

At Butler Memorial Hospital, where he is rushed, he resists a CT scan, worried that it could show "plaque" and that people might say he is getting Alzheimer's.

With his small entourage—Susie Wiles, Natalie Harp, Ross Worthington, Dan Scavino—he flies to Newark Airport and then on to Bedminster.

Most candidates, when their nomination is a foregone conclusion, arrive late in a convention's proceedings in an effort to be above low politics and promotion and to claim the prize on the last night in as dignified and gracious a manner as possible. But Trump previously determined to arrive on Sunday, the night before the start.

Now, though, here is a seventy-eight-year-old man who was grazed in an assault-weapon attack and then hit by a squad of spring-loaded security people. His staff, uncertain about his physical and mental state, gently suggest he delay his arrival in Milwaukee by a day or two. What's more, he has to make his VP choice, far from being decided, in the next twenty-four hours. Why doesn't he just take the time at Bedminster?

"We can't look weak. If we don't show up, we'll look weak. We can't look weak," he insisted. The show must go on. And Donald Trump, the most extraordinary showman in the history of American politics, is not going to waste this exemplary moment. He picks up Boris Epshteyn;

Jason Miller; Lindsey Graham, with whom he is scheduled to play golf; and his former White House physician, currently a U.S. congressman, Ronny Jackson ("Dr. Ronny"), at Newark Airport. The staff tries to cancel the two right-wing reporters—Byron York from Fox and Michael Goodwin from the *New York Post*—who have been scheduled to accompany him. "That would be rude!" Trump countermands, with the reporters joining him less than twenty-four hours after his attempted assassination with Trump taking the opportunity to begin to shape his story.

"I'm not supposed to be here, I'm supposed to be dead. The doctor at the hospital said he never saw anything like this, he called it a miracle," he tells the reporters. And lest he appears to be humbled by the furies—the shooter, he says with both awe and delight, was taken out "with one shot right between the eyes."

Meanwhile, Natalie is bringing him color printouts of all the photos taken at the moment of the shooting and in its immediate aftermath. *The New York Times*'s 1/8,000th-of-a-second shot capturing the bullet going by will, he remarks, "live forever in history."

The shooting is no different from all the other efforts that have been made to fell him, and with no greater chance to succeed than any other, which has been proven by his having the presence of mind, at exactly the perfect moment, to pump his fist. (Curiously, his call for his shoes to be returned, which suggests that not just Ron DeSantis, but Trump as well, might be wearing lifts that caused him to fall out of his loafers, is little noted.) And, too, it is the Democrats in their hatred of him, and their demonization—theirs is the truly nasty language, not his!—who caused this.

But perhaps most of all, certainly for those around him, this is the ne plus ultra demonstration of Trump's luck. You can't fight it. Not only has he survived, with others dead and wounded around him, but his wound has made him a martyr and a hero with no physical cost at all. But beyond that, this seems to have happened at the exact best moment: the ultimate political boon. Once again, he has imposed himself on events, rather than the other way around.

The CNN anchors and panel are unable to hide their frustration and perplexity at this remarkable fortune. MSNBC preempts the Biden-boosting *Morning Joe* show to avoid any reflexive off note of resentment. The clear consequence of the near miss, sticking in the craw of every liberal commentator, is that this was a political event that came as close as you might come to guaranteeing the election of Donald Trump.

. . .

Throughout the week before, Trump, in a low panic, had been grasping at ways to compete with the Democrats' Shakespearean drama. As much as, in traditional political terms, one is always advised to let the opposition, if it be so inclined, immolate itself, Trump understood that in today's world, whoever held media time, that single most valuable political asset, deprived someone else of it. Prior to the Trump shooting, the big event on the first night of the uneventful Republican convention seemed certain to be another can't-take-your-eyes-off-it, unedited (NBC promised) interview with Joe Biden. Would Biden snuff out the flames, or would he continue to burn—and with what verbal howlers? Whereas the RNC was likely to be more of the same Trump bluster. Who would care when there was this minute-by-minute Biden meltdown in progress? What was better television? "Our ratings are going to suck," Trump had complained.

Before the assassination attempt, his speechwriters, working on his acceptance speech, kept returning to him with what Trump called "pablum," same old, same old, not anything that was going to take away a headline from the Dems.

All he had was the VP choice. He was yet shuffling the candidates like playing cards, needing a surprise but not having one.

Melania continued to be an additional freak-out, absolutely refusing every entreaty to speak or even to appear side by side with her husband. He had never faced point-blank questions from the media about their relationship. But what if "Where's Melania?" started now in earnest? There was a move to get Barron to speak, but Melania nixed that, too.

But that was all before the shooting . . . now the attempt on Trump's life not only made him again incontrovertibly the central figure of the moment, if not the age, giving him a maximum hero's electoral mantle, but it also repositioned his convention as the joyous and abject coronation of which he dreamed. What's more, it distracted the media from their mortal filibuster against Biden, which could help save Joe, Trump's weakest-possible opponent.

What's more, if Trump needed it, which he did not, future Supreme Court justice Aileen Cannon delivered him one more legal coup de grace on July 15, the opening day of the Republican convention. In a cream-on-top, shoot-a-corpse, don't-get-mad-get-even ruling, Trump's judge declared the special prosecutor himself unconstitutional and out of a job. As the Democrats appeared to falter in every effort to dispatch their own weak king, Trump grew ever stronger—and his supporters bolder.

All obstacles had been cleared for him as he arrived in Milwaukee.

* * *

JD Vance, that official son of Trump's core message of the dystopian Midwest (a vision in stark contrast to the gentrified Milwaukee neighborhood surrounding the Fiserv Forum, with its rehabbed nineteenth-century factories, its neighborhoods of boutiques and coffee shops, and the city's financial services and med tech industries), was finally announced as the VP choice on Monday, the opening day, a decision put off, in the interest both of dramatic suspense and of Trump's own ambivalence, to the absolute last minute.

Up until virtually seconds before Trump placed the call, he had still been waffling. His flight out to Milwaukee had been a movable focus group. As he had indecisively waffled among Mike Pence, Newt Gingrich, and Chris Christie in 2016, he was yet stuck now among Vance, Burgum, and Rubio. Or others.

Bill Hagerty called mid-flight, and Trump asked if he wanted to be VP—a joke, possibly, or possibly not.

There was a string of other calls: *So glad you're okay, but this is who you should pick for VP.* Lindsey Graham was pushing for Rubio. Sean Hannity and Kellyanne Conway, a Rubio consultant, were weighing in hard, too, for him. Boris edged in to say, "If you're still open, why not go back to thinking about Elise," who had hired Boris as one of her political consultants.

Actually, Trump wanted a woman, he had decided. But *not* Elise Stefanik.

Why hadn't he been given better women?

What about . . . Maria Bartiromo? he wanted to know.

Or Harris Faulkner? The Black woman on Fox.

Haley? They couldn't go back to "Birdbrain"—or could they? Trump displayed a series of CEO and other billionaire texts supporting Doug Burgum, the one candidate whom he personally liked. And Murdoch, Burgum's chief supporter, would be attending the convention—"What am I going to say to Rupert if I don't pick Doug?" Trump mulled.

Susie Wiles, Rubio's most significant supporter, had shifted to Vance, and her support now finally brought the decision to a close, helping to land the plane, in essence, as the plane landed.

"I thought you loved Marco?" asked a surprised Trump.

"I do. But it should be Vance. I'm sold on the reasons for Vance." Although, in fact, those reasons remained quite unclear.

Oh, yes, and Elon Musk told Trump his support for the ticket was contingent on Trump's picking Vance. Tucker Carlson, a chief Vance promoter, was at the finish line with his support. Peter Thiel, always ambivalent in his support for Trump, was willing to re-engage if it were Vance.

Still.

A mistaken leak of a video, in a world where there are no mistaken leaks, capturing a call the day before between Trump and Bobby Kennedy Jr.—with Trump in active flattery mode, trying to get Kennedy to support him and give up his own campaign—seemed to suggest that Trump was still considering his choice and looking for a Trump–Kennedy opening. (It was a characteristic call, Trump monologizing, Kennedy able to register only monosyllable agreement—"yeah"—and Trump, typically, never really getting to the point.)

On Monday morning, Trump authorized Wiles to call Burgum and Rubio and tell them it wasn't them. He called Vance, who was waiting by the phone in Cincinnati.

Perhaps Trump saw the young man, as he saw his own children, as someone whom he could overshadow and browbeat into a factotum. On his first day in office, this second time around, Trump would be a lame duck. In a few months, the jockeying around him would begin in earnest, power slipping from him. But it might be a different story if his vice president, and logical successor, were more acolyte than replacement.

A quicksilver Vance had shape-shifted himself quite as shamelessly and adeptly as it might be possible to do. He had been one thing— a serious public intellectual of a difficult and uncertain new era, agonizing over difficult choices and limited answers and groping to a post-right or -left point of view and, to say the least, dismissing Donald Trump as an unserious man, and a joke figure and possibly a dangerous one— Hitler, even, said Vance. But then, catapulted by his bestselling-author profile (as Trump himself, with *The Art of the Deal* had been remade into a pop figure) and the adoration of the liberal press, Vance had seen a political opportunity. This was an opportunity directly facilitated by his mentor, the political and business contrarian Peter Thiel, who had frustratingly tried and largely failed in his own courtship of Donald Trump—and, indeed, who continued to see Trump as both pilot fish for political contrarianism and piss-poor standard-bearer for it. If Vance was game for a political career, Thiel had been willing to help him try. Hence, Thiel had floated a ten-million-dollar contribution, earning Trump's endorsement of Vance for the Senate. (Then, in the give-and-take of politics, Thiel was happy not to deliver it.) But in addition to the ten million, Vance had had to convert himself from an intellectual skeptic and *New York Times*-approved prose stylist to a reductive, happy MAGA warrior and Trump fanboy, all the more so when Trump's presidential prospects came amazingly back to life.

Anyway, the plane would arrive shortly in Cincinnati, waiting to take the Vances to Milwaukee.

· · ·

A brief time capsule on the recent order of events: Over the course of little more than six weeks, Trump has been convicted of thirty-four felonies; a ninety-minute debate has upset all the reasonable assumptions of the race and even the certainty of whom Trump will be running against; days later, the Supreme Court upends the entirety of the legal challenges and peril he faces, including the threat of a jail sentence days before the convention is to begin; with Biden insisting he'll continue as the Democrats' nominee, the tight margin-of-error polling, which has largely held steady for a year, has shifted to a clear Trump advantage in every swing state and a weakening in solid Democratic states; and now, just two days prior, a gunman took aim and fired.

And then a bandaged Trump, now a magical figure, appears on the convention floor, amid Corporale's exultant staging, in a celebration of the Republican Party's inevitable destiny.

The first night is meant to deliver a precise message: If you have not voted for Trump before but are looking for a reason now—because the Democrats are hopeless—Trump is the alternative, the *only* alternative, and inevitable anyway. This is a tactical bid to chip away at the Democratic margin, where slight shifts can move important states. Add a few more points to the Black Trump vote and Hispanic Trump vote and union Trump vote, and you start to come into landslide territory.

It's a message of inclusion, but one fashioned not out of policy—beyond broad strokes, the policy is light—but instead out of the vividly demonstrated circumstance that Trump is obviously strong and the Democrats are obviously weak. *Obviously!*

There will not be one speech at the convention that does not reverently return to the shooting and, with awe, recount the once-and-future president defying his fate.

The "get" of the night is Sean O'Brien, president of the International Brotherhood of Teamsters. No Teamsters president has ever spoken at a Republican convention. But Trump's chatty and convivial sit-down at Teamsters HQ earlier in the year was him playing an unaccustomed long game. O'Brien is not here to endorse Trump, but his presence certainly gives his membership permission to vote for him. It is nearly a formal and official acknowledgment of the historic shift: The working man, labor, has left the Democratic Party, taking key Democratic states with him. In a big Trump victory, O'Brien's appearance could be the footnote for which this convention is most remembered.

But the evening is surely most noted for the arrival of the warrior-hero-king. The showman-huckster-felon-pugilist-disrupter, having defied fate, has been transformed in gait and mien and expression into a figure of serenity and, even, magnanimity. And yes, the crowd, primed for this by the fluffers circulating around the floor—"He's coming shortly"—goes wild, with the awe and wonder and thrill of being on the certain winning side. There is no longer the sense of fight, of us against them, of an all-or-nothing future—the future is here, and it is all. And it is amazing. There is something similar to the sense in 2008 at the Democrats' convention: the otherworldly surprise that they had nominated a Black man. Well, here now, the Republicans have somehow defied logic and the furies and are nominating Donald Trump once more, and he is better and more incredible than anyone has ever imagined.

He slowly makes his way, with his young vice presidential choice at his side, to his VIP box—although, there is only one real VIP. He will spend the entire convention in this seat. The real purpose of the proceedings, as he sits in his box, will be to pay tribute to him.

But, looking closely, there is perhaps a further story. He seems remote. Inexpressive. Haggard. Unfamiliarly, he seems to be listening as people talk to him, whereas his retinue, in almost all other circumstances, only ever listens to him. And at the regular intervals of standing ovations, for God and country and other moments of great self-congratulation, he seems reluctant to rise, and when forced to, he requires a labored two-step slide-and-push motion. His young VP sidekick looking on with . . . patience.

Trump's wife, people seem at pains *not* to note, is absent.

• • •

Presidential nominating conventions last for four days as a relic of their former purpose: the time-consuming process, often running into early-morning hours, of nominating speeches, without time constraints offered for many candidates; with multiple seconding speeches and delegate politicking and caucusing in between; and then state-by-state roll calls, a ritualistic and long-winded affair and, in the past, often involving multiple ballots. This process was then repeated for the vice president. None of this happened anymore, but the four days remained, with the hours (trying not to run beyond prime time) filled by encomiums and self-promotional opportunities.

The thematic point of the second day of RNC24 was to demonstrate the rare unity of the Republican Party by having Trump's two most dedicated and quite likely vengeance-minded opponents pay public obeisance to him. Nikki Haley and, immediately following her, if the point was not made, Ron DeSantis, both begrudgingly playing the long game of politics—conscious that, at least for the time being, a Republican career had to be a Trump career—and biting the bullet. Likewise, Vivek Ramaswamy, who, in this election season, had risen from total political obscurity to substantial political prominence on the odd coattails of slavish adoration of Trump as he ran against him, delivered more inexhaustible love.

Trump, from the VIP box, looked on, his head occasionally seeming to loll to the side.

The topper of the evening, with a segment time far longer than any other, was Lara Trump, Eric Trump's wife, another in-law reaching for high and unaccountable status in Trump politics. A former producer on the tabloid news show *Inside Edition*, she had risen as a family adjunct and eager public speaker into various honorary and paid political roles and had even, briefly, considered a run for the Senate, before being adroitly blocked by the professional political class. She was now the co-chair of the Republican National Committee, another role more related to name than to function (but in which she was increasingly assuming the actual chairperson responsibilities). Her job, at the podium, her muscular arms bare, and with flowing tresses in keeping with all the other *Charlie's Angels* types surrounding Trump, was to represent the theme of the Trump family and its dynastic love and the patriarch's personal warmth: a determined narrative of the convention. The insistence on family was both a highly uncharacteristic and puzzling effort to soften Trump's image—a good man, a caring man, an amazingly sensitive man—and to hurriedly and aggressively distract from Melania's absence, if you were inclined to notice it.

The third night's theme was meant to address what was regarded as a persistent Trump forced error and liability: his draft-dodger disdain for people in the military, particularly for people who had suffered in the military. From his dismissal in the 2016 campaign of Gold Star families and of John McCain's imprisonment in Hanoi, to his "losers" and "suckers" remarks on his visit to commemorate the war dead in France, Trump's knee-jerk contempt for fallen soldiers was a weakness he had managed to survive only because the Democrats had at least as much ambivalence about the military. For one of the longest segments of the evening, family spokesmen for some of the soldiers who died in the disastrous melee of the U.S. retreat from Afghanistan told their stories of a heartless Joe Biden and a despairing Donald Trump, who surely would never have let such a thing happen on his watch.

Also on the third night—because, as an almost in-law, she necessarily merited airtime, too—there was Kimberly Guilfoyle, Don Jr.'s live-in partner, inexplicable to almost everyone, including Trump. The former wife of California governor (then San Francisco mayor) Gavin Newsom, a plausible Trump opponent, Guilfoyle had converted herself from California lefty to right-wing agitprop personality and gotten herself a job on Fox News, where she became one of the few women—perhaps the only woman—to be felled by #MeToo issues, fired for sending dick pics to colleagues and for harassing a young assistant. Taking the podium, she used her few minutes to deliver a flailing, screeched, near-hysterical homage to her not-quite father-in-law.

Don Jr. got his own turn. It was a cautionary display of the hard duty and slavish requirements of being Donald Trump's son.

But the real purpose of the night was for the prospective vice president to formally accept his nomination. It seemed apt that Vance follow so closely on the heels of Don Jr., both with their beards, making it seem that they might share Donald Trump as a parent and, indeed, that Vance owed Trump, the father, the same servility.

Vance is an able writer—he seems, in fact, unusual for a politician, even a future one (Barack Obama being another notable exception), to have written his own book—and had tried to fashion himself as the *intelligent* MAGA explainer and spokesperson. But here Trump's speech-writers had reduced him to basic pro-workingman talking points. This cheering crowd was witnessing his transformation into high-flunky status.

. . .

Trump had arrived in Milwaukee with an unfinished speech—a "dull" speech, a "nothing" speech. On Monday, with a small team in his suite on the seventh floor of the Pfister Hotel, an unfamiliar Trump, generally doubtless and peremptory about what he wanted in a speech, began to agonize.

One of the things that marked Trump's speeches from the beginning of his political career had been his noted lack of interest in attempting the personal background stories that almost all other politicians seem compelled to include.

"That's phony stuff. Everybody sees through that bullshit," he'd told Steve Bannon in 2016. "I can't do it."

Now was different. "I think I need to tell the story," he said to his surprised staff. "Everybody keeps calling me, and that's what they want to know. I need to explain it. It would be weird not to. I'm going to tell the story. The only reason people are going to tune in is to see what I'm going to say about this."

It was clear that he had continued to tell the story to himself and that he still had questions.

"I only want to tell the story once. That's all I'm going to tell it. Let's just say this is the only time you'll hear it," lest people started to expect a touchy-feely Trump.

In the Pfister Hotel, in front of his amazed staff, he started to grope through the story of the attempt on his life, pulling together the disparate details and trying to describe his own amazement and confusion and fear. Nobody was meeting anyone else's eyes—this was uncharted territory. The man who knew everything always—whether he knew it or not—now was deeply uncertain about what had happened.

He was . . . baring his soul.

"This is tough to say . . . It's hard to say this . . . You think you can . . . You do a eulogy, and you think you can do it . . . but then when you're up there . . ."

He moved forward and then returned to the beginning, remembering details, adding more details—the staff now just transcribing the fragments. He continued and then returned to the beginning again. This was therapy more than speech prep. Again and again . . . *I was standing there . . . What a great crowd . . . I was on time . . . What a great day . . . At first I had no idea . . . but maybe I sensed something . . . I went down . . . and for a moment . . . but I thought I'm okay . . . I had to let people know I'm okay . . .*

"Read that back to me . . ."

And back to the beginning: *It was such a fine day, and we were on time . . . and for some reason I decided to put up the slide at the beginning . . .*

By the time Monday's prep was over, they had a first draft. He didn't want to have to tell it again. This would be the first time a former president had told something like this. He was satisfied they had gotten it. They wrapped the top of the speech on Wednesday and then hurried through the bottom.

• • •

In the preceding several weeks, Trump had continued to call either Wiles or LaCivita to force speakers onto the convention program. Most of Trump's choices, none of them quite germane to the themes or goals of the convention, ended up being pushed to the last night. By then the general thread was mostly lost anyhow, so the team was resigned to the odd-lot program: Tucker Carlson; Hulk Hogan; Kid Rock; Linda McMahon, the former professional wrestling entrepreneur (and the unlikely small-business administrator in the Trump administration); Steve Witkoff, golf buddy; and Dana White, CEO of the Ultimate Fighting Championship.

Early in the evening, before Trump arrived at Fiserv Forum, ninety-three-year-old Rupert Murdoch had shown up at Trump's suite in the arena building and, unrecognized by the staff, was kept waiting in the hallway for almost thirty minutes.

"You don't keep Rupert Murdoch waiting!" Trump declared when he arrived, a usage he often applied to the innumerable people who found themselves waiting for him.

Miriam Adelson, mega-billionaire Sheldon Adelson's widow and Trump's nominee for the most boring human being on the planet, who had committed ninety million dollars to the campaign and was hinting she might be willing to double that, also showed up for a pre-speech tête-à-tête.

He sat in the VIP box through the early speeches. Only when he exited the box to go backstage to prepare for his own entrance did Melania finally—*finally!*—appear. She would be there, she had *finally* agreed, but would arrive in the VIP box only after *he* had left. Still, even that was a relief.

And then he was on the stage . . .

There was something of a political hush, at least in pundit circles, if not on the chatty and chaotic convention floor. It was a new Trump; even, it could seem, a transformed Trump. Here's what had been promised, a man looking beyond this convention and beyond the party to the nation. He had had the kind of experience that necessarily changes a man—even Donald Trump. He began . . . and it seemed like it could be a great speech, a genius one. It might have even seemed that the half of the country that had, for more than eight years, continually asked what people could possibly see in Trump might now get their answer. It was a tale told with humility and awe. One might not believe, as Trump himself probably did not, that God, as he was saying, had saved him, but *something* had. In front of that, his pettiness, bile, and long list of standard grievances seemed to fall away. For minutes there, it was clear to all, perhaps truly everyone, that another Trump presidency was inevitable—and even deserved to be.

But then, having delivered his story, having struggled against his own natural character to give it—and succeeded—he relaxed, put his elbow down on the lectern, and, in his rally lean (a near snuggle with the lectern), continued as though nothing whatsoever had changed.

If, in hindsight, there is a search for the moment of the bubble's bursting, the tide's turning, the shark's jumping . . .

As written, the speech had been clocked by his staff at just under sixty minutes. He went on for ninety-two. It was a mere variation on his stump speech, huffing, puffing, snarling, mocking, insulting, mugging, smirking . . . a jarring and even embarrassing juxtaposition between, minutes ago, the man humbled before God and now the same old, same old.

It fell hopelessly flat. The lines that had reliably delivered a big roar— nothing. Instead of his energy building, feeding off his crowd—his fans—he was scattered, flagging, and then, redoubling his efforts, cramming more in. The slacks-and-blazer crowd, the country chairs, here for their every-four-years Republican trade show, were not the jeans-and-cut-off-shorts crowd, the outdoor-concert types, of his rallies. For once, Donald Trump had misread his audience.

He had set the evening up with him as the happy carnival barker— Hulk Hogan, Kid Rock, the UFC. In his ideal happy life, he would have been a sports and entertainment promoter. Then, in a revelatory turn, here was a chastened man with his soul bared. But, bait and switch, the raging, petulant id was back again. Suddenly, there was a pressing question about a man who had heretofore, in perhaps the greatest of all political virtues, been quite a simple creature: Who was Donald Trump?

"What a weird fucking night," read a text from a guest in the VIP seat.

PART SIX

You Say Kamala . . .

CHAPTER 21

Reversal

JULY–AUGUST 2024

A recumbent Democratic Party had failed to overcome its disbelief that Donald Trump, whom it saw as a threat to every aspect of its existence, was electable, until it faced the hard numbers projecting his landslide. It had happily watched the criminal justice system add a fail-safe pile-on of all-but-insurmountable, likely even mortal, legal challenges, and then had looked on with incredulity as, quite beyond legal logic, those challenges had come undone. The party, with the support of its vast media apparatus, had chosen, for the most part, not to notice the day-by-day physical and mental degradation of its candidate, despite the outpouring of evidence, plenty of it a torturous video record, of the president's confusion. It took the public spectacle of the bewildered standard-bearer, utterly helpless in the face of not just a relentless Trump, but a nearly martyred one, to finally move the party to urgent concern and then outright panic and then decisive action.

It is perhaps understandable that the Trump campaign, complacent in its extraordinary success, and having built its strategy around the Democrats' willful denial of Biden's incapacities, with every good reason to trust the Democrats' continuing, if inexplicable, blindness, found itself open-mouthed and stunned when the end came—on Sunday, July 21, three days after the close of the Republican convention, at 1:46 Eastern time, in a tweet.

The top members of the Trump team were each trying to take at least some of the weekend off, and when it happened, when the tweet hit and the end came, it was hard to corral everyone. It was with confusion and even anger, and as though without warning, that they now faced a re-made race. And recriminations: *How did we not know?* But of course they had known. How could they *not* have known? But that sense of disbelief—of destiny being on your side and then, suddenly, denied—is not the flaw of just one political party.

The senior team discussed, as though for the first time, how they wanted to begin to reposition the campaign in a race that was no longer against Joe Biden, the yin to their yang, the contrast loser to their contrast gainer.

With Wiles, LaCivita, Fabrizio, and assorted others gathered on the phone, they tried, with care, to consider a consequential reframing of attitude, posture, and strategy and how to come out of the gate. Then they got Trump on the phone to discuss their thinking. But Trump said, well, I already put out a statement that I worked up with Boris and Natalie. It was a best-of Trump's favorite Biden aspersions—he did not even mention Kamala. He was still running against Joe, even his ghost. And now redoubling his venom, with added bitterness, because Biden had left him home alone, jilting him practically at the altar.

• • •

Overnight—literally, overnight, from Sunday afternoon until midday Monday—Kamala Harris, next to Biden, the candidate whom Trump had heretofore seemed most readily poised to beat, became the inspiration, mission, and future of the Democratic Party. For three years, few in the party or media had ever had a good word to say about her; seldom had the pathos of the vice presidency seemed so pathetic. Now, though, in her instant and head-spinning transformation, she had become the hidden gem of liberal politics, a singular figure of political energy and perspicacity. A Trump killer. Likewise, Joe Biden—who had refused to recognize or been unable to understand the glaring implications of almost every poll; and who had, in almost Trumpian fashion, made himself his only concern; and, to boot, who had seemed to take his exclusive counsel from, of all people, his deeply wayward son—was now a figure of extraordinary selflessness and wisdom. He had been, in clear view of the world, pulled out of office by his fingernails—a full, public emasculation. You need to get the fuck out. But Hillary Clinton, that paragon of straight talking, now called his decision "as pure an act of patriotism as I have seen in my lifetime."

And what of that strong bench of Democratic swing state governors the party regularly extolled? Smarter-seeming minds had urged the party to mount a reality show–type bake-off that would dominate the news, rivet the nation, and deprive Trump of the media air he needed to breathe. Hadn't George Clooney, in his game-changing public excoriation of Biden, called for an open convention? But in the blink of an eye, those energetic governors and would-be presidents had wilted. They had concluded either that the odds of beating Trump were not worth the gamble; or that the prospect of being mauled by him too gruesome; or, simply, that time and money were too short . . . so let Kamala do it. Or, here was proof of her extraordinary political skills or of at least a singularly efficient power grab: In a matter of hours, she had swept away the wishes of a significant part of the Democratic leadership, and short-circuited the plans of all her possible opponents. The prize was there and she took it.

Anyway, the game had changed.

Seven days after Biden's withdrawal, the newly inaugurated Harris campaign had commitments for upward of three hundred million dollars.

• • •

Thus the Republicans' convention bounce was posthaste exceeded by the Democrats' out-with-the-old, in-with-the-new bounce.

The media, in the first week of Harris's acclamation, seemed intent on giving her all the attention it had previously withheld, wall-to-wall in its coverage, and to make up for its past unkindness, rudeness, and dismissal of her with awe and adulation (. . . her stepchildren really, really loved her; she could crack an egg with one hand; she was *only* fifty-nine!).

Trump, of all people, understood that neither the media's motives nor even its point of view mattered as much as its attention. Zero-sum. Since the race began, there had hardly been a news cycle that Trump had not dominated, thwarting any possibility that his Republican opponents might compete with him. Biden in the past year had barely registered against Trump. The Democrats' meltdown had, briefly, taken Trump's headlines, but then, with his preternatural luck, the shooting and his walk-away survival restored the stage to him. But now this, Kamala—Kamala everywhere, a political sensation—and he could hardly get arrested.

American politics had seldom experienced such an overnight transformation—and this was just the latest overnight transformation of the many overnight transformations in the space of a few weeks.

Trump now reverted from indomitability to hunkered-down resentment and rancor. Of course, all along, in his bitterness, he had known it was a question of not if, but when . . . Again and again, he had made his injured case . . . If the legal stuff didn't work, the Democrats wouldn't just lay down their swords. There was one point and one point only for the Democrats in 2024 and that was to keep him from winning. If it meant ripping Joe Biden out of the White House, yup, they would.

"They" were all the component pieces and figures of the system itself—Justice Department, deep state, Nancy Pelosi, the media, Hollywood, tech.

It had always been thus: He would beat the system, or the system would beat him.

As Kamala soared—coming even with him in the polls, and moving past him if you figured Bobby Kennedy Jr. in the race, with Trump seeing these polls as more of the concerted effort against him—Trump was in an odd form of denial. He now found satisfaction that the Democrats had not opted for a bake-off and an open convention, deciding that his worst fear would have been Gretchen Whitmer. Against Gretchen, "we'd be losing big." Kamala was nowhere near competitive in Georgia or Arizona. Winning Georgia and Arizona, Trump just had to pick off a single swing state, Pennsylvania, Wisconsin, or Michigan, and she wasn't leading in any of those three.

Harris was bad on the border, bad on crime, radically liberal, and totally incompetent . . .

And yet . . . he was raging. At the Democrats, certainly; and at the system; and at the deep state; and at *The New York Times*; but also at his own staff. The Trump campaign's message was that they were entirely ready for Kamala, of course they were. But they weren't. Their research on her was, at best, light. They hadn't tested their VP choices against Kamala as the opponent. Indeed, they hadn't ever believed it would be anyone else but Joe.

Why—given that their main campaign platform was precisely that Joe couldn't make it? Didn't a doddering Joe mean an inevitable Kamala?

The senior leadership, many believed, had become an insular and inward-looking group. Their mission was humoring, containing, and delivering good news to Trump—a difficult job they had seemed to master—and running against an incumbent who, at best, had only a low-wattage ability to fight back. Self-satisfied with their perfectly executed strategy, the top trio—Wiles, LaCivita, Fabrizio—was wholly uninterested in any further, unnecessary discussion of the game plan. We've got this (yawn).

In the days after Biden's withdrawal, at a senior staff meeting at Palm Beach HQ, James Blair, a Florida political operative whom Wiles had hired as the campaign's political director—that is, the chief tactician, and one of the few staffers who had the temerity to speak up in the top-down structure—tried to sound the alarm.

"I'm sorry if this makes me seem like I'm overly abrasive," he began his critique.

"We already thought that before," responded an annoyed Wiles.

But Blair went on: If there was a plan, no one knew it. Even senior people felt excluded from the decision-making process. They weren't ready. They weren't prepared. There was a total disconnect between the campaign's strategy and what was actually happening in the race. The campaign, said Blair, seemed hopelessly caught in its own echo chamber.

Blair's office was promptly moved off the sixth floor, where Wiles, LaCivita, and Fabrizio sat.

As the race had been transformed overnight, so, too, was the Trump campaign organization. Its great discipline, remarkable lack of friction, adept management of its candidate, and flawless execution of a singular plan to keep Trump at the forefront of the news cycle had, overnight, revealed itself to be utterly flat-footed. It was the clear victim of that most singular flaw: It believed its own bullshit. An unbeatable Donald Trump had cornered a hopeless beaten-down Joe Biden and, as well, had seemingly overcome the legal onslaught against him. All that remained was to pile up the votes. Except not—and now they were left blinking in the sudden light. Trump, who again and again—so often that it had become mere Trumpian nonsense—had predicted Biden's exit from the race, was, too, like his campaign, unable to process what had happened or to pivot to a world that, with a new opponent, would require a new strategy. Trump the counterpuncher had been counterpunched.

And, glued even more than usual to his phone, he was in a rage loop: They were always going to get him. They had tried the legal stuff, and that hadn't worked; now they were trying this. They were always going to find something. He'd beaten Joe Biden, but nobody wanted to give him credit for that. He'd won. Biden's getting out meant *he* had won. He had forced Biden out. Now they were changing the rules on him again. Bait and switch! Furious at his people for not having anything on Kamala (refusing or unable to pronounce her name correctly), he manically trolled for rumors about her and polled people on a nickname for her—"Laffin'," "Lyin'"—kicking himself for being unable to find one that would stick. And the assassination, the almost assassination—"they're trying to take that from me." Trying to cancel the assassination! The FBI saying he might *not* have been hit by a bullet. Eargate. It *was* a bullet! He had the worst staff. They weren't prepared for any of this. How could they have nothing on her? Everybody knows she's crooked, and they have nothing at all! And JD; they fucked up on JD. They hadn't given him a good *woman* to choose from. And now all the media was talking about was JD. What the fuck was wrong with that guy? What the fuck?

. . .

The phone is Trump's instrument for mulling things over, for talking to himself, even if someone else is party to the conversation, an ideal echo chamber—when he is thinking, he is effectively always thinking out loud.

When he gets on the phone and does a round of calls, asking people what they think of someone, that's seldom good for the person he's asking about. He's not really seeking an opinion. Rather, he's rhetorically framing an opening to express his own doubts. In fact, if he's asking you if you know anything, you know you're merely the mirror here . . .

"What do you think about how JD is doing?" he asks.

"Well, he seems—"

"Yeah. What the fuck is with that name-change stuff? How many name changes has he had? That's shifty, that's very shifty. That's my staff fucking up. They know what I think about people changing their names. I think it's shifty. And they didn't tell me."

The fear that a thirty-nine-year-old Vance might make Trump look old suddenly seemed to be playing in the exact opposite fashion. Vance, in contrast to the political field—even if a fifty-nine-year-old Kamala was passing as a generational shift—seemed hopelessly, comically callow and lightweight, wet behind the ears. The baby face, the transparent beard, the effort to be a bro, the need to impress—the need to impress *Tucker Carlson*! Really, the aspiration to *be* Tucker Carlson. All the right-wing bros wanted to be Tucker!

There is a curious subset of the conservative movement that aspires to be the smartest kid in the class, to take the intellectual mickey out of the lefties and the snobs. The conservative smarties often adopt a Jesuitical approach, mounting a contrarian, disputatious, and theoretical form of argument—clear parallels can also be found in the law school case method—that can easily make somebody seem like a smart aleck, or a troll. A la JD Vance, a lawyer *and* Catholic convert. (Ted Cruz, Princeton and Harvard, was a famous conservative smarty-pants, alienating nearly everybody with his theoretical constructs and constant one-upmanship.) In less than a week after his national introduction, the reveal of his past efforts, studied and composed, to say clever and contrarian things—generally more nasty than clever—together with the details of his conversion from loathing to loving Trump, as well as the highlighted focus in his short career on the particulars of his greasy-pole climb, had turned Vance into, at best, an unpleasant figure, if not a sinister one.

A theory of the JD case was that he would supply ballast to the base—the nationalist, isolationist, wing-nut policy, Project 2025 crowd—leaving Trump to freely wander where his sharper electoral instincts took him. But what had suddenly seemed to be exposed was the Tucker Carlson fallacy. Carlson, who had long considered joining the race, had instead promoted two central figures in it: Bobby Kennedy Jr. and JD Vance. Each had forged quite a vivid, mean-minded, unsympathetic, and absolute view of the world. To an extent, this might seem Trumpian. Except that you did not have to take Trump—ungrounded, performative, even unhinged—literally. Whereas Carlson, Kennedy, and Vance, manifesting apparent logic and intelligence, did seem to want to be taken at their word. This continued to work for Carlson as entertainment, but curiously—surprisingly—Vance and Kennedy in their political climbing revealed that there was at least a subtle difference between entertainment and politics. What, in one context, might be a social and political inversion that was engaging enough to be amusingly contemplated, demanded, in another context—at least among that slim segment of swing voters—that you actually engaged with the meaning of what was being said. Was there something fundamentally wrong with women who didn't have children? Your sister, your friend, your aunt, your cousin? Everybody knew somebody. Would people without children—the single largest-growing demographic—really be okay with paying more taxes than those with children?

Nobody had told him, Trump fumed. Why hadn't anyone told him about the cat lady stuff?

And the couch. Vance had confessed in his book that he had masturbated into a couch. *Except he hadn't.* He hadn't written this at all. It was born out of thin air. It was like so many right-wing tropes that stuck because Republicans got the joke. Now the Democrats had one that was sticking because, *finally,* the Dems had gotten the joke.

Trump hadn't wanted Vance. He had wanted a woman. Why hadn't he been given a woman? In fact, there was Elise Stefanik, Sarah Huckabee Sanders, Kristi Noem (before the dog), Katie Britt (before her terrible State of the Union rebuttal in her kitchen), Marsha Blackburn, and Nikki Haley, and he hadn't wanted them.

He suddenly couldn't get off the topic of Maria Bartiromo, the 1990s CNBC "Money Honey," now on Fox. Once upon a time, with her slavish deference, every American CEO and billionaire had fallen in love with her. Why hadn't they considered Maria? How crazy was that? And Fox's Harris Faulkner—a Black woman named *Harris*! Come on. That was Natalie's idea. And it could have been a great idea!

And who had done the vetting, anyway? Because she had been so squirrely about the whole thing, keeping everybody else out of it except "her" people, making it so clearly not a campaign decision but a "chief of staff" decision, it was squarely at her feet—Susie Wiles. Now in crouch mode.

He had been forced to pick from a group of people none of whom he had wanted to pick. None of the guys he was left with had brought anything to the table. Nobody was thinking outside the box. Why didn't he have people who could think outside the box?

"She"—Kamala—was getting great press. And JD—"JD" or "J.D."? (Which was it? And why didn't he use his real name, anyway? "JD" because he was a lawyer? Put it on your license plate where it belongs!) JD was getting terrible press. And he, Trump, was getting no press.

Could they bounce JD? *Could* they?

JD, for his part, seemed to remain blissfully ignorant of the nature of Trumpworld and how difficult it might be to hold on to this tiger's tail.

• • •

Michael Wolff

Trump had had two meetings right before he gave his convention speech. He had tried to mollify Murdoch about picking Vance over Burgum, suggesting again that Burgum would be secretary of state and would be there to advocate for all of Rupert's hawk opinions. But since then, Murdoch's *Wall Street Journal* had done nothing but shit all over Vance. Trump had also met with Miriam Adelson, the multibillionaire widow. He had endured an entire hour of having to listen to Miriam, the most boring woman in the Republican Party, in order to reel in the one hundred million she had promised and the one hundred million more she was dangling. The Adelson money required kid gloves, and then she might fuck him anyway, like he believed the late Sheldon did to him in 2020, skimping on his promise. He listened to Miriam and let her drone on. Except, in the week after the convention, Natalie brought him an article about how Miriam was hiring a slew of Never Trumpers to run her Trump PAC: Charlie Spies, whom they had fired from the RNC because they found out he was a Never Trumper (and, to boot, one of Ron DeSantis's lawyers), and Dave Carney, a Rick Perry guy who had said terrible things about Trump. What's more, Miriam seemed to have promised her money to Ike Perlmutter's PAC, but then had decided to start her own—meaning Ike was whispering in Trump's ear about Miriam's undependability. Off-the-cuff, Trump dictated a text for Natalie to send: ". . . Your late husband would never have done this to me. . . . You're my enemy if you're hiring never-Trumpers to work for you . . ." His stream-of-consciousness invective, as relayed to Natalie, continued.

• • •

The period between the Biden–Trump debate on June 27 and Biden's withdrawal from the race and endorsement of Harris on July 21—with the Democrats' meltdown marked by the sweeping pro-Trump Supreme Court decisions, an assassination attempt, and the Republicans' celebratory convention—likely represents the most screwball reversal-of-fortunes month in American political history. And suddenly, it didn't seem to matter at all. Dropping Biden, quite as though he hardly ever

existed ("pay no attention . . .") and replacing him with Harris (heretofore thoroughly disdained, now universally adored among Democrats),
had reset the race back to the day before the debate. It was a toss-up,
a fifty-fifty election, a country of implacable Trumpers versus a country
of implacable Democrats (no longer embarrassed by their stumbling
standard-bearer).

An exact reset except for one soft caveat. Trump's yearlong domination of the news before June 27, and ceaseless hectoring about Biden's
failing faculties, had allowed him to even the race against the incumbent
and put the momentum at his back. Now, with the Kamala ascendency
and her startling reinvention dominating the news and wiping out and
perhaps even reversing the age issue, the big mo—what Tony Fabrizio
was, with something like panic, trying to dismiss as her "honeymoon"—
was at *her* back.

"Why is the media in love with her? They know she's an idiot. For
years, they've said she's an idiot. Why aren't they saying she's an idiot
now?" Trump raged in phone call after phone call and, at the same time,
was deeply mystified. "Why? Can you tell me? Can anybody tell me?
She used to be an idiot; now she's not an idiot?"

An elemental part of the Trump attack strategy—and he had no
other strategy but to attack—is repetition. Over and over and over again,
you repeat the same few needling words. It's a branding strategy. It's a
reliable approach that takes time, together with a certain unrelenting
shamelessness. Now, suddenly, Trump didn't have the time. There were
only one hundred days to go. It was suddenly a European campaign of
quick-to-it impressions rather than the American subdural hammering
of billion-dollar ad spends and limitless cable television blah-blah.
What's more, Trump didn't have a nickname for her, nor a tagline about
her. The campaign's line about Biden, "weak, failed, dishonest," was
lamely tweaked to "weak, failed, and dangerously liberal" for Harris.

What's more, they really knew nothing. They were outside the news,
victims of it. It was impossible, they reasoned, that the Harris movement
had come together overnight. Obviously, this must have been weeks or
even months in the works—assembling the party support, prepping the

media, diverting possible opponents, working delegates . . . But, if so, the Trump camp hadn't known. Nothing. Nada. And their information wasn't getting better. Here's how little they knew: Paul Manafort and Roger Stone were suddenly back as unlikely figures of authority in Trumpworld because they were claiming that they had actually known something about what the Democrats were up to.

And with the hundred-day countdown begun, and Harris yet to be touched—turning out ten thousand people for a rally in Atlanta, crowds not seen for the Democrats since the days of Barack Obama—she was now looking at two news-killing events that each promised a massive boost:

A VP pick, which would be measured against the stumble or *crack-up* of Trump's Vance selection, and a convention, less than three weeks away, which would be a four-day Kamala festival.

Still . . .

You can only surge so much.

And, in fact, while her numbers were going up, his numbers were not going down.

Trump's country was not moving away from him; and the Democrats' joy was simply the product of being back in a fifty-fifty race.

• • •

An appearance at the National Association of Black Journalists convention was put on his calendar weeks before Biden withdrew from the race and Harris grabbed the mantle. Even then, it would have been a curious choice, a Venn diagram of two groups reliably hostile to him. But when the invitation came, there was a sense within the campaign of him being the effortless publicity gainer in any conflict; and of him being fearlessly out there, making unprecedented strides with Black voters. That is to say, nobody thought too much about it.

But by the appointed day, he is no longer facing an unpopular, faltering white man, but a surging, electric-with-promise, next-generation Black woman.

Sometimes the train wreck just can't be stopped. He will claim to friends that he didn't know anything about it until the day before. And, certainly, in the hours before, he is like a man clawing back from the abyss. "I never signed off on this . . . Nobody ran it by me . . . We're walking into a trap . . ." From the plane and then from the car, he's calling Susie Wiles . . . "Who the hell signed off on this?" he keeps asking. "Who the hell?"

It gets worse. Rachel Scott, the ABC reporter who will lead the panel of three Black women journalists, announces that his remarks will be fact-checked in real time. He's hearing this and, backstage, Justin Caporale and Steven Cheung by his side, won't come out. He's dug in, railing against the fact-check stuff and trying to forestall the inevitable. He's level-ten pissed off. Still, though, this is Trump. He's in a fetal position, but now he rises looking for a fight. In his aggression are his best instincts—the bravado that has gotten him this far in his preposterous climb; and his worst—the unforced errors that shift the wind from at his back to against him. And, too, here is his inability to tell the difference.

Onstage, he unfurls a vivid display of utterly unreconstructed racial attitudes, expressed with not just ignorance, but a special joie de guerre—Kamala, he tells his Black audience, isn't actually Black; maybe she's Indian, maybe not.

He rises to every occasion; he gives more than he gets. He never opts to skirt or deflect. He punches back, whatever its ultimate effect. No matter; it's always great television. But it's also a dumpster fire. If the election isn't about past versus future, about a minority-white America versus a new and varied majority nation, about a retro view of women versus a new empowered reality . . . he seems helplessly to make it so now.

But . . . no matter. If it is a dumpster fire, let it be *his* dumpster fire. After the event, he's flying high. It's the panel who messed up: "They overreached. Everybody could see that. Get everybody out there to reinforce the message: She's a fake." The next day's rally features a Jumbotron headline about Kamala's Indian identity. Whatever it is, ever pursuing the best/worst flip sides of his instincts, lean into it and double down.

*   *   *

The campaign, along with the candidate, is utterly stumped. Kamala has gone from Cruella de Vil to Mother Teresa in a political minute, and they can't figure out how that happened nor how to make everyone realize that's what happened. In a torrent of ad spending—and fundraising—Harris has been successfully positioned as positive, young, attractive . . . and baggage-free. She's new, everybody else (Trump and Biden) not.

The Trump campaign puts dozens of different messaging attacks into the field for testing. Nothing resonates. They seem unable to connect Kamala to Joe, or to inflation, or even to the border. Biden's negatives, it turns out, are overwhelmingly related to his age and faltering appearance—and Kamala is the opposite of that. The best they seem to have is the ambiguous case of linking a prosecutor, often faulted by the left of her party for her get-tough policies, to crime.

But Trump decides on his own where he wants his messaging to go: DEI hire, low IQ, and a slut.

"She had a very good friend named Willie Brown, I like Willie Brown," he says, going off script at a Georgia rally in early August about the California political power whom Harris may or may not have dated thirty years ago. "He knows more about her than anybody's ever known. He could tell you every single thing about her. He could tell you stories that you're not going to want to hear."

As the campaign tries to find an alternative to Trump's dubious instincts, he's on them about Harris dominating social media—that is, he's "hearing" from "everybody" that she's dominating social media. "Killing us."

That same day, Trump launches a gambit to cancel the ABC debate of September 10 that he has agreed to and swap it for a September 4 date on Fox. (This will not only give the venue advantage to Trump, but will be the sop he promised Murdoch.) Trump proposes a post:

> Kamala Harris doesn't have the mental capacity to do a REAL Debate against me, scheduled for September 4th in Pennsylvania. She's afraid to do it because there is no way she can justify her Corrupt and Open Borders, the Environmental Destruction

of our Country, the Afghanistan Embarrassment, Runaway Inflation, Terrible Economy, High Interest Rates and Taxes, and
her years long fight to stop the words, "Merry Christmas." I'll see
her on September 4th or, I won't see her at all. She is acknowledged to be the Worst Vice President in History, which works
very nicely against the Worst President, Crooked Joe Biden. The
combination of these two Low IQ individuals have destroyed
our Country, but we will Make America Great Again!

The team goes into crisis mode trying to rewrite the post to focus on
its newly evolving message points—"Why are we talking about the environment?" complains Fabrizio. "The environment is not one of our core
messages!"—and to move off the candidate's "IQ" slur, which they correctly see as a racial signal. Trump posts it unchanged anyway.

· · ·

Lara Trump and Kellyanne Conway, together, come out to Bedminster
to meet with Trump that first week of August.

Among the most notable aspects of the 2024 Trump campaign is
that this is the first of his campaigns not to have a leadership shake-up.
Consistently rising poll numbers, Wiles's astute handling of the candidate, and the distraction of his legal morass have saved the team.

But Lara Trump and Kellyanne Conway have come in now to tell
him that if he is to save his campaign, he needs a total housecleaning. It's
a moment that arises in most campaigns when there's a reversal of fortunes, a power grab, or a clash of ideologies.

At this point in 2016—early August, with his campaign flatlining—
Robert Mercer and his daughter, Rebekah, big spenders on conservative
causes, came to him with the offer of a cash infusion if he fired Paul
Manafort and installed Steve Bannon and Kellyanne Conway in
Manafort's place, which, indeed, arguably rescued his campaign. In the
summer of 2020, consistently underwater against the Democrats and in
something close to financial extremis, Trump and his son-in-law, Jared

Kushner, the effective head of the campaign, ousted Brad Parscale, a family favorite, and put in the GOP operative Bill Stepien, arguably *almost* saving the campaign.

A power grab of his underlings generally becomes a competition about who is most loyal to him and adulatory; hence, he is inclined to indulge it.

In a grasping, needy, and insecure family, Lara Trump has emerged as a climber of the first magnitude. She considered a run for the Senate, hoped she could break through as a talking head on Fox, and is now trying to turn her honorific post at the RNC into an actually powerful position. And, indeed, with quite a Leni Riefenstahl vividness, she delivered the most panegyrical speech at the convention. Her ambition is a White House job—and it seems to be nothing less than Jared Kushner's in-law position of great influence and power.

Kellyanne Conway wants what she believes her husband, George, deprived her of in the first Trump administration: the chief of staff job. She has been operating in the past months on the edge of the campaign with increasing temerity, harshly critiquing both Wiles and LaCivita, who are both directly in her way. Most recently, she has been pouring scorn on Vance, blaming the campaign for this choice.

The *Times*'s Maggie Haberman gets a heads-up about the meeting—all eyes here on Kellyanne as the leaker—and the Susie–Chris–Tony view is to defuse the situation by having Trump get on the phone with Haberman and issue a forthright denial about discord and offer a public vote of confidence. Instead, Trump gets on the phone and starts to mimic Haberman's voice and mock her nattering questions, which results in exactly the hostile story Susie, Chris, and Tony were trying to avoid.

LaCivita is probably the most imperiled. Wiles seems always to adroitly recede as LaCivita, inopportunely, steps out front. What's more, he seems to have a good-bottle-of-wine-and-posting problem, with an X account that is rivaling the candidate's Truth posts in its impulsiveness and true feelings.

"Are you all right?" Trump, on one recent occasion, after a particular public venting, calls him to ask.

After his meeting with his daughter-in-law and Kellyanne, in an act of troublemaking transparency, Trump seems to act as if the attempted putsch were out of his hands—"She's family."

LaCivita posts a picture of James Gandolfini as Tony Soprano giving the finger.

CHAPTER 22

"Weird"

The doubtless opinion in the Trump camp was that Harris would pick Josh Shapiro, the governor of Pennsylvania, for her running mate—the Jewish governor of Pennsylvania. This was threatening because Shapiro was overwhelmingly popular in his swing state, where Trump had, at best, only a razor-thin margin. In the Biden-and-now-Harris electoral math, it was a must-win for the Democrats, but it was also pretty vital for the Republicans. If putting Shapiro on the ticket gave Harris Pennsylvania, then, Trump was convinced, he'd lose the election.

But then she picked Tim Walz, the virtually unknown governor of Minnesota. Nebraska-born, a former schoolteacher and coach with a long career in the National Guard, and a degree from a college you'd never heard of, Walz was out of shape, evidently genial to a fault, white-haired and balding, and though only a year older than Harris, looking like he could be her father, except that he was white—very white.

He had—guilelessly, it appeared, and inadvertently (although his team would later brag that this was part of a calculated rollout)—gained some media attention for himself with his apparent offhand description of Trump and the people who surrounded him as "weird." Come the hour, come the word. The resonance here seemed to be the word's small-bore characterization in contrast to the existential moral and ideological condemnation that for so long seemed to have fed rather than diminished the Trump rise. "Weird" was a commonplace usage that everyone understood and no one wanted to be. (Curiously, there was at this moment the story of Bobby Kennedy Jr. and how he, revealing this now after ten years, had come into possession of a dead bear cub and, on the spur of the moment, decided to abandon it in Central Park and make it look like the bear had been the victim of a bicycle collision—an occurrence that had long puzzled the city. Weird.)

As had so often happened in the bubble of Trumpworld, the Walz pick caught everybody off guard. At Trump HQ, they were using the Google pronunciation helper to get his name right. The repeated failure of Trump's team to anticipate and plan for variables, even the predictable ones, was partly about the risks of getting ahead of Trump himself. He had decided it was going to be Shapiro; therefore, anything else was a contradiction and a challenge. So, don't go there. At the same time, there was little advantage to preparation, given that Trump was almost wholly reactive—the inveterate "counterpuncher"—and no amount of planning would alter his instinctive response.

The immediate contrast was with their vice presidential pick. Democrats were supposed to be the out-of-touch city elites. But against the avuncular, even goofy Walz, JD Vance was clearly the yuppie; in his case, a tech bro yuppie, a climber, a striver, and a step-over-your-mother guy—Vance had certainly used his own mother to lucrative effect—a type whom salt-of-the-earth Republicans had long viewed as part of the nation's moral rot. Beyond the psychographic considerations, Harris had—hereto in contrast to the Trump team's too-clever-by-half choice—tried to return to running mate basics. Pick someone who first and foremost will do no harm and who won't compete for headlines with the top of the ticket—the Democrats hoped.

Trump, defensively, was now saying *he* wasn't the one being accused of being weird; it was JD.

. . .

A useful attribute of the word *weird* was that things could become even weirder. Weirdness, an unfortunate state, is able to compound itself.

Trump had melted down onstage in front of the panel of Black women journalists and, afterward, had pronounced himself extremely happy with how he had handled them. He absolutely rejected any possibility of the September 10 ABC debate he had agreed to with the Biden campaign. He would do a debate only on Fox, in front of his own approved Fox moderators, declaring that he had "fixed her wagon," that *she* would now have to do *his* debate. He spun out a scenario wherein Joe Biden would come back and reclaim the nomination that had been wrongfully stolen from him—and then defended this as a reasonable possibility. "Could absolutely happen this way." He went to Georgia, an important swing state, and took pains during his rally to vilify its popular governor, Brian Kemp (and, by the by, Kemp's wife). Andy Stein, his old friend and a frequent caller, mildly wondered if it wouldn't have been as easy to ignore Kemp or even offer some platitudinous praise. "Why," Trump asked, "would I possibly want to do that? He's a scumbag." That, Trump decided, was his message, and the message people wanted to hear.

Stewing about Harris's constant headlines, he staged an instant news conference at Mar-a-Lago on August 8 and, for an hour, focused largely on how stupid she was, continued his complaints about how unfair it was for her to have replaced Biden on the ticket, defended the legitimacy of his wound in the attempted assassination ("I'm a fast healer"), returned to his stolen 2020 election, quarreled about the reporting on the size of the Harris rallies, wildly exaggerated the size of his own, and reversed himself and agreed to the September 10 ABC debate. Plus, he recounted a harrowing ride in a helicopter with Willie Brown, the California politician and Kamala Harris's long-ago paramour, during which Brown told him all of Harris's dirty secrets, before a near crash and emergency landing. "We thought maybe this was the end," said Trump. Except, it shortly transpired, he had never been on a helicopter with Willie Brown, though, it seemed, he *had* been on one with *Jerry* Brown, the California governor, but they hadn't come close to crashing or being in danger of any sort, and they hadn't discussed Kamala Harris; and there had been another plane ride, with another Black California official—not, though, Wille Brown. All in all, it was a classic Trump presser, which, in its illogic, unpredictability, and wealth of attacks and oddball statements, reliably delivered headlines—though these headlines were also now, in the new Harris–Walz context, clear, *incontrovertible* evidence of weirdness.

But what this all added up to for him, after his week of Sturm und Drang, was that, in his mind, the pendulum had swung back 100 percent for him. Pay no attention to what anyone said. He had turned it around.

The fact that the polls appearing on the heels of his Mar-a-Lago news conference were showing improved numbers for Harris in Michigan, Pennsylvania, and Wisconsin, with victories there certainly giving her the race, could only mean that the polls were wrong.

· · ·

But twenty-four hours after the "totally fake" polls appeared, the pendulum in his mind swung 100 percent in the other direction, and once again, the world was coming to an end for him. It was the dark nadir of the Trump campaign. They had been 9–0, and then in the eighth inning, it had reversed, and now they were 9–10.

There was a creeping sense in Trumpworld that something was off with him, that he was just not into it. "Something mentally going on," in one inner-circle view, "something in his head." When the campaign had started in earnest twenty months before, it was never quite clear if he was running mostly to be president or mostly to deal with his legal problems. Running to win or running not to go to jail? Now, suddenly, it could seem he was running for president *not* to be president. He was revolting against his will to win. He had been spooked.

And who wouldn't have been? As much as he might have wholly lacked an interior life or an iota of introspection or self-awareness, he had missed a bullet by the purest fluke. He simply did not want to die. And, beyond metaphor, he was a target. He went through a constant catalogue of who might be after him.

He was now focusing obsessively on the Iranians, with the recent arrest of a man said to be the leader of an Iranian hit squad that was out to

avenge the Trump administration–ordered assassination of Qasem Soleimani, the general who ran Iranian intelligence and was the principal architect of its foreign aggression and director of its terrorism proxies.

"These guys are trying to kill me in real life. We don't say Soleimani.
No Soleimani. This is serious."

In the convoluted depth of his unconscious thinking, this fear of
death might have been why he was insisting on more rallies. Yes, they
certainly exposed him to more threats, but why else, except courting
defeat, wondered the campaign leadership, would you open yourself up
to repeated and inevitable blunders and then cycles of negative news?
The clear fact was that the rallies satisfied the hard core and, increasingly,
in light of the Democrats' new candidate and new facility for weapon-
izing Trump's words against him, alienated the swing voters. No matter;
he wanted rallies.

On Friday, August 9, the Trump team set out for a fundraising swing
through the western states, with Trump in the blackest moods anyone
had yet seen, continuing with his assassination fears and bitterly objecting to fundraising and demanding to know why they weren't holding
rallies in swing states—"she" was in the swing states; why wasn't he?
"Forget the money. I can always get money." Indeed, he stormed in a
steady stream of aggrieved phone calls, he had just been with a "crypto
guy" who would put up any money he needed.

And then, as things seemed to always do when his mood was bad,
things got worse. As they were heading to Bozeman, Montana (Trump:
"Why the fuck are we going to Montana?"), and then on to Big Sky for a
fundraiser, the pilot came back and said the plane was having mechanical problems, so they'd have to land in Billings instead of Bozeman—
and nothing put him in a bad mood more than the plane breaking
down. Worse news, they'd invited *The New York Times*'s Doug Mills,
Trump's favorite photographer, on board, and Mills instantly tweeted
out an image of Trump and the plane hobbled by mechanical failure—
a further insult, because Trump had somehow come to equate his plane's
capabilities with his own. (Trump had also become convinced that the
plane's problems were the result of the pilot, who just didn't want to fly.)

Several small planes were then needed to get everybody to the fundraiser, and then a caravan on long and winding roads, through perilous mountain passes, to the Yellowstone Club in Big Sky. Then back to Bozeman for a rally for Republican Senate candidate Tim Sheehy. On-stage, Sheehy, an Iraq War vet, told the story of how he hadn't originally been a Trump fan, but then . . . "he dropped a bomb on that son of a bitch Qasem Soleimani and blew him to pieces!" Trump visibly blanched, the Trump team holding its breath. "You're the guy who dropped the bomb on that son of a bitch Soleimani, and I'll always have your back for that!"

Another plane had to be rounded up and chartered to the fundraiser in Jackson Hole—Trump in a nonstop rant that he needed to be doing swing state rallies; that he didn't have to do fundraising, the crypto guys would fund it all; that the Iranians were going to kill him; and that he couldn't be on an unbranded plane. In Jackson Hole, a new plane was rustled up and a big Trump–Vance decal quickly plastered onto it.

It was on to Aspen for the worst plane ride in the collective experience of everybody on board, many who had spent much of their professional lives in the air. White-knuckle, head-banging lurches. Stomach-dropping turbulence. Sudden stone-falling drops in altitude and air pressure. People actually praying. Then, in the middle of it all, a report tracking the Trump team's peregrinations identified that they were riding on the former plane of Trump's old friend, the infamous sex abuser Jeffrey Epstein—the one name he had perhaps struggled most not to be associated with.

"I'm going to die," howled Trump, "on Jeffrey Epstein's plane!"

They went back to Palm Beach from Denver in a plane his golf buddy Steve Witkoff, an absorbant sounding board for so much of the turmoil and so many of the grievances cycling through his head, sent for him (grateful, Trump gave fifty-dollar bills to the flight staff—a signed one to keep, another to spend).

• • •

Meanwhile, various reporters have anonymously been passed a document purported to be the Trump campaign's vetting check on JD Vance.

The Washington Post informs the campaign that it is preparing a story based on the vetting report.

There's a five-alarm panic about where the leak came from and a rush to get out of harm's way once Trump looks to blame the campaign team. In fact, the report was prepared by an outside group hired by Wiles, which passed through lawyers and then through the campaign—at least a dozen or more people would have had access to it.

Simultaneously, Microsoft has informed the FBI and publicly announces that it believes Iran or its proxies are attempting to hack a "high-ranking official of a presidential campaign." With no more evidence than this, the campaign sees the solution to covering up its leak—blame it on Trump's most up-to-the-minute nemeses: the Iranians! They'd been hacked by the Iranians! The Iranians were trying to help the Harris people—it was possible, even working with them! This has the effect not only of removing blame for the leak from the campaign, but, in a moment of knee-jerk soul-searching about the moral difference between "leaked" and "hacked," of keeping press outlets from reporting on the material.

As it happens, and unbeknownst to the campaign at the time, the "high-ranking official" victim of the phishing attack might actually be Susie Wiles.

So . . . they made up the Iranian thing, and then, it turns out, it just might be true—maybe. Well, probably not. (There is nothing, as it happens, all that interesting in the Vance vetting report [indeed, if it had been a thorough report, they might not have picked him]—that's the best they could phish from Wiles's files?)

Well, go figure.

• • •

He had spent one hundred million dollars to "defeat" Joe Biden, and now that was money down the drain, and he wanted it back. For real. How this would happen was, to say the least, unclear. But he seemed perfectly confident in his view that this should somehow be able to happen. He was speaking to lawyers and on the phone obsessively repeating his grievances and outlining his case. It was "unconstitutional." You could not just replace Joe after he had defeated him. How could that be "legal"?

The way he was acting now could well be compared, alarmingly so, to how he had behaved after the 2020 defeat. Here was an inability to accept quite a simple circumstance and a head-banging willingness to devote all his energy to altering an inalterable fact.

In a purely objective view, you might reasonably describe what was going on as an utter inability to cope or, even, a breakdown. But it could not, of course, be characterized that way, so the usage had become "focus." *It's just his focus. He's not focusing. He needs to get his focus back.*

Trump elders were called in: Steve Wynn, Steve Witkoff, Ike Perlmutter, Sean Hannity, Lindsey Graham (there was a reach-out to Rupert Murdoch). Their message was that this was yet a winnable campaign. If . . . he *focused.*

The economy . . . the border . . . the economy . . . the border . . .

On Thursday, August 15, at Bedminster, at Trump's own request, a news conference was called *specifically* to address the economy. *Specifically,* the price of food, that gut measure and experience that brought the daily grind of inflation home to all. To this end, in an illustrative setup, there was, along with posters and graphs, actual food: chicken, ground beef, steak, pork chops. The inflationary spiral was laid out on tables at Bedminster.

Trump began on topic, reading the prepared remarks—it was all *focused.*

But the temperature was also in the high eighties and getting hotter in the golf club's sun. And one thing about Bedminster—which must never be brought up with Trump—is that there are a lot of flies. Incessant flies. Always flies. And now, with all that food baking in the sun, so many more flies. And he was batting them away as he tried to *focus.*

It was a fatal distraction. He went exactly where he was not supposed to go—straight at *her.* It was an ad hominem filibuster: She was an idiot, "an incompetent individual," mentally deficient; and she was ugly— "beautiful Kamala," he said risibly. And the laugh—how could anyone vote for anybody with a laugh like that?

And it was not just this news conference; it was every news conference, and he wanted to put more on the schedule. He had, he pronounced, the "right" to attack her. His singular interest—his *focused*
interest—was attacking her. Forget her politics—it was her person he
wanted to attack. She *personally* had taken something from him, a
woman had taken something from him, a *Black woman* had taken it. His
one hundred million dollars. His certain victory.

He had agreed to the ABC debate on September 10, but now he was
asking everybody—everybody: staff, donors, supporters—should he do
it? Could he get out of it? "Is there a way to back out? I've got to get out
of this."

· · ·

The staff has worked to bury the story of Kellyanne Conway's attempted
putsch, not least of all because Trump seems to be entertaining it. He
doesn't like the ads the campaign is running—people are telling him
that they're bad. And why are people getting paid so much money? He
means LaCivita. And the polling isn't right—that's on Fabrizio. Why do
we need him?

Meanwhile, the hapless Corey Lewandowski has been lobbying
Trump for a job in the campaign. (He's been on the payroll at the RNC.)
Trump, ever wedded to his hangers-on, asks that something be found
for Corey. This now presents as a Kellyanne workaround. Corey is coming in along with a list of others—so really . . . the campaign isn't being
challenged, it's expanding.

But then Lewandowski—again and again, pushed to the margins of
the Trump circle precisely because he can't contain his exaggerated sense
of self or, often, his hands—starts saying he's being brought in as "chairman" above Susie and Chris.

Trump clarifies—well, he's going to be "my special envoy" to the
campaign; that is, Corey explains, the campaign will report to him, and
then he to Trump, which actually does *sound* chairman-ish.

Indeed, this could well be a shake-up, but one that you won't know
has actually taken place until long after it's happened: Trump seeding

the ground for dissension and rivalries and maximal discomfort and uncertainty. The betting is that Kellyanne could well shortly have her own "special envoy" status.

. . .

If Trump is thinking that victory has been stolen from him, the campaign has a critically different view. The campaign's financial position is strong; the ground organization is solid in every swing state; election authorities in key states are stacked in their favor; winning issues (the economy, the border) are in hand. Here is the Wiles management victory. So if they lose, it won't be because of *them,* but because of *him.*

Equally, though, as campaign and supporters try to restrain him, he cannot be more convinced that the only way forward is ad hominem, his strategy for every political fight he's ever had; indeed, every career battle, every legal challenge, every marital breakdown. It's the taunt that people remember. The more outrageous and outlandish, the more cartoonish, the more memorable. Say it enough, and it sticks. Everybody, at their most frustrated and sputtering core, is a would-be name-caller. Donald Trump is their voice.

CHAPTER 23

Deadlock

AUGUST 2024

The Democrats have had nine years to figure out how to take down this beast. Neither defeating him nor prosecuting him has worked. But trading out Joe Biden for Kamala Harris is, if not a silver bullet, then at least a clear sign (and the theme of the Chicago convention) of overwhelming resolve that the party really will do anything at this point to turn the page. In the space of a few weeks, they have gone from utter hopelessness to the self-satisfaction of, so it would seem, getting their act together.

The big advantage, it turns out, of Harris's being ignored and dismissed during her nearly four years as vice president is that she is unknown yet well known. The curious effect of this is a sudden sense of great confidence and familiarity in her now hastily filled-in story. We might have thought she was lackluster, but in the sudden reveal—our bad for not knowing—it turns out she's radiant.

This compares, of course, directly to Donald Trump, among the darkest human beings who has ever lived. Here, then, is the singular premise of the Democrats' four-day convention: her light and his darkness.

The Democrats' new structural edge in the election is that this is only a two-and-a-half-month campaign. There just doesn't seem to be enough time for Donald Trump's relentless and repetitive invective to reduce Harris and her new star power, as it did with both Hillary Clinton and Joe Biden. That's the root of his fury now. An eighteen-month campaign truncated to fewer than eighty days is a fundamental change in the nature of the game—a cheat, a steal.

The Democrats are, of course, making the most of this—her virtue, his mendacity. Other than abortion, there isn't much in the way of policy presented at the Democratic convention. Since 2016, they have run most heavily against Donald Trump and only secondarily toward any Democratic platform. So . . . does all that virtue—in contrast to his sleaze—mobilize a high turnout of Democratic voters and, crucially, gain her a margin among the swings?

The problem with the Democrats' goodness is that it can easily turn into their weakness. Hillary Clinton wrapped herself in it, and to say the least, it strained her credibility. Virtue helped Joe Biden in 2020, but— even with the shadow of January 6 on Trump—began to erode while he was in office, not least as the dissembling about his age so evidently challenged his principled stand.

If professional goodness begins to seem smarmily phony—and God knows, it *is* phony—that then threatens to make Donald Trump's utter lack of artifice a reasonable alternative (or at least a fuck-you alternative). And if the message seems like corporate branding and double-speak, a default of the Dems, that may only reinforce the divide between empty-suit elites and the peanut gallery.

• • •

Other than the novelty of the defenestration of the party's sitting president, and the subbing in of the new nominee, the Democratic convention was largely made up of the party's greatest hits. Back again . . . Hillary Clinton, one of the most equivocal figures in American politics, who lost to Donald Trump; Bill Clinton, out of office for nearly a quarter of a century and yet, somehow, seeming as current as ever in the Democratic sensibility; the Obamas, as much an official political duo as the Clintons, and at the highest level of virtue—no matter that the Obama White House directly led to the Trump White House; oh, and Joe Biden . . . but pay no attention. And Oprah. Assuming that the phenomenon and staying power of Donald Trump indicates an existential hole in American politics—that is, the evident desire among so many to reject most every political conceit—the Democrats were yet doubling down on theirs.

This was no doubt the cautious strategy: Embrace what *mostly* or, at least, *sometimes* worked in the past—losing, yes, in 2016, but by a hair, and winning in 2020, if only by a hair. Don't rock the boat more than it has already been rocked. Look to stabilize the party, a large, complicated, and fractious enterprise. They would hold firm and wait him out. After all, he was seventy-eight and, not an outlandish bet, irreplaceable— the existential crisis could very well die with him. Of course, in that plan, Harris has to get elected and deprive his chaos and toxicity of another opportunity.

. . .

On the last night of the convention, she was good. Possibly very good. The revelation that she could hold her own had a compounding effect. She was her own contrast gainer, between what we thought we knew of her and what we were now seeing. She was forceful. She was direct. And she looked great. She had a glint in her eye. And wit (and the laugh was gone or suppressed). She was fifty-nine; she could have been forty-nine. Perhaps most important, she seemed to be enjoying herself. She spoke succinctly, too, handily avoiding much liberal filler and blah-blah.

Donald Trump's acceptance speech was ninety-two minutes; hers, thirty-eight minutes.

She presented herself as someone motivated only to do good. Helping people was her second nature. Selflessness her calling card. As a prosecutor, she had been compassionate to a fault. She had only ever fought for the underdog. Her career as a politician was as a fighter—for equity, inclusion, women's rights, and the greatest benefits to the greatest many that the system could provide. The true-believer crowd seemed very pleased to believe her.

The problem could be, however, that other than among people who attended political conventions, it was no longer a country of believers.

Donald Trump's transparent appetites and cravenness may have shattered the last illusions. He offered a new standard: We no longer had to pretend that he, or anyone else who aspired to getting more, much more, than the rest of us got, was like the rest of us. It was a dirty business—so, admit it.

The name of the game was ambition. Donald Trump might have been among the worst examples of it, but no one—billionaires, politicians, and celebrities alike—was free from its characteristics. Say this for Donald Trump, and it had distinguished him: He was not a phony about it.

Kamala Harris was, of course, none of those things she represented herself foremost to be. She would do most anything, if not everything, she had to do to win, stepping over innumerable bodies on the way. She had clawed her way up, distinguishing herself in moral, practical, and temperamental terms from those who had not—and now she had little in common with most Americans. She headlined her middle-class bona fides, but her middle-classness had long since disappeared. But pay no attention: For Democrats, careers made of rank and bloody careerism, as cold and cutthroat as any, as eager to be distinguished from the hoi polloi as power always is, were nevertheless redeemed in pursuit of the common good.

Donald Trump was who he was, and that identity—the real thing—was always on display. He had sold that as an alternative to the Democrats' phony virtue. His frustration now—indeed, incredulity—was that people actually seemed to believe Kamala Harris was who she said she was, or at least they were willing to suspend disbelief. This was killing him.

• • •

August, for Donald Trump, is for golf. (All times of the year are for golf, but August is for nothing else but golf.) But to keep him from being hate-focused on the Democratic convention, he was kept on the road.

Monday, he was in York, Pennsylvania, for a speech on the economy, which largely went all over the place. Tuesday was a speech about crime in Howell, Michigan, which similarly went into a free-form diatribe on many grievances, a perfidious Harris, of course, among them. On Wednesday, he met Vance in Asheboro, North Carolina, for an address that was supposed to be narrow-focused on national security, but it was an outdoor venue, so it turned into a chum-the-waters-with-bile-and-bitterness rally. On Thursday, he went to the border, where he managed to stay on the subject.

Having returned from the Arizona border to Las Vegas, and his suite at the Trump International Hotel, he is supposed to begin debate prep for his first matchup with Harris, on September 10, less than three weeks away. He is still maintaining that the debate probably won't happen, and anyway, if it does, he'll just say over and over again that she's an "incompetent bitch." (Although a spokesman has officially denied that Trump often refers to Harris as a "bitch," by the end of the week, the inside estimate is that he ranted about the "fucking bitch" hundreds of times.) His alternative to debate prep is to have everybody in his suite to watch the Harris convention speech. It's Natalie to his right and Tulsi Gabbard, Matt Gaetz, Stephen Miller, Jason Miller, and John Coale (Greta Van Susteren's husband) gathered around him over plates of chicken fingers and mini burgers. In the room is a Tucker Carlson video crew to whom Trump himself has granted wide access. As Trump watches the Harris speech, he barks out instant posts to Natalie. This, then, is rationalized as . . . debate prep.

His takeaway from her speech: He's been saddled with abortion—the "A-word." So, the next morning, Friday, he wakes up and pronounces himself in support of a woman's reproductive rights. That's the new message, he instructs—get it out there. Vance, the Catholic convert who has adopted a strict pro-life agenda, is scheduled to appear on *Meet the Press* on Sunday, and immediately panics. "Deal with it," he's told. "We're pro-choice, however you want to put that in your own words."

Having Harris in his face (on the screen) has increased both Trump's wrath and his determination to take her out. Hillary, Biden, Ron DeSantis—he knows what to do. All advice to the contrary is wrong; this is personal—personal is what he does. Friday morning, Trump tapes a *Dr. Phil* show. In his most therapeutic voice, Dr. Phil tries to guide Trump back to an issue focus with deferential softball questions; Trump rejects it all and beats down on Harris.

After a no-tax-on-tips Vegas event, it's back to Arizona for a rally in Glendale, a WWE pyrotechnic–style event, where he receives RFK Jr.'s support. The RFK campaign, which, in the beginning, was a concoction of the far right, Tucker Carlson and Roger Stone its principal authors, now comes back full circle. The RFK effect seemed with Biden in the race to pull equally from both sides, but with the Harris elevation, RFK's Democrats have largely returned to the party, leaving Kennedy holding on to his otherwise Trumpers. In a series of reach-outs, including RFK slipping into Milwaukee, Trump, surprisingly, and even with sudden enthusiasm, offers the possibility of a healthcare role for Kennedy in a Trump administration. (Trump regularly makes large promises about eventual jobs, while his team takes them back.) Kennedy, in the estimation of Trump campaign staffers, is "fucking crazy," but he could clearly be helpful to them by returning the Trump voters attached to him. The endorsement is scheduled to compete with whatever events the Democrats might add as follow-ups to their convention momentum. But, in fact, the Democrats are resting. Suddenly, it is a Trump weekend. Trump's calculation is in news cycles—with the last news cycle being the winning one. So, suddenly, he is back. The internal somewhat-resigned reality-check guess in the Trump campaign is giving Harris, at this moment, a 55ish percent chance of winning. Trump, however, by all signs, has not considered the possibility that he might lose (and, as a direct result, spend time in prison). He is, he considers, despite the evidence, ten points ahead.

"Rasmussen"—a pollster generally tilting in his favor—"has us ten points ahead," he tells a caller.

Gently informed that it is actually *three* points ahead, he instructs, "Have them fix that; it's ten points."

• • •

Trump has spent the Democratic convention week traveling with Corey Lewandowski, his "envoy." Lewandowski has been setting up interviews and meetings for Trump as well as communicating directly with the swing state and regional campaign offices and key surrogates, including making his own invitations to the debate-response team. And putting himself on television. Glued to Trump's side, Lewandowski has been deftly going around Chris and Susie, or overriding them, and taking on key campaign issues and decisions.

In an interview, Lewandowski is asked about his role versus those of Wiles and LaCivita. He praises them both and says the three are working together—"the three amigos"—elevating himself from what the campaign thought was a mere pity hire and satellite adjunct to co-equal.

The Washington Post, in a story the impetus of which no one has to wonder too hard about and formally announcing the internal leadership war, dredges up 2021 charges of sexual harassment of a Republican donor, along with other Lewandowski headlines, the slapped buttocks and financial grabs of his past.

In the week before Labor Day weekend, there is a "third-party complaint"—that is, someone reporting that Lewandowski has made "inappropriate comments" to someone else—to Trump campaign HR. By the weekend, the campaign is aware that both *The New York Times* and *The Washington Post* are following up on this story.

Trump himself is unaware both that an internecine battle is brewing and that Lewandowski is once again threatening to become a lowlife headline. You don't want to bring it up with Trump that somebody may be under fire, because his instinct might well be to double down on defending that person. Indeed, Lewandowski has survived the many depredations on his reputation because his defense of Trump is always adamant and absolute—and, if there was hope this report might bring Corey down, there's now a rush to cover up the story lest Trump defend his guy.

• • •

The Trump campaign was anticipating as much as a six-point convention bounce for Harris—but there is hardly any. The supposition on the part of nearly all Democrats and not a few Republicans is that the momentum is with her, but it has really covered only Biden's deficit. The race appears to be deadlocked heading into Labor Day and the historical start of a presidential campaign season—but now its last, determinative and exhausting leg.

For Trump, the difference between victory and defeat has come down, he believes, to the A-word. He can't stop talking about it. The best position, he knows, for swing voters is a position at radical odds from his base.

On a Midwest swing just before Labor Day weekend, he's polishing a speech he'll give just after the interview with NBC reporter Dasha Burns. "Ross," he says to his speechwriter, Ross Worthington, "I've got an idea—one more thing to add. Let's say we're giving away IVF treatments. Let's make 'em free."

Whaaa?

Is the government going to pay for this? Are they going to force insurance companies to pay? And how much are we talking, anyway?

"Just put it in. Just put it in." He's certainly not interested in the details—likely he doesn't *know* the details of IVF.

It's just the A-word fucking him.

And then in an interview with NBC reporter Dasha Burns, he's asked how, as a Florida resident, he'll vote on the abortion initiative that will be on the Florida ballot in November. It's a constitutional amendment that will overrule Ron DeSantis's ban on abortions after six weeks. The amendment brings the right to an abortion up to the point of viability—that vague cutoff. It's *Roe v. Wade*—and Trump appears to say he'll be voting for it.

And he's fucked again. The pro-life constituency in the Republican Party—among its most organized, dedicated, and uncompromising—loses its shit. Donald Trump, pro-life's most vaunted candidate, the slayer of *Roe v. Wade,* is supporting late-term abortions!

Well, he can't. That's immediately clear. He has to oppose the Florida amendment. He's told by allies who have been fielding the pro-life wrath in perhaps the clearest political reality that he has ever had to confront that if he supports the amendment, there will be a rank-and-file revolt in the party that will surely cost him the election.

So, okay, right, upon further thought, of course he's opposed to late-term abortions—so, no, he won't be voting for the amendment; sure, maybe not six weeks, but not, you know, no restrictions. Peculiarly, the pro-choice base seems mollified, even though he's perilously close to Harris's own position.

What is *his* position? He's on the phone, calling everyone. He needs a "real" position on the A-word that "works." He doesn't want to be the A-man. How does he make this issue go away?

Stop talking about it, virtually everyone tells him.

Can he?

* * *

If you want a perfect snapshot of the nature of the deadlocked campaign, look at the shocked, *shocked* reactions of both sides to the incident at Arlington National Cemetery.

Trump walks into it by trying to grab a photo op with some of the Gold Star families whose relatives were killed in the Abbey Gate suicide bombing during the exit from Afghanistan. The support of many of the thirteen Abbey Gate families has been a notable counter to the Democrats' attack on Trump's oft-maligning of the military—these are some of the families who appeared at the Republican convention. But the Trump team is stopped by a cemetery employee on the way into the graveyard; she stands in their way. Justin Caporale tries to go past her and brushes her or bumps her. She throws her hands up, saying he hit her. No, Caporale says; she touched me.

The Harris campaign, barely containing its glee, rolls out its disgust at someone who would be so disrespectful of such hallowed ground and, too, rehashes all Trump's past defaming of the military. Whereas Harris mourns "America's fallen heroes . . . and I will never politicize them," as she is now doing.

Score for the Dems! It might seem.

But then the Trump side, as gleefully, rolls out a series of videos by various of the Gold Star family members, all now deeply attached to the Trump campaign and, in grief or to self-promotional advantage, virulent in their bitterness and fury toward the Biden administration—and now connecting Harris specifically to the bungled withdrawal, with a social media bonanza of views, likes, and retweets.

PART SEVEN

....

50/50

CHAPTER 24

The Debate

SEPTEMBER 2024

Staff, donors, family, and friends—a mobilized effort—were pushing Trump to tighten his focus on that key campaign pillar, the economy. In his first major post–Labor Day speech, on September 5, at the Economic Club of New York, he laid out an expansive, Trumpian vision of how to pay for deep tax cuts and vast new benefits with trillions in savings and mountains of new revenue. "We're going to have so much money coming in." Although immediately derided as balderdash by most economists, it was at least in keeping with the standard political convention to lay out a plan for great new prosperity full of politically attractive promises. What's more, he stuck to the prepared speech. Big sigh of relief.

The next morning, for no seeming practical reason other than to confirm his own sense of indignation and belief in the power of absolute and implacable denial, he showed up in a Manhattan courtroom to hear oral arguments in the appeal of the five-million-dollar judgment against him for having sexually abused E. Jean Carroll decades before in a Bergdorf Goodman dressing room. From there, he repaired to the lobby of Trump Tower to stand before Justin Caporale's draped-in-red-white-and-blue set for a news conference.

"Watch the DJT presser," a Trump friend texted one reporter. "Guaranteed to be off the rails."

To the degree that political journalism is the study of cause and effect, of reporting on and understanding a politician's goals and his or her
method of obtaining them, here, once again, Trump brought the collective press corps to wonder and bafflement. Not only was he calling attention to the trial and its judgment against him of sexual abuse—pushing
Carroll into the Bergdorf dressing room and attacking her—but then,
with considerable apparent effort to spite his own face, he recounted in
particular detail two other claims of sexual abuse against him.

It was hard to read this insistence on his own guiltlessness and righteousness, and effort to blame anyone who would challenge him, as anything other than what kept him going. And, to boot, with his lawyers
lined up abjectly behind him, he singled out *their* poor performance—
looks of shame, panic, and bewilderment on each of their faces. Boris,
immediately thereafter, went into damage control, both for his own
benefit and, he seemed to hope, for his boss's, too, ushering in, over
lawyers' and advisers' objections, several reporters to see Trump. Boris's
reasonable hope here was that Trump would make new headlines that
would diminish the press conference's headlines about his long, uncomfortable sexual history but also about the diss of his lawyers. Alas, for
once, Trump stayed on subject.

Later that day, Judge Merchan postponed Trump's sentencing on his
thirty-four felony convictions, scheduled for September 18, until after
the election. It was easy to imagine that much of Merchan's consideration involved what he knew would surely be Trump's virulent, implacable, relentless, and inevitably damaging attacks on him, his family, the
jury, the court system, and anyone else the former president could think
of. If Trump lost in November, Merchan might have reasonably figured,
then his bite would be far less; and if he won, he would be little con-
cerned with his New York sentence, or there would be a sober pretext for
Merchan to delay again—so, safer all around, for the courts, democratic
comity, and Merchan himself, to push the date. So, yes, chalk up another Trump victory: His media strategy was his legal strategy.

• • •

In the immediate Labor Day aftermath, a palpable sinking sensation seemed to overcome Democrats and the media. Far from having it wrapped up, Harris was in clear danger of sliding back, her gains against Trump equivocal, her remarkable August fading fast, her convention bounce all but non-existent. And this sudden lackluster turn in her fortunes was against an opponent who not only had failed to mount a forceful or even coherent case against her, but who continued to make a public spectacle of his rage toward her, his reflexive antipathy to all other women and to African Americans, and what might reasonably have seemed his feelings of helplessness in having to face her.

Trump, whatever he did, seemed to remain a wholly known quantity, entirely satisfactory to his supporters, and she a largely equivocal presence, not yet passing a second smell test.

The New York Times, that barometer of the Democratic great and good, which had euphorically boosted the first month of the Harris candidacy, now came squarely back to earth with a national poll that put Trump in the lead, however equivocally, and a succession of opinion columns suddenly tempered if not curdled in their view of Harris.

The race was a toss-up in search of the next new perspective, jolt of enthusiasm, or media re-evaluation or revelation. In other words, the ideal curtain opener to the coming debate.

• • •

Trump continued to view Harris as not so much his opponent as a plot against him or an indignity to him, and Joe Biden as having taken something from him. He continued to want to sue someone. All the money he had spent successfully besmirching Biden he wanted back. (Not dissimilarly, he had, without hyperbole, once felt he should be granted an additional two and a half years to his presidency because of the interruption of the Mueller investigation.) Could he sue? he wondered in round after round of phone calls. Could he sue the Democratic National Committee? Should he try? And his demand had now risen from $100 million to $150 million.

His odd-lot collection of friends, staff, golf buddies, and, it some-times seemed, whoever wanted to be in the room, assembled for the catch-as-catch-can debate prep, confused and dumbfounded by Trump's sense of vendetta and grievance toward Harris and the Democrats and struggling to force its Trump-square-peg into a round hole. The debate was the clear opportunity to right the focus: With Harris's flash novelty fading, now was the time to firmly tie her to Biden's economic and im-migration policies, inflation and the border. And then sit back. "You broke our economy. You broke our border." Ideally, he would repeat that as often as was possible over the ninety minutes onstage. Simple strategy. Ninety minutes was the measurement. Would more of that time be taken up with the economy and immigration, or would more be taken up with abortion, women, Trump's legal cases, and Project 2025? Was it more about her or more about him? If the former, he would win; if the latter, she would win. The prep sessions worked on his "redirects." He would, in theory, easily dismiss those subjects harmful to him and di-rectly turn to any of the variations on immigration and the economy—crime, drugs, cartels, lost jobs, food prices, gas prices, mortgages, China . . . Here was one of the advantages of his scattered mind: He felt no obligation to continue with his or anyone else's train of thought. For him, unbound by logic, sequence, or sense, changing the subject was as basic as flipping an On/Off switch—that is, if he could hit the switch before she pushed his Rage button.

Unlike for the Biden debate, he was blowing off prep sessions. He was just not that into it. He turned the sessions his political team man-aged to hold him to into open-call sycophant forums—suck-up sessions: Jason Miller, Stephen Miller, Matt Gaetz, Ross Worthington, John Coale (Greta Van Susteren's tobacco-lawyer husband), and visits by a steady stream of flatterers, family members, and glad-to-help lawyers. His reliable lack of attention, which had turned into an unlikely focus in preparing for the Biden debate, was back. Matt Gaetz, for one, now sounded the alarm to the broader Trumpworld: He was stuck. "He's just not getting his pivots." He was obsessing about the subjects he needed to quickly move off of, sputtering in his indignity of having to face her. There was, in fact, not a pretense of facing her—nobody was playing the

Harris role; there was no podium; there was no clock; there was no . . . debate prep. Still, the many advisers, visitors, and boosters consoled one another and felt that at least there should be no surprises. They had reviewed every question and every subject with him, hadn't they?

• • •

While, behind one set of doors (a revolving set of doors, because debate prep was, at best, on the fly, wherever he was), the prep team was struggling against a coming disaster, behind another set of doors, every other aspect of the campaign seemed to be coming apart—an implosion that might even put to shame all other internal Trumpworld breakdowns and car crash moments.

In addition to grabbing Trump's ear, Corey Lewandowski had aligned himself with Ike Perlmutter. Perlmutter, a constant billionaire presence in Trump's circle, had continued to wage an unrelenting campaign against Wiles. During the week before the debate, Perlmutter and Lewandowski went in to see Trump to outline their case for why this campaign, by miles the most orderly of any of his three runs for the presidency, was, in fact, the product of vast mismanagement and staggering incompetence. Lewandowski left the meeting with a more or less specific nod from Trump to review the budget and offer his views.

Almost immediately, this was framed, in an announcement from Lewandowski, as the "president" having authorized him to oversee the campaign's finances. He would review all existing expenditures and everything going forward; the budget would now run through him. He started moving desks around and reassigning offices in the West Palm Beach headquarters. Lewandowski was arriving at campaign HQ at six thirty every morning, patrolling the floors, "taking names" of when people arrived, and demanding that staff members—many of whom had been working for the campaign since the fall of 2022—explain and justify their jobs. His new ownership of headquarters included giving Kristi Noem, the married governor of South Dakota who had employed Lewandowski as an adviser and with whom he'd had quite a public affair—officially denied by her spokesperson—a tour of the offices.

Meanwhile, Wiles, LaCivita, and Fabrizio were bunkered inside their offices, unsure what exactly was occurring.

Here again was Trump management—that is, non- or anti-management. He existed far above ordinary, workaday concerns. His interests were only his interests. Because he did not listen (by inclination or ability) and was not sympathetic (by temperament or basic human interest), he was never quite aware of, nor mindful of, the concerns and problems of others. And if you worked for him with any success, you knew the hardships and disadvantages of trying to talk to him—even if this were possible, and mostly it was not—about what he was not interested in. Hence, nobody truly knew who was in charge.

"We knew chaos would have to come, now it's here, blood in the streets to follow," said one Trump intimate.

And with that, it was off to Philadelphia and the debate stage.

• • •

As he arrived in Philadelphia, he was slipped another letter of abject devotion from Natalie, though this one was also full of how her enemies were trying to cross her, not least because she had only one interest: him.

Trump seemed aggrieved to be here, forced into doing this when all his instincts said not to, and yet entirely confident that he'd handle it easily.

The tip-off of what was ahead might have been in Harris's decision to seamlessly march toward him and put out her hand—and his second of bewildered hesitation, if not disgust.

Harris took the first question on the economy. Trump, in his turn—instead of ignoring her in his first response and laying out, as planned, his thematic linking of her to the Biden years—disputed her direct assertions and then spiraled off to immigration and Springfield, Ohio, and his vision of an immigrant onslaught there, based on recent social media tropes and fictions that had gotten stuck in his head. "Well, this is not fucking good," said Matt Gaetz, backstage.

Every passing reference Harris made—Project 2025, quoting the Wharton School against him, her family background—seemed to sting him. He struggled against each of her assertions. And then, not far in, the abortion question hit, and his increasingly tortured views turned into jaw-dropping nonsense. Next, immigration, that Trump pillar— but instead of making his case, clearly wounded by her claim that people were leaving his rallies early, he vainly tried to justify the devotion of his crowds. And then he was off on the immigrants in Springfield, eating dogs.

Backstage, the size of the disaster was in clear view. "Everybody was just paralyzed by the fucking car crash," said one member of the Trump entourage.

"My God," said John Coale to the group, registering his shock.

The Democrats, in the estimation of the backstage team, had researched all the Trump hot buttons that might be pushed, and one by one, Harris was pushing them.

Then the ABC moderator David Muir, stunned, pushed back on Trump's "they're eating dogs" claim, challenging its veracity and quoting a specific denial from a city official.

This now became the behind-the-stage focus of the otherwise dumbstruck Trumpers.

The team believed that in sorting out the details of the debate—and largely accepting the rules that the Biden team had first offered in the spring—ABC had specifically agreed not to allow its moderators, Muir and Linsey Davis, to challenge answers and fact-check on the air. This had been negotiated by Jason Miller—or, at least, Miller had assured Trump and the team that this had been locked down: no real-time fact-checking. This now—they were counting the many more times Trump had been interrupted against what they saw as the bend-over-backward respectful attention that greeted Harris—shifted the blame for the catastrophe-in-progress off Trump himself and put it onto the perfidy and deceit of the network. A series of outraged phone calls to ABC producers and executives ensued.

LaCivita, on the phone, threatened to storm the stage. (This backstage scene being filmed, to everyone's irritation, by the Tucker Carlson film crew to which Trump had given free rein.)

Onstage, Trump, meanwhile, dug himself in deeper, taking up virtually every swipe or accusation Harris made and magnifying her digs, dismissals, and disdain. In the history of presidential debates, with Joe Biden's the nadir, this one certainly was near it at the bottom, a how-not-to in almost every aspect, with Trump not only unsteady on his own issues, but wearing his resentment, self-pity, and profound lack of cool on his sleeve. For several people in the Trump camp, there was a shared sense that if Joe Biden was too old and unsteady for a prime-time debate stage, Trump himself was not all that far behind, not quick, facile, confident, or present enough.

But, as usual, actual reality took a back seat to his aggressive and implacable rendering of it. Shortly after ten thirty, Trump came off the stage pronouncing, "That's the best debate I've ever had." He followed up: "I think we should go out into the spin room and take a victory walk."

Several cautionary voices offered the obvious, including Miller, otherwise a reliable yes-man: "The media will say you're there trying to spin . . ."

"I don't think it's a good idea," weighed in a judicious Wiles.

"I think it's a great idea, sir," said Boris, and the plan was set.

With annoyance, the Trump team had to wait until the vice president's motorcade departed. But then the entourage, backstage at the audience-less debate, jumped into the caravan for the few-block trip to the spin room. Trump made a surprise entrance—actually, a confounding one—out on the floor of the convention center, with its hundreds of reporters and its cadres of Republican and Democratic surrogates. Stepping into a fast-forming press scrum fifty feet deep, he willfully, perhaps happily, insisted in the flat-out extreme that it had been a great night and his best debate anywhere and that, already, the polls were overwhelmingly saying he was the winner. Then, from the spin room, he went live with Sean Hannity to reiterate his vast satisfaction at his own victory and to critique Harris's pathetic performance.

While it was logically inconceivable that he believed this, in the ensuing days, including a trip to New York for a 9/11 memorial where he would stand close to the vice president, and in a speech extolling his great debate victory in Arizona, no one saw anything close to him breaking character. It was the best debate he had ever had. It was the best debate anyone had ever had.

Meanwhile, he was on the phone with everybody—staff, lawyers, donors, friends: ABC had promised no real-time fact-checking. They'd reneged. He was going to sue.

. . .

On Thursday in Arizona, after Wiles and LaCivita had played out the variety of scenarios about how to deal with the continuing Lewandowski coup in progress—their earlier leaking against him having largely backfired, winning him more support from Trump—they played their strongest hand. In a throwdown with Trump, the duo outlined the chaos Lewandowski had wrought and the impossibility of things continuing in this way, clearly implying that Trump had to make a choice between Lewandowski and them. They then dragged Lewandowski himself into the meeting, confronting him with their charges, not least of all that he had paraded his reputed lover, Kristi Noem, the dog killer, around the offices.

Trump's hand was forced. He now suggested to Lewandowski that he concentrate on New Hampshire, a state Trump, however unlikely, thought he might actually win. Privately, he committed to Wiles and LaCivita his promise that he would truly rein Corey in. Here Trump seemed to have made good: Lewandowski, in a snit, left the entourage and went home on his own.

On Friday, the *Daily Mail*, a leaker's destination of choice for stories about Trump women, broke a story linking Laura Loomer to the campaign's dysfunction, and the dysfunction to Wiles and LaCivita: "How Donald Trump's close friendship with glam conspiracist Laura Loomer, 31, is threatening to blow up his presidential run—as insiders say his campaign managers don't care if he wins or loses," ran the extended headline. And further: "Multiple sources familiar with the campaign structure are questioning whether the two running the operation, co-managers Susie Wiles and Chris LaCivita, should keep their jobs."

Loomer's odd presence with Trump had been particularly noted in his 9/11 trip to New York and to Shanksville, Pennsylvania, where one of the 9/11 planes crashed—not least because she was a 9/11 "truther," enthusiastically propounding her theory of an inside job. Entertaining to Trump, and an adept flatterer, Loomer had been a peripatetic presence since the beginning of the campaign, mostly kept at a distance or at least out of sight by the campaign principals, but craftily finding her way in, often at Natalie Harp's invitation (that is, likely, at Trump's suggestion).

Almost everything about Loomer, other than that she amused and flattered Trump, presented an emergency situation. There was almost no furthest-extreme, straining-the-bounds-of-all-credulity, right-wing conspiracy theory she had not adopted and aggressively promoted. Her virulence both marked her and protected her. This profile was combined with the fact that she was a Trump-style thirty-one-year-old woman whom he liked to have around for reasons psycho-sexual or as a reliable source of flattery—attributes that made her presence beyond question. She was one more self-inflicted wound.

The blame now for having the wound opened so vividly in the *Daily Mail* was put on Lewandowski or his proxies. (Loomer, whom some regarded as a Lewandowski ally, was, anyway, thrown under the bus.)

Among Lewandowski's fabled attributes in the Trump universe— from the lovers he had taken, to the lunges he had made, to the outré comments he had offered, to rages he'd unleashed—were the leaks he had planted. In a court of weaponized leaks, Lewandowski was the guerrilla general.

The *Daily Mail* piece laid out the take-no-prisoners case against Wiles and LaCivita:

Wiles, according to the *Mail* source, "had 100 percent control of the preparations for the debate and the Trump plane manifest," and hence responsibility for the debate performance and for allowing Loomer on the plane.

The story went on, outlining Wiles's previous connection to a lobbying firm and her purported conflicts of interest, blind sources saying, "'Wiles just wants to hold on to the end [of the election,] because she has the potential to get herself some lucrative contracts,' the sources say. 'This is good for her corporate business whether Trump wins or loses.'"

LaCitiva, for his part, according to the *Mail*, was a loose cannon accomplishing little and ignoring what Trump told him to do.

"Meanwhile," said the *Mail*, "outrage among prominent Trump allies over Loomer's relationship with Trump is now exploding into public view." With her presence in the entourage credited to the failures and perfidy of Wiles and LaCivita.

The Loomer story promptly spread to even more free-form media than the *Mail*, including to posts by Milo Yiannopoulos, the right-wing provocateur long discredited and long out of the news. Here was excited speculation over Trump's sexual relationship with Loomer, which shortly made it onto the Bill Maher show.

By the weekend, Trump was back on the phone asking friends and donors what they thought about him bringing Kellyanne Conway in and putting her in charge.

. . .

In a lucky break from the bad headlines—and lucky for all the more obvious reasons, too—on Sunday, playing with his friend and steadiest companion Steve Witkoff on the Trump-owned golf course in West Palm Beach, where he could be found most mornings when he was staying at Mar-a-Lago, there was a just-in-time sighting of a would-be shooter. Ryan Wesley Routh, fifty-eight, a drifter who had adopted Ukraine as his cause, was hiding in the bushes, rifle in hand. This confirmed for Trump, if it needed confirming, the mortal stakes in this campaign: "It's me they want," he went on in one phone call to a friend, marveling more, in the friend's view, at the momentousness of the event ("two assassination attempts!") than at the threat itself. "They will do anything to take me down. They will try to stop me by any means necessary." (Plus, he was put out to have lost his golf time, now foreclosed by the Secret Service.)

The first assassination attempt, in Butler, Pennsylvania, had—bitterly, in Trump's view— all but disappeared from mainstream media interest.

But it had continued as part of the hero narrative among the faithful, with the suggestion that the plots against him were far greater and darker than could be imagined and that his continued presence on the campaign trail, albeit with dramatic new security, confirmed his indomitability. Within a few hours, this new attempt was converted into a fundraising appeal.

He was being singled out as a historic figure and an agent of history, with unknown forces trying to stop him. Thomas Crooks, the first would-be assassin, had been using encrypted platforms based in Belgium, Germany, and New Zealand, evidence, repeated by people in the Trump camp, of something larger than a lone figure. "Foreign adversaries" is the description Trump darkly used. "We just don't know if these guys are speaking to foreign adversaries, I hear they might be." The Iranians, probably. But possibly Ukraine. In his conversations, the plot on his life, his legal difficulties, the scheme to replace Joe Biden—all easily ran together, portents of the case he would make if he lost or of investigations to come if he won.

Meanwhile, following the first attempt and now with redoubled fervor, security had been overhauled and upgraded, more evidence to him of plots in progress. Trump Force One had become the decoy plane, his staff and guests available to be shot out of the sky, with Trump himself on a secret flight.

CHAPTER 25

The Closer

OCTOBER

In the lore of Trumpworld, Trump always closed strong. He found a certain discipline in the final weeks. That was how he had prevailed against Clinton in 2016 (even surrendering his phone to Jared Kushner in order to prevent his self-sabotaging tweets) and how he had almost won in 2020. (Beyond his insistence that he had won, he would actually have done so in an indisputable landslide, he believed, if only he had had another week.) The Sun Belt swing states were holding with Trump in the lead; Michigan and Wisconsin were now a dead heat . . . if, now, in the final days, he could just refrain from being too Trumpy.

In the last days of September, with speeches in Pennsylvania, Wisconsin, North Carolina, and a news conference in Trump Tower, in which he mostly balanced his invective and puzzling digressions with attention to his two main issues, immigration and the economy, Trump might, his team hoped, be signaling that he was moving into close mode. A possible indication here of a change in tenor, that he was connecting in a more focused way, was that Fox News was cutting to his speeches live and then carrying them in their entire, wayward length. That was his success measure: Fox was the premium outlet, and if Fox was carrying his winding speeches, he was getting ratings. Perhaps related to this, he was bragging that Rupert Murdoch—at that moment, in a Nevada probate court waging a bitter battle against three of his children, caused, not least of all, by Fox's support of Trump—was calling him every day. (Trump added to friends that the ninety-three-year-old Murdoch could not remember that he had called him the day before.)

Still, with the debate behind them and none scheduled for the final weeks, there was the sense on the part of the Trump team of no clear climax to build to, no final impression to clearly make, no closing opportunity. The natural arc—or, at least, the one around which modern campaigns had structured themselves—had lost its shape.

In 2016, Steve Bannon, then running the Trump campaign, had averred that in a tight election, nothing mattered more than the last two weeks and the last gut judgment produced by a candidate's powerful summation or by the good or bad luck of exogenous events (e.g., then-FBI director James Comey's sudden last-minute re-opening of the Clinton email server investigation).

During the last weekend of September, with thirty-seven days to go and with early ballots being cast in more and more states, Trump relapsed from his hoped-for new discipline in a series of swing state speeches in Pennsylvania and Wisconsin, that devolved into rants on jailing his opponents, including Harris and Mark Zuckerberg; his picture of a dystopian America that would require extra-constitutional purges and crackdowns; and a furious insistence that Harris suffered from mental impairments.

"He just can't stop," said a Trump insider resigned to the randomness of both his worst instincts and his saving graces.

• • •

Likely, the October 1 vice-presidential debate, the one face-off between Vance and Walz, would be inconsequential for the ultimate vote, the Trump team understood. The Tuesday debate would be forgotten by Thursday. But the campaign doubled down on Vance—and the conscientious student and would-be VP worked to get it all. In the team's Cincinnati retreat with its mock stage, the proceedings were formal, structured, timed, and repeated. Tom Emmer, a congressman from Minnesota, played Walz. (Of note, the Trump team, at Trump's behest, had gone out of its way to defeat Emmer in his bid for House Speaker because Trump judged him less than 100 percent in his support.) Monica Crowley, the on-air right-wing commentator and gadfly always buzzing around Republican political circles, played the moderator. Here was the campaign's dream strategy: Lean away from MAGA instead of into it. Soft-pedal the hard core. Don't fight. Be nice. Vance, heretofore the attack dog, was now the default make-nice and make-sense strategy. Objectively, Vance, with his fuck-you hard-right views, both staunchly anti-abortion and retrograde in his regard for women, was being forced into an unlikely role. But he seemed to relish the opportunity to verbally shape-shift his identity. He had shape-shifted from writer and conservative intellectual to Trump acolyte. Now he would shape-shift to calming the waters and finding common ground.

In the CBS network's aging headquarters—in long decline, the company was now being taken over by the son of tech billionaire and Trump backer Larry Ellison, with his father's money—with the VP candidates in an empty sound studio, and the spin room in the company's cramped cafeteria, the final one-to-one clash of the 2024 campaign played out. It was Vance's show.

Smart and clever were exactly the characteristics he brought to MAGA world. Performance and sophistry were the high talents. There were Tucker Carlson attributes here. It was MAGA careerism of a sophisticated order—far more sophisticated than Donald Trump. Trump survived his contradictions by chaos and denial. Vance was proposing to outsmart them. The issues were of terminology. In Vance's many prior attacks on Trump, which showed a deep alarm about the intelligence and intentions of his benefactor, he had gone so far as the "Hitler" designation—but now Trump (or Hitler), on second look, turned out to be a rather nice fellow. Donald Trump wasn't denying climate change, because Trump and Vance and the MAGA party were as much for clean water as anybody; pay no attention to their stonewalling of the scientific consensus and their resetting the environmental movement back to the first Earth Day in 1970. And pay no attention to the right to abortion: What women really wanted were policies to help out families—and, he said, he had three beautiful children. And January 6 and the actual winner of the 2020 election—*why go there?* he asked with long-suffering patience. He was focused on the future.

Dismantling these neon contradictions could have made this Walz's moment. But the hyper-performance, locked-and-loaded media values of the MAGA party were now sniffed at by the Democrats. Harris's lack of spontaneity in front of the press and her guarded media schedule were, to Democrats, something like the high road in a down-and-dirty world. Tim Walz's not-ready-for-prime-time demeanor was a hoped-for ultimate MAGA contrast gainer. Except, when the opportunities were presented in the moment to starkly expose the MAGA world—Hitler, climate disregard, no abortion rights, election denial—he simply wasn't up to it. Only in the final moments did Walz call out Vance on his defense (the necessary defense in MAGA world) of Trump's continuing election denial baloney. Indeed, here was a model response ("that is a damning non-answer"), leaving Vance flat-footed. But too late. By then, JD Vance had made Trump seem, in the reflection of his potential vice president, something like cogent and reasonable. At least, in the moment.

• • •

On October 3, two days after the VP debate, the federal court in Washington unsealed the government's argument about why the Supreme Court's immunity ruling should not apply to Trump's actions to undermine, or overthrow, the 2020 election results. It was a detailed narrative of both a would-be conspiracy, however ham-handed, and the unyielding refusal of Trump to take any counsel even from his closest advisers—indeed, from anyone actually in a position of responsibility and sobriety to appreciate reality—that the election had been lost.

Was this the October surprise? The political and media world was poised for one. Hurricane Helene, with its death path through North Carolina, a swing state? The nation's Longshoremen walking off the job? Israel on the brink of war with Iran and in Lebanon?

The January 6 case, the most damning of all the legal assaults on Trump, one that Jack Smith might never be allowed to present in court, was—to howls of protests from the Trump side—being presented in public now. None of Trump's myriad legal difficulties had yet had much evident impact on him or the election, but this salvo, in by a squeaker, as the Dems were trying to make saving democracy a key issue, might leave a last damning impression. Thirty-three days before the election, the special prosecutor, with a wealth of new and incriminating details, was once again telling the oft-told tale of how Trump had tried to subvert the last election. Smith spelled out the ultimate point that the result of the election for Trump was merely a variable to overcome and that the effort to do this had been vast and elaborate. It was *Trump* who had tried to steal the election—not remotely the other way around. (Arguably, the Democrats had failed to properly articulate this, making the issue about whether he had accepted the election, rather than that he had tried to hijack it.)

The tale that Smith told was a near-Trollopian view, encompassing the range of characters in Trumpworld, both the relative normies and the extreme cuckoo birds, more than fifty of them.

But, in surveying the list of names, from Giuliani to Bannon to body man Nick Luna to the wide assortment of lawyers opportunistically entering the picture or making panicky escapes from it, what members of the present campaign and extended legal teams noticed most glaringly about the list was that Boris wasn't on it. No mention at all. The one lawyer most actively involved with the election aftermath, from immediately flying into Arizona to help coordinate the Trump efforts there (which had earned him his nine-count criminal indictment); to effectively becoming the chief of staff and aide-de-camp to Rudy Giuliani, the steal's mastermind; to being a key conduit back to the campaign and the White House in the post-election weeks, was nowhere present in Smith's retelling. If there was any explanation other than that Boris was cooperating with Smith, no one could imagine what that would be.

• • •

The "Return to Butler" rally, back to the scene of the first assassination attempt, is a Fox News–conceived idea, specifically Laura Ingraham's, but it is immediately embraced by Trump. (Others around him thought it might be morbid.) It's a headline, a news cycle hook, and a mystical offering to the most fervent in the Trump base. It's a reunion tour.

As important, it's a signpost in the courtship of rural voters in Pennsylvania—the most must-win state. The Trump camp believes they are winning there, or at least that Harris isn't winning. She's stalled, it seems, her previous bumps flattening. This, too, confirms Trump's own view: If Harris had picked Josh Shapiro, the Jewish PA governor, the White House would be hers. (But now, wasn't it in the interest of the ambitious Shapiro for Harris to fail here and leave 2028 as the year of the first Jewish president? That is, Harris's "Shapiro problem.")

Everybody is on the Pennsylvania train for the Return to Butler. John Paulson, in closer and closer proximity to Trump; Steve Witkoff, nearly always by his side; Pennsylvania Senate candidate Dave McCormick and his wife, former Trump White House staffer Dina Powell (who, in her post-Trump career at Goldman Sachs regularly lunched out on the chaos and treachery of the Trump White House and the know-nothingness of her old boss). Doug Mills, the *New York Times* photographer who has been elevated to nearly an official position in the campaign, is on the plane and positioned to capture the family of Corey Comperatore, the firefighter killed in the assassination attempt, there on the tarmac to greet the returning warrior Trump. JD Vance has flown in. The entire campaign team is here. Boris is back to traveling everywhere with Trump, keeping up an almost constant patter in his ear about how good things are going. Natalie, always trying to quicken her step to catch up, is competing with Boris to say it first. Seb Gorka, a strange yes-man from the margins of the first Trump administration, who went on to retail his Trump expertise through C- and D-level media outlets around the world, is suddenly back on hand. A doleful Corey Lewandowski, largely banished after the internal showdown, is shuffling along. And with them, the largest Secret Service and security detail ever at any time assembled for a presidential candidate. And somehow, Justin Caporale and his specialized team have accomplished the visual sleight of hand to make all this new security not look like Trump is walling himself off— like he is afraid! Instead, they have made it look as though he were more presidential, more in need of protection, and worthier of it than any president. He is raised up instead of distanced by it.

And Elon is here, waiting when they arrive, which is cause for a moment of consternation among the team. Elon! Next only to Trump, there is Elon. In the last weeks, he has inserted himself as a new, overwhelming, and discordant presence in the campaign, his new presence and importance expressing themselves in an ever-rising tide of bewildering, if not opaque, requests, orders, and recommendations from him or his people. Musk appears to have elevated the Trump campaign in his own mind to a personal mission and religious cause, with the Trump circle already anticipating the earth shaking when he and Trump invariably fall out.

When they arrive, Elon—wandering about by himself, with only a thin layer of assistants or security—is hungry. This causes a kerfuffle and results in uncertainty over how to attend to him. Someone produces a bag of pretzel sticks.

The suggestion is made that JD is here and would love to speak to him.

Musk, sitting down and eating his pretzel sticks, politely declines: "I've really no interest in speaking to a vice president."

Later, called onstage, with no one having any idea what he might say, Musk bounds up and, suddenly—in Mick Jagger style, prancing and jumping—becomes the headline, his T-shirt rising far above his midriff.

"What the fuck is wrong with this guy?" says a bewildered Trump. "And why doesn't his shirt fit?"

At any rate, if they win, the theorizing already goes, it could well be because of the Return to Butler rally and the advantage of a few thousand votes in rural Pennsylvania.

• • •

The other theory about where they might place the credit for victory—if victory comes, and it's a positive sign that they are trying to explain the causes of hypothetical victory rather than hypothetical defeat—is Corey Lewandowski's being relegated to the back of the plane.

In the telling, Lewandowski came very close to winning the power struggle. He had Trump's ear, he knew Trump's history, he understood how panicked Trump was by the Harris rise, and he wasn't waiting for permission; he was seizing the day—and he had aligned himself with other powerful forces in Trumpworld, including Ike Perlmutter. But Trump, reluctantly, was forced, in this telling, by Wiles and LaCivita into making an up or down decision, and in a sign of their Trump acumen, they didn't let him monologize his way out of it. He upgraded them and downgraded Corey.

If Lewandowski had succeeded, the "close" would certainly have been a chaotic and unscripted one (even less unscripted than it was and than Trump always is). The fact that he did not succeed (recognizing that failure in Trumpworld today might yet be success tomorrow) says less about Trump's desire to avoid chaos than it does about how much Trump depends on Wiles and LaCivita and, as crucially, how much he understands he depends on them.

That understanding, then, might very well be considered the reason for victory and might further cement Wiles and LaCivita's standing— one, or the other, or both—as the pillars of a next hypothetical Trump administration. If so, then this was a victory, at least a relative one, for reasonably steady management (largely absent in the last Trump White House) and for relative Republican establishment values over MAGA ones. For now.

. . .

Enter Melania, at last.

On October 8, her book, *Melania,* was published.

This was, to the campaign—largely unaware that the book was even in the works and with, practically speaking, no idea what was in it—an October surprise. The book itself, or what was in it, was largely without consequence. It was, in fact, so bland and anodyne that it might easily have been written by AI. (Curiously, it has no acknowledgments page, possibly because there was no human to acknowledge.) The only flutter was Melania's pro-choice view, which could be subsumed into Trump's own contortions on that issue (and was more helpful moderation on the issue for him).

It's not what's in the book that's notable, but the existence of the book itself.

There's an observable aspect of competition between the Trumps and their efforts to trade on the name (or, arguably, wipe out the name, with her book making her singularly "Melania")—as though they both think this is something of a last-chance moment. As the campaign comes down to a no-time-to-spare end, Trump himself is spending an awful lot of time on his odd-lot endeavors: the sneakers, the watches, the crypto wallets, the new golf course in Scotland, the Bibles, the NFT trading cards, a forthcoming picture book. Melania, meanwhile, had been charging for speeches and was now rolling out the book and charging for interviews.

The "why exactly now?" question hangs over the book.

The book's publisher was Skyhorse, an independent, upstart house without its own sales force, best known for publishing "canceled" authors who couldn't get published by mainstream houses. This has become the Skyhorse business model: It customarily pays no advances and offers a royalty that is half as much as that offered at major publishers in the book industry, to authors with nowhere else to go.

It would surely be the case that, if Melania became the First Lady again, she would have her pick of publishers, might name the size of her advance, and have the world's best platform from which to sell her book. But if you believe you will not be the First Lady again, or you are hedging against it, then now would certainly be the moment, the last moment, to publish.

How do we read this? That was the question, perhaps most of all for Trump, not about the book itself, but about its deeper message—a diss or a kiss (of course, from afar)?

• • •

For both sides, their winning issue, each believes, is the other side: Donald Trump and the deep aversion to him on the part of so many

Americans is the Democrats' winning hand; and Kamala Harris and the visceral dislike and deep suspicion of her in MAGA land is the Trumpers' ace. There has been a nearly daily straight-up comparison of their negatives. Here has been a steady pace of Trump rallies—notably, this week, in the blue states California and Colorado—in which his language becomes ever more threatening toward people and groups against him, vengeful about the future he promises, virulent toward his opponent, and vivid in his description of the hellscape coming for illegal and other categories of immigrants. And, too, lest you haven't noticed, at uncontrolled length, he has been, for much of the time, no more than semi-coherent and spiraling into tangents that have to be confounding even to his most dedicated supporters. She, on the other hand, has remained locked down, precisely programmed, calculated and guarded in every utterance, and quite a cipher in most of her views. The more you see of her, the less you seem to know of her.

A tight race—as tight as any in the modern history—could default to the enemy you know.

· · ·

On October 11, a sign of greater Trumpworld's growing optimism broke out in *The New York Times* with reports of transparent jockeying for the penultimate job in the prospective new Trump White House. Internally, the Trump camp assumed that Susie Wiles would, doubtlessly, become the White House chief of staff. Now the *Times* was pronouncing the near likelihood that Brooke Rollins would be the chief of staff. This was both bewildering to the inside Trump circle—no one had heard even a whisper of Rollins's name for the job—and, yet, at the same time, a piece of predictable and transparent Kremlinology.

Rollins had been a Kushner lieutenant in the White House. A fifty-two-year-old Texas lawyer and political technocrat—there weren't too many of them in Trumpworld—she had, with Kushner, been one of the authors of the 2020 Platinum Plan, meant somehow to win over Black voters in the election, a plan widely hated by the MAGA team. (Stephen Miller became one of Rollins's chief adversaries.) She had gone on to run the America First Policy Institute, the Kushner-aligned group that, with the Heritage Foundation, had served as an exile camp and staging area in anticipation of a new Trump regime. AFPI had raised huge sums and, to Trump's irritation, spent lavishly on itself (including hundreds of thousands to have Wynonna Judd play at its annual party at Mar-a-Lago) to support hundreds of employees in the wait for a coming Trump White House. More recently, the Heritage Foundation, AFPI's main competitor in vying for Trump's attention and future influence and jobs, had largely been blown up by its sponsorship of Project 2025 and months of headlines that had infuriated Trump. At any rate, here again was the Jared barometer: He would be nowhere if they lost and back pulling strings if it looked like they might win. Rollins and a *Times* story meant, in other words, that Jared, a famously astute leaker, was on the move, which in turn meant that victory was truly looking possible.

And perhaps, too, as a sign of Trump's surging (if a surge can be measured in increments) was another story in the *Times*—another calculated leak. This was about how contemptuously Trump was treating his major donors. In a small meeting in Trump Tower that included Paul Singer, the hedge fund billionaire, and Joe Ricketts, the TD Ameritrade founder, and Ricketts's son Todd, Trump blasted them for being ingrates and not giving enough. This was a pattern that had been evident for some time: He would gather large investors and then single out individual donors and, in front of the whole group, reprise their giving history, whether it had been too early or too late ("Where the fuck were you?"), how it compared to others' ("There's cheap, and then there's what you came up with"), and how it compared to their overall fortunes. (He tended, particularly, to single out Jews for not giving enough, for not being grateful enough.) This was part of his new confidence that the tech billionaires would give him all he needed and his belief that he would win and everybody would need to come crawling to him, so fuck them. It was also, however, with the *Times* story as evidence, an indication of a potential rebellion—the story had clearly come from one of the donors at one such meeting and was detailed enough for him to suspect that someone had taped the gathering. And, again, twenty-four days out, a reminder that Trump could yet bring this all down.

And what was read as another sign: Natalie filed an eye-popping expense reimbursement bill. Immediately noted: a new wardrobe. She said
the "president" had encouraged her to go shopping because she would
be so much more in front of the cameras when he won.

. . .

The new confidence—that they had broken through the Kamala wall;
that after erecting it, Harris had weakly defended it—was manifesting in
Trump himself as a new level of wrathfulness or defiance, of people getting destroyed on a daily basis, of him going full flamethrower. Or, alternatively, as the days ticked down, he was growing more fearful, the
stakes clear to him. Whatever had brought him to this state, hubris or
dread, injected perhaps the ultimate variable into the final days.

Jason Miller, who (with Dan Scavino) was his longest-serving aide,
was singled out, a warning to everyone of the new intensity of Trump's
blast radius, a legend minutes after it happened. Preparations had been
ongoing for Trump to do specific interviews on the economy, including
one with Christine Romans, a business correspondent for NBC News,
and a live interview at the Economic Club of Chicago with Bloomberg
News editor in chief John Micklethwait. This was a clear closing-week
strategy. Sean Hannity seemed, however, to question it: Why NBC, why
Bloomberg? This, then, was echoed by Boris. And then, in a weather
report that reverberated throughout Trumpworld, the question was directed into maximal destruction toward Miller: "You've done this to
fuck me! You're fucking me! This is a trap! This is sabotage. You've always
been out to fuck me! Who approved this? I want to know who approved
this. This was you, wasn't it? Who else knew about this? How many
people are in on it?"

"Who approved it? *He* approved it!" said a staffer, relating the incident. "Miller took it for the team, but, Jesus, it was *Mommie Dearest*
stuff. Everybody just had to avoid eye contact after that."

Nor was the target of Trump's rage and sense of constant injury limited to his staff. Natalie, operating in her own singular and powerful

fiefdom, had set up a meeting for him with Rupert Murdoch; Robert Thomson, the CEO of Murdoch's newspaper company; and Keith Poole, the editor of the *New York Post*. It was not necessarily clear why the meeting was being held, at least not to the Murdoch team (who were bragging about it and yet clearly confused by it for days afterward), except that Natalie called it. But Trump turned it into a bitter castigation of Fox News for the few Democratic voices, reliably weak ones, the network allowed on the air and for paid Harris ads it was running. (In fact, almost all these ads were local inserts the network had had nothing to do with, targeted to the Bedminster and Mar-a-Lago markets, and meant, pointedly, to irritate Trump.) Trump focused on ninety-three-year-old Murdoch, assailing him for having fired Roger Ailes, the Fox founder whom Murdoch had dismissed in 2016 over sexual harassment charges. Ailes, Trump insisted, would never have screwed him like this.

Similarly, at a meeting that same week with the *Wall Street Journal* editorial board—the Murdoch-owned paper with its staunchly conservative editorial page—Trump read from a list of grievances he had with the paper, enumerating a ten-year litany of all the times the *Journal* had been wrong and he had been right.

This was the private backdrop. In the public foreground, and in a first in presidential campaign behavior, he petulantly stopped a town hall meeting in suburban Philadelphia—he doesn't like town halls and wants rallies—and peremptorily decided to play music for thirty minutes, calling out the songs and either pulsing jerkily to a percussive beat or swaying beatifically to a sentimental melody. (In the history of politics, who would have done this? Nero, maybe.) And in his series of continuing "closing messages" appearances—including a rally in Pennsylvania where he focused on 1950s and '60s golfer Arnold Palmer and the size of his penis; and another at the Alfred E. Smith Memorial Foundation Dinner in New York, an event of traditional bonhomie and amusement, sponsored by the archdiocese, where his insults seemed neither good-natured nor droll—Chuck Schumer is transitioning; Tim Walz has a period; and "I don't give a shit if this is comedy or not. [Bill DeBlasio] was a terrible mayor"—he seemed to have lost all sense of a filter or of having any need of one. He would win and was therefore beyond restraint; or he wouldn't, and he was then preparing some shocking, no-holds-barred, let-Trump-be-Trump alternative.

. . .

Meanwhile, Corey Lewandowski, vowing continuing revenge, disruption, and with personal experience that wars in Trumpworld were long and that you could never predict where you'd end up in them, had focused his ire on Chris LaCivita—particularly reflected in a leak to the Daily Beast. Lewandowski's campaign "audit" had, among other line items, according to the story, spelled out the monies flowing to LaCivita, eye-popping top-line amounts. Presidential campaigns can be dark holes of cash, especially as that cash flows to a variety of consultants and campaign officials who, while working directly for the campaign, are also providing it with third-party services. This is true for both Democratic and Republican campaigns and exists in the largely unregulated world of campaign expenditures. (Raising the money is highly regulated; spending it, less so.) LaCivita's deal, not especially unusual, was essentially to have his personal company act as the media buyer for portions of the hundreds of millions of dollars in Trump campaign advertising. He was, in this, functioning as an advertising agency might, receiving a commission as an agency might. At any rate, LaCivita's deal when he came into the campaign was that he could maintain the fees he might otherwise have made as an outside consultant to it. In total, according to Lewandowski's report (or, anyway, the leak of the report), LaCivita had received, over two years, $22 million in fees and commissions. This is a gross amount and does not account for the various costs he might have incurred, either for his own staff or for vendors he might have hired. Lewandowski's line item for LaCivita was leaked—with the Occam's razor surmise that the likely leaker was Lewandowski personally or Lewandowski ally Dave Bossie—to the Daily Beast in a story by Michael Isikoff, a righteous anti-Trump reporter. (In the face of LaCivita's legal threats, the website subsequently corrected the $22 million to $19.2 million.) And this is where the leak might have died among the catchall of too-good-to-be-true Trump leaks.

However . . . LaCivita, wielding his new power over the plane manifest, had recently excluded not only Lewandowski, but others whom he disapproved of, didn't like, or didn't want. Among them, Alina Habba. Habba went immediately to Trump, who restored her seat on the plane. With an extra kick, she showed Trump the Daily Beast article about LaCivita's $22 million.

While, to say the least, it is unlikely or bizarre that a candidate would be unaware of the compensation levels of his topmost aide, a gobsmacked Trump now torched LaCivita for stealing his dough, and turned on Wiles, too, for not protecting his money.

Both Wiles and LaCivita, one after the other, offered an instructive response:

They took it. Eyes down. Breaths shallow.

Depersonalize. Step out of your body. Go blank. Let it wash over you.

CHAPTER 26

Finale

OCTOBER–NOVEMBER

Victory seemed as possible as defeat. That in itself should have been relatively good news. In the two weeks prior to his finale at Madison Square Garden, on October 27, the final week of the campaign, many in the Trump camp judged that they had moved firmly and confidently ahead. Tony Fabrizio—"Fucking" would effectively become his first name because his polling did not necessarily match the polls Trump wanted to read (and because Trump could get from the media for free the same information he believed he was paying inordinately for)—was giving them the best swing state margins since Harris had become the candidate. The day before the Garden rally, Melania, surprising friends and family, had sent word to her husband that she was willing to introduce him at the event. While this might possibly have been a pity move, it could be read, too, as a clear olive branch, his wife sizing up the victory to come and her own place in history. Yes, this was more good news.

Trump himself, however, seemed possibly on the verge of cracking. There was a rolling subtext of trying to diagnose him. He was tired, for sure. Who wouldn't be? But had it gone dangerously beyond that? He had been pushing to schedule more rallies, and this had prompted anyone looking for an opening to drop something else in: the everyday rallies plus donor meetings, plus finance meetings, plus penny-ante interviews, plus phoners, plus . . . There now was not an unscheduled moment. Since the second assassination attempt, his golf game had been taken away from him—his eighteen holes of downtime had been sucked into the campaign. And he was, after all, seventy-eight. Yellow hair and an orange face and instinctual aggression could mask only so far that he frequently gave up trying to complete sentences; that he turned left when he should have known it was right; that he elided obvious names, repeated himself beyond the one or two allowances, and erupted in rages that, even for him, seemed irrational. Mar-a-Lago patio cronies believed that Trump, like so many others on the patio ("everybody's shrinking"), was taking Ozempic or another weight-loss drug and that it was increasing his fatigue. But the other interpretation was that he was face-to-face with the reckoning: He would win and go on being Donald Trump; or he would lose, and then everything in his life would change—his life and, likely, his freedom would be taken away. At some point, even for him, indomitable will breaks; losing, even for him, is . . . losing. In some sense, this was the subtext of his rally speeches. He was drafting his audience into his existential fight. So much of his exhortations and his energy was about his own survival.

· · ·

And so began what was perhaps the worst week of the campaign.

Arriving at Madison Square Garden, amid back-to-back finance and donor meetings, with Trump raging about why they had been set up and what fuck-face idiot had set them up—answer: *he* had insisted they be set up—he lost it over the speech he was shortly to give at what was, arguably, the triumph of his New York life. Having been exiled from New York City—indeed, convicted by it—the conquering antihero was back at the very center of it. Twenty thousand people were in Madison Square Garden to celebrate him—a further overflow of thirty thousand outside watching on the Jumbotron. He was given the same speech that had reliably worked before. But why wasn't there a *new* speech? Why wasn't it a *special* speech? Why weren't there new ideas here? New proposals? Why was it always the same old, same old?

At various points in the campaign, a triumphal turn at the Garden had seemed like a tempting idea, but was then put aside because of the expense, doubts about the crowd size, and fear of the negative New York press it might kick up. But it was never wholly abandoned, and with large donors stepping up to offset the costs, confidence in the crowd size, and the positive of negative press generating multiple news cycles on it, and with Caporale's staging, the Garden rally was turned into a redo of the GOP convention.

Except that, in the pressure of the closing of a presidential campaign, and the Garden a late addition to the calendar, it was not at all clear who exactly was in charge of the mini-convention. Where the actual convention had been closely vetted, with Wiles and LaCivita taking the platform under their direct control and constant review, the Garden reprise was effectively a say-whatever-you-want-to-say free-for-all. Not least, among the bewildering indications of the general vacuum was that Rudy Giuliani, who at that moment was being cleaned out of his last possessions in one of the 2020 election fraud civil cases against him, had somehow found himself a slot. Rudy was the disappeared man in Trumpworld. He reliably called campaign staff and Trump cronies, and just as reliably, no one returned his calls. Rudy, in Trumpworld, officially did not exist— and yet, here he was.

Then, too, with unvetted insouciance, reading between the lines, you might even have taken the remarks of Tucker Carlson and Robert Kennedy Jr., two more among the long list of speakers preceding Trump, to be less about their support for Donald Trump than their own forward-looking positioning for 2028.

If there was any guiding hand, it belonged to Alex Bruesewitz. Alex who? All presidential campaigns are porous to the relatively unemployed who will work for little or nothing and who have an unnatural amount of enthusiasm and a high tolerance for, no matter how unappreciated, always showing up. Alex Bruesewitz was a would-be right-wing-world fanboy and promoter with a contact list of online influencers and personalities and the letterhead of his own political consulting firm.

The Garden doors opened at noon for the thousands of people who had begun to line up the night before and who needed to be entertained until the once and (for all here) certainly future president took to the stage that evening. Along with Rudy, Tucker, RFK Jr., and other less-than-obvious Trump boosters and opportunists, Bruesewitz introduced Tony Hinchcliffe into the mix. Part of the ever-greater fracturing of sub-set media, Hinchcliffe was one of many young white male comedians— at forty, he looked younger than he was—competing to insult wokeness, offend liberal propriety, and find their inner Trump.

Later, Bruesewitz would seek praise (or, at least, sympathy) for hav-ing interceded with Hinchcliffe to cut the word *cunt* from his set.

Nevertheless, as Trump, backstage, railed against his speechwriters for finding nothing new to say, word started to filter back that Tony Hinch-cliffe, whom few had ever heard of, was, onstage, throwing a bomb into the Latino voters whose margin might well provide the Trump victory.

"There's literally a floating island of garbage in the middle of the ocean right now; I think it's called Puerto Rico."

Well.

The quip, at the moment it was delivered, was mostly unheard by the Trump command, and hardly heard by the audience pushing in and trying to find seats and choose from the array of MAGA merchandise, not there so much to pay attention to the stage as to join in the bonho-mie of the experience. But as his remark began to echo through social media and, shortly, jump to something like universal renown, there was a slow, dawning appreciation that this was the moment (standing out among all the others) that might have lost Trump the election.

Beyond the immediate finger-pointing at both Hinchcliffe and Bruesewitz—and, once more, a sense of the rings of incompetence that surrounded Trump—there was in Trumpworld, again, a deep resent-ment of the media's unwillingness to understand the real Trump spirit.

The New York Times et al. were portraying the rally as something like darkness at noon, a Brownshirt event recalling the German American Bund's 1939 Nazi rally at the Garden. (Indeed, this coverage had been going on for days.) Where, in truth, this Trump rally (like all Trump ral-lies, in spite of the unvetted words) was a festive occasion. Not dark at all. Instead, like a UFC or WWF event—or, even, in its familiarity, a Grate-ful Dead concert. It wasn't the message; it was the experience. Really.

Except, there it was, "a floating island of garbage."

A media moment. Another media moment.

In fact, the Trump camp, and Trump in particular, remained stalwart and, in Trumpian style, uncontrite. No need to address it. Ignore. Forget about it. Here commenced an almost forty-eight-hour nonstop window of media focus on the inherent paradox of Latino openness to Donald Trump with hardly even a veneer over his tolerance for bigotry. Condemnation now part of every Democratic talking point: How could Latinos actually swallow this? Trump, who in his own (not precisely correct) calculation, had never apologized for anything, was certainly not going to address this. (In calls with friends, he polled whether anyone thought the line was funny and then simply concluded that "people get it, everybody gets it—it's a joke.")

Then, on Tuesday, on the third day of the "garbage" outcry, Joe Biden, clearly intending to turn the knife, teetered in with his own version of Hinchcliffe's remark: "The only garbage I see floating out there is his supporters." Hence, in an instant, turning the "garbage" label into a badge of honor, with the Trump team, delightedly, cranking up the outrage machine. Whatever arguable damage had been done by the comedian's "garbage" joke was now balanced, or superseded, by Biden, once more haplessly tangled up in his own words.

The next day, on the way out to Wisconsin—with Harris scheduled that afternoon to give her own closing summation—Trump, on board the plane, got the idea to have a garbage truck waiting at the airport, which, with barely a few hours of prep time, Justin Caporale arranged. A brand-new garbage truck with full Trump branding met the plane. Trump's only worry was that the truck cab was too high for him to gracefully climb into.

But lest this be seen as any kind of confidence, Trump's mood remained as dark as anyone had seen it—and everyone around him had seen very dark Trump moods. Brooding, with its suggestion of deep inner thoughts, might not be something normally associated with Trump. And yet, now there was an impression of some well of bitterness and even fear that Trump's manic loquacity couldn't expel or hide.

"Come on, really, who could take this, you're going to the executioner or you're going to become the executioner in a few days' time. It's all or nothing. I want to repeat that: It's all or nothing. Life or death, pretty literally. Hours away," said one Trump friend and adviser with him on the flight out to Green Bay.

Meanwhile, Harris's closing speech, before a crowd of as many as 75,000 at the Ellipse in Washington, D.C.—exactly where Trump urged on a similarly sized crowd to march on the Capitol on January 6, 2021— was as powerful and cogent an argument for the dire future of a government returned to Donald Trump's hands as she had made in the campaign.

He was, yes, implacable in his conviction that he was going to win, as implacable as in his conviction that the last election had been stolen from him—and yet, as in 2020, no one really believed he was so certain. Rather, he was trying to will it. Studying him—and everybody was— one saw, other than the clear exhaustion, no break in his outward swagger and indomitability. The more you played the part, the more the part became real. Reality followed pretense.

Nevertheless, he *was* tired, dragging, short-fused . . . and most of all, he was seventy-eight. He was repeating himself. He was having noticeable trouble rising from his chair. He was blanking on all kinds of names (including "Vance," in one instance).

Whatever—the way and path were still his. He saw a poll indicating that he might even have a shot at winning New Mexico—not, in anyone's calculation, a reasonable chance—and suddenly, he wanted an event in Albuquerque. Then, because his previous annoyance with and distrust of Tucker Carlson had been converted over the campaign year into full man crush and father–son adoration, he added a Tucker event, joining him, along with RFK Jr., on Tucker's "live tour" in Glendale, Arizona—helpful, no doubt, for Carlson but of little apparent benefit to Trump. Prodded by Carlson, whose own particular bête noire was Republican neo-cons, about "Dick Cheney's repulsive little daughter," Trump responded, "She's a radical war hawk. Let's put her with a rifle standing there, with nine barrels shooting at her, okay? Let's see how she feels about it when the guns are trained on her face." That, in the

Democrats' outrage machine, immediately became a death threat against Liz Cheney and, for the Trump campaign, another worry about the residual influence she might have with wavering Republicans.

Harris, to Trump's great fury, was on the campaign trail in the closing days with A-list celebrities, the theory being that their support might move their fan bases, even though there might not be any direct political correlation. Meanwhile, Trump gathered the endorsement of Joe Rogan, whose vast fan base was directly political.

On Saturday, in *The Des Moines Register,* Ann Selzer, an Iowa pollster with something of a cult following (at least among other pollsters), put Harris three points over Trump in Iowa, a heretofore solidly red state. This might seem to be the biggest news of the campaign since Biden left the race. "It's hard for anybody to say they saw this coming," pronounced Selzer. Harris, she said, "has clearly leaped into a leading position." Even pollsters who reasonably saw Selzer's poll as an outlier were yet seeing movement, including in the final *New York Times* poll and in ABC's last look, to Harris. The smart money was putting the Trump peak as having happened just before the Garden event and drifting down from there, and Harris's margin of safety increasing in the blue wall states.

On Sunday, the second-to-last day of the campaign, in Lititz, Pennsylvania, Trump returned to the 2020 election, sounding still as bitter about his loss—the steal—and as profoundly convinced of the historical wrong against him as he had four years before. He digressed briefly to calling attention to the configuration of the protective glass enclosure around him, noting that for an assassin to get to him, it would be necessary to shoot through the reporters in front of him. "I have this piece of glass here," he said. "But all we have really over here is the fake news. And to get me, somebody would have to shoot through the fake news. And I don't mind that so much."

Once more, Trump being Trump could lose the election.

Then, with three other rallies on the penultimate day, it was on to Grand Rapids, where a superstitious Trump had closed out both 2016 and 2020. He arrived back at Mar-a-Lago at four in the morning on Election Day.

• • •

It was, by all available measures as the day began, the closest election in modern history.

No one, Republicans or Democrats, had good reason, other than that the odds of being right were fifty-fifty, to feel confident about the outcome.

If there was movement—and both sides claimed the winds were blowing in their direction—it was minor movement within the margin of error, from which no polls had emerged in more than sixty days. Curiously, the same polls that had failed in 2016 and in 2020 and in 2022, which apparently could not accurately measure the Trump phenomenon, were yet guiding the outlook.

"I think we will win, but with a lot of carnage," a Trump intimate texted—not too confidently, it seemed—anticipating a period of trench warfare, merely picking up from where 2020 had left off.

Trump, in an early call on Election Day with an old friend, seemed to balance precariously between positivity, reciting cherry-picked polls (and not necessarily accurately), and a falling back into 2020, reliving the offenses against him. "They have it in place to do it again. They do. We know all about it. Too bad Rudy is a drunk. That's too bad. I need a new Rudy"—just as he needed a new Roy Cohn. (In fact, the example of Rudy Giuliani's utter humiliation and defenestration, and Trump's own abandoning of him, might well have put a damper on any new election denial and legal fight.)

Melania sent word that she would not appear with him unless it was an outright win. Her message seemed to be that she did not want to go through 2020 again.

In a sense, the evening was set up to replicate 2020. In the White House in 2020, a war room had been set up in the basement Green Room; now the war room was in the dining room at Mar-a-Lago. In the White House in 2020, there had been a dinner for hundreds of friends and donors in the East Room; now, at Mar-a-Lago, dinner for a largely similar cast of friends and donors was held in the Grand Ballroom. As president, Trump had been scheduled to go before the crowd in the East Room to give his acceptance speech—and where, instead, he gave, as the polls began to turn, his harangue of defiance. Now the convention center in Palm Beach would be the scene of his victory or of a new and unimaginable chapter of denial and truculence.

Not long before Election Day, Barry Diller, the media mogul, billionaire, and Democratic heavyweight donor, expressing a shared wariness with the deadlocked state of play and, perhaps, too, a Democratic fatalism, offered in an interview that even more than an eked-out Harris victory, he wanted a definitive result. He wanted a clear choice—one that the nation would then have to accept that it had made. The full monty. Perhaps Diller felt free enough to entertain this exercise in clarity—and risk the full Trump monty—because it was so unlikely to happen.

In the calculus of most Democrats and most Republicans, the evening's outcome and the immediate fate of the nation would yet teeter on Pennsylvania. It would be Thursday or Friday before the night was truly over. Or longer. "Hanging chad–level craziness," said one Trump adviser, recalling the Bush–Gore election in 2000 and the weeks of hand counting and the ultimate deciding vote of the Supreme Court.

. . .

At 5 P.M., as dinner guests slowly start to arrive at Mar-a-Lago—largely a crowd of blue-haired club members—Tony Fabrizio is bringing Trump the first exit polls.

They are up in every swing state by two points, except Pennsylvania, where it's tied, and Michigan, where they're down by two.

"Well, that's not good," responds Trump in what perhaps could be read as a sign of his resignation.

"No, no," Fabrizio tells him. "This is an electoral college victory."

"I'm going to win?"

"You're going to win."

For a moment, Trump seems deflated, even confused.

The word, with still some disbelief, begins to spread.

The war room, which in 2020 was filled with people on IV information drips, trying to will the numbers to add up, with, as the evening went on, more and more people crowding in to hear the latest numbers, seems this time to lose its purpose, more people leaving than arriving.

The action, such as it is, shifts to the Grand Ballroom.

But in a way, it seems more of a club event than a historic event. It's bluehairs and men in sports jackets. An easy victory—and that's what, bewilderingly, it increasingly appears to be—might seem to deprive everyone of the sense of battle. Where's the fight? There's a push by family and assorted VIPs (Elon Musk) trying to get close to Trump—with Boris adroitly putting himself next to Musk and Trump.

The sense of disbelief shifts from doubting that they will win to disbelieving that, yes, after all, after everything, they have won. Indeed, instead of willing it to happen, as they had in 2020—on the phone, pushing against all sources of information, searching for whoever could read the data streams positively, the most exciting Election Night . . . ever—many at Mar-a-Lago now seem content to passively watch it happen on television, with a sense both of wonder and anti-climax.

At 8 p.m., the room at the Palm Beach Convention Center is no more than a quarter full—an aimless bunch of young Republicans, bikers, and more bluehairs. It will never reach more than half full.

At 8:30, Rudy Giuliani arrives and immediately begins speculating to a small gaggle of reporters about where fraud might yet have occurred in 2024. Other low-level notables—including Nigel Farage, the British Trump wannabe; Lady Victoria Harvey, a press-ready British socialite and former reality star; and the North Carolina ladies, a group of evangelical women who have followed Trump from rally to rally—hit the floor, looking, it appears, for a much greater celebration than is apparently on offer.

Victory seems to lack the energy and passion of believing that victory has been stolen.

By midnight, the celebration, such as it is, has turned to many puddles of vomit, with a scattering of Trumpers asleep on the floor—quite a party that never happened.

LaCivita and Lewandowski square off briefly—a "Fuck you," "No, fuck you," sort of confrontation that turns out to be the singular excitement of the evening.

The point, of course, is to wait for the jubilant arrival of the winner—and by 11 P.M., it's clear that's exactly who he is. His Mar-a-Lago guests start to arrive at the convention center at around midnight. But he isn't coming yet. For one thing, Melania doesn't want to go out until victory is officially certain. And he, too, of course, has been out here before without having what he believed was his. He wanted this night to be different.

At 2:25 A.M., he comes out onstage, followed by Melania, and then the rest of the family, and then staff. He seems less than himself. This turn of events is certainly not evidently filling him with joy—not yet, anyway. Where is the dancing? He is, you might read the weary body language, in a kind of stoic mood; it's a flat affect—almost, in fact, the manner of a conventional politician in defeat. How to get through this? He proceeds to deliver his standard rally speech. A subdued Donald Trump is not Donald Trump.

Has victory robbed him of his reason for being?

Because this is Donald Trump, a train heading for the wall, there has always been, even among those loyally by his side, the understanding that this could end, perhaps even inevitably would—and by any standards of reasonable risk management, probably should—in a fiery wreck. And perhaps that, in some sense, has still been the expectation—even what everyone has truly been waiting for.

The fact that he will take every swing state; that in his third try he will easily win the popular vote; that he will significantly reconfigure many safe assumptions about an otherwise predictable electorate; that somehow, at this moment, he might seem to be the most successful figure in American politics since Franklin Roosevelt is a new and bewildering reality even for those who were a part of it. Even for him, perhaps most of all.

What new fire must he now set?

Epilogue

Back Again

In the days after the election, Trump named Matt Gaetz, Pete Hegseth, and Robert Kennedy Jr. as among his important cabinet picks.

In a phone call with a friend, he singled out, with amusement, that each of his headline nominees had gotten in trouble, lots of trouble, over women—"girl trouble"—and he was eager, with quite some cheerfulness, to see how his reprobate nominees handled this.

This friend, a longtime New York acquaintance, offered the observation that what excites Trump most is not the fire but the clanging fire engines and sirens rushing to the scene. The drama, the conflict, the sound and fury of it all.

Meanwhile, his most significant appointment was to make Susie Wiles, undoubtedly the single most important person in his victory, his chief of staff. Never before was there a chief (and four proceeded her in four years) with whom he had a long working relationship. Never before has he had a chief who, like himself, is at an age beyond further professional ambitions—she won't be looking to protect her own career path. She will be there as she was in the campaign, and this might be good news, to make the trains run on time and deal with the details he won't want, or isn't able, to deal with. The bad news, however, is that she might help free him up to do exactly as he wants to do: If the backstage works smoothly (more or less—and without microphone fuckups), he can be out front, holding the attention of the public by whatever inspiration, cruelties, or effronteries cross his mind.

In among the most difficult to imagine developments, in some sense dwarfing most of the other difficult to imagine developments, Boris Epshteyn—along with Rudy Giuliani and Donald Trump, among the most culpable figures in the 2020 election overthrow attempt, and, indeed, under indictment in Arizona for it, and, to boot, *widely suspected of being ready to sell out the new president-elect, if that became necessary*— was given effective carte blanche over the legal function and reach of the executive branch. The bet Boris had made on wholly backing Trump's preposterous all-or-nothing legal strategy—he would not bend, he would not give an inch, and by making all prosecutors and judges his enemy, he would win on Election Day, solving all his legal problems— had paid off. Boris was on the verge of becoming the most trusted legal adviser to the President of the United States—and already his people were taking the top legal slots. This included ludicrous Matt Gaetz, delighting Trump (no less delightful to Trump for his quick exit), as the prospective acting attorney general; Emil Bove, from the Trump trial, the assistant attorney general; Todd Blanche, Boris's own former attorney and the lead counsel in the New York trial as deputy attorney general; and John Sauer, Trump's appeals attorney, the new solicitor general. These were all Boris's picks. Wars are fought over lesser power grabs.

In effect, Boris Epshteyn had become what Michael Cohen once imagined himself to be but never quite became: the president's personal lawyer and most trusted voice in his ear. Boris was, truly . . . the new Roy Cohn. Here was the one person who Trump could always rely on because he would always say what Trump wanted to hear.

The flaw was that such shameless sucking up, greater even than everyone else's shameless efforts, had meant during the campaign—and now continued to mean—that he'd alienated most everyone else. He existed, his indisputable and ever-growing power existed, only at Trump's sufferance. Were Trump's regard to waiver, Boris would instantly be set upon and cut to pieces.

Days after the election, a new chapter of the Boris watch began: Could he take on real power? Could he survive a knives-out power struggle? And the true measure here: Would Trump continue to find him useful and entertaining—and what did that *mean* for everyone else?

Alas . . . three weeks after the election . . . Boris, in a midnight roll-out of leaks from what seemed to come from the highest levels of the incoming administration, was tagged for behavior he had long been famous for: charging his personal clients to represent their interests to Trump (this was now appreciably more serious because of the hint that he was running a protection racket, threatening prospective clients, if they didn't pay him, to screw their interests). It was now, finally, a full effort to pry Boris from the boss.

Many believed the sudden rise of Elon Musk had meaningfully shuffled the deck—and, indeed, Musk had apparently expressed incredulity about Boris to Trump. There was certainly no question that Trump might be capricious enough to entertain an attentive Musk at Boris's expense. But, to say the least, Trump-Musk yet remained a sporting dynamic: the two most swollen, bumptious, overbearing, and successful men in America, each lacking basic social skills, in the same room.

Anyway, it was a daily grab bag of appointments, similar to the in-and-out parade at Trump Tower in 2016. Most of the pretense of vetting was dispensed with, as were so many of the reasons that the vetting process existed in the first place. Trump liked familiar names—that is, television faces ("unknowns don't get headlines"). He liked a résumé of loyalty. He liked not to spend too much time on any of this. A safe prediction might be that, as so many of the slapdash meetings in Trump Tower in 2016 became investigative fodder, so would the basic lack of process, structure, and compliance at Mar-a-Lago eight years later.

And as in 2016, by the first weeks of the transition, its lack of process reduced the selection of key figures in the new White House to a primal power grab, a near-life-and-death virulence creating enmities which, as it did before, would track through the next four years.

Indeed, many who might logically enter the new administration were thinking twice about it. Here was a career gamble: Entering the White House might give you direct power and influence, but at the risk of being caught in lethal fights, turned into the targets of poisonous leaks, dismissed by the president in humiliating fashion, and, of course, always the possibility of facing indictment. At the same time, never would the market for someone who might be able to navigate such muddy and riled, not to mention shark-infested, waters be so great. The unpredictability, on-the-fly decision-making, and arbitrariness of the Trump style put a premium on anyone who might provide reliable knowledge of and access to the right voices.

Still, if you were already a billionaire, or a television star, or a Kennedy, then here, by the unlikely hand of Donald Trump, was a gamble that might take you to a next giant step of notoriety and perhaps even history—of course yet with the risk of disgrace, ignominy, and ridicule, too.

And what of the big man, or, in the most secret of monikers inside the campaign, "the old man," himself?

He had achieved everything he had sought. His comeback arguably dwarfed all others in modern political history. He had bet it all and won. In his life of pressing for the next rung of fame, recognition, attention, there was really nowhere else to go. He would exit office at 82—no one ever older. There was nothing else.

He will have some goals. He will reach out to punish enemies, and because of his threats, some knees will surely bend before him. But then he will make more enemies, which will distract him from his original targets. He will get a tax bill—though he's uninterested in details, thus it will be an accomplishment more in name than purpose. He will pursue draconian immigration policies—at least until they become too unpopular and the headlines too rough for him to tolerate anymore (Stephen Miller is back again—to experience the limits of his fantasy of a pure America). He will try tariffs until their consequences became too complicated and too many CEOs complain to him. He will meet with Vladimir Putin, and good cheer will be announced. But accomplishing goals is not really central to Trump's mission or conception of the presidency, because he will claim that all has been accomplished anyway.

So, now, what, really?

Perhaps he will try to enjoy himself.

Certainly, he will be guaranteed an unending supply of obsequious foursomes. Chaos and audacity will continue to be his friends, because that combination keeps him at the center of attention—his real enjoyment—and, as well, distracts from problems that might actually require his attention. And he will focus as he always has—his real life's mission—on his own PR and how to put himself on Mount Rushmore.

But there is, too, the inescapable fact of his age, term limits, second-term malaise, and his lame-duck status—power ebbs. At some point, as hard as it might seem to imagine, events will have a life of their own without Donald Trump at the center of them. And then the story will end.

Meanwhile, amid the disorder, and perhaps in place of what surely seems to be his consistent inability to find peace and satisfaction, Natalie will be just outside the Oval Office door writing letters to him.

Acknowledgments

My great thanks goes to the many people whom I have met over the Trump years who have been as compelled to understand this story as I have been—his friends, staff, donors, lawyers, and others. They have shared with me their time and thoughts, and while they will surely not want to be publicly thanked, I am in their debt. At Crown, Gillian Blake, who was there with Steve Rubin and John Sterling at the beginning with *Fire and Fury*, David Drake, Kevin Doughten, Chris Brand, Dan Novack, and Dyana Messina have been wonderful collaborators. For twenty-five years, my cohorts at the Wylie Agency have been an extraordinary brain trust—and once more, I am pleased to be able to express my gratitude to Andrew Wylie, Jeffrey Pasternack, and James Pullen. The insights of my podcast partner, James Truman, are everywhere in this book—and perhaps one day we will be able to talk about something other than Donald Trump. With thanks, too, to the Kaleidoscope/iHeart team, Oz Woloshyn, Mangesh Hattikudur, Adam Waller, and Emily Marinoff. David Rhodes at Sky, and the Sky documentary team, Jonathan Parker, Yasmine Permaul, James Marsh, and Georgina Turner, have been my companions on much of this journey; it has improved this book to have often seen events through their eyes. The faults here are my own, but Amy Morris's fact-checking means there are far fewer. As always, my thanks to Eric Rayman, the best literary lawyer in the business. And . . . with the greatest thanks of all to my wife, Victoria, and my children, Elizabeth, Susanna, Steven, Louise, and Jack.

About the Author

Michael Wolff has written four *New York Times* best-sellers since 2018, including the #1 *Fire and Fury*. In addition to his three prior books about the Trump White House, his twelve books include *The Man Who Owns the News,* a biography of Rupert Murdoch; *The Fall: The End of Fox News and the Murdoch Dynasty*; and *Burn Rate,* his memoir of the early internet years. For more than a decade, Wolff was a regular columnist for *New York* magazine and *Vanity Fair.* He is the winner of two National Magazine Awards.